MALAYSIA'S FOREIGN POLICY
THE FIRST FIFTY YEARS

The **Institute of Southeast Asian Studies (ISEAS)** was established as an autonomous organization in 1968. It is a regional centre dedicated to the study of socio-political, security and economic trends and developments in Southeast Asia and its wider geostrategic and economic environment. The Institute's research programmes are the Regional Economic Studies (RES, including ASEAN and APEC), Regional Strategic and Political Studies (RSPS), and Regional Social and Cultural Studies (RSCS).

ISEAS Publishing, an established academic press, has issued more than 2,000 books and journals. It is the largest scholarly publisher of research about Southeast Asia from within the region. ISEAS Publishing works with many other academic and trade publishers and distributors to disseminate important research and analyses from and about Southeast Asia to the rest of the world.

MALAYSIA'S FOREIGN POLICY
THE FIRST FIFTY YEARS

Alignment, Neutralism, Islamism

JOHAN SARAVANAMUTTU

ISEAS

INSTITUTE OF SOUTHEAST ASIAN STUDIES
Singapore

First published in Singapore in 2010 by
ISEAS Publishing
Institute of Southeast Asian Studies
30 Heng Mui Keng Terrace
Pasir Panjang
Singapore 119614
E-mail: publish@iseas.edu.sg
Website: http://bookshop.iseas.edu.sg

The responsibility for facts and opinions in this publication rests exclusively with the author and his interpretations do not necessarily reflect the views or the policies of ISEAS or its supporters.

ISEAS Library Cataloguing-in-Publication Data

Saravanamuttu, Johan
    Malaysia's foreign policy, the first fifty years : alignment, neutralism, Islamism.
    1. Malaysia—Foreign relations.
    I. Title.
DS596.3 S24   2010

ISBN 978-981-4279-78-9 (soft cover)
ISBN 978-981-4279-79-6 (hard cover)
ISBN 978-981-4279-80-2 (E-Book PDF)

Cover photo:
Malaysian Prime Minister Abdul Razak Hussein, accompanied by Vice Premier Li Hsien-nien, acknowledges the cheers of Chinese girls waving the Malaysian and Chinese flags and streamer ribbons on 28 May 1974. The Malaysian Premier's visit to China was the occasion for Malaysia's establishment of diplomatic relations with the People's Republic of China. *(Picture by Noordin Sopiee, courtesy of NSTP).*

Photo Credit: Reproduced with kind permission of The New Straits Times Press (Malaysia) Berhad.

Typeset by Superskill Graphics Pte Ltd
Printed in Singapore by Photoplates Private Limited

For

Adil & Rosa

CONTENTS

PREFACE

The idea of writing a major work on Malaysian foreign policy has been many years in gestation. The idea came to fruition when the Institute of Southeast Asian Studies (ISEAS) kindly offered me a visiting research fellowship in 2007. As with all projects of this sort, deadlines became elastic, not least of all because of the volatile and changing times we live in. In the course of researching and sourcing material for the book, there have been tumultuous developments in Malaysia along with significant global developments. Accounting for such changes is a constant hazard of good writing. However the test of any academic work must be its enduring relevance and I do hope my readers will not be disappointed.

A good part of the material for my book was largely derived from a previous work and this provided a rather comfortable cushion on which to recast old and new in the context of the current times. Although I have drawn on previous writings I wish to assure the reader that the material has been duly reconfigured to suit the arguments and overall theoretical thrust of this present work. Where convenient, I have sourced and acknowledged my previous publications as articles in journals or chapters in books, citing them by the usual academic conventions. This notwithstanding, I wish to acknowledge Penerbit USM for the use of substantial factual portions of my previous book, *The Dilemma of Independence: Two Decades of Malaysia's Foreign Policy 1957–1977*, published in 1983.

The subject of this book spans some fifty years, a large expanse of time by any measure. My first responsibility was to render correctly the facts covered over this wide swathe of time. The second task was perhaps even more difficult, namely, to frame these facts within certain conceptions of meaning. While facts can never be altered, the manner by which we interpret them is clearly marked by certain currents of thought, intellectual constructs, and paradigms. Remarkably, the fields of international relations and foreign policy study have been highly stable. There remain broadly two kinds of analysts, realists and idealists, sometimes found in their new incarnations as "neo-realists" and "constructivists". I lean more naturally on the side of constructivism. However, this should not be taken as a slavish adherence to any particular school of thought. Indeed, an appreciation of realism and sensitivity to critical theory are important epistemic antidotes to certain modes of idealistic thinking, at times too liberally indulged by the social sciences.

Readers not interested in theory should read the book as a chronicle of the highly eventful and often controversial meanderings of Malaysian foreign relations over fifty years.

Let me take the opportunity here to thank the two anonymous readers of my manuscript who gave me useful and constructive criticisms in revising it for final publication. Deepest thanks go to Maznah who is at once my severest critic and staunchest ally.

Johan Saravanamuttu
December 2009

ACKNOWLEDGEMENTS

In writing a book such as this, there are usually too many persons to thank and the inevitable danger is of excluding many persons who have contributed in one way or another to the effort.

Firstly, I wish to thank Ambassador K. Kesavapany, director of ISEAS, for his generous support and constant advice and encouragement. Secondly, my sincere thanks go to Dr Chin Kin Wah, deputy director of ISEAS and Dr Ooi Kee Beng, coordinator of the Malaysian Studies programme at ISEAS, both of whom read an early draft of the book and offered valuable comments.

Many thanks are due to Mrs Triena Ong, head of publications, who provided much needed assistance towards seeing the manuscript to its printed form. In particular I would like to thank Ms Fatanah Sarmani for her invaluable assistance. Many thanks also go Ms Chng Kim See, chief librarian, Mrs Y.L. Lee, head of administration, who have also assisted me in various ways during my tenure at ISEAS. Thanks also go to Ms Sharifah Shifa Al-Attas who assisted in sourcing materials from the IDFR library.

To Barry Wain and Lee Hock Guan, many thanks for the many long conversations about Malaysia, and in particular, to Barry, for an advanced reading of the chapter on Mahathir's foreign policy in his book, *Malaysian Maverick: Mahathir Mohamad in Turbulent Times*. Thanks also go Izzuddin Mustafa with whom I bounced off many ideas on foreign policy, particularly the notion of "middlepowermanship".

Many other colleagues at ISEAS, especially Tan Keng Jin, Rodolfo Severino, Mark Hong, P. Ramasamy, Daljit Singh, David Koh, Hui Yew Fong, Terence Chong, A. Mani, Vijay Sakhuja, Arun Balasubramaniam, and Omkar Shrestha expended much time in conversations with me and extended encouragement in one form or another.

Finally, I wish to acknowledge and record my thanks to the many senior diplomats, government officials, and others who were interviewed by me or had conversations with me through the years of 2007/2008/2009 when I was writing the book. Where appropriate, they have been duly attributed in my text and footnotes but I can assure them that I have also assiduously avoided unwanted attribution on sensitive questions. Similarly, let me also take the opportunity to acknowledge previous interviews and communications with important individuals which I completed in 1975 when I was conducting my doctoral fieldwork. In my citations I have retained their original formal positions and mostly left out honorifics and titles. Some of these individuals would have received new honours and taken up new positions and some have passed on, so I do seek their families' indulgence for having cited their names again in this book.

Johan Saravanamuttu

ABBREVIATIONS AND GLOSSARY

ABIM	Angkatan Belia Islam Malaysia (Islamic Youth Movement of Malaysia)
ABC	ASEAN Brussels Committee
ACCIN	Allied Coordinating Committee of Islamic NGOs
ACA	Anti Corruption Agency
ACCRIS	ASEAN Coordinating Committee for the Reconstruction and Rehabilitation of Indochina States
ACFTA	ASEAN-China Free Trade Area
ARF	ASEAN Regional Forum
AFTA	ASEAN Free Trade Area
AJCEP	ASEAN-Japan Comprehensive Economic Partnership Agreement
AMDA	Anglo-Malayan Defence Agreement
AMED	Asia-Middle East Dialogue
ANZAM	Anglo-New Zealand-Australia-Malaysia Defence Area
ANZUZ	Australia-New Zealand-US Defence Area
APEC	Asia Pacific Economic Council or Community
APR	Asia Pacific Roundtable
ARMM	Autonomous Region of Muslim Mindanao
ASAS/ASA	Association of Southeast Asian States
ASEAN	Association of Southeast Asian Nations
ASEM	Asia-Europe Meeting
ASG	Abu Sayyaf Group
ASLI	Asian Strategy and Leadership Institute
Berdikari	Self-reliance
BITAC	Bilateral Training and Consultation
BN	Barisan Nasional
BNPP	National Liberation Front of Patani
BRN	National Revolutionary Front (Patani)
CEPT	Common Effective Preferential Tariff
CHOGM	Commonwealth Head of Government Meeting
CIQ	Customs, Immigration and Quarantine

CLOB	Central Limit Order Book
Colombo Plan	British Commonwealth association of countries
Danaharta	Asset Management Corporation
Danamodal	Special Purpose Vehicle (for capital management)
DAP	Democratic Action Party (Malaysia)
EAEC	East Asian Economic Centre
ECAFE	Economic Commission for Asia and the Far East
EON	Edaran Otomobil Nasional or National Car Sales Company
EU	European Union
FAO	Food and Agriculture Organization
FDI	Foreign Direct Investment
FIC	Foreign Investment Committee
FIDA	Federal Industrial Development Authority (predecessor to MIDA)
FPDA	Five Power Defence Arrangement
FPI	Front Pembela Islam (The Islamic Defender Front)
FTA	Free Trade Agreement
GAM	Gerakan Aceh Merdeka (Free Aceh Movement)
GATT	General Agreement on Trade and Tariffs
GERAKAN	Parti Gerakan Rakyat Malaysia (People's Movement Party of Malaysia)
GRP	Government of the Republic of the Philippines
GSP	System of Preference
HDC	Halal Industry Development Corporation
HICOM	Heavy Industries Corporation of Malaysia
HINDRAF	Hindu Rights Action Force
IBRD	International Bank for Reconstruction and Development or World Bank
ICAO	International Civil Aviation Organization
ICJ	International Court of justice
ICMI	Indonesian Association of Muslim Intellectuals
IDB	Islamic Development Bank
IDFR	Institute of Diplomacy and Foreign Relations
IDR	Iskandar Development Region
IDA	International Development Association
IGO	Inter-Governmental Organization
IIU	International Islamic University
IKIM	Institute of Islamic Understanding
ILO	International Labour Organization

IMF	International Monetary Fund
IMT	International Monitoring Team
INTERFET	International Force East Timor
IPCMC	Independent Police Complaints and Misconduct Commission
IRCON	Indian Railway Construction Company
ISA	Internal Security Act
ISNA	Islamic Society of North America
ISIS	Institute of Strategic and International Studies
ITC	International Tin Council
ITU	International Telecommunications Union
JAKIM	Jabatan Kemajuan Islam Malaysia (Department of Islamic Development Malaysia)
JAMECA	Japan-Malaysia Economic Association
JMEPA	Japan-Malaysia Economic Partnership Agreement
JAWI	Jabatan Agama Wilayah or Kuala Lumpur Religious Department
JI	Jemaah Islamiyah or Islamic Congregation
JIM	Jakarta Informal Meetings
JIM	Jemaah Islah Malaysia or Islamic Reform Congregation of Malaysia
JPA	Jabatan Perkhidmatan Awam or Public Services Department
Ketuanan Melayu	Malay supremacy
KLSE	Kuala Lumpur Stock Exchange
LDC	Less Developed Country
MAJECA	Malaysian-Japan Economic Association Malaysian External
MAPHILINDO	Association of Malaysia, Philippines and Indonesia
MATRADE	Trade Development Corporation
MCA	Malaysian Chinese Association
MCCBCHS	Malaysian Consultative Council for Buddhism, Christianity, Hinduism and Sikhism
MCP	Malayan Communist Party
MEA	Ministry of External Affairs
MFA	Ministry of Foreign Affairs or Foreign Ministry
MIC	Malaysian Indian Congress
MIDA	Malaysian Industrial Development Authority
MIFC	Malaysia International Islamic Financial Centre Initiative

MIHAS	Malaysia International Halal Showcase
MISC	Malaysian International Shipping Corp
MTJA	Malaysia-Thailand Joint Authority
MILF	The Moro Islamic Liberation Front
MITI	Ministry of International Trade and Industry
MMC	Malaysian Mining Corporation
MNLF	Moro National Liberation Front
MSRC	Malaysian Strategic Research Centre
MTCP	Malaysian Technical Cooperation Programme
NAFTA	North American Free Trade Area
NAM	Non-aligned Movement
NDP	New Development Policy
NEP	New Economic Policy
NIC	Newly Industrialized Country
NIDL	New International Division of Labor
NIEO	New International Economic Order
NGO	Non-Governmental Organization
NOC	National Operations Council
NRPC	Association of Natural Rubber Producing countries
OAU	Organization of African Unity
OIC	Organization of The Islamic Conference
OPEC	Organization of Petroleum Exporting Countries
PAP	People's Action Party (Singapore)
PAS	Parti Islam SeMalaysia (Islamic Party of Malaysia)
PERNAS	Perbadanan National or National Trading Corporation
Petronas	National Petroleum Corporation of Malaysia
PKFZ	Port Klang Free Zone
PKN	Parti KeADILan Nasional (National Justice Party)
PKMM	Parti Kebangsaan Melayu Malaya (National Party of Malays)
PKR	Parti Keadilan Rakyat (People's Justice Party)
PMIP	Pan-Malayan Islamic Party
PMO	Prime Minister's Department
POA	Points of Agreement (Malaysia-Singapore)
PPP	People's Progressive Party (Malaysia)
PRM	Parti Rakyat Malaysia (Peoples Party of Malaysia)
Proton	Perusahaan Otomobil Nasional or National Car Corporation

PSRM	Parti Sosialis Rakyat Malaysia (Socialist People's Party of Malaysia)
PULO	Patani United Liberation Organization
PUM	Persatuan Ulama Malaysia (Malaysian Ulama Association)
RELA	People's Volunteer Corps
ROO	Rules of Origin
SCCAN	Coordinating Committee of ASEAN Nations
SEAFET	Southeast Asia Friendship and Economic Treaty
SEANWFZ	Southeast Asian Nuclear Weapon Free Zone
SEARCCT	Southeast Asia Regional Centre for Counter-Terrorism
SEATO	Southeast Asian Treaty Organization
SME	Small and Medium Enterprise
SRV	Socialist Republic of Vietnam
Tabung Haji	Muslim Pilgrims' Fund
TERAS	Teras Pengupayaan Melayu (Malay National Force)
TWN	Third World Network
UEM	United Engineers Malaysia
UMNO	United Malays National Organization
UN	United Nations
UNESCO	UN Education, Scientific and Cultural Organization
UNCTAD	United Nations Conference on Trade and Development
UNTAC	United Nations Transitional Authority in Cambodia
UNTAG	United Nations Transition Assistance Group
UNHCR	United Nations High Commissioner for Refugees
UNPROFOR	United Nations Protection Force
UPU	Universal Postal Union
USIP	United States Institute of Peace
Wisma Putra	Malaysian Ministry of Foreign Affairs
WHO	World Health Organization
WMU	World Meteorological Union
WTO	World Trade Organization
ZOPFAN	Zone of Peace, Freedom and Neutrality

Two former prime ministers meet on 17 June 1986. Tunku Abdul Rahman receives Tun Hussein Onn at the Tunku's residence in Penang.
Source: *The Star*, Malaysia.

Malaysian Prime Minister Tunku Abdul Rahman, in jovial mood at a tea reception, is seen with Singapore's Prime Minister Lee Kuan Yew and former Chief Minister David Marshall on 16 November 1961. The Tunku was en route to the London Talks on the formation of Malaysia. *Source: The Straits Times* © Singapore Press Holdings Limited. Reprinted with permission.

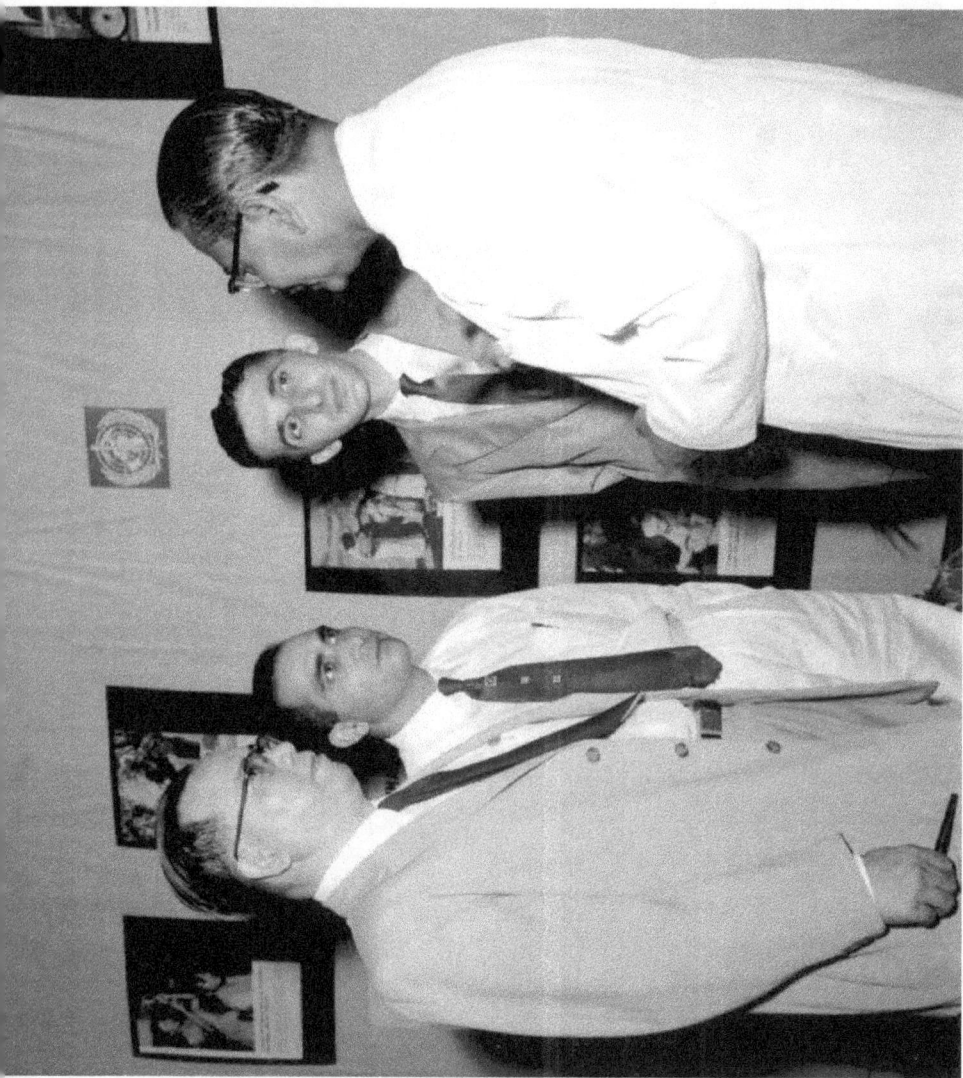

Malaysian Prime Minister Tunku Abdul Rahman visits a United Nations' exhibition on 28 October 1957. He is seen talking with several foreign dignitaries. *Source*: National Archives of Singapore.

Malaysian Prime Minister Abdul Razak is escorted by his Singapore counterpart Lee Kuan Yew and is greeted by Singapore's Defence Minister Goh Keng Swee on 13 November 1973. The Malaysian Premier was on his first three-day official visit since Singapore became independent on 9 August 1965. *Source: The Straits Times* © Singapore Press Holdings Limited. Reprinted with permission.

Malaysian Prime Minister Mahathir Mohamad bids farewell to Palestinian leader Yasser Arafat after their meeting in Kuala Lumpur on 17 October 1999. Arafat was on a one-day visit to discuss bilateral cooperation and the Middle East peace process with the Malaysian leader. *Source*: Photo by Getty Images.

U.S. President George W. Bush shakes hands with the Malaysian Prime Minister Mahathir Mohamad on 14 May 2002 at the Oval Office of the White House in Washington, D.C. The two leaders talked about the war on terrorism during their meeting. *Source*: Photo by Getty Images.

The KD Tunku Abdul Rahman docks at the Teluk Sepanggar Naval Base in Sabah on 17 September 2009. This is the first of two French Scorpene submarines delivered to Malaysia. The submarines measuring 63.5 metres long have a displacement of 1,590 tonnes. Each is manned by a 31-man crew and has a submerge depth of up to 200 metres. Each is also equipped with six torpedo tubes, which can launch simultaneously, as well as anti-ship and anti-submarine torpedoes and anti-surface missiles. *Source: The Star*, Malaysia.

Malaysian Prime Minister Abdullah Ahmad Badawi is seen waving with Japanese counterpart Shinzo Abe (2nd L), Philippine President Gloria Macapagal Arroyo (C), Singapore Prime Minister Lee Hsien Loong (2nd R) and Myanmar leader General Soe Win at the meeting of the ASEAN-Japan leaders during the 12th Summit of the Association of Southeast Asian Nations (ASEAN) in Cebu, Philippines on 14 January 2007.

Source: Photo by Getty Images.

Malaysia's sixth Prime Minister Najib Abdul Razak shakes hands with President Hu Jintao of China in the Malaysian Premier's office in Putrajaya, Malaysia on 11 November 2009. China and Malaysia signed a loan agreement for the Penang second bridge project, according to a joint statement.

Source: Photo by Getty Images.

1

INTRODUCTION
Framing the Study of Foreign Policy

INTRODUCTION

On 27 May 1974, a Malaysian entourage led by Prime Minister Tun Abdul Razak left for the People's Republic of China in the first high-level official contact of the two governments since Malaya's independence in 1957. On 31 May, Malaysia and China announced the normalization of relations, to be followed by an exchange of ambassadors. At the same time, Malaysia terminated diplomatic (consular) relations with Taiwan. In a joint communiqué, the two governments considered "all foreign aggression, interference, control and subversion to be impermissible" and held that the social system of a country should be chosen and decided by its own people and "opposed to any attempt by any country or group or countries to establish hegemony or create spheres of influence in any part of the world" (see Chapter 5). Malaysia's opening up to diplomatic relations with China was part of an overall transition in its foreign policy from a pro-Western to a non-aligned stance and recognition of the imperative for coexistence among non-Communist and Communists states in the global system. In so doing Malaysia was no doubt moving along with a global trend set by the foremost anti-Communist state, the United States of America, which had recognized the PRC, in 1972. Nonetheless, Malaysia was first among Southeast Asian states to have formally recognized the PRC which remained locked within a Cold War regional politics. For a small country with a Communist insurgency and a Chinese minority population, the recognition of China resolved a number of matters for Malaysia, which will be further discussed in Chapter 5. From the perspective of foreign policy, I believe it exemplified what the literature in International Relations has termed "constructivism". In plain language, the Malaysian state "constructed" a new foreign policy and acted in its interest *qua* state to move in a direction consonant with its national needs and its internal social dynamics and political culture. To be sure, the change of policy was executed by a political leadership or elite, but its construction was based not only on the cold calculation of material gains, but also on an "intersubjective" interpretation of domestic sensitivities and needs.

The main purpose of this introductory chapter is to show the importance of constructivist thinking or theory in the study of Malaysian foreign policy, while at the same time to critique it with a view of the specific task at hand; a critical study of Malaysian foreign policy. The literature on International Relations (IR) has witnessed a challenge to, if not a shift away from, rationalist-realist, institutional, and transactional approaches.[1] Many studies may be said to now fall under the broad rubric of "constructivism" or are influenced by the constructive turn in IR theory propounded by Alexander Wendt.[2] Although constructivism has been made out to be highly complex,[3] Wendt has stated the premises of constructivism as it pertains to international relations plainly in the following manner:

1. States are the principal units of analysis for international political theory
2. The key structures in the states system are intersubjective, rather than material; and
3. State identities and interests are in important part, constructed by these social structures rather than given exogenously by the system, by human nature, or domestic politics (Wendt 1994, p. 385).

In the example above of the shift in Malaysian foreign policy, Wendt's first point about the agency of the state is well illustrated, along with the second and third points that the state does not only act mechanically according to the dictates of the international system or even domestic structure, but is also influenced by "non-material" elements of the global and domestic environment in decision making.

We could, therefore, take it that a corollary of constructivist theory is that actions of states are "constitutive" of social structures and processes embedded in the domestic and external environment rather than merely a function of exogenous factors.[4] The basic tenet in constructivism has to do with the role of human agency acting within certain social or structural constraints. It posits that human agency, while not fully independent of structure, is not wholly limited by it. Furthermore, human agency is to be understood as "reflexive", that is, that social action is mutually dependent and dynamic and consists of the constant interplay of social forces and actors with their own particular ideas, identities, and interests. Many of the notions of constructivism hark to the work of sociologist Anthony Giddens.[5] Alexander Wendt may be said to be among the first to apply this to the realm of international relations. In his important and still hotly debated work on *Social Theory of International Politics* (1999), Wendt proffers a new paradigm for IR in contradistinction to the dominant neo-realist and neoliberal theories underpinning the bulk of the IR literature.[6] My interest here is to see how constructivism can be applied to foreign policy studies, particularly in the Southeast Asian region and more particularly, to the Malaysian case.

In the main, my critique emanates largely from the body of literature in the social sciences known generically as "critical theory", which is sometimes thought to have also influenced the constructivist turn.[7] I would argue that critical theory challenges realism and neo-realism in a somewhat different fashion from constructivism by problematizing institutions and processes, and by "deconstructing" their ideological and ideational underpinnings. Thus a critical theorist would consider the state of "anarchy" in the international system as no more inevitable and natural than dominating the system due to some preordained law of nature. In fact, hegemonic orders arise out of a particular course of history, not just through conquest and wars, but also the outcome and emergence of various social forces and social formations. The neo-Gramscian approach of Robert Cox, for example, attempts to uncover the sources of such hegemony, as well as the forces of counter-hegemony, so as to steer human society in the direction of a non-hegemonic or even a "post-hegemonic" global order. It is evident that Cox's notion of post-hegemony stands in diametrical opposition to Robert Gilpin's neo-realist notion of "hegemonic stability", seen as a necessary ingredient of the neoliberal global order.[8] As such, critical theory demands that the analyst does not merely explain global phenomena, but in so doing, also attempts to steer it towards a particular intellectual trajectory.[9]

To appreciate foreign policy through the lenses of constructivist theory and critical theory would give an analyst two distinct theoretical advantages. First, through constructivist lenses, one would presumably be able to uncover how policy outputs and outcomes are not only a function of rationalist-realist construction by decision makers, but that they are also constitutive of domestic and external processes in which the decisions of policymakers are embedded. Put differently, one could posit that foreign policy outcomes do not necessarily only flow from "rational-actor" assumptions or presumptions; they are the product of multifarious processes usually intimately linked to particular identity and interests, and even more importantly, often the product of societal needs, social contestation, and the character of domestic politics.

Second, appraising foreign policy from the perspective of critical theory allows one to raise important questions and issues with respect to the direction or trajectory of foreign policy. What have been the ideological, ideational, and "cultural" underpinnings of foreign policy? What are the vested interests, social forces, actors, and agents behind these ideational impulses? Have these changed over time, along with changes of leadership or societal movements, developments and transformations? Is a foreign policy hegemonic, counter-hegemonic, *status quo*-oriented in the global and regional contexts, and *vis-à-vis* the global order? What societal forces have been able to influence, if at all, foreign policy? What other domestic or international elements of civil society impinge on the shape and character of foreign policy in what phases of its history? It is clear that a constructivist perspective on foreign policymaking would not be complete without its critical facet.

Another dimension of foreign policy analysis needs to be engaged in the study of a country such as Malaysia. I refer in particular to a literature that may be best described as middle-gauge rather than grand theories. Some of this literature deals with notions of middle power statecraft and the idea of "middlepowermanship".[10] Some other literature has alluded to the statecraft of small states, which construct strategies and policies going well beyond the stock realist paradigms of international relations. More specifically, some analyses of small state and middle power diplomacy have invoked notions such as balancing, bandwagoning, and hedging, to explain more nuanced foreign policies.[11] This study will draw on this literature and particularly, middle power diplomacy as an idea to illuminate Malaysian foreign policy in its more matured phases.

TOWARDS A CRITICAL CONSTRUCTIVISM

It may be suggested that Wendtian constructivism could be said to have made its mark either explicitly or implicitly on Southeast Asian studies although it has not impacted directly on foreign policy studies of particular countries in the region. Constructivism seems to have inspired or influenced a spate of more critically poised ASEAN (Association of Southeast Asian Nations) studies, which may be said to have tried to uncover the relationships between the ideas, identities, and the interests of Southeast Asian states through the agency of the generic ASEAN entity. Some studies have implied that an ASEAN "pluralistic security community"[12] has resulted through statist construction.

In the language of Wendtian constructivism, these relationships have evolved along with socially and politically constructed structures and dynamics which are not exogenous givens of the anarchic international order. In the brief literature review below, let me take a few recent examples of constructivist-inclined or constructivist-inspired writings on ASEAN and then relate this to the state of security discourse and practice in ASEAN. In the process, I will also develop my own understanding and critique of constructivism.

The work of Acharya (1999, 2001) seems to bear the strong influence of constructivism. The latter work cited above which is titled *Constructing a Security Community in Southeast Asia* clearly bears the hallmark of constructivist theorizing. Thus, the book examines the interplay between norms and socialization, the "ASEAN way", for example, as well as the regulatory and constitutive effects of ASEAN, that is, its various processes and institutions, in its quest to become a security community. However, in my view the flavour and thrust of Acharya's work fall within the broad sphere of state-centric constructivism, more or less in keeping with Wendtian theory.

Ruland in a self-consciously critical engagement with the constructivist literature examines the Asian crisis of 1997/1998 and its implications for ASEAN's brand of regionalism. He suggests that at the end of the day, "ASEAN's policy mix is closer to the realist than institutionalist pole." (Rüland 2000, p. 443). Looking at ASEAN's handling of the financial crisis, he further argues that the "institutional and constructivist requiems for realism were premature". Another work on ASEAN's diplomatic and security culture (Haacke 2003) falls squarely within a state-centric paradigm while adopting only some of the language of constructivism. The author suggests that the core of the ASEAN security culture, known famously as the "ASEAN way", can be decomposed into the following elements, namely:

- Sovereign equality
- Non-recourse to the use of force
- Non-interference and non-intervention
- Non-involvement of ASEAN in bilateral conflict
- Quiet diplomacy
- Mutual respect and tolerance

While Haacke's study shows great sensibility to a constructive approach and points to how ASEAN security culture was the basis of all of ASEAN cooperative ventures, it begs the important question of how such a culture is paradoxically also the chief impediment to the attainment of a full-fledged security community in the region.

My own writing on ASEAN (Saravanamuttu 1999) has tried to steer analysis away from a state-centric paradigm and, I would argue, falls in line with another strain of constructivism, which is not Wendtian in origin. Taking the cue from Falk's notion of "geo-governance" (Falk 1995), I have implicitly argued that in ASEAN and Asia-Pacific regionalism, there emerged a plethora of competing visions and missions stemming from the interests and identities of state and non-state actors has emerged. ASEAN security processes and agendas have, however, remained profoundly state-centric. Quite often the non-state visions with their "alternative" discourses were mirror images of their state counterparts, with paradigms verging on a total rejection of the statist visions for regional order (Saravanamuttu 1999, p. 108). Hence, I have argued for the dialogic interaction between civil society and state to fashion more non-violent, humane approaches to geogovernance.

Writing on the security discourse of ASEAN, William Tow, in his essay on "Alternative Security Models: Implications for ASEAN" (2003), avers that constructivism "invites policy-makers and analysts alike to delve beneath perceived (or misperceived) interest and intentions of potential opponents". Positing that the "human security model" poses the most significant challenge to traditional security referents, he states:

> Ultimately, security is about all of us and each of us, regardless of how we may choose to organize institutions or instruments at a given time to achieve it. This model supplants the collective human rights concept (Tow 2003, p. 304).

He further calls for a linking of traditional and alternative security perspectives and agendas. Taking the area of conflict prevention as an example, he suggests that time-honoured strategies to achieve regional stability could converge with the attempts of alternative security proponents "to discern and eradicate the root causes of conflict, based on economic deprivation, social cleavages and human suffering." (Tow 2003, p. 308). Further extrapolating from Tow's essay, I would add that the agency for such a convergence would be the engagement of the state by civil forces, groups and NGOs whose work is indeed focused on issues and questions of human security. State-civil society dynamics could, therefore, be seen as an important plank for new constructions of regional security agendas, which are in greater sync with societal concerns and problems.

To my mind, it becomes increasingly clear that when constructivism is applied to a situation such as ASEAN's, it would be imperative to see how it could be conjoined with "critical theory", which I will subsequently attempt to do below. However, let me now turn specifically to foreign policy studies to determine if constructivism has had any impact. At first glance, foreign policy studies of ASEAN states, even in more recent years, or for that matter foreign policy studies for the most part, have remained innocent of the constructivist turn.[13] Let me take just a few examples from the ASEAN region for the sake of discussion, aside from Malaysian foreign policy studies, which will be reviewed further on.

The vast oeuvres of the late Michael Leifer,[14] which include one study of Indonesia's foreign policy and one of Singapore's foreign policy, clearly fall under the rubric of realist or neo-realist studies,[15] although Leifer does not employ or explicitly commit to any particular paradigm. A deconstruction of the study of Indonesian foreign policy may suggest that Leifer is basically guided by a commonsensical understanding of major political developments and changes affecting the country. For example, even prior to the September 11 attacks, he came to recognize the increasing importance of Islam as a factor influencing foreign policy, and demonstrates this in his study. In contrast, Dewi Fortuna Anwar's study of Indonesian foreign policy could well have been cast into a constructivist vein or may be said to have some constructivist sensibility although she herself makes no mention of this school of thought. She instead explains that she is influenced by the much earlier work of Franklin Weinstein (1976), now considered a classic, which debunked or downplayed the "idiosyncratic" factor and elitist interpretations of Indonesia's foreign policy. Weinstein rejected James Rosenau's (1980) framework of "pre-theories" of foreign policy and instead locked into a political economy approach in appreciating Indonesian foreign policy. More recent works on Indonesian foreign policy tend to eschew theorizing altogether, an example being Suryadinata's study of foreign policy under the Soeharto period (1996). Suryadinata admits to using a "determinants" of foreign policy approach, and places considerable emphasis on "political culture" in explaining the character of Indonesia's foreign policy elite. The interesting study by Rizal Sukma on Islam in Indonesian foreign policy (2003) employs no explicit theoretical approach and acknowledges an intellectual debt to Michael Leifer, to whom he has dedicated the work. Sukma's concluding that "Islam has entered Indonesian foreign policy only in form rather than substance" (p. 140) provides a hint of a constructivist theoretical sensibility. A constructivist analysis may thus have been better able to unearth how Islam may have been constitutive of a deepening Islamist perspective in Indonesian foreign policy.

The classic study of Thai foreign policy by Ganganath Jha (1979) is essentially realist and historical as the author himself intimates (p. 5). A more explicitly IR approach is adopted by Charivat Santaputra (1985) in his study. Submitted as doctoral thesis to SOAS (the School of Oriental and African

Studies), the author acknowledges an intellectual debt to Joseph Frankel and employs a decision making framework for analysis. Interestingly, in his study of the role played by early Thai political leaders, Pridi Phanomyong and Phibun Songkhram in foreign policy, the author is able to weave in the notion of a "weak state" as the underpinning of Thai foreign policy in the years of 1932–46.

The work on Philippine foreign policy has been more varied and somewhat uneven. There have been studies by foreign policy practitioners, that is, those who have served as diplomats (Ingles 1982; Domingo 1993), critiques of foreign policy, sometimes reading more like political tracts (Simbulan 1991), and academic studies (Wurfel 1983, 1990). The tone of the first genre would be something platitudinous such as, "Philippines has embarked on an independent course that is guided by a clear and coherent conception of the values, aspirations, needs and interests of the Filipino people" (Ingles 1982), in contradistinction to its mirror opposite which would argue that the Philippine foreign policy is a function of American foreign policy (Simbulan 1991, passim). The essay by Wurfel (1990) provides an antidote. Rejecting a rational choice model as a basis to understand Philippine foreign policy decision making, he argues that domestic constraints and resources, coupled by intra-elite politics and a high economic dependency borne of Spanish and American colonialism, have been the basis of foreign relations. The debilitating presence of corruption and the failure of social reform are also part and parcel of a Philippine political culture that contextualizes foreign policy. While Wurfel's effort is premised on the political economy approach of the book in which it appears, it could well have been enhanced by a constructivist sensibility.

Finally, let us take look at the study of Singapore's foreign policy. The major studies have been by Rau (1974), Wilairat (1975, 1976), Leifer (1999), Ganesan (2005), and a recent effort by Acharya (2008). All three writers except Acharya have stressed the vulnerability of the Singapore state. Wilairat's now classic study was a doctoral thesis submitted to Georgetown University in 1975 and provides a veritable benchmark. After reviewing the foreign policy literature, he devises a framework of analysis based on four dimensions: external environment; internal environment, including political culture and domestic politics; structure and process (foreign policymaking elite and bureaucracy) of the foreign policy system; foreign policy content and undertakings (objectives, decisions, consequences, and effects). The core thesis of Wilairat's work is the allusion to the crucial role of a foreign policymaking elite, which consisted of an inner circle (Lee Kuan Yew, Goh Keng Swee, S. Rajaratnam, and Toh Chin Chye), a second echelon (selected politicians and business elite), and a technical elite of foreign affairs bureaucrats (Wilairat 1976, pp. 291ff.). Some may argue that a similar elite, with a greater smattering of technocrats, continues to dominate foreign policy decision making today.

Ganesan's 2005 study begins with a reaffirmation of realism as the most applicable theory for Singapore, much in keeping with Leifer's earlier study. Consisting of eight chapters, Ganesan's book begins with a theoretic chapter, followed by one on policy principles and "policy arena", and proceeds to examine early policy outputs (1965–68), Cold War and post-Cold War outputs and important regional bilateral relations, that is, with Malaysia and Indonesia, followed by a chapter on economic and defence diplomacy, and a conclusion. Stressing the "helplessness" of a small state such as Singapore, Ganesan avers in his conclusion that neutrality in foreign policy remains an elusive option for weak and vulnerable states such as Singapore. I wonder if a constructivist sensibility to Singapore's foreign policy would not reveal nuances of the so-called vulnerability of Singapore, namely that a recursive reproduction of an ideology of "siege and insecurity" (Leifer's phrase) could actually be the basis of psychological strength (rather than weakness) in a foreign policy clearly anchored on high economic capacity, if not superiority, as well as the skilful manipulation of regional and global politics.

MALAYSIAN FOREIGN POLICY STUDIES[16]

In this section, I will first try to review all known studies of Malaysia's foreign policy (MFP) to date and provide a "genealogy" as it were,[17] after which I will make the case for the framing of Malaysian foreign policy in terms of a constructivist-critical approach. Crudely speaking, there may be several "generations" or subsets of Malaysian foreign policy studies,[18] two of which may be said to have constructivist sensibilities, but I have detected none that self-consciously possess elements of critical theory.[19]

The first generation of Malaysian foreign policy studies comprised essentially descriptive studies or chronicles (Silcock 1963; Hazra 1965; Dalton 1967; Tilman 1969; Ott 1971; Tongpricha 1970; Khaw 1976). An early attempt to be somewhat more analytical was Ott's article on Malaysian "foreign policy formulation", which suggested that foreign policy was "the virtual prerogative of a small stable elite comprising four or five men." (Ott 1973, p. 225). At the same time, Ott does not completely deny the importance of the Ministry of Foreign Affairs (MFA) in foreign policy (Ott 1971, pp. 191ff.).

My own efforts (1976, 1983, 1987) in tracing the "sources and content" of Malaysian foreign policy within chronological frames employ an analytical framework which I had devised, culled from foreign policy theoretical literature. It identifies four sources of foreign policy: external sources, eco-historical sources, and idiosyncratic/elite sources, which are linked to four types of foreign policy outputs: objectives, postures, strategies, and actions.[20] The study argued that for a developing, Third World country such as Malaysia, foreign policy was intimately linked to the pursuit of certain nationally defined needs and interests. The study by Liow (2001) uses a similar generic analytical framework, but focuses on the Mahathir administration.

A third, larger slew of studies of the 1980s, 1990s, and 2000s examines specific periods under the tutelage of particular prime ministers (Abdullah Ahmad 1985; Chamil Wariya 1989; Camroux 1994; Pathmanathan and Lazarus 1984; Liow 2001; Rozeman Hassan 2003; Dhillon 2005, 2009). One particular study by Faridah Jaafar (2007) focuses entirely on the idiosyncratic or *keperibadian* (personality) factor in Malaysian foreign policy. Another set of studies has focused on bilateral or foreign relations with particular countries or powers such as with the United States, Australia, and Indonesia (Sodhy 1982, 1988; Camilleri 2001; Liow 2005), or with the "South" (Ahmad Faiz 2005).[21] An important set of studies has been specifically framed in particular contexts; that of political economy (Stubbs 1990) and with respect to Islam (Nair 1995; Abdul Razak Baginda 2004)). There are a number of studies on defence policy and alliances pertaining to Malaysia (Chin 1974, 1983; Jeshurun 1980). One recent work has placed diplomacy and the MFA at the centre of its narrative (Jeshurun 2007). Finally, there are edited volumes on overall foreign and defence policies, often published as readings or training modules (Mohammed Azhari et al. 1990; Abdul Razak Baginda and Rohana Mahmood 1995).

In this section let me focus on three recent book length works, each of which represent interesting and important genres in the study of Malaysian foreign policy. I have in mind Pamela Sodhy's 1991 study of Malaysian-American relations, Ahmad Faiz's 2005 study of Malaysia's South-South relations, and Shanti Nair's 1997 study of Islam in foreign policy.

Sodhy's 570-page tome is originally derived from a doctoral thesis submitted to Cornell University in 1982, with two added chapters to bring the book up to speed with events and relations in the Reagan-Bush and Mahathir eras up until 1990. The work, which is chronologically structured, is a macro historical study which employs the tools and perspective of a trained historian. The nine substantive chapters deal with relations up till 1945, the post-war period till 1949, the Korean War years of 1950–53, the "dawn" of independence from 1946–57, the post-independence period of 1958–62, the Confrontation years of 1963–66, the Vietnam War years of

1967–75, and the last period already mentioned above. For the historian Sodhy, particular years marked important events either on the American or Malaysian side that heralded a new phase or temper in relations. Sodhy employs no particular discursive paradigm, but implicitly accepts the state as a unitary actor in foreign policymaking, the state being basically equated with a putative political leader, that is, a prime minister or a president as the case may be. This sort of fact driven rendering of foreign policy reveals important predilections of leaders in foreign policymaking, but leaves a lacuna of unexplained linkages between state and society, or between leaders and their political constituencies, which could be important factors constitutive of foreign policy practices and outcomes.

The second work by Ahmad Faiz (originally a doctoral thesis for Waikato University, New Zealand) purports to employ some of the tools of foreign policy literature to dissect determining factors and their implications in Mahathir's South-South policies for the years 1986–96. In Chapter 2 the author suggests that "a new assertiveness" is evident in the foreign policy under Mahathir, which has led to greater forays into South-South cooperation. Ahmad Faiz contends that the shift under Mahathir first entailed a "top-down" process where the leaders' preferences were evidently dominant, but this evolved into a phase where players such as private sector elites became important agents of policy and where policy outputs were often the results of even interdepartmental debates, consultations, and discussions. Empirical rendering of the relations with the Indochinese states, with South Pacific states, and particularly with Papau New Gunea and Fiji, and Melanesian forestry constitute the substantive chapters of the book. Ahmad Faiz's study of foreign policy may be considered to comprise a microanalytical political economy approach, especially in terms of his case study of Malaysian private sector involvement in Melanesian forestry. It is also interesting that he points out in his conclusion that an element that had become constitutive (to use constructivist parlance) of Malaysian political economy and foreign policy was the New Economic Policy (NEP). There is, however, no engagement with constructive theories in Ahmad Faiz's work.

Shanti Nair's study of Islam in Malaysian foreign policy, initially a doctoral dissertation submitted to the University of Geneva, clearly shows a sociological and even a "cultural studies" sensibility. She avers that her book hoped to demonstrate the imperatives of rapidly changing patterns of division within political society (in particular, that of the Malay community) and that power structures within the general system hold as much if not greater relevance for Malaysian foreign policy than the particular character and style of its leader. (Nair 1997, p. 10). While the author does not herself locate her study within constructivism, in essence, it is a study in that vein. The first chapter deals with Islam in Malay politics and also in its multi-ethnic context, the second, the internationalization of Malaysia's Malay-Muslim identity; the third, Mahathir's constituting of "right (moderate) Islam" in various facets of policy; the fourth, the management of "wrong (extreme) Islam" by the state; the fifth, relations with Muslim minorities or "building of the *umma*"; the sixth, the issues of Palestine and Afghanistan; the seventh, post-Cold-War issues. Throughout all chapters, she conveys the sense of a seamless linkage between domestic processes and structures, and foreign policy practices and outcomes. The constructivist tenor of the author's concluding chapter speaks for itself:

> Like all religious ideas, Islamic ideas are products of their times — of different political and historical periods. As such, "Islam" in Malaysia (as elsewhere) has responded to the social, economic and political influences of its particular contexts. Islamic culture in Malaysia is produced and reproduced by every generation. Each particular context has thus been influenced by historical "conjunction" (Nair 1997, p. 271).

If there is one obvious lack in the study, it is the absence of any full discussion of the resistances and contestations of non-Muslim constituencies *vis-à-vis* the Islamization agenda of the state, especially during the Mahathir period.

The three studies I have reviewed point to important academic and intellectual directions to which a new study of Malaysian foreign policy should aspire. While macrohistorical surveys are crucial to capture broad patterns and developments of foreign policy outcomes over time, evidently, political institutions and processes which drive these policies also need to be explained. While Sodhy's study shows the importance of capturing foreign policy "in the large", Ahmad Faiz demonstrates how constituents and agencies beyond state actors are crucial factors operating at different levels of policy practices and formulation. And Shanti Nair's study shows how a sensibility to political culture and the domestic contexts of politics enhances greatly our understanding that foreign policy is not merely a function of structures and processes, but constitutive of its societal norms and values.

DEFINING FOREIGN POLICY OUTPUTS

This study posits that "foreign policy" consists of various broad levels of policy outputs such as objectives, postures, and more specifically directed outputs such as strategies and actions.[22] Concepts such as these have intuitive appeal since the practitioners of foreign policy themselves often use these very terms. I have attempted to provide some degree of conceptual clarity and definitional rigour to these concepts as they apply to foreign policy practice. In my framework, then, foreign policy objectives and postures occupy a central position, and in combination, determine the kinds of strategies and actions implemented in the actual conduct of foreign policy. Before elaborating on the exact nature of the relationships among these key concepts, it is necessary to define them more fully.

OBJECTIVES

The first category of foreign policy outputs may be termed "objectives". The most permanent of these objectives are the "core values" of political independence, territorial integrity, and national survival, which all states must value *qua* nation states. These basic goals of self-preservation are likely to be pursued by states for a long time more, considering the low likelihood of any substantial changes in the present anarchic condition of the international system. Since all nation states by definition seek to protect these core goals, they require little explanation beyond what I have already said. Apart from these basic goals, Arnold Wolfers has distinguished between "possession goals" and "milieu goals" (Arnold Wolfers 1962, pp. 73–74). The former are goals aimed at enhancing national values and needs, while the latter refer to the pursuit of conditions which transcend national boundaries. An example of a possession goal is bargaining for trade concessions with the view to gaining economic advantage, while a common milieu goal is the pursuit or promotion of international peace. Following K.J. Holsti, core goals are then short-range objectives of immediate importance, possession goals are middle-range objectives, normally involving demands on other actors, and milieu goals are long-range goals with no specific time limits and of grander pretensions.[23]

POSTURES

Postures are the general orientation of a state towards other world actors. They are different from objectives in that they are aspirational and are not functionally specific in purpose. Together with foreign policy objectives, they determine the kind of strategies and actions carried out by a state. However, since postures are aspirational in character, they may not directly result in any foreign policy strategy or even actions. Thus strategies and actions may be more a function of foreign policy objectives than postures. Nevertheless, since postures are the reflection of the various sources of a state's foreign policy, they give the general complexion and character to a foreign policy.

For example, although the core value goals exist solely by virtue of national existence, the manner in which these goals are sought (strategies and actions) will be affected by a state's foreign policy postures. In this case the causal sequence is:

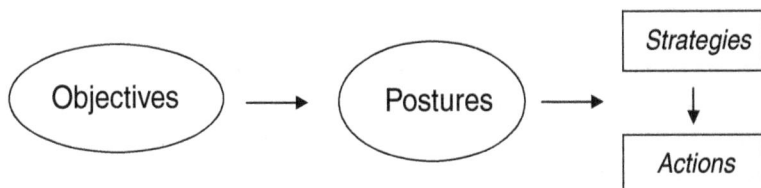

```
                                                    ┌──────────────┐
                                                    │  Strategies  │
                                                    └──────────────┘
  ( Objectives )  ──────▶  ( Postures )  ──────▶           ↓
                                                    ┌──────────────┐
                                                    │   Actions    │
                                                    └──────────────┘
```

In other instances, foreign policy objectives are to a large extent determined by foreign policy postures. In general, the middle-range goals fall into this category. For example, a "developing-world" posture in foreign policy usually leads to the pursuit of developmental goals such as those sanctioned by many Third World forums. In this case the causal direction is:

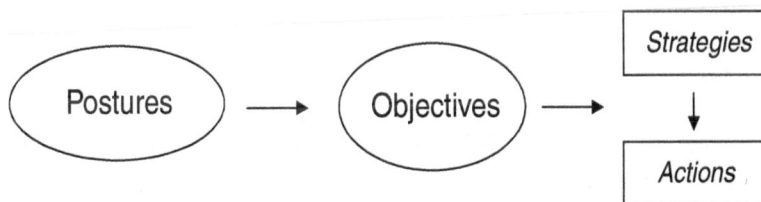

```
                                                    ┌──────────────┐
                                                    │  Strategies  │
                                                    └──────────────┘
  ( Postures )  ──────▶  ( Objectives )  ──────▶           ↓
                                                    ┌──────────────┐
                                                    │   Actions    │
                                                    └──────────────┘
```

The relationship between objectives and postures is a two-way flow. It has already been mentioned that postures may not directly result in foreign policy strategies or actions. As the word suggests, postures do imply a degree of "posturing", that is, the attempts by states to play to the gallery and to take stands largely for "home consumption", or for purely symbolic and political motives without any real intention of following through the pronouncements with concrete actions. Malaysia's adoption of a strong, developing world posture in economic issues often has the ring of posturing particularly, in the early and mid-1960s. For the most part, however, we will use the concept in its more formal and serious sense as the general orientation of a state along various dimensions or issue areas of foreign policy. What is clear is that a state's foreign policy postures are of primary importance in the depiction of its foreign policy.

STRATEGIES

These refer to the middle-range schemes, plans, and general lines of action which a state presents or employs as a means of securing its objectives. A strategy may be single-purpose or multi-purpose. That is, it may be aimed at securing one or more foreign policy objectives. While strategies are directly related to objectives, their particular texture and character are also a function of a state's foreign policy postures since there are many ways of securing any one objective. To take a simple Cold War example, a country not having the capability to protect its territorial boundaries may turn either to the Americans or the Russians for military assistance. Whether it goes to the Americans or Russians will be determined by whether it has a pro-Western or pro-Eastern foreign policy posture, or if it is non-aligned, the strategy would be to steer clear of either side or play off the interests of one against the other.

ACTIONS

These refer to the actual steps taken at the diplomatic, political, or military levels to implement policy. Actions normally flow from foreign policy strategies, but can also flow directly from foreign policy objectives or postures. It is unusual — but certainly not unknown — to have actions that are unrelated to any foreign policy strategy, objective, or posture. Thus it has been shown quite decisively by Graham Allison, employing non-rational-actor paradigms, that actions sometimes simply occur as standard bureaucratic procedures or as political resultants of an explicit or implicit bargaining process (Allison 1972). This raises the issue of the assumption of rationality in my foreign policy framework. Such a bias is perhaps not totally unjustified given that we are examining the foreign policy of a small, developing country with relatively limited external goals, and considering that organizational structures relating to policy formulation are not highly complex. A more important argument, however, is that while non-rational-actor paradigms are important in the explanations of decision making behaviour, my focus on the substantive aspects of foreign policy makes the rational-actor paradigm the most suitable candidate for my purposes. In any case, the foreign policy framework presented in this study does not exclude the consideration of "organizational process" and "bureaucratic politics" variables, which in constructive parlance would be constitutive of foreign policy decision making.

Thus in the language of more standard social science we could view foreign policy outputs — objectives, postures, strategies, and actions — as the dependent variables, that is, the phenomena we seek to explain, while the various sources (or inputs) of foreign policy represent the independent variables or the factors with which we explain the phenomena under study. It is clear, however, that one does not explain foreign policy merely by examining each of the policy outputs discretely, but rather in the manner in which they relate to one another and to societal forces. In using a dynamic framework of analysis such as the one presented here, there may be a tendency to confuse the dependent and independent variables. This could occur if one thinks of the constant feedback process functioning as a recycling device whereby the policy outputs of time T are converted back into sources of foreign policy at time T2. For instance, a country may wage a war at a particular time (policy output), but at a later time the war will have become internalized as an important past experience and thus as a societal source of foreign policy.

NEUTRALISM, REGIONALISM, GLOBALIZATION, AND ISLAM — THE FIRST FIFTY YEARS

To capture Malaysia's foreign policy from the date of its formal independence (1957) until the time of writing, which is about five decades, will surely not be an easy task, depending on what is one's overall objective. As I have set the stage for a constructivist and critical appreciation of foreign policy, my main tasks would be essentially twofold. The first would be to convey accurate "macro historical" narratives of foreign policy practices and outcomes over specific time periods.[24] For convenience, I have taken the tenures of the five prime ministers as distinct periods of foreign policy formulation and construction.[25] The second task, a much more daunting one, would be to provide critical-constructivist appreciation, understanding, and analysis of foreign policy, understood as outcomes of socio-political-economic processes embedded within a Malaysian political culture.

Given the overall chronological structure of the book, the narratives of each period of foreign practices and outcomes would be followed by analytical sections that will try to show the constitutive forces and actors both within state and civil society which have been responsible for the character, tendencies, and inclinations, as well as actual outcomes of foreign policy. The schema in Figure 1.1, certainly not cast in stone, is the heuristic device,[26] which will guide this analysis of foreign policy.

Malaysian foreign policy can be examined across broad issue areas, such as "defence and security", "developmental and economic concerns", "international cooperation", "terrorism", and the like. I have also chosen four themes, which could also be appreciated as broad foreign policy postures, namely, Neutralism-Neutrality, Regionalism, Globalization, and Islam. These

FIGURE 1.1
Foreign Policy Theoretical Schema

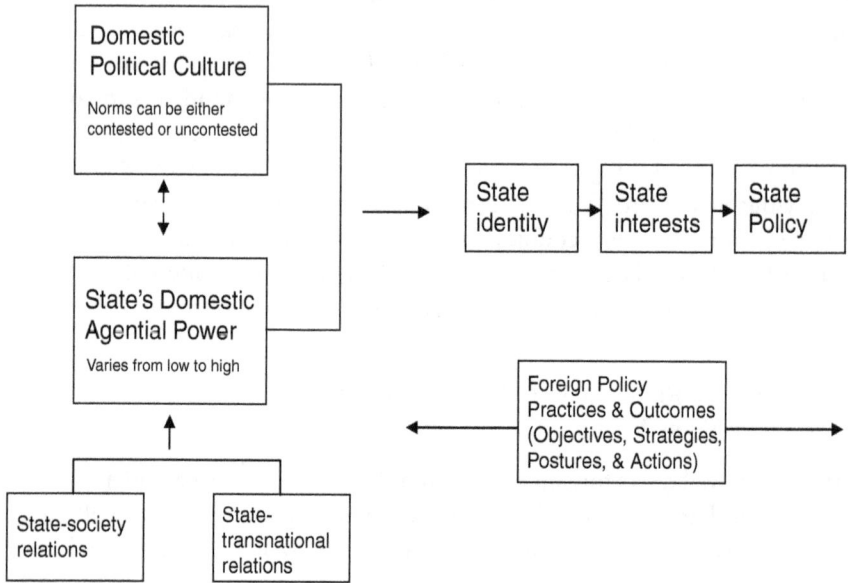

Source: Author's figure.

are largely intuitive categories which are again often used in the vocabulary of statesmen. The choice also underlines the constructive orientation of this work. The categories are not meant to be exhaustive of the broad range of foreign policy outputs that any state may evince. While there are certainly many possible ways of delineating issue areas, in general, the three kinds of foreign policy goals or objectives identified earlier tend to relate with various concerns in issue areas identified above in the following suggested manner:

Issue Areas	Foreign Policy Postures	Foreign Policy Objectives
Defence & Security	Neutralism-Neutrality, Regionalism	Core value Goals
Developmental & Economic Concerns	Regionalism, Globalization, Islam	Possession Goals
International Cooperation	Regionalism, Islam, Globalization	Milieu Goals
Global Terrorism	Regionalism, Islam	Core value Goals

I have chosen four broad themes of neutrality, regionalism, Islam, and globalization to provide the substantive elements and political context for the foreign policy narratives of the five periods under study. Of course, there could be more aspects of foreign policy that could be covered, but most can be subsumed under these four broad themes. The problem of maintaining neutrality, especially in the Cold War era, or its obverse, adopting pro-Western stances, provides the backdrop for the first period of foreign policy from 1957–69 in the tenure of Abdul Rahman. Neutralism came to the fore in the second period when Malaysia became a full-fledged member of the Non-aligment Movement (NAM) under the tenure of Abdul Razak from 1970–76. The consolidation of regionalism, already initiated in the Razak period, became prominent in the periods of Hussein Onn (1976–81) and Mahathir Mohamad (1981–2003). Islamic perspectives and politics have arguably been important from early years, but came to the fore in the Mahathir period and have remained crucial up to the present time beyond the tenure of Abdullah Badawi. Globalization has arguably been prominent since the 1970s.

Thus, it is evident that the themes I have chosen are not exclusive to each period, and there could be other aspects of foreign policy in the various periods perhaps not even subsumed under these themes,[27] but the four themes, I believe, provide the most important signposts of thrusts and contexts in Malaysian foreign policy alignments and outcomes over five decades. One of the important aims of this study is to show the often seamless manner in which foreign policy transits from one period or era into another, even as substantive aspects of policy morph into new policies. Going beyond the chronological narratives, the study also examines Malaysia's most important bilateral relations, namely, with the Philippines, Indonesia, Thailand, and Singapore. The chapter illustrates that proximate dyadic relationships are laced with antipathies of history and ethnicity. A chapter on the political economy of foreign policy delves into the intricacies of Malaysian's foreign economic relations. A constructivist rendition shows that foreign economic policy is embedded within the contours of a developmentalist state. A concluding chapter illustrates that the drive for postures, strategies, and policies of "middlepowermanship" are limited by the idiosyncratic or leadership factor, global constraints, and a lack of engagement with civil society forces.

NOTES

1. See Ruggie (1998), who was in the forefront of such a shift. Works which draw most directly from Wendtian constructivism are Hopf (2000) and Kubálková (2001). Another sort of related turn in IR has been to interface "culture" with

foreign policy analysis. See Hudson (2006, 1997) who suggests that it is time to explore the effects of culture on the "actor-specific" study of foreign policy in terms of culture as shared meaning, as value preferences, and as a template for human action (1997, p. 19). The interesting essay of Sanjoy Banerjee (pp. 27–44) in the volume on "the cultural logic of national identity formation" in late colonial India uses a constructivist paradigm.

2. See Wendt (1992, 1994, 1995, 1999). Wendt posits that: "[A]gainst materialism constructivism hypothesizes that the structures of human association are primarily cultural rather than material phenomena, and against rationalism that these structures not only regulate behavior but construct identities and interests…Analysis should therefore begin with culture and then move to power and interest, rather than only invoke culture to clean up what they leave unexplained." Wendt (1999, p. 193). See also the volume edited by Guzinni and Leander (2006) in which various critiques of Wendt's constructivism have surfaced, while Wendt himself has fashioned an "auto-critique' in the last chapter. A book of this sort goes to show that the "Third Debate" in IR is well underway, if not gained full respectability.

3. See the excellent review essay of Houghton (2007) which surveys the multifarious strains of constructivism, including constructivism 'before' constructivism.

4. According to Wendt, constitutive theories, contra causal theories, seek answers to different questions, namely, "how possible" and "what" rather than merely "why" or 'how" (Wendt 1999, pp. 77–78). See also, Hobson (2000), who calls for a "structurationist" theory of the constitutive state and global politics.

5. See, among others, his now classic work on the theory of structuration (Giddens 1984).

6. The classic text of neo-realism (or re-statement of realism) is of course Kenneth Waltz's Theory of International Politics (1979). For an idea of the extent to which constructivism has penetrated recent IR literature, see Lebow's exposition of "Thucydides the Constructivist" (2001) and Widmaier's "Keynesianism as a Constructivist Theory of the International Political Economy" (2003).

7. Critical theory harks to the Frankfurt School whose figures count the likes of Theodor Adorno, Hebert Marcuse, and Jürgen Habermas. In IR, Robert Cox's neo-Gramscian, international political economy approach is taken to be iconic. See Cox (1996).

8. Cf. Hobson (2000). The Figure 4.2 on page 131 presents graphically the differences between neo-realist and the neo-Gramscian paradigms.

9. It is also evident that constructivism has a clear intellectual project, in the words of Wendt, that it should be seen as "a kind of 'structural idealism' " (1999, p. 1). However, Cox's project is more political, namely, the dismantling of hegemonic orders. See Cox's essay and plea, to wit, "Can there be distinct, thriving macro-societies, each with its own solidarity, each pursuing a distinct telos, which could coexist through a supra-intersubjectivity? This supra-intersubjectivity would have to embody principles of coexistence without necessarily reconciling differences in goals" (Cox 1996, p. 168).

10. See, among others, Ping (2005) and Cooper (1997). On Malaysia, see Nossal and Stubbs (1997) and Mustafa Izzuddin (2007).

11. See, for example, Liow (2005).

12. The concept is credited to Karl Deutsch, who, while not a constructivist, was certainly one of the more original and innovative theorizers in international relations. See Deutsch (1968).

13. Two major exceptions are Vendulka Kubálková's (2001) and Ted Hopf's application of the constructivist paradigm to the study of Russian foreign policy (2000). See also the Christopher Hill's (2003) new textbook approach to the study of foreign policy incorporating constructivist notions. In contrast, a recent book on "comparative foreign policy", edited by Sidney Hook (2002) treats readers to a broad selection of foreign policy expertise, offering chapters on "great powers" (the United States, Russia, China, Japan, and the European Union) and emerging powers (Brazil, India, Indonesia, Iran, South Africa) with no mention of "constructivism" by any of the authors nor did the name of Alexander Wendt find its way into the index and bibliography.

14. See the volume of collected works compiled and edited by Chin and Suryadinata (2005).

15. Consider Leifer's own words in the preface to his 1999 study of Singapore's foreign policy, viz.: "It represents an attempt to explore and explain Singapore's conduct of foreign policy with reference to the same realist outlook that has characterized the approach to economic development and urban planning." (p. xiii).

16. I have used the generic label "Malaysian" for convenience, even though Malaysia came into being only in 1963 and Sarawak and Sabah had no part in "Malayan" foreign policy from the years 1957–62.

17. Perhaps not fully in the Foucaldian sense although I would like to uncover the ideational and paradigmatic assumptions and underpinnings of these studies, including my own.

18. The major authors in chronological order are: Silcock (1963); Hazra (1965); Dalton (1967); Tilman (1969); Tongpricha (1970); Ott (1972); Saravanamuttu (1976, 1983, 1987); Sodhy (1982, 1991), Abdullah Ahmad (1985); Sodhy (1988); Chamil Wariya (1989); Stubbs (1990); Pathmanathan and Lazarus (1984); Pathmanathan (1984, 1990); Zakaria Ahmad (1990); Mohd Yusof Ahmad (1990); Camroux (1994); Shanti Nair (1995); Liow (2001); Camilleri (2001); Ahmad Faiz (2005); Dhillon (2005, 2009).

19. The two are Nair (1997) and Liow (2005). Nair's work will be reviewed on pp. 11–12.

20. See Saravanamuttu 1983, Figure 1 (p. 8), and pp. 46–61.

21. It should be noted that Ott's 1971 dissertation focused on relations with Indonesia and the Philippines, and Tongpricha's was on relations with the Commonwealth.

22. These ideas were first developed in my 1976 doctoral thesis and have been further modified in my 1983 book.

23. K.J. Holsti, *International Politics* (1967, pp. 131–32). While in Wolfers' classification, possession goals include core-value goals, I prefer to use the two terms as mutually exclusive. Wolfers also distinguishes between "direct" and "indirect" goals, that is, those directly serving national interests, and those serving the interests of private individuals. This distinction is not pertinent here since this study is in general concerned with only national or state goals. See Wolfers, (1962, p. 77).

24. For the dependent variable side of the equation, that is, foreign policy outputs, I will rely on the schema that I developed in my 1983 study, to be explicated further below.

25. The sixth, going beyond fifty years, under Najib Razak, was added as a postscript.

26. I have adapted this figure from Hobson's depiction (Hobson 2000, p. 167) of Katzenstein's basic theoretical scheme. Katzenstein (1966) is depicted as a "state-centric constructivist" by Hobson.

27. Regionalism, developmentalism, and iconoclasm will also be important themes which feature strongly in various periods and will be dealt with in the appropriate chapters.

2

THE MINISTRY OF FOREIGN AFFAIRS

ATTAINING A GLOBAL REACH

Before I delve into the substantive chapters of the book, it may be germane to touch on the structure of the Malaysian Ministry of Foreign Affairs (or Wisma Putra), its growth since independence, and its policy formulation process. There is little reason to doubt that the ministry has functioned primarily in accordance to its formal goals, namely, as a bureaucracy of trained and professional officers providing expertise on and in the implementation of foreign policy and related matters. It has however undergone considerable change, particularly in terms of size, since independence. Over time there has also emerged the view that Wisma Putra has lost some of its capacity and capability.

Wisma Putra was established in 1956 shortly before the country's independence in 1957. The Ministry of External Affairs (MEA), as it was initially called, began with the training of a batch of eleven career diplomats to man it and the country's diplomatic missions overseas. This pioneering batch was trained in Britain and Australia. The MEA was modelled after the British Foreign Office, as was its bureaucracy, which was patterned after the British Civil Service. The first Permanent Secretary was Dato Othman Mohamed, who held the post from 6 July 1956 till 23 March 1958. Three officers "shared" the world among them as areas of geographical responsibility (see Figure 2.1).

Malaysia initially had diplomatic missions in London, Washington, Canberra, New York, New Delhi, Jakarta, and Bangkok. In 1963, there were fourteen Malaysian missions and twenty-five countries were represented in the country (four by way of concurrent accreditation). As late as 1964, at the height of Indonesia's Confrontation, the diplomatic corps consisted of

FIGURE 2.1
Organizational Chart of the Ministry of External Affairs, 1958

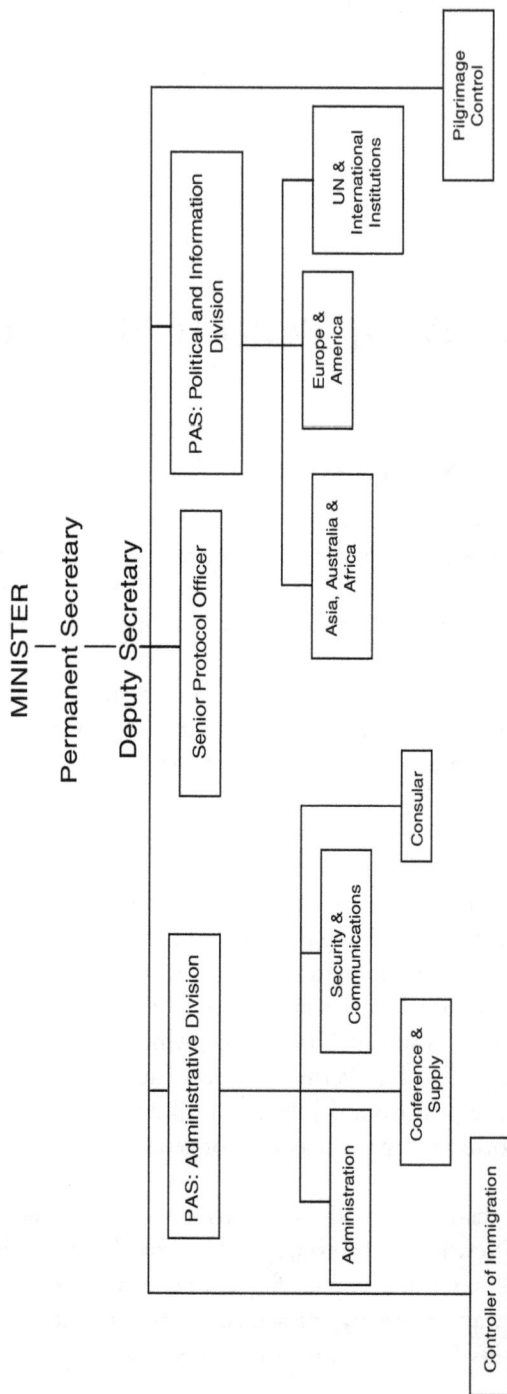

MINISTER

Permanent Secretary

Deputy Secretary

Senior Protocol Officer

PAS: Political and Information Division

UN & International Institutions

Europe & America

Asia, Australia & Africa

Pilgrimage Control

PAS: Administrative Division

Security & Communications

Consular

Administration

Conference & Supply

Controller of Immigration

Note: PAS = Principal Assistant Secretary

Note: PAS = Principal Assistant Secretary
Source: The Treasury, Government of Malaysia.

only thirty Division One officers while the home office in Kuala Lumpur was manned by a handful of officers. All of Asia was looked after by four officers; the Americas and the United Nations by two; the Middle East, one; Africa, South of Sahara, Western Europe and the Commonwealth, two.

At the time of the first major reorganization in 1965, the country had a total of twenty-one diplomatic postings and resident diplomatic representation in Kuala Lumpur numbered twenty-five. The expansion of Wisma Putra over the years can be gauged from the increasing number of missions abroad in the third, fourth, and fifth decades: from nearly forty in 1980 to double that in 2002 and with more than seventy between 1980 and 2000. By 2007, with eighty-one embassies, inclusive of high commissions, two liaison offices, three permanent missions in New York, Geneva, and Vienna, Malaysia had a grand total of 104 overseas posts, including consular missions (Jeshurun 2007, p. 325).

The year 1966 was a watershed year marked by an accelerated growth, particularly with regard to personnel and financial allocation. The name of the ministry was changed to the Ministry of Foreign Affairs (MFA). The year also saw its physical relocation and consolidation. From its original habitat at the Moorish-styled Bangunan Sultan Abdul Samad, commonly known as the Federal Secretariat Building, located in the heart of Kuala Lumpur, the MFA moved to a new RM2 million complex in a lush garden setting at the foot of Bukit Petaling and became known as Wisma Putra — in honour of YTM Tunku Abdul Rahman Putra Al-Haj, the first prime minister and foreign minister.

By 1967, the mini staff at home increased to sixty-one and the diplomatic staff overseas totalled 171 by 1968 (Ott 1973, p. 229). The structure, while remaining fundamentally unaltered over the first decade of independence, had undergone a significant overhaul in the second decade. Geographical coverage, for example, had expanded considerably as indicated by the proliferation in the number of "desks" manned by principal assistant secretaries (see Figure 2.2(B)). The most important changes, however, consisted of a redesignation of important officers and the addition of new tiers vertically, and new divisions horizontally. Essentially, though, geographical and functional desks at the principal assistant secretary level continued to be the basic organizational level of operation.

In a simple ceremony on 5 September 2001 Foreign Minister Datuk Seri Syed Hamid Albar stepped into the new Wisma Putra Complex at No. 1, Jalan Wisma Putra in Putrajaya, the new administrative capital of the country. Its new complex cost the government RM170 million. The new Wisma Putra Complex is built on a 4.848-hectare (12.12 acres) site and combines traditional and modern architectural features. The Institute of Diplomacy and Foreign Relations (IDFR) now occupies the old building at Jalan Wisma Putra in Bukit Petaling.

During the first decade under the tenure of Premier Tunku Abdul Rahman, the MFA was headed by a Permanent Secretary, assisted by a deputy, who could act on the former's behalf in his absence. As stated in Figure 2.1, together they supervised the three divisions of the ministry — political and information, administration, and protocol. The largest was the Political and Information Division headed by a principal assistant secretary who supervised the various geographical desks. The Administration Division, also headed by a principal assistant secretary, handled day to day administrative functions, the allocation of funds and expenditure, training and posting of personnel, and immigration matters. The senior protocol officer looked after matters of diplomatic privilege and immunity, precedence, ceremony, and official visits. A significant addition in the second decade was the economic division which was created largely to handle first ASA (Association of Southeast Asian States) and then later ASEAN matters. By 1979 this division had become the Secretariat of the Director General of ASEAN (that is, the ASEAN national secretariat).

The Permanent Secretary in the second decade was redesignated as the Secretary General, heading the whole of Wisma Putra (Foreign Ministry), and by 1979, was accountable to a minister as well as to a deputy minister. Below the secretary general, was a tier of deputy secretaries general, created for the Political and Information, Economic and Administration and General Affairs Divisions, as well as the ASEAN director general, a chief of protocol and a head of inspectorate. A new tier of undersecretaries was also created in the second decade, below the deputy secretaries general, and by 1979, all three deputies had such undersecretaries, with the ASEAN and Protocol chiefs also having deputies of the same rank (see Organizational Chart in Figure 2.2). Below the undersecretaries are the familiar desk officers or principal assistant secretaries, the backbone of the ministry.

Now that the structure of the Foreign Ministry has been sketched, it may be useful to examine its day to day functioning in the first and second decades. A Foreign Ministry undersecretary denied that decision making in Wisma Putra was an ad hoc process.[1] Instead he said there was an institutionalized procedure for making and implementing policy. This consisted of a daily round table meeting of all the senior officers (down to the principal assistant secretaries) in the ministry. Any matter requiring attention is brought up at the daily morning meeting and every officer is given a chance to air his views on the subject. If action is to be taken, a recommendation is made to the

FIGURE 2.2(A)
Organization Chart of the Ministry of Foreign Affairs, 1979 (A)

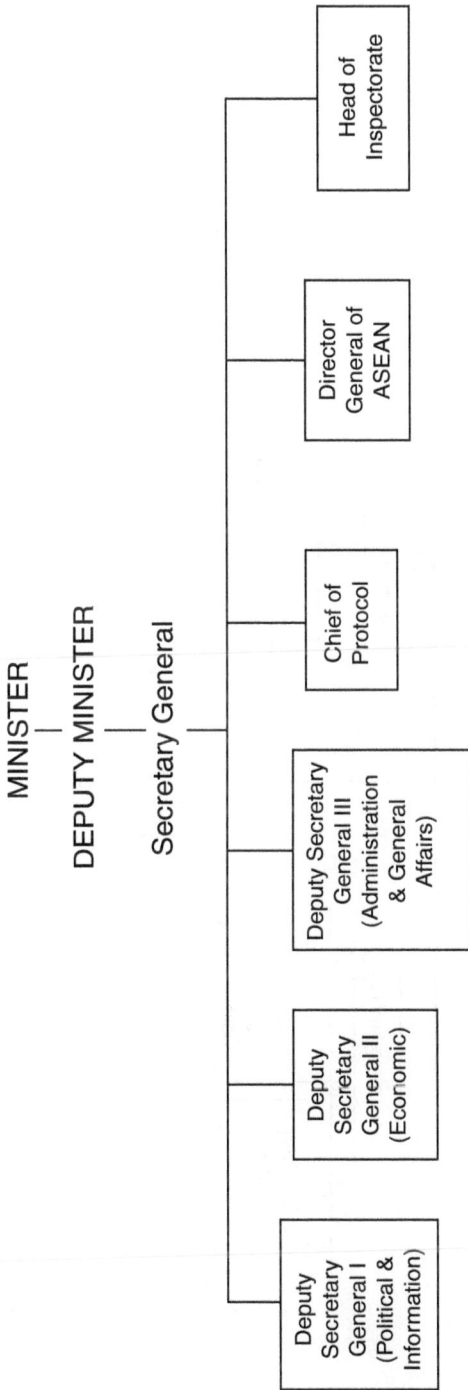

MINISTER
—
DEPUTY MINISTER
—
Secretary General

Deputy Secretary General I (Political & Information)

Deputy Secretary General II (Economic)

Deputy Secretary General III (Administration & General Affairs)

Chief of Protocol

Director General of ASEAN

Head of Inspectorate

Note: PAS = Principal Assistant Secretary
Source: The Treasury, Government of Malaysia.

FIGURE 2.2(B)
Organization Chart of the Ministry of Foreign Affairs, 1979 (B)

DEPUTY SECRETARY GENERAL
(POLITICAL DIVISION)

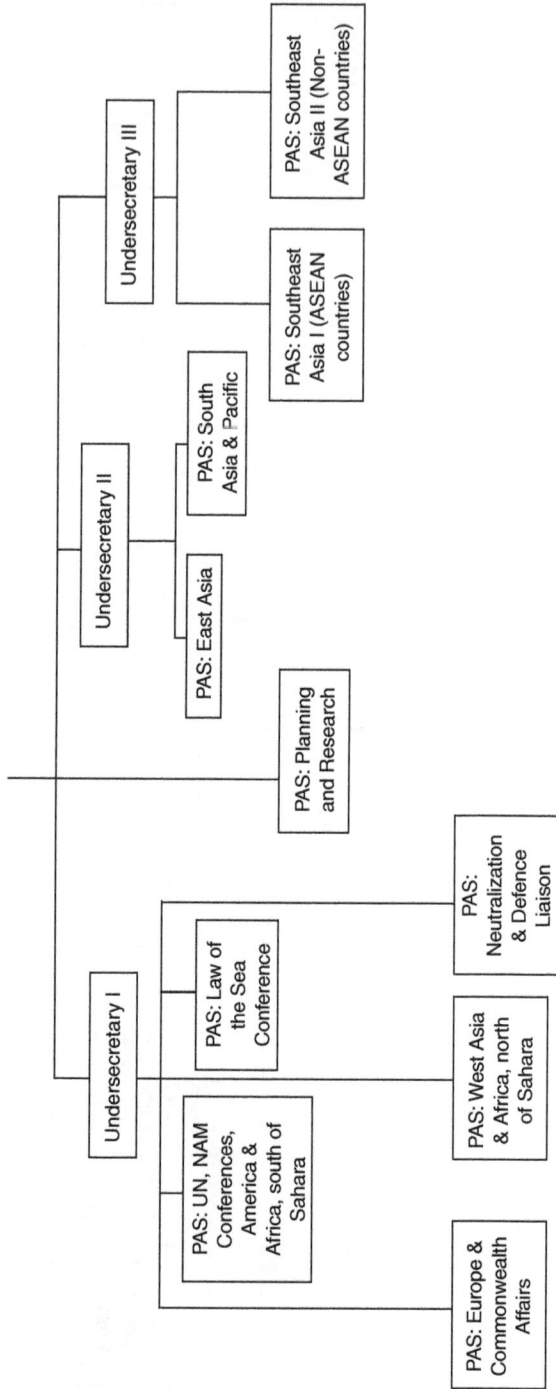

Note: PAS = Principal Assistant Secretary
Source: The Treasury, Government of Malaysia.

FIGURE 2.2(C)
Organization Chart of the Ministry of Foreign Affairs, 1979 (C)

DEPUTY SECRETARY GENERAL
(ECONOMIC & INFORMATION DIVISION)

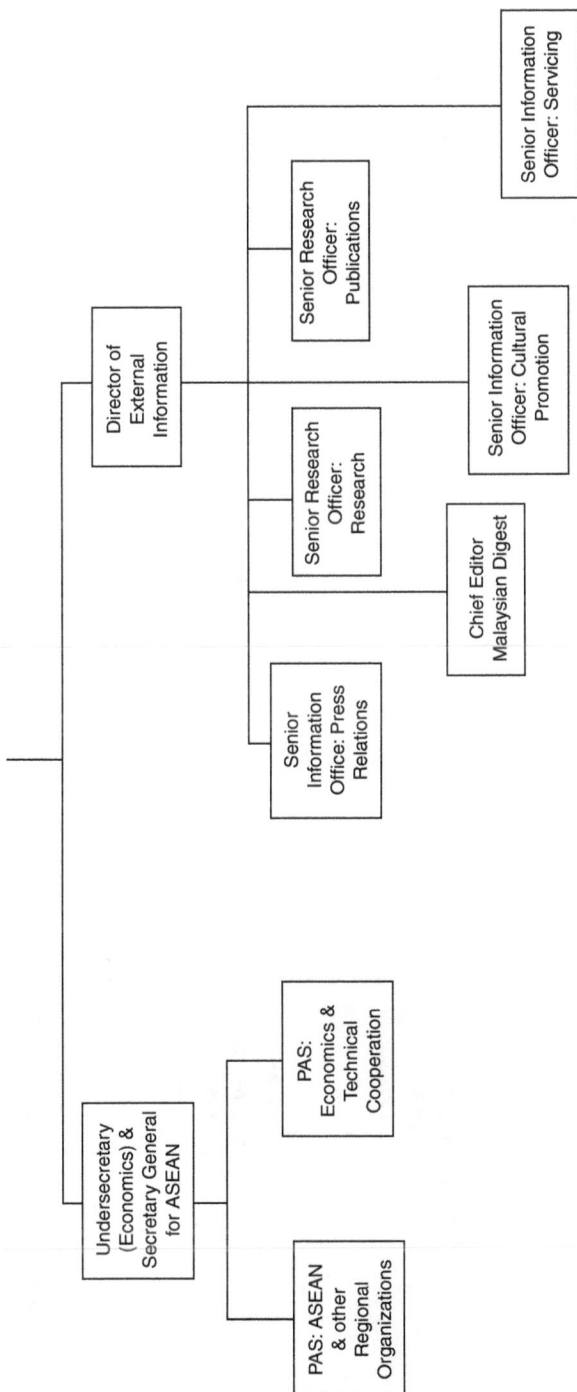

Note: PAS = Principal Assistant Secretary
Source: The Treasury, Government of Malaysia.

FIGURE 2.2(D)
Organization Chart of the Ministry of Foreign Affairs, 1979 (D)

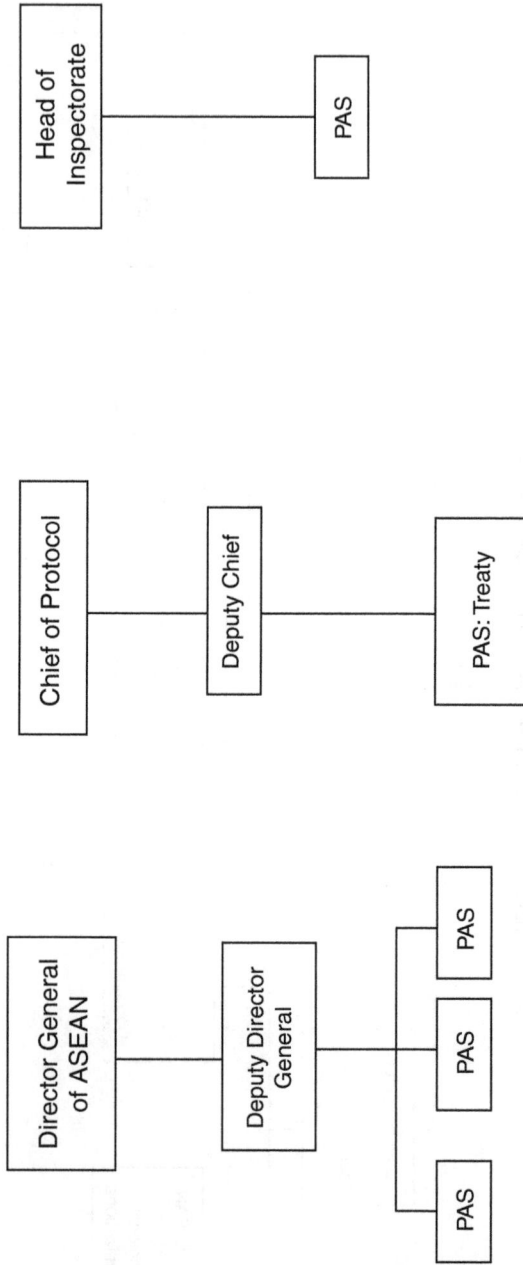

Note: PAS = Principal Assistant Secretary
Source: The Treasury, Government of Malaysia.

minister and the cabinet via the Secretary General after all the officers have had their say. If it was an important matter, but did not require immediate attention, such as a policy position on an issue or for some conference, the document would go through various drafts, starting at the principal assistant secretary level before being finally presented to the cabinet. This description of the second decade policy formulation process in Wisma Putra does not appear to differ very significantly from Marvin Ott's account of "the morning prayers" in the first decade:

> Ordinarily a problem requiring action would come to the Ministry in the form of a question from a Malaysian embassy or high commission. The question could be forwarded to the Principal Assistant Secretary responsible for the geographical area involved. He would in turn probably refer it to one of his Assistant Secretaries dealing with the country concerned. The two of them might discuss the problem together and work out a proposed reply or policy. The problem and proposed solution would then be presented to a daily round table meeting ("the morning prayers") of all the officers in the Ministry. The resulting discussion gave everyone a chance to present his views on any question and kept each officer informed about what his colleagues were doing. The officer who originally presented the question would then compose a minute outlining the recommendations of the meeting and this would be forwarded to the Permanent Secretary. When it was not a particularly important matter and Ghazali approved the contents, he would initial the minute and send a copy to the Prime Minister for his information. If it was an important question, a paper would be drawn up by the Permanent Secretary and the relevant section of the Ministry, outlining the problem and possibly recommending a solution (Ott 1973, p. 232).

There is some evidence to suggest nonetheless that the ministry of the subsequent years was a closer approximation of the classic bureaucratic model than it was perhaps in the days when Tun Ghazali Shafie (later, minister of home affairs) was Permanent Secretary. Ghazali Shafie, the third man to hold that position, has himself written the following about the ministry of the early days:

> We did follow the British structure a little for our ministry — we had our Minster, we had an Intelligence Officer, whose studies and observations we used to later form the basis for our policies, etc. Two British officers were in fact allowed inside our new ministry after Independence — one officer to handle accounts and money matters. But they had no official posts or titles then. Neither of these British officers stayed very long. Shortly after receiving their Golden Bricks, they left (Ghazali Shafie 2006, p. 13).

Tan Sri Ghazali was noted for his rather non-bureaucratic, interpersonal, and flamboyant style, and also for his receptiveness to new ideas. On the other hand an official described his successor, Secretary General Tan Sri Zaiton Ibrahim, as "more or less a straight-laced bureaucratic type". Marvin Ott has suggested the interesting if non-verifiable estimate that "80–90% of the important decisions which shaped the course of … foreign policy derived from the interaction of Ghazali with the Tunku". According to Ott, the relationship may best be characterized as one in which Ghazali and his ministry provide the initiative and ideas while the Tunku acts as a "screen of acceptable and feasible policies", selecting and modifying. (Ott 1973, p. 234). At the same time, the bureaucracy had a considerable influence on the political elite and, "from all evidence … the Tunku, the Ministry, and the Cabinet have seen eye to eye on most questions. The Ministry enjoys the respect of the Cabinet and the Prime Minister and attitude is largely reciprocated" (Ott 1973, p. 235).

Wisma Putra, with the absence of Ghazali, was perhaps no less influential, despite being a closer approximation to the classic bureaucratic model. The simple reason is that second decade leaders were more likely to consult it on foreign policy matters.[2] Tun Razak himself, who rose from civil service ranks, was well known for his pragmatism and was not known to make important decisions without extensive consultation. Hussein Onn did not seem to exhibit any strikingly different characteristics from his predecessor in this respect. There is also evidence of a great degree of rapport between the political leaders and the ministry, of the kind suggested by Ott in the Tunku era. Besides, the large majority of Wisma Putra officials were themselves convinced the soundness of elite perception on most foreign policy matters.[3] A book, *Number One Wisma Putra* (2007), commemorating Malaysia's 50th Anniversary, with chapters written by senior diplomats, gives an inkling of how they were involved in important foreign policy initiatives and events, ranging from the recognition of China, the Cambodian peace process, the birth of Timor Leste, to the "constructive engagement" with Myanmar on behalf of ASEAN.[4]

In his book on fifty years of Malaysian diplomacy, Chandran Jeshurun (2007) offers the view that, for the most part, there was a close, even intimate, relationship between the presumed formulators of policy — prime ministers — and the professional diplomats housed in Wisma Putra. Such a relationship was especially evident during the premierships of Tunku Abdul Rahman and Tun Abdul Razak, although, from his account, the relationship was rather estranged during the Tun Mahathir Mohammad era. Dhillon (2007) in his study of foreign policy in the Mahathir era is much more explicit about the prime minister bypassing or ignoring the MFA in most of his major foreign policy initiatives. Senior retired diplomat Dato Yusof Ahmad, who wrote a doctoral dissertation on Mahathir's foreign policy, said that MFA was left with the unpleasant task of rationalizing policies and carrying out "damage control".[5] In my own further discussions and informal chats with Malaysian diplomats, I got the rather distinct impression that as the diplomatic service turned larger and increasingly professional, the kind of domination of specific prime ministers, foreign ministers, and individuals such as Ghazali Shafie, became less prevalent. Over time prime ministers and foreign ministers began to draw on the growing expertise of their professional officers as a matter of routine. To pose the matter rhetorically, who else but the officers of Wisma Putra would be able to churn out the hundreds of speeches and position papers required on a month to month basis for the affairs of the state, which by the fifth decade, saw a truly impressive global reach of foreign or international undertakings by Malaysia (see Figure 2.3(A), (B), (C), and (D), for Organizational Chart of Wisma Putra, 2008). By mid-2008, Wisma Putra had a total of 2,500 establishment posts, a sprawling team of senior officers under the Secretary General, who now had under his charge, three deputy secretaries general, two heads of centres, one for training and the other for counterterrorism, and the director general of ASEAN. As shown in the organization chart, there is now also a Division of Public Diplomacy and Media, a Department of Policy and Strategy, a Chemical Weapons Task Force and a Law Division, led by department heads.[6] The establishment of two centres under the purview of Wisma Putra perhaps deserves some of our attention as it relates to Malaysia's increasing regional and global reach, and its posture and policies as an aspirant middle power, which I will address in the conclusion of this book.

The Institute of Diplomacy and Foreign Relations (IDFR) was established under the prime minister's department in 1991 and became part of the MFA in 2004. It provides basic and mid-career training to Malaysian foreign service officers and also basic training for diplomats of participating developing countries (under the MTCP or Malaysian Technical Cooperation Programme). Together with the National University (UKM), it also offers a one-year master's degree programme in international relations, strategy and diplomacy.[7] IDFR is headed by an executive chairman, who is assisted by a team of administrative personnel and trainers, and houses a library and resource centre of documents of relevance to the MFA. Its stated goals are "to develop a corps of diplomatic officers who will be able to promote and defend the country's interests in keeping with the ever increasing pace and breadth of modern day diplomacy resulting from global changes" and "to

FIGURE 2.3(A)
Organization Chart of the Ministry of Foreign Affairs, 2008 (A)

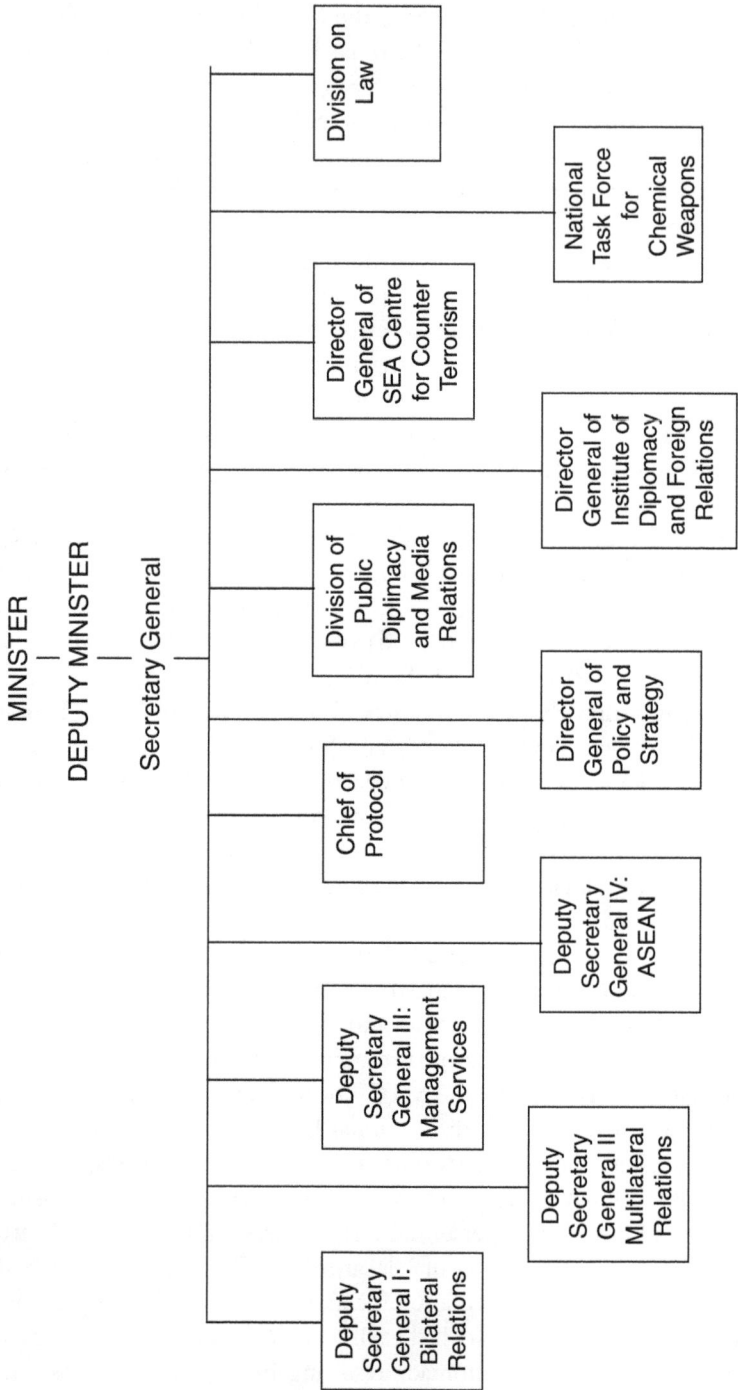

Note: PAS = Principal Assistant Secretary
Source: The Treasury, Government of Malaysia.

FIGURE 2.3(B)

Organization Chart of the Ministry of Foreign Affairs, 2008 (B)

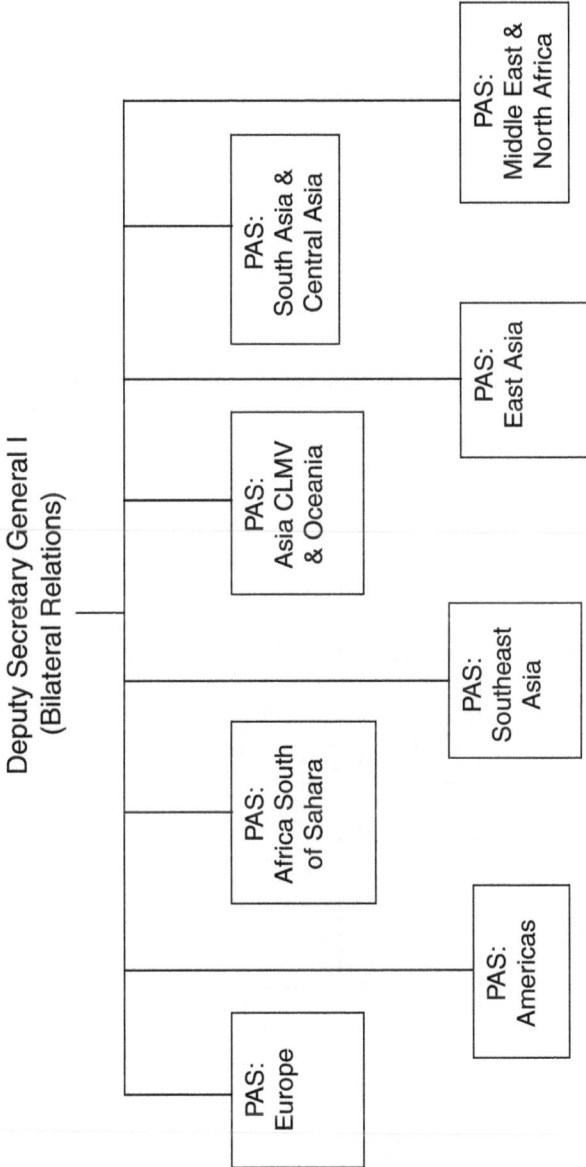

Note: PAS = Principal Assistant Secretary

Source: The Treasury, Government of Malaysia.

FIGURE 2.3(C)
Organization Chart of the Ministry of Foreign Affairs, 2008 (C)

Deputy Secretary General II
(Multilateral Relations)

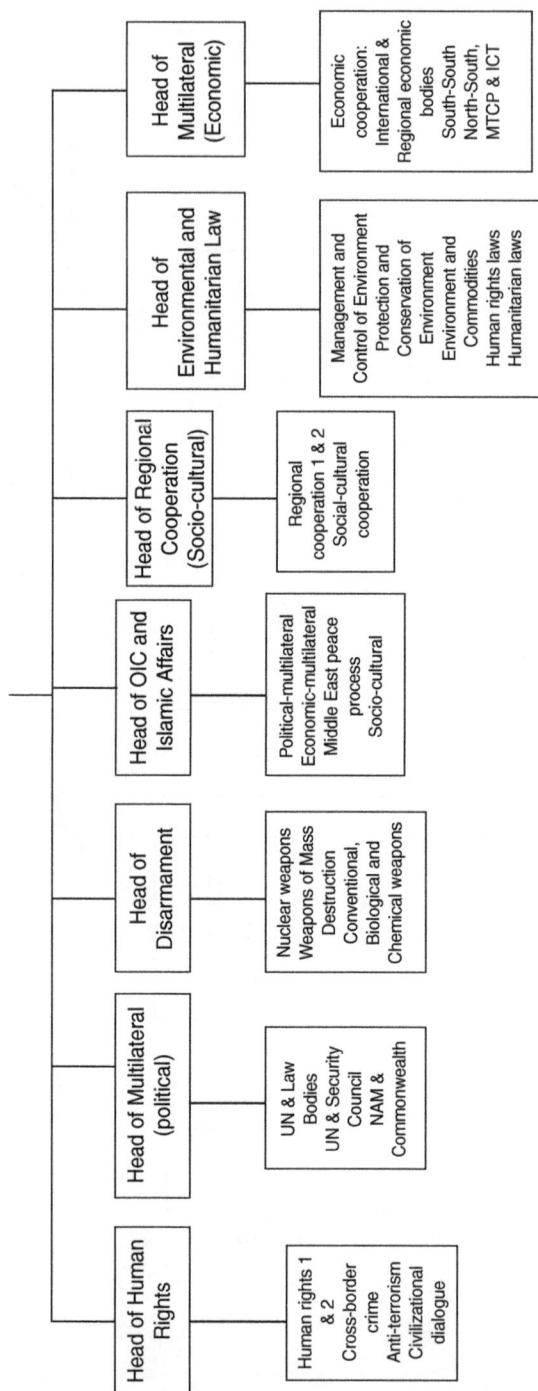

Head of Human Rights	Head of Multilateral (political)	Head of Disarmament	Head of OIC and Islamic Affairs	Head of Regional Cooperation (Socio-cultural)	Head of Environmental and Humanitarian Law	Head of Multilateral (Economic)
Human rights 1 & 2 Cross-border crime Anti-terrorism Civilizational dialogue	UN & Law Bodies UN & Security Council NAM & Commonwealth	Nuclear weapons Weapons of Mass Destruction Conventional, Biological and Chemical weapons	Political-multilateral Economic-multilateral Middle East peace process Socio-cultural	Regional cooperation 1 & 2 Social-cultural cooperation	Management and Control of Environment Protection and Conservation of Environment Environment and Commodities Human rights laws Humanitarian laws	Economic cooperation: International & Regional economic bodies South-South North-South, MTCP & ICT

Note: PAS = Principal Assistant Secretary
Source: The Treasury, Government of Malaysia.

FIGURE 2.3(D)
Organization Chart of the Ministry of Foreign Affairs, 2008 (D)

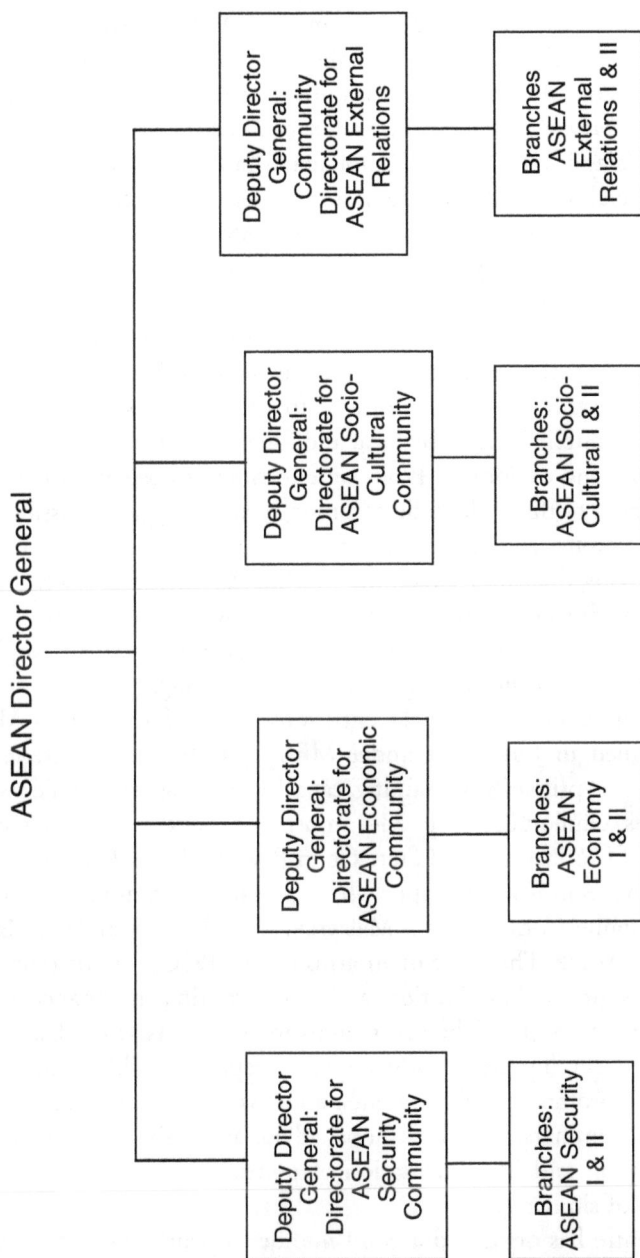

ASEAN Director General

- Deputy Director General: Directorate for ASEAN Security Community
  - Branches: ASEAN Security I & II
- Deputy Director General: Directorate for ASEAN Economic Community
  - Branches: ASEAN Economy I & II
- Deputy Director General: Directorate for ASEAN Socio-Cultural Community
  - Branches: ASEAN Socio-Cultural I & II
- Deputy Director General: Community Directorate for ASEAN External Relations
  - Branches ASEAN External Relations I & II

Note: PAS = Principal Assistant Secretary
Source: The Treasury, Government of Malaysia.

equip officers with in-depth knowledge, professional skills and the right attitude required in the conduct of foreign relations".[8]

The team of lecturers at IDFR comprises IDFR and Ministry of Foreign Affairs officers, officers from other ministries, NGOs, as well as university lecturers and consultants from various private organizations. IDFR publishes the biennial *Journal of Diplomacy and Foreign Relations*. In 2008, it was headed by one of Malaysia's distinguished diplomats, Tan Sri Hasmy Agam, a former director general of the ASEAN desk, former permanent representative to the United Nations and Ambassador-at-large for NAM (Non-Aligned Movement). Training is offered through courses, seminars, workshops, conferences, and consultancy services, for Malaysians as well participants from ASEAN, Commonwealth, and Colombo Plan countries, and a number of newly-independent countries recovering from war, such as Afghanistan, Iraq, and Timor-Leste. IDFR's courses are offered to 136 countries worldwide. IDFR also organizes public lectures by local and foreign speakers, including former heads of state and diplomats. From time to time, it hosts informal talks on issues pertinent to the diplomatic community and foreign embassies situated in Kuala Lumpur. IDFR has hosted international conferences on topics such as bridging the gap between the Muslim World and the West, a public lecture by the distinguished scholar of religion, Karen Armstrong, and more mundane activities such as the meeting of deans and directors of diplomatic training institutes of the ASEAN Plus Three grouping.

The Southeast Asia Regional Centre for Counter-Terrorism (SEARCCT) was established in July 2003 under MFA as a regional counterterrorism facility, focusing primarily on training, capacity building, and public awareness programmes. Dhillon (2007, p. 234) informs us that the centre was set up at the behest of U.S. Secretary of State Colin Powell. SEARCCT operates from its own premises in Kuala Lumpur which is headed by a director general and engages personnel from MFA, the Malaysian Armed Forces, and the Malaysian Royal Police Force. The three main arms of SEARCCT are its training and planning, research and publication, and administration and finance divisions. As stated on its webpage, the centre aims to achieve its vision based on the following: to develop and conduct quality capacity building and training programmes; promote public awareness and disseminate information through conferences, seminars, and workshops; advise and assist the government in the formulation and implementation of policies; and, network with other institutions of similar goals.

The centre has organized a good number of workshops, seminars, and training schemes involving the participation of the United States, ASEAN countries, as well as the South Pacific and Oceania countries. A selection of the topics covered in 2007 and 2008 will provide a flavour of the work of SEARCCT: Cell Phone Forensic Consultation, Managing Terrorists whilst in Prison, Regional Terrorism Scene Investigation, Seminar on Comparative Analysis of Counter-Terrorism Laws in Cambodia & Malaysia, South East Asia Bio-terrorism Workshop: Multi-Sectoral Policy Responses to International Bio-terrorism, Regional Program on Money Laundering and Terrorist Financing through Charities and New Technology, Prevention and Crisis Management of Chemical and Biological Terrorism, ASEAN-Japan Counter Terrorism Dialogue.

Finally, let me conclude this discussion of the evolution of the MFA with brief sketches of four prominent Malaysian diplomats and their work and roles at the MFA. I have chosen Tan Sri Zakaria Mohd Ali, Tan Sri Zainal Abidin Sulong, Tan Sri Zain Azraai Zainal Abidin, and Tan Sri Razali Ismail. The four men could be said to have been diplomats of high calibre who had excelled in their careers as well as impacted on the conduct of Malaysian diplomacy. This depiction will serve as an example of the professionalism and global reach of Malaysia's Foreign Service, as well as profile the role of prominent bureaucrats in influencing foreign policy decision making. All four individuals played direct and important roles as lynchpins between the foreign ministry and the highest levels of decision making, that is, the Prime Minster's Office (PMO) or the prime minister himself. My depiction is in no way an attempt to show that individuals determined all aspects of foreign policy. Indeed, given the professionalism of the four men depicted, foreign policy decision making was probably greatly attuned to many factors, international and domestic, which these men were bound to include in the decision making process.[9]

Tan Sri Zakaria Ali joined the MFA in 1957 and was Malaysia's permanent representative to the United Nations in New York and concurrently high commissioner to Canada from 1970 to 1974.[10] In 1984, Tan Sri Zakaria Ali became secretary general of MFA and later served as high commissioner to Australia before retiring in 1989. He played a pivotal role in Malaysia's normalization of relations with China in 1974. Zakaria Ali has himself written that the passage of time has not diminished the importance and relevance of this event. Recent developments have proved him right. The 2004 and 2009 state visits to China of two Malaysian premiers suggest that it is hard to deny that Malaysia's China policy crafted in the mid-1970s continue to yield economic and political benefits. Zakaria Ali points out that this turn in relations with China represented a change of attitude and perception from one based on "exclusion, mistrust, and suspicion to one of acceptance and cautious constructive engagement" (Zakaria Ali 2006, p. 121).[11] Being Malaysia's chief negotiator in talks on normalization with the Chinese, Zakaria Ali was clearly at the centre of this major foreign policy initiative. He made initial contacts in June 1973 with Chinese Ambassador Huang Hua who was later to become China's foreign minister. The Malaysian delegation to the exploratory meetings in New York included Zain Azraai from the PMO, and Khor Eng Hee from Wisma Putra, both senior bureaucrats. Zakaria Ali was assisted by his deputy at the United Nations, Ahmad Kamil. As intimated to me by Zakaria Ali, Malaysia's idea was to have a treaty with China, but Chinese demurred at the idea and eventually convinced the Malaysians to settle for a formal visit to China by the Malaysian premier who would then sign a comprehensive Joint Communiqué on all outstanding issues.[12] In retrospect this has proven to be the most efficacious way to handle relations with China.

Tan Sri Zakaria Ali who initially began his career as an MCS officer for external affairs under the British represents a crop of MFA career diplomats who were not just solidly grounded in their field of work, but who also exhibited a political wisdom characteristic of that old school of Malaysian civil servants. There is now growing critique that the MFA, as a service, may have lost some of its early lustre, with the departure of such individuals, a matter we will address further below.

My second example, Tan Sri Zainal Abidin Sulong, who is a protégé of the redoubtable Ghazali Shafie. Zainal Abidin is seen today as one of the veteran diplomats of Malaysia and one of MFA's early pioneers, having joined the service in 1957.[13] Zainal Abidin served almost three decades with the MFA and was ambassador to Indonesia from 1972–77; to the Soviet Union, from 1977–80; U.N. permanent representative, from 1980–84, and secretary general from August 1984 until he retired in March 1988. He won his spurs when Ghazali asked him to lead a task force to explain the Malaysia Project to rural folk in Sabah and Sarawak in 1961. He travelled the length and breadth of the two East Malaysian states, and as he recounts with some amusement, gained much needed cultural knowledge about his own country (Zainal Abidin Sulong 2006, pp. 16–17). Zainal Abidin intimates that the MFA was a highly influential establishment in the early years, not least, because the prime minister was also foreign minister:

> We could undertake a lot of programmes because every government department and ministry would comply with whatever the Foreign Minister wanted. So the Foreign Ministry then was truly a powerful organization, with Ghazali Shafie as our Permanent Secretary; he headed the Special Research Unit in the Prime Minister's Department as well. We therefore collaborated closely with this unit which got involved in preparing programmes and papers on strategic issues for the government. This collaboration eventually

became an important network for us in facing the Indonesian Confrontation (Zainal Abidin, p. 17).

Zainal Abidin was also assigned to be the secretary to the Malaysian delegation led by Lee Kuan Yew to counter Indonesian propaganda against Malaysia in the Afro-Asian states. The mission took him across Saharan and Sub-Saharan Africa and to India where he learned to be adept at using the diplomatic tools of propaganda and counter-propaganda. He recounts that Malaysia became a member of the Afro-Asian People's Solidarity Organization, "even though it was known to be a leftist organization", in order to make Malaysia's voice heard and presence felt (Zainal Abidin, pp. 18–19). Zainal Abidin considered this mission to be huge success whereby Malaysia won recognition to be admitted to the non-aligned conference originally planned to have been held in Algiers.[14] Apart from his stint with Wisma Putra, Tan Sri Zainal Abidin Sulong had served as chairman of the International Institute of Strategic Studies (ISIS), and for two decades, as chairman of the Malaysian Industrial Development Authority (MIDA). By all accounts, this is a civil servant who has not just done the usual tour of service, but one who h as contributed significantly to his country's foreign relations.

The late Zain Azraai (1936–96), an Oxford graduate, was recruited by "King Ghaz"[15] and may be said to have "epitomized the persona of a Foreign Service Officer" (Jeshurun, 200, p. 55). Zain Azraai joined the MFA in 1958 and was then hand-picked by Prime Minster Tun Abdul Razak to be his principal private secretary and then, on Razak's untimely death, went on to serve as Malaysian ambassador to the United States from 1976–83. He then served as Malaysian permanent representative to the United Nations until 1986. On his return he assumed the post of secretary general of minister of finance, a post he held until he retired in 1991. Because of Zain Azraai's close relationship with the prime minister, the MFA had a constant and close contact with the highest level of decision making. I was able to interview Zain Azraai in 1975 and was most impressed by his knowledge and erudition on matters of foreign policy. Malaysia's China initiative and the tilt towards a non-aligned foreign policy were clearly influenced by men such as Zain Azraai. Diplomatic historian Jeshurun is unequivocal about the important role played by Zain Azraai in Malaysia's foreign policy and its professionalization:

> When Zain Azraai — one of Razak's key foreign policy advisers — was moved from the Prime Minister's Office to the prestigious appointment as Ambassador to the United States, it marked a subtle transition in the relations between Wisma Putra and the "inner circle" of Malaysian decision-making. It was also something of a historic change in the country's overseas representation: the Washington mission had hitherto been entrusted only

to senior Alliance Party politicians such as Dr. Ismail, Ong Yoke Lin and Mohmed Khir Johari. (Jeshurun 2007, p. 139)

We now turn to our fourth personality. Joining the service in 1962, Razali Ismail went on to become the MFA's deputy secretary general in 1985. Before that, he had diplomatic stints in France, the United Kingdom, Laos, Poland, and India, Razali then went on to be increasingly involved in the work of the United Nations. He also served as special adviser to the prime minister in 1998. From 1989–90, he headed the Malaysian mission to the United Nations and was elected to be chairman of the Security Council. He became involved in the United Nations Conference on Sustainable Development, the "Rio Summit" of 1992, and was elected to chair the 53-country Commission on Sustainable Development on the implementation of "Agenda 21". From 1996–97, he became the president of the U.N. General Assembly. Razali has headed Malaysian delegations to various regional and international bodies and in 2000 was appointed U.N. Secretary General's Special Envoy to Myanmar, a position which he relinquished at the end of 2005 after the Myanmar military junta repeatedly denied him entry to the country. Razali writes candidly about his forays into Myanmar, which came to naught in spite of fourteen meeting with Aung San Suu Kyi and several with the junta. This said, Razali's work laid the ground for further engagement with that country by the international community.

Besides the role of senior diplomats in foreign policy issues such as those mentioned above, prominent individuals in government-backed think tanks also played various roles in foreign policy matters. With the formation of the Institute of Strategic and International Studies (ISIS) in 1983, under the helmsmanship the late Dr (later Tan Sri) Noordin Mohd Sopiee, and with the prime minister as its patron, ISIS and its director became a significant player in national policy formulation.[16] Dhillon (2009, p. 17) writes that ISIS was created by Prime Minster Mahathir and he hand-picked Noordin and other loyal individuals "with exceptional writing and analytical abilities to staff the think tank". As Dhillon notes, Noordin's loyalty was amply displayed in the Al Gore incident at the APEC Summit of 1998 in Malaysia. Noordin took out a full-page advertisement upbraiding Gore for his lack of manners in supporting the *Reformasi* movement, but also apologizing to the prime minister for having inadvertently applauded the American vice-president's speech.[17] Let me briefly highlight a number of well known contributions to foreign policy matters by the late Noordin Sopiee and ISIS before concluding the chapter on the Wisma Putra. Under Noordin, ISIS became the think tank which represented Malaysia in the ASEAN-ISIS second track diplomacy. ISIS has since 1987 held the annual Asia Pacific Roundtable (APR) in Kuala Lumpur.

As a Track Two forum, the APR brings together think tanks, academics, media representatives, and senior government officials to engage in candid dialogue regarding the major security challenges confronting the region. The APR has gained a reputation as the main second track forum in the Asia Pacific region, bringing together more than 250 participants and observers to its annual conferences. As a consequence of Malaysia's advocacy of East Asian regionalism under Mahathir, ISIS created the East Asian Economic Centre (EAEC) with the same sound byte to Mahathir's proposal since 2003. The EAEC engages in independent policy-oriented studies, conferencing and networking, hosting the East Asia Congress, an annual quadripartite gathering of policymakers, scholars, the private sector, and the media.

A critique of the diplomatic service has emerged in recent times on the question of whether Wisma Putra has the qualified personnel to cope with the ever changing and increasingly more sophisticated international environment of diplomacy. A former senior ambassador has written the following:

> There is a wide range of well known global and regional issues, which hardly rated as policy subjects a generation ago, today preoccupies huge amounts of attention. Additionally, interest groups, domestic and foreign, are more active and sophisticated than ever. And Wisma Putra simply does not have officers to match these new actors. Indeed, it does not seem to be attuned to the new thinking of a younger generation of citizens with a keen interest in foreign affairs. (Mohd Ridzam 2009).

Moreover, the critique incorporates the idea that foreign policy formulation in Malaysia should become a more open process. The same writer proposed an independent Council on Foreign Relations to provide alternative viewpoints in the promotion and shaping of the Government's position on regional and global issues in the context of the country's own worldview.[18]

In my interview with a senior retired diplomat, who did not wish to be attributed, he said that Wisma Putra very early in the day lost the opportunity to set up a strong, independent service. Tun Ghazali Shafie was said to have promoted such an idea, but had failed to convince the Public Services Department or Jabatan Perkhidmatan Awam (JPA), which recruits all government servants, to do so. This meant that the MFA follows the policies of promotion, terms of service, including salary structure, determined by the JPA, that is, MFA officers are no different from other civil servants. Indeed, civil servants can be transferred from other services to the MFA and vice versa.

In January 2009, under Foreign Minister Rais Yatim of the Abdullah Badawi government, there was a response of sorts to these issues. The MFA put out a "Strategic Plan" spanning the years 2009–15.[19] The plan purports to provide the broad vision, mission, and core values of the MFA from this period of time. For our purposes here, let us briefly examine the objectives of this document, which is stated as follows:

1. Safeguarding and protecting national sovereignty in the international arena
2. Strengthening bilateral diplomacy
3. Strengthening multilateral diplomacy
4. Strengthening ASEAN
5. Information dissemination and enculturing diplomacy
6. Improving and strengthening the institution and human capital

Of the above six objectives, the first four sound much like motherhood statements about Malaysia's pursuit of foreign policy goals rather than a strategic plan. Perhaps objective five and six may have some "strategic" dimensions in dealing with the issues at hand, including the possible deterioration of the MFA as a service in terms of its professional culture and capacity. The plan in objective five is a laudable one, which is to encourage Malaysian public to understand and appreciate Malaysian foreign policy, as well as to increase its awareness of it (p. 83). The broad theme or ideal of "public diplomacy" is entailed in this strategic plan. Thus, as we have noted above, a special division in the MFA has been set up for public diplomacy. As for the development of human capital, the plan's strategy is to get the most qualified individuals to serve in the MFA (pp. 88–89). Continuous training is envisaged for officers, but as explained in the text, this goal remains general in nature, with no indication that the MFA should be developed as a special or autonomous service arm of the government. From my experience and numerous contacts with the IDFR, the ministry's in-house training institute, a lot of emphasis has been given to the mastery of English as most Malaysian graduates often fall short in English competency. I also understand from talking with retired diplomats that most plans for postgraduate training have been ad hoc at best. Without mentioning names, I will point to an egregious case of a former IDFR officer who, after receiving a Ph.D. in international relations, found himself in another ministry.

CONCLUSION

This discussion of the structure and functioning of the Ministry of Foreign Affairs lends credence to the view that it probably behaves like most bureaucracies of a democratic format. Interviews with government officials in economic divisions of other ministries tend to confirm this perception, with the majority of these officials themselves perceiving the policy formulation process to be pluralistic in the sense that there is at least a plurality of stages in the decision making process, as well as considerable input at various horizontal levels.[20] Foreign Ministry officials in general also tended to see the policy formulation process as pluralistic although they were careful to note that the major guidelines were largely laid down by the politicians and not subject to question. Some two decades ago, one Wisma Putra official suggested that in the political sphere, one has to use "the underdeveloped societal model" to appreciate foreign policy, an allusion to a situation in which the bureaucracy does not challenge the premises of policy, but rather rationalizes them. This would hardly be the case in late 2000s, when, as we have shown, the MFA spread it wings far and wide and deepened its internal capacity by degrees. Even some twenty years ago, government officials tended to be partial towards the pluralistic policy formulation model while politicians and journalists interviewed invariably saw the process as elitist.[21] The same could be said for the situation today.

The work of Chandran Jeshurun (2007), in purportedly providing a "historiography" or fifty years of diplomatic practice, sheds some light on the non-formal foreign policy decision making processes. Drawing on narratives and anecdotes of the interventions or role played by particular diplomats in important events, he derives the conclusion that, for the most part, there was a close, even intimate, relationship between the presumed formulators of policy — prime ministers — and the professional diplomats housed in Wisma Putra. Such a relationship was especially evident during the Tunku and Razak years although, by implication from his rendering of events, the relationship was rather estranged during the Mahathir era.[22] Jeshurun (2007, p. 198) also makes the point that in the earlier Mahathir years, the prime minister was served by "the cream of the crop" at Wisma Putra, the likes of Zain Azraai, Razali Ismail, and Ahmad Kamil Jaafar, secretary general from 1989–95, all noted for their Wisma Putra "activism". However, one could also well argue that the Mahathir era saw a burgeoning relationship with ISIS, as suggested above, and one that may well have supplanted the role of Wisma Putra in many areas of policy. Writers such as Jeshurun, drawing on narratives around personalities, often conclude that foreign policy formulation is virtually the preserve of prime ministers, who are its "chief architects" (Jeshurun 2007, p. 365) in spite of the activism of some senior diplomats to whom the author himself had alluded throughout the book.

One is left with the sense that there is the inevitable problem of selective perception among the practitioners and observers about foreign policy decision making processes and that the truth lies somewhere in the middle of elitist and pluralist conceptions of these processes. There is nevertheless a sufficiently strong *prima facie* case for the contention that Malaysia's formal and broader foreign policy formulation process is fundamentally pluralistic, with perhaps the qualification that informal channels may, of course, sometimes be used to bypass this process and that this will have varied considerably during the tenures of different prime ministers and foreign ministers. This notwithstanding, at an even higher plane of generalization, as we have argued in Chapter 1, foreign policy formulation *qua* national policies are, at the end of the day, constitutive of larger societal processes, which are at play at different historical and political conjunctures.

NOTES

1. Interview with Yusof Hitam, Undersecretary for Southeast Asia I and II, 27 June 1975. The account of the decision making process in Wisma Putra is largely derived from this interview. Yusof Hitam rose to become the secretary general of Wisma Putra and permanent representative to the United Nations. Now retired from the MFA, Tan Sri Yusof Hitam is still active in voluntary service in various public bodies. I met him twice at separate events in Kuala Lumpur in 2008 at the Institute of Diplomacy and Foreign Relations, and in 2009 at the Universiti Technology of Malaysia (UiTM).

2. It is interesting to note that Tan Sri Ghazali Shafie considered that Malaysia's foreign policy formulation process was "no different" from that of the developed democratic countries (interview with Tan Sri Ghazali Shafie, 30 October 1975). In his own memoirs (1998), Ghazali wrote only about his role in helping to bring to fruition the formation of Malaysia, which he intimated was the primary task assigned by the Tunku to him when he was Permanent Secretary of the MFA.

3. All Wisma Putra officers to whom I spoke in 1975 gave me this impression. In more recent umpteen encounters, including friendships, with diplomats in the late 2000s, although I never asked them directly about decision making processes, my overall sense was that the service has become even more engaged in day to day management of foreign relations. Many of them do admit that it was trying times during the Mahathir years because polices were decided without reference to previous positions and established policies (interview with Dato Mohd Yusof Ahmad, former ambassador and director of IDFR, 16 July 2007).

4. See, for example, the chapters by the ambassadors Zakari Ali, Mohd. Ridzam Deva Abdullah, Abdullah Faiz Zain and Razali Ismail (Fuaziah Mohamad, 2007).

5. See Dhillon (2007, p. 54). Dato Yusof used about the same phraseology in my interview with him. (Interview with Dato Mohamad Yusof Ahmad, 16 July 2007).

6. Interview with Saiful Anuar Mohamad from the administration section of Wisma Putra, on 11 August 2008. The latest organizational charts of MFA were obtained from Albert Ch'ng (Treasury). I'm grateful to both individuals for their assistance and help in this matter.

7. The IDFR–UKM joint degree programme for the Master of Social Science in Strategy and Diplomacy degree was started in May 1999. The first intake comprised eighteen local students and five foreign students. Since then the programme has had foreign students from Guinea, Sudan, Philippines, Croatia. Russia, Albania, Mauritius, Bosnia and Herzegovinia, Senegal, Liberia, Australia, Fiji, China, Oman, Libya, Myanmar, Guinea, Maldives, Sri Lanka, Laos, Indonesia, and Yemen. 2006 is thus the eighth year IDFR has conducted the course, which is being attended by a total of fifteen students, including eight foreign participants. The master's class consists of diplomats, government servants, private sector individuals, and fresh graduates. These students have backgrounds in a variety of undergraduate specializations.

8. As stated on the IDFR webpage, <http://www.idfr.gov.my/en/index. php?option=com_content&task=view&id=5&Itemid=5> (accessed 15 August 2008).

9. As I have had occasion to interview or communicate with all four individuals, I have reason to believe that my assessment of their role and significance in foreign policy decision making is largely valid.

10. He intimated that he was sent to the London School of Economics and Political Science for his diplomatic training as a young MFA officer (interview with Tan Sri Zakaria Ali, 6 October 2009).

11. In my interview with Tan Sri Zakaria, he emphasized the importance of the move by pointing out that Tun Razak's China initiative was aimed at involving all sectors of Malaysian society in the normalization effort, including the opposition parties and all regions of Malaysia (inclusive of Sabah and Sarawak). The Communist insurgents were dead against the idea and demonstrated this by carrying out many acts of sabotage in Perak during this time and soon after that the inspector general of police was gunned down (interview with Tan Sri Zakaria Ali, 6 October 2009).

12. Interview with Tan Sri Zakaria Ali, 6 October, 2009. For the details of the negotiation points, see also Zakaria Ali (2006).

13. Like Tan Sri Zakaria Ali, Zainal Abidin Sulong was sent for training at the London School of Economics and Political Science (interview with Tan Sri Zainal Abidin Sulong, 7 October , 2009).

14. Interview with Tan Sri Zainal Abidin Sulong, 7 October 2009. The Algiers conference was held in 1973. Malaysia attended the non-aligned conference for the first time in Lusaka in 1970. See Chapter 4.

15. This was the playful pseudonym given to Tan Sri Ghazali Shafie in the service and clearly alluded to his authoritative, if not authoritarian, style.

16. In my interview with Tan Sri Zainal Abidin (7 October 2007), he considered the late Noordin Sopiee to have been an important adviser to Dr Mahathir, especially on economic policies. I have myself met Noordin Sopiee many times and it was patently clear that he had a close relationship with the prime minister. He intimated to me that at times he had crafted various speeches for the premier.

17. See Chapter 8, note 25.

18. In an interview on 22 October 2009, Dato Mohd Ridzam Deva shared his candid views with me on this subject. One of the major problems, he opined, was the poor and loose recruitment policy of the civil service authority, the Public Service Department or JPA. In the 1980s the "Isi Penuh" (Fill Up) exercise of the JPA greatly affected the quality of the PTD officers (Diplomatic and Administrative Service) from which the MFA sources its recruits.

19. The document, entitled "Strategic Plan 2009–2015" of some 139 pages, is complete the Wisma Putra anthem, composed by former Foreign Minister Syed Hamid Albar.

20. Interviews conducted in 1975 with M. Shanmughalingam (Treasury), Fong Kwek Yuen, *Encik* Zainal Aznam (Economic Planning Unit), Yee Che Fong (Ministry of Trade and Industry), Yusof Hitam, Looi Cheok Hin, Hasmay Agam and M. Ben-Haron (Foreign Ministry), and L.C. Vohra (Ministry of Law). At the point of writing, after many meetings over the years with Wisma Putra personnel and diplomats, I can confirm this impression. In 2008, I had formal interviews with Tan Sri Hasmy Agam, director of IDFR, on 13 July 2007, and Tan Sri Fuzi Ahmad, ambassador-at-large, on 16 July 2007, who again gave me the same sense of regular MFA involvement in decision making.

21. Interviews in 1975 with Dr Tan Chee Khoon (Pekemas), Fan Yew Teng and Lim Kit Siang (DAP), Lee Siew Yee, Samad Ismail, Dhahari Ali, and Dr Noordin Sopiee (journalists).

22. This is certainly the point made by Dhillon (2009, p. 54) who cites a senior diplomat saying that during the Mahathir period, "MFA role in policy formulation was either minimal or virtually nil."

3

ENGAGING THE COLD WAR 1957–63

CONSTRUCTING FOREIGN POLICY

Early analysts of the foreign policy of the fledging Malayan state were wont to suggest that it was the preserve of one man, the prime minister (Silcock 1993, p. 42) or that of a stable elite of four or five men (Ott 1973, p. 225). This book argues that foreign policy formulation in its multifarious dimensions is the product of a "construction" by political agents, the most important of whom, admittedly are prime ministers, foreign ministers, and important cabinet ministers, acting on behalf of the state. Having said this, however, I will advance the argument throughout the book that such a construction must ultimately dovetail with, or correspond to, embedded ideas, interests, and identities, inclusive of the norms and political culture of a society. In this chapter I will begin by examining foreign policy as foreign policy outputs, described and explained in the introductory chapter. These outputs saw their construction in the three issues areas of "defence and security", "developmental and economic concerns", and "international cooperation". These were clearly the areas of greatest relevance to the newly independent state, which sought first to secure its territorial boundaries (a core objective), use its foreign policy for economic gain (a medium-range objective), and maintain a level of international cooperation with other actors and states (a long-range goal).

DEFENCE AND SECURITY

The new Malayan state's external defence policy banked almost entirely on the Anglo-Malayan Defence Agreement (AMDA) of 1957 whereby Britain and Malaya promised to provide each other with mutual aid in the event of an armed attack on either Malayan or British possessions in the Far East. Article IV of the agreement stated clearly that, "[I]n the event of armed attack against any of the territories or forces of the Federation of Malaya or any of the territories or protectorates of the United Kingdom in the Far East or any of the forces of the United Kingdom within any of those territories or protectorates or within the Federation of Malaya, the governments of the Federation of Malaya and the United Kingdom undertake to cooperate with each other and will take such action as each considers necessary for the purpose of meeting the situation effectively."[1] The two governments were also to consult each other if the peace of the mentioned territories was threatened. Should hostilities involving either party occur anywhere else in the world, "the Government of the United Kingdom shall obtain prior agreement of the Government of the Federation of Malaya before committing United Kingdom forces to active operations involving the use of bases in the Federation of Malaya…" Another provision obligated the parties to consult each other "when major changes in the character or deployment of the forces maintained in the Federation…were contemplated". This proviso was supposedly recognition that Britain could not introduce nuclear weapons into Malaya without the latter's approval (Tilman 1969, p. 7).

The Malayan government's objectives in securing AMDA were fairly obvious, given the size of its armed forces at the time of independence. It did not even have a division of men, but only several battalions of the Malay Royal Regiment, and no air force or navy to speak of.[2] Then Deputy Prime Minister and Defence Minister Tun Abdul Razak gave this candid rationale for Malaya's defence policy:

> As far as the Federation of Malaya is concerned we are a relatively small nation with many demands on our resources. We have to concentrate our efforts on improving the standard of living of our people and provide them with amenities and social services which are necessary for an independent and civilised country. Therefore, we can only afford to maintain a small defence force and must depend for our external defence on the help of friends and allies in times of need. That is why…we entered into a mutual defence pact with the United Kingdom Government, associated by the governments of Australia and New Zealand…Our defence policy is, therefore, to contribute toward a common commonwealth effort in the protection of our territories in this area and for the maintenance of external peace and security of our country, to ensure that the authority of the lawful government is effectively enforced anywhere in the Federation, including its territorial waters.[3]

For Britain, the pact was used as a means to protect its national interests in the region, with an eye towards its obligations to the Southeast Asian Treaty Organization (SEATO). Beneath its formal language, the pact couched a preoccupation with the communist threat to the region. Malaya's long and bitter internal war with the communists, in which the British played a major role, left the Malayan policymakers with the continued perception of the threat of communist expansionism in Southeast Asia.[4]

Prior to the signing of AMDA, the ANZAM Agreement of 1949 between Britain, Australia, and New Zealand had provided for Malaya's defence. The Commonwealth Far East Strategic Reserve was formed in 1955 and stationed in Malaya, its functions being to contain communist insurrection, provide defence from external attack, and carry out SEATO commitments (Dalton 1972, p. 64). The protracted negotiations over AMDA saw the exchange of letters until as late as 23 August 1957. According to Dalton, Malaya had evidently "won a maximum of security with a minimum of obligation and it had not compromised on two basic policies of rejecting nuclear weapons and refusing to join SEATO" (Dalton 1972, p. 66).

AMDA was not accepted at home without a brief groundswell of opposition against the pact from nationalist elements in the United Malays National Organization (UMNO) of the ruling Alliance party, the opposition parties, and various trade union leaders and public figures. Interestingly, the most vocal support for the pact came from the non-Malay partners in the Alliance — the Malayan Chinese Association (MCA) and the Malayan Indian Congress (MIC).[5] The UMNO backbench revolt began when a party member, Tajuddin Ali, attacked the treaty for being "harmful to independent Malaya". This sparked off the Johore UMNO Youth claim that the pact made Malaya indirectly a member of SEATO and led the UMNO Kedah branch to call for an emergency general session to discuss the implications of the treaty as it considered some of the clauses too binding. Then Prime Minister Tunku Abdul Rahman stood his ground amidst mounting criticism of the treaty, but was forced to call an emergency meeting of the UMNO Executive Committee to "explain" the pact. The Tunku placed his leadership at stake by making AMDA a "confidence issue", stating that an emergency UMNO assembly debate on the pact would be taken by him to be a vote of no confidence. The Tunku's tactic succeeded and he won a unanimous vote from the Executive Committee and the agitation for a general session subsided. The Tunku, however, did make the concession that the treaty would be reviewed within a year.

Subsequently, in October, AMDA was presented and debated in the Legislative Council. A number of backbenchers, the opposition parties, and the trade union representatives continued to oppose the pact, arguing that it compromised Malaya's sovereignty and independence, that military pacts invited military threats, and that Malaya was unnecessarily rushing into a military pact without having had a full debate on foreign policy.[6]

The Tunku reiterated the government's position that the pact was a matter of necessity:

> [L]et us face facts, and the facts are that we have at our command an army of less than one division in strength; we have no air force, not even a single plane or a single man; we have no navy, not even a single sailor and we have not even a sea-going craft. With the revenue at our command we can never be able to build our forces to the strength which we would require for the defence of our country.[7]

The Tunku in winding up the debate again staked his leadership over the issue, stating "… if the people of this country do not want (the treaty), a simple thing can done and that is — this is all I ask of the people of this country and of my party — to call a meeting, a general meeting, of UMNO and pass a vote of 'no confidence' against me and my friends and colleagues, and we can just make way for some other clever 'Dicks' to come and run this country [*sic*]." As it turned out, the motion of support for the treaty was unanimously passed, with those opposing it, abstaining. In the light of the UMNO and other opposition to AMDA, it is perhaps not at all surprising that Malaya had not joined SEATO. The Malayan leaders dared not hazard a formal tie with the Western bloc even though SEATO was specifically aimed at containing communism, which, presumably, was the purpose of AMDA. Among the other reasons given for non-participation in SEATO was that Malaya would not have gained any military advantage by joining and that the organization was unpopular with India and Indonesia, the two non-communist Asian bulwarks to which Malaysia showed a great degree of deference. The Tunku, when asked about Malaya's decision not to join SEATO, was quoted in Canberra in 1959 as saying: "Well, I don't count, you know. As the representative of my people, I have to do as they want, and SEATO is rather unpopular among my people. I don't know for what reason." (Tilman 1969, p. 22).[8] A more complete and honest answer would have been that there were strenuous objections from the various segments of Malaysian society to SEATO even beyond UMNO voices, which were surprisingly vociferous. There is a strong suggestion that Chinese groups were also against SEATO and the Tamil Association sent a memorandum to the Tunku on the issue while opposition parties such as the Pan-Malayan Islamic Party (PMIP) and Parti Rakyat also objected to SEATO membership (Khaw, 1976, pp. 78–79).

Despite the Malayan government's many denials that it had anything to do with SEATO, Robert O. Tilman has compiled evidence, produced below, that Malaya's voting in the United Nations closely approximated that of the SEATO countries. In comparing Malaya's voting pattern on East-West issues in the years 1957, 1960, and 1963, he shows a 72–96 per cent fit with the voting pattern of SEATO countries, Australia, New Zealand, United Kingdom, United States, Pakistan, the Philippines, and Thailand (Tilman 1969, p. 23).

The Tunku himself did not deny the government's indirect links with the organization. In answer to a question in Parliament, he said: "[A]l I can say is that we are not in SEATO. In this respect, if SEATO countries are involved in any war, we are not committed to the war, but on the other hand, if Britain entered the war and one of the countries which we are committed to defend, like Singapore, a British territory, or Borneo, is attacked, then we are treaty bound to fight. Perhaps you may say we are indirectly connected with SEATO, but I can say quite openly here and assure the House that we are not in SEATO."[9]

The manifest anti-communism in Malayan foreign policy was especially evident in the country's orientation towards and relations with great powers other than Britain. The Tunku in 1958 proclaimed to Parliament Malaya's non-neutrality on questions of East-West conflict:

> There is no question whatsoever of our adopting a neutral policy while Malaya is at war with the Communists. Only when we are certain that people here have become truly Malayan-minded and have set their minds on making Malaya their only home can the government declare our policy of neutrality. So long as this fight continues, I consider that we would be breaking faith with the people if this government were to enter into any form of diplomatic relationship with the communist countries... let me tell you that there are no such things as local communists. Communism is an international organization which aims for world domination, not by aggression if they can avoid it, but by the use of tactics and methods among the sons of the country to overthrow democracy and to set up in its place a government after the pattern of all communist countries. (*The Straits Times*, 7 December 1958)

With respect to Vietnam, the Malayan Government gave its wholehearted support to the United States and the South. Indeed, the prime minister's first official visit was to South Vietnam in 1958 during which he made pledges of solidarity with President Ngo Dinh Diem. Ngo returned the Tunku's visit in 1960.

The government's opposition to communism was perhaps most evident in its relations with China. While it accorded diplomatic recognition to the Soviet Union and the Eastern European countries, the government was unwilling to recognize China, being content to espouse the "two-China" policy at the United Nations.[10] This policy supported in principle the admission of China with the understanding that Taiwan would continue to be a U.N. member and that a vote for China's admission did not imply recognition. At the United Nations, the government had also been forthright in criticizing China's actions in Tibet in 1959, and in the Sino-Indian hostilities of 1962. The Tunku even launched a "Save Democracy Fund" which raised RM1 million "to help India defend herself against Chinese aggression". The excessive fear of Chinese communism even prompted Malaya's representative at the United Nations in 1963 to depart somewhat from the formal two-China policy:

> [W]e have been and are indeed, too close to China to take an academic or theoretical view of the situation…For ten long years and more, while the world has been shivering in the chill winds of the Cold War, we in (Malaya) were right in the storm centre of a shooting war arising out of a communist campaign which threatened to overthrow our government…China started unprovoked aggression on India. China has recently resisted…violently the moderating influence of even its greatest ally…China regards a global class war not only as inevitable but desirable…In all these circumstances, we cannot avoid asking ourselves what good, in practical terms should we do China or to ourselves by bringing it to the United Nations. (Tilman 1969*b*, p. 7).

There was nonetheless a seeming paradox in Malayan foreign policy with respect to its anti-communism and its pro-Westernism. Tilman has noted that Malaya was "no more a lackey of the West than she was a fellow traveller of the communists". There is some evidence that Malaya tried to steer a course of political independence while at the same time making no secret of its Western alliances. This often led to policy contradictions which opposition parliamentarians were quick to point out. One of the favourite opposition issues was that the presence of foreign Commonwealth troops compromised Malaya's political independence. Malaya's attempts to steer the narrow course of political independence was perhaps less an effort towards non-alignment than one which can best be described as a foreign policy posture of impartiality in foreign dealings, and "non-interference" in the business of other states. Thus, speaking soon after admission to the United Nations, Malaya's representative, Dato' Ismail said:

> Our position in the world today is…unique in that we are fairly content with what we already possess. We do not need vast sums of money from our friends to tide us along in our own affairs. We do not covet the goods and chattels nor the territory of others… The greatest need of my country

today is peace and the goodwill of all countries with which it is our desire to live in friendship and mutual understanding. We venture to suggest that our unique position permits us to play an impartial role in the affairs of the world. (Tilman 1969*b*, p. 11)

To summarize, Malayan foreign policy with respect to questions of defence and security displayed a distinct pro-Western, and concomitantly, anti-communist posture, tempered by a rather ineffectual attempt towards neutrality, or what would be more correctly described as a posture of impartiality and non-interference. Robert Tilman, an early keen observer of Malayan foreign policy, characterized it as the political ambivalence of a "committed neutral".[11] We would probably be nearer the mark if we described Malayan foreign policy as being more committed to a particular set of ideological beliefs, than that of a neutralist state steering clear of the established political fissures of the Cold War era. Using constructivist lenses, one could well argue that Malaya, *qua* state, had an identity and interests like most states, namely, its major foreign policy objectives were the protection of its political sovereignty and its territorial boundaries against outside interference and aggression. These, in realist parlance, represented the basic core value goals of self-preservation. However, the approach to attaining these objectives were clearly coloured by a set of highly coherent ideological and normative constructs wrapped around a profound anti-communism stance, which was deeply imbibed by its major policymakers. Given the worldview of its policymakers, the pursuit of these objectives translated as the imperative to seek protection against communist expansionism and aggression. The Anglo-Malayan Defence Treaty was the direct response to meeting such eventualities. As far as foreign policy strategies were concerned, there was perhaps no great deal of thought given to planning complex policies. Defence was the basic objective and AMDA was an almost automatic response to Malaya's defence needs.[12] However, since Malaya had unequivocally camped on one side of the East-West divide, it also naturally behaved strategically as a minor "cold warrior". There was, therefore, a conscious effort on the Malayan Government's part to align with the Western powers and concomitantly to disassociate itself from the communist powers.

I summarize below in table form the foreign policy of the period with respect to issues of national defence and security in terms of foreign policy objectives, postures, strategies, and the most important actions. The summary should be taken only as a listing of the various examples of policy outputs, without their more complex relationship specified. This task will be accomplished in a later section at the end of this chapter.

TABLE 3.1
Defence and Security Policy Outputs, 1957–63

Objectives	Postures	Strategies	Actions
Maintaining Political Independence	*Pro-Western Orientation* – supporting ideals of Western democracy and their dissemination	Aligning with Western powers Non-association with communist States	Signing Anglo-Malayan Defence Pact Supporting US policy in Vietnam, Cuba, and on Gulf of Tonkin incident
Protecting Territorial Integrity	*Anti-Communist Orientation* – opposing communist ideals and their dissemination *Non-interference* – respecting territorial integrity and political sovereignty		Not recognizing and/or having diplomatic relations with most Communist states Following a "two-China" policy at the United Nations

Source: Author's own compilation.

DEVELOPMENTAL AND ECONOMIC CONCERNS

The impact of British colonial rule on Malaya's economy was perhaps more profound than in any other area. The British left Malaya as a resource-based economy largely geared to the expanding industries and needs of the metropolis. Thus, independent Malaya emerged as essentially an agricultural country in which rubber and tin accounted for approximately 85 per cent of all exports, and in which 69 per cent of its two million working population was engaged in agriculture. In addition, continued British economic interests in the country effectively controlled much of its economy. As a former British civil servant noted, most of the major agency houses and giant holding companies that dominated agriculture and commerce were still in British hands after independence and that, "at present (1963) all the tin dredges, three-quarters of the large rubber estates, almost all of the new oil palm estates, possible two-thirds of Malayan foreign trade, and much of the new secondary industries are in overseas, mainly British, ownership and control." (Tilman 1969*a*, p. 36).

Malaya's espousal of a *laissez-faire* economic policy made the continued participation of foreign enterprise not only possible, but to a large extent, welcome. In most part, this philosophy was prompted by the belief that only foreign economic enterprise could provide the necessary capital for growth and stability. At the international level such a policy construct implied a strong commitment to international commerce and private foreign investment. As a direct consequence, Malaya concluded bilateral investment pacts with West Germany, Japan, and the United States soon after independence, was a party to the ECAFE (Economic Commission for Asia and the Far East) multilateral Investment Charter, and also granted tax relief to "pioneer industries" in the country in 1958.

In contrast to its *laissez-faire* posture towards foreign investment, Malaya's narrow-based economy caused it to press vigorously for international control of the prices of raw materials. In particular, it has been a leading participant in the international tin agreements and the International Rubber Study Group. But before we examine the specific policies in this area, it may be illuminating to consider more thoroughly the composition and direction of Malayan trade. Economists had in early years noted that the country had a very high export orientation, measured in terms of Gross Export Proceeds over Gross Domestic Product. Malaya ranked first among a cross-section of Asian and European countries with an export orientation of 40 per cent, while the United States at the other extreme had a figure of only 4 per cent. In Lim Chong Yah's words:

> The extent of export orientation can reveal a good deal about the nature of a country's economy. For one thing it suggests a high degree of dependence on foreign markets, which leads in turn to the dependence of the country's economic welfare on foreign economic forces. Insofar as a country produces goods that have high foreign marginal income elasticities of demand, as do most (Malayan) exports, the prosperity of its export industries is directly correlated with the prosperity of the importing countries. (Lim 1969, p. 205)

Thus, Malaya's economic prosperity was heavily tied to its external trade, which in turn was heavily dependent on its two major exports, rubber and tin. The table below shows that rubber was by far the most important Malayan product, accounting for more than 60 per cent of its exports, with tin ranking a high second with a figure of around 20 per cent. Malaya's heavy dependence on these two primary commodities made it indirectly dependent on the major industrial countries which were the chief buyers of rubber and tin.

The next table shows the direction of Malayan exports in terms of the major buyers of Malayan goods. Of the six major importers, three were

TABLE 3.2
Composition of Malayan Gross Exports, 1947–60 (%)

Commodity	1947–50	1951–55	1956–60
Rubber	64.0	64.0	63.0
Tin	19.0	21.0	17.0
Iron	0.3	1.0	4.0
Timber	1.0	1.0	2.0
Palm Oil	2.0	2.0	2.0
All Others	13.7	11.0	12.0
Total	100	100	100

Source: Lim Chong Yah (1969, p. 210).

advanced Western countries (the United States, the United Kingdom, and West Germany), one was an advanced communist country (the Soviet Union), another, an advanced Asian country (Japan) and, the last, a major trading centre and international entrepot (Singapore). However, there was an important difference between Singapore and the other five countries. Unlike the five, which were final consumers of Malayan exports, Singapore mainly re-exported Malaya's domestic products to other countries. Thus, the chief buyers of Malayan exports were the advanced industrialized countries.

The picture on imports is a little more complex. Britain, however, dominated as Malaya's most important supplier, again emphasizing the colonial links. Malaya's substantial imports of manufactured and capital goods made the country doubly dependent on industrial countries, which, as noted, were also the main buyers of its products. Malaya also imported considerably from its Southeast Asian neighbours, largely food and raw materials for domestic use and its processing industries.[13]

This discussion of Malayan trade figures provides us with a lucid understanding of the country's heavy dependence on external trade and the extreme vulnerability of the Malayan economy to external forces quite beyond the country's control. It was not surprising, therefore, that Malaya ardently espoused all international efforts to stabilize the prices of primary commodities. Its participation in the various international tin agreements was a direct response to the need to protect tin prices. Malaya also strenuously protested against the United States' release of its strategic stockpiles of rubber and tin acquired during the years of the Korean boom. Such releases, whatever the real U.S. motive, adversely affected the market prices of the two commodities and became the chief irritant in U.S.–Malayan relations. In addition, U.S.

TABLE 3.3
Direction of Malayan Exports, 1958–63 (%)

Country	1958	1959	1960	1961	1962	1963
Singapore	23.8	23.0	21.5	19.8	19.8	20.0
United Kingdom	18.5	13.3	13.0	11.9	9.3	8.3
United States	10.6	11.5	10.3	12.6	14.5	14.4
Japan	9.4	12.8	12.6	14.5	13.8	14.7
West Germany	5.0	5.8	7.7	8.6	4.2	4.3
USSR	3.9	8.2	3.7	6.0	8.5	7.7
Sub-total	71.2	74.6	68.8	73.4	70.1	69.4
Italy	3.8	3.5	3.6	3.8	3.7	4.1
China	2.9	0.9	0.2	—	—	—
India	2.7	2.1	2.8	2.9	2.8	2.4
France	2.6	3.2	3.8	3.8	3.7	2.8
Australia	1.7	1.6	1.9	1.0	1.7	1.7
Canada	1.6	1.4	1.3	1.8	1.9	2.4
Netherlands	1.5	1.1	0.8	0.8	0.9	0.8
Total	88.0	88.4	83.2	87.5	84.8.	83.6

Source: Calculated from Lim (1969, p. 216).

TABLE 3.4
Composition of Malayan Imports, 1958 & 1963 (%)

	1958	1963
Food, beverages, and tobacco	36.5	28.5
Crude materials and mineral fuels	19.1	17.6
Manufactures, capital, and consumer goods	42.9	51.1
Others	0.6	2.8
Total	99.1	100.0

Source: Calculated from Lim (1969, pp. 223–24).

production of synthetic rubber and its reluctance to support commodity arrangements provided a further source of annoyance to Malaya.

Tin, unlike rubber has had a long history of price-fixing arrangements and Malaya willingly joined the 1953 Tin Arrangement under Britain's aegis, and participated after independence in the 1960 agreement.[14] Apart from the pragmatic matter of obtaining better prices from the industrialized, tin-consuming countries, the tin conferences also provided Malaya with the opportunity for expressing solidarity with other primary-producing Third World countries. Typical of Malaya's utterances at such conferences was the statement produced below that was made by a Malayan delegate when complaining about producing countries having to bear the burden of maintaining the buffer stock, the mechanism for cushioning price fluctuations:

> It hurts none but the producer; the principle seems to be: "To him that hath, more shall be given; from him who giveth, more shall be taken away," The producer's burden will not be lightened for another five years. Condemned to the same old floor price, he would also be required to subsidize the consumer by providing out of his own meagre earnings the means with which to keep the price at or below the ceiling. (Saravanamuttu 1972, p. 87)

Apart from tin agreements, Malaya also employed the strategy of negotiating bilateral trade agreements to overcome trade barriers, and thus ensure a ready market for its goods. These trade agreements typically accorded to Malaya and the other country mutual, most-favoured-nation treatment, as well as the exemption of duty in certain specified areas. The agreements were in force for one to three years, and usually renewed at the expiry of the period. Malaya concluded the first such agreement with Australia in August 1958, with the result that rubber and tin imports were allowed into Australia free of duty in exchange for similar treatment and purchase of certain Australian products. The second trade agreement was concluded with Japan in May 1960, which had the immediate impact of increasing its export of pineapples and timber to that country. Subsequently, trade agreements were signed with New Zealand in February 1961, United Arab Republic in February 1962, and South Korea in January 1963. Attempts were made to conclude a trade agreement with India, but it never materialized. In a statement, the Ministry of Commerce and Industry said that it was Malaya's policy to sign trade agreements with any interested country. The strategy of signing trade agreements may be related to Malaya's commitment to a *laissez-faire* posture in international commerce, but pragmatic considerations of direct economic benefit were perhaps the more important motive.

To recapitulate: Malaya's foreign policy in the area of trade and development was marked by a strong developing-world orientation that betrayed the vulnerability of its economy. At the same time, it would seem that Malaya's colonial ties tended to foster a liberal, *laissez-faire* policy towards international commerce and foreign enterprise in the country. Malaya's trading ties tended to reinforce its western-world leanings, although this orientation did not preclude trading with the Soviet Union and China. A summary of its foreign policy with respect to development and trade appears in Table 3.7.

TABLE 3.5
Main Sources of Malayan Imports, 1958 & 1963 (%)

Country	1958	1963
United Kingdom	25.0	21.0
Thailand	11.0	9.5
Indonesia	13.8	8.3
Singapore	8.4	9.3
Japan	5.7	9.9
Sub-total	63.9	58.0
China	5.7	5.2
Australia	5.4	5.1
Hong Kong	2.9	3.3
Burma	2.9	2.1
India	2.5	2.6
United States	2.5	5.2
West Germany	2.4	3.7
Netherlands	1.7	2.3
Total	89.9	87.5

Source: Lim (1969, pp. 225–26).

INTERNATIONAL COOPERATION

We have already noted that Malaya portrayed itself as an impartial actor in world affairs at the United Nations. Malaya looked upon the United Nations as a rallying point for the smaller nations and thus actively supported the ideals and work of the international organization, and, not without distinction.[15] Tilman writes lucidly on this point:

> The United Nations has played a large part in the enunciation of (Malayan) foreign policy, and (Malaya) has played a significant role in the work of the UN. Malayan troops performed distinguished service under the UN flag in the Congo, an operation that Malaya supported not only with troops but also financially through the purchase of UN bonds. The Malayan representative opposed Soviet attempts to weaken the Secretary-Generalship after the death of Dag Hammarskjöld[,] supported the appointment of U Thant to the vacant post, and has consistently applauded all the efforts of the Secretary-General to make the UN a more effective influence in international affairs... As a result of its enthusiastic support of the activities of the UN, it is not surprising that Malaya was early designated to take a non-permanent seat on the Security Council, a chair that it held during the 19th Session. (Tilman 1969*b*, p. 7)

TABLE 3.6
Developmental and Economic Concerns, 1957–63

Objectives	Postures	Strategies	Actions
Promoting Economic development – industrialzation – rural development – commercial development	*Laissez-faire Orientation* – commitment to international commerce and free enterprise	Providing a good investment climate in the country (having no nationalization policy)	Concluding bilateral investment agreements with W Germany, Japan, and U.S. (1957)
Stabilizing the prices of primary commodities	*Developing-world Orientation* – supporting price fixing of primary goods	Supporting and participating in trade groupings of developing countries	Negotiating Multilateral Investment Charter in ECAFE (1958)
		Negotiating bilateral trade agreements to overcome trade barriers	Participating in International Tin Agreements (1953, 1960)
			Denouncing US GSA releases of tin and rubber stockpiles
			Concluding trade Agreements with Australia (1958) Japan (1960) New Zealand (1961) United Arab Republic (1962) and South Korea (1963)

Source: Author's own compilation.

Malaya's most significant action in support of the international organization and its ideals was the country's participation in the Congo peacekeeping mission in 1960. It initially contributed 613 personnel, but increased this to a total of 1,413 men when the secretary general sought reinforcement.[16] Backing Dag Hammarskjöld strongly when the secretary general came under attack from the Soviet Union, the Malayan delegate stated during the emergency session of the United Nations on the Congo crisis in September 1960 that:

> Many unjustified and erroneous accusations have been levelled against the United Nations Command. whose integrity and sincerity have been unfairly questioned by these accusations.... Under normal circumstances these

charges because of their fallacious character could easily be dismissed but when they seem to have the intention of publicly discrediting the Secretary-General, and thereby endangering the authority of the UN, in which we small nations place our hope and faith in this troubled age, my delegation feels it incumbent upon it to speak up and take strong exception to these unwarranted and unjustified accusations. (Hazra 1965, pp. 54–55)

Thus, throughout the duration of the Congo crisis, the Malayan policy was to forestall any efforts of eroding the U.N. authority in the handling of the crisis and also to prevent its engulfment in Cold War politics. This apparently non-aligned position, however, was not motivated by adherence to a truly neutral or unbiased appreciation of the problem as the Tunku amply demonstrated in explaining Malaya's stand to Parliament, arguing that external interference in Malayan internal affairs will not be tolerated, and that the Republic of Congo was akin to Malaya by reason of the fact that it was recently independent, and "must not be exposed in her tender years to the dangers of subversion as perpetrated by international communism". He further stated:

> Let us not be beguiled by the veneer of friendship like that offered by the communists when their declared aim is to gain control of the world and place it under a system where there were no personal freedoms and democracy as we understand them… In the communist book, peaceful co-existence is a fraud designed to reduce into a state of non-existence those trapped victims…. We are firmly convinced that to keep the Congo free of unnecessary power bloc interference, aid must be channelled through the UN. (*The Straits Times*, 30 September 1960)

The Tunku also described Soviet Premier Khrushchev's proposal of replacing the secretary general with a three-man "troika" secretariat as "despicable" and a "mischievous idea" aimed at turning the United Nations into the "Disunited Nations". It would seem that the Tunku unwittingly drew Malaya into Cold War politics during the Congo crisis in his pronouncements on the subject although Malaya had formally taken an impartial stand at the United Nations on the matter.

Among the topics that came up regularly for debate at the United Nations was the question of disarmament. Malaya supported the idea in principle, but tended to back the more conservative, usually Western-bloc proposals on the problem. For example, at the 12th Session (1957) of the General Assembly, fresh from independence, Malaya voted against a Soviet draft resolution proposing a five-year ban on the use of nuclear weapons, with the provision to reconsider the moratorium at the end of that period, and abstained on a second resolution calling for the establishment of a Permanent Disarmament Commission. Yet it voted for the Western-sponsored draft resolution urging international control covering reduction of armed forces and armaments, open inspection to guard against surprise attacks, and immediate suspension of nuclear testing. Malaya's voting at the 13th Session was similar. Dr Ismail, the Malayan delegate, explained his country's support for a limited plan for disarmament in the following colourful manner:

> It is painfully obvious to the world at large that under the strenuous conditions of modern life, disarmament has become a sprawling complex of interrelated parts, a many-headed hydra which will test our human ingenuity and resourcefulness to the limit if we are to overcome it and yet survive in the process. It is no longer possible to slay the monster with one clean sweep of the diplomatic sword. We must, therefore, turn to the venerable ancients for wise precedents and attacking each individual part of the problem, take care to seal it off forever from its dreadful capacity of multiplying itself after every attempt to destroy its many heads. (Hazra 1965, pp. 37–38)

In general, then, Malaya did not vote with the neutralist countries wanting to propose compromise resolutions. For example, Malaya was not among fourteen neutralist countries drafting a resolution calling for immediate discontinuance of nuclear tests until agreement was reached by the states concerned on controls necessary to ensure the stopping of such tests. Malaya abstained from voting in both the First Committee and the General Assembly on the resolution. Thus Malaya adhered basically to a realist, if conservative, stand on disarmament, and unlike its unequivocal support for U.N. collective security, did not see the United Nations capable of controlling the arms race without the compliance of the armed.

On questions of colonialism and human rights, Malaya's position was decidedly more Third World oriented. Its response to the Algerian situation perhaps typifies the reaction to colonial issues. Except on one occasion, it supported all the Afro-Asian resolutions on the Algerian question. Only in 1958, when reference was made to the "Provisional Government of the Algerian Republic", did Malaya cautiously abstain on a resolution, but in general it voted for the recognition of the right of the Algerian people to self-determination and independence. In the words of Dato Kamil, Malaya's U.N. delegate, in 1960:

> As a nation which has just attained its independence from colonial rule, however beneficent the regime may be, the Federation of Malaya has dedicated and continues to dedicate itself to the just cause of peoples and nations everywhere for the right to self-determination and freedom from alien bondage in all forms, manifestations and guises. This dedication to the cause of freedom has become one of the cardinal principles that

form the cornerstone of (my) government's foreign policy. (Hazra 1965, pp. 48–49)

Malaysia's attitude and voting behaviour on the West Irian question also took a similar line.[17]

A prominent aspect of Malaya's foreign policy with respect to international cooperation was its active participation in the many specialized and regional intergovernmental international organizations.[18] Participation in these organizations has in general been a boon to Malaya in the areas of economic and technical advancement. For example, the International Bank for Reconstruction and Development (IBRD) in 1958 made a loan of $28.6 million to Malaya to help finance the Cameron Highlands hydroelectric project, the biggest single development project then for the Federation. A second loan of $51.9 million was given in 1963 to finance the second phase of the project. We have already noted earlier Malaya's strong support for the role of international organization in assisting Third World socio-economic development. This extended to virtually all other specialized or specific-purpose organizations and is a manifestation of what we may term a "functionalist" orientation in this area of foreign policy.

Next in importance to the United Nations was perhaps Malaya's association with the Commonwealth. From the standpoint of defence, the Anglo-Malayan Defence Pact (associated by the Governments of Australia and New Zealand) automatically made Malaya an integral part of Commonwealth defence. As Tun Razak put it, Malaya's defence policy was to contribute towards "a common Commonwealth effort in the protection of our territories in this area…". In addition, participation in the Commonwealth also ensured certain economic advantages to a developing country such as Malaya. In particular, the benefits included capital aid grants from advanced Commonwealth countries, technical and educational assistance from the Colombo Plan, and indirect advantages through membership in the Sterling Area and participation in the system of Commonwealth trade preferences. The most significant of these benefits accrued from Malaya's participation in the Colombo Plan, originally designed for Commonwealth members only, but from 1958 included non-members as well, notably the United States. The plan benefited Malaya mostly in terms of technical assistance in the training of experts in various economic, educational and professional pursuits. The supposed benefits derived from participation in the Sterling Area and the Commonwealth trade preferences were somewhat more controversial.

The most contentious issue in Malaya's Commonwealth politics has been South Africa and apartheid. It was on the Tunku's initiative that the question of apartheid was raised in the 1960 conference leading eventually to the South

African Republic leaving the Association in 1961. The Tunku never minced words on the question of apartheid and as he told Parliament in 1960:

> Those who rule South Africa and control its destiny do not conform to our Commonwealth ideas and ideals of human rights and justice and I am beginning to think whether a country like South Africa has any right to be within this family of nations…. If those who control the destinies of South Africa will not listen to our protest in the cause of humanity and justice as a member of the Commonwealth, then again we should ask ourselves what right has South Africa to be a member of this Commonwealth of Nations. (Hazra 1965, p. 109)

After South African Premier Dr Verwoerd decided to withdraw his country's application for membership in May 1961, the Tunku opined that nobody was sorry: "On the other hand, the Commonwealth now means something and has been given a new stature, the Commonwealth nations can now speak up boldly on all peaceful issues which include social and religious subjects." (*The Straits Times*, 17 March 1961)

Finally, let us examine Malayan efforts towards regional — Southeast Asian — cooperation. It must be noted that Malaya was instrumental in the formation of the Association of Southeast Asia (ASA), the first truly indigenous association in the area in that all its members belonged to countries of Southeast Asia. ASA, formed in 1961, appears, however, to have been an offshoot of the Tunku's efforts at a broader grouping of non-communist (if not, anti-communist) Southeast Asian states. As early as April 1958, the Malayan premier was reported to be toying with the idea of a "defence treaty organization consisting of Malaya, Burma, Thailand, Laos, Cambodia and South Vietnam … outside the framework of the Southeast Asian Treaty Organization". He had previously rejected a Soekarno suggestion of an Islamic bloc comprising Pakistan, Malaya, Indonesia, North Borneo, and Southern Philippines as "impossible".[19] The Tunku discussed his plans with President Garcia of the Philippines on a visit in January 1959, at this stage denying reports that he was considering an "anti-communist pact for Southeast Asian countries". The upshot was a surprisingly prompt announcement of a plan for the formation of the Southeast Asia Friendship and Economic Treaty (SEAFET), an association with apparently only economic, trade, and educational objectives. Malaya undertook to draft the treaty and the diplomatic work in inviting Indonesia, Thailand, Cambodia, Laos, South Vietnam, and Burma to participate. However, the plan received lukewarm response except from Thailand and South Vietnam. Indeed, Indonesia objected and was even hostile to the idea. This Indonesian sentiment was expressed by *The Times of Indonesia* in the following unfriendly tones:

It would be a charitable act on the part of the Indonesian Government if it nipped in the bud the puerile, vain and flamboyant hopes expressed by Malaya and the Philippines in the Rahman-Garcia communiqué issued in Manila on Tuesday for the setting up of an economic and cultural union of Southeast Asia. (Hazra 1965, p. 129).

The Indonesian objections were explained more succinctly by the consul-general in Singapore that "the Philippines is a member of SEATO and Malaya has ties with Britain" and that "as long as all the member countries of such a pact are not really independent, there will be splits which will spoil the ties of unity".

SEAFET was eventually abandoned and in its place an Association of Southeast Asian States (ASAS, later, ASA) was proposed in July 1960, with Malaya, the Philippines, and Thailand as the sponsor nations. The Indonesian response was again, if not hostile this time, certainly unreceptive, while other Southeast Asian states were apparently indifferent to the project. Nevertheless, the organization was formed on 31 July 1961, with the three sponsors as founder members. The expressed aims of the association were non-political. As embodied in the Bangkok Declaration, they were:

- To establish an effective machinery for friendly consultations, collaboration and mutual assistance in the economic, social, cultural, scientific and administrative fields;
- To provide educational, professional, technical and administrative and research facilities in the respective countries for nationals and officials of the associated countries;
- To exchange information on matters of common interest or concern in the economic, cultural, educational and scientific fields;
- To cooperate in the promotion of Southeast Asian Studies;
- To provide a machinery for fruitful collaboration in the utilization of their respective natural resources, the development of their agriculture and indirectly, the expansion of their trade, the improvement of their transport and communication facilities, and generally raising the living standards of their peoples;
- To cooperate in the study of the problems of international commodity trade; and generally to consult and cooperate with one another so as to achieve the aims and purposes of the Association, as well as contribute more effectively to the work of existing international organizations and agencies.[20]

The aims of ASA were thus very general and broad. At no point was the association geared towards defence and security. The accomplishments of

ASA tend to confirm its largely cultural and diplomatic orientation as even the economic objectives were never seriously pursued. ASA's achievements included the abolition of visa requirements for officials, and the waiver of visa fees for nationals visiting one another's countries, an ASA express train service between Kuala Lumpur and Bangkok, several athletic and cultural exchanges, and consultations on an ASA airline, and a Multilateral Trade and Navigation Agreement. The last two projects never materialized. Soon after its inauspicious birth, the fate of ASA began to be adversely affected by the Tunku's Malaysia plan which brought in its wake the renewed Philippines claim to Sabah, and Indonesian Confrontation which we will discuss in the next chapter.

In summary, Malaya's foreign policy on questions of international cooperation and peace was marked by a strong commitment to the United Nations and many of its ideals, with the notion that perhaps the United Nations embodied the aspirations of small, developing states, and that any attempt at reducing U.N. authority in such matters as peacekeeping meant a threat to the position of the militarily weak states indirectly. This foreign policy posture was best manifested in Malaya's stand in the Congo crisis and to some extent is reflected in its support for the functional U.N. agencies. However, Malaya's posture and actions with respect to such issues as disarmament revealed a conservatism and a tendency to lean towards the Western-bloc nations, while on questions of colonialism and human rights, Malaya was more forthrightly Third World oriented. This was evident in its position on the Algerian, West Irian, and apartheid issues. Apart from the United Nations, Malaya also showed a commitment to the Commonwealth largely because of its mutual defence arrangement with Britain, but, one might argue, also for sentimental, if not ideological, reasons, since the Commonwealth is decidedly a Western-bloc or Western sponsored association. Finally, Malaya initiated a concerted effort at regional cooperation in Southeast Asia, but typically the efforts, which culminated in the formation of ASA, were marred by undertones of anti-communism or a pro-West flavour, which tended to foreclose the participation of countries such as Indonesia. The basic foreign policy strategy seemed to be to promote the authority of the United Nations and other international organizations so that this would also indirectly promote and protect the interests of smaller countries such as Malaya.[21] There were two definite facets to this general strategy which may be seen as two substrategies of (a) promoting and participating in general purpose or functionally diffused international groupings and associations such as the United Nations and the Commonwealth, and (b) promoting and participating in specific purpose groupings and regional bodies. In general, the strategies in this issue area tended to be somewhat diffused since the goals were long-range and distant in nature. There was, therefore, a greater fusion between postures, objectives, strategies, and actions. A foreign policy posture or objective does not always have to have a corresponding foreign policy strategy. A strategy is a premeditated, specific plan of action, whereas a good number of foreign policy actions often flow directly from policy postures and objectives. This seems to have been the case in Malaya's posture of anti-colonialism. Adopting a standard posture such as this led naturally to certain kinds of actions, in particular voting in support of Third World issues at the United Nations. Where no clear-cut foreign policy strategy existed, foreign policy postures were often also of the "posturing" type, that is, they were largely designed for public consumption. In this sense, they were related to status and prestige questions which will be discussed in the next, concluding, section of the chapter.

SOURCES OF A MALAYAN FOREIGN POLICY

In surveying Malayan foreign policy from 1957–63, we have used a number of descriptive labels to depict its texture or character. We have called these its postures and have also identified its major policy objectives, strategies, and actions. The overall picture of the emergent Malayan foreign policy is that of a Western-leaning, conservative foreign policy with a low profile in Third World orientation, except on economic issues.

Applying a constructivist sensibility towards an understanding of Malayan foreign policy need not imply a total debunking of the idiosyncratic or individual variable as a major factor in decision making. It may be hard to deny that Malayan foreign policy "owes more to the personality of its Prime Minister, Tunku Abdul Rahman, than is usual". (Silcock 1963, p. 42). However, one cannot ignore the more fundamental, underlying sources of foreign policy in explaining it fully. It is certainly overstating the case to say that the formulation of Malayan foreign policy was "the virtual prerogative of a small stable elite comprising four or five men". (Ott 1973, p. 225).[22] Much of the difficulty with the early (or even latter day) analyses of Malaysian foreign policy is that they invariably latched upon the idiosyncracies of prime ministers as the crucial explanatory variables, to the exclusion of other factors such as political culture or domestic needs. Part of the problem is the emphasis on decision making style, rather than foreign policy as such. If such analyses were to appreciate and define the full range of foreign policy outputs or dependent variables, their conclusions might be somewhat different. They may find, for example, that the importance of idiosyncratic variables will vary from issue area to issue area, just as it will likely vary depending on whether

TABLE 3.7
International Cooperation Policy Outputs, 1957–63

Objectives	Postures	Strategies	Actions
Promoting U.N. ideals – collective security – self-determination – decolonization – human rights & social justice – disarmament	*International Orientation* Supporting exercise of U.N.'s authority *Functional Orientation*	Promoting & legitimizing the authority of the U.N. and other well known NGOs to promote the interests of small nations	Participating in U.N. peacekeeping mission in the Congo (1960) Participating in U.N. specialized agencies and their work
Promoting regional cooperation	Supporting work of functional international organizations *Anti-colonialism* Supporting self-determination & Human rights *Regionalism* Encouraging Regional cooperation	1. promoting goals of general- purpose groupings 2. promoting goals of specific-purpose international groupings & regional bodies	Participating in the Commonwealth – joining Colombo Plan, imperial trade preferences & Sterling Area Sponsoring & voting in the U.N. on resolutions calling for self-determination in Algeria, West Irian Denouncing in the U.N. & Commonwealth policy of apartheid & boycotting S. African goods Founding, with the Philippines, and Thailand, the Association of Southeast Asia (ASA) in 1961

Source: Author's own compilation.

one is explaining foreign policy postures, objectives, strategies, or actions. However, such minimalist analytical gestures may fail to triangulate fully the plural elements involved in the construction of foreign policy in all its major dimensions. This study does not pretend for a moment that it provides any final resolution to these thorny analytical and theoretical issues. Suffice it to say that by employing constructivist sensibilities, we may derive a fuller and better understanding of the whole foreign policy process.

In my view, the idiosyncratic dimension or elite predilections in Malayan foreign policy may best be appreciated as intervening variables in the policy formulation process, in the sense that they do represent a final filter, seen by traditional IR specialists as the inscrutable "black box", through which policy is formulated. However, in our explanation of Malayan foreign policy, these idiosyncratic factors could be subsumed under a construct, such as a dominant elite ideology, with the assumption that it is the more general political beliefs and attitudes of leaders and policymakers rather than the peculiar, quirky, personality traits that are more important in the analysis of overall foreign policy.[23] The notion of a dominant elite ideology suggests a convergence of ideational and political perspectives at the uppermost level of decision making. In constructivist parlance, it could well be the enabling factor in the state's agential power. It could also be partially embedded in the domestic political culture of a state if one considers elites to be connected to society also. Put differently, the agential power of this elite ideology, which drives the foreign policy outputs, is ultimately constrained by the societal forces which constitute a political culture under which various political actors play out their preferences. In other words, state identity and state interests can perhaps be best appreciated as the summation of such preferences mediated by an elite ideology to generate state policies, such as particular foreign policy outputs. Seen in this light, the state's agential power personified in prime ministers, foreign ministers, and other agents of foreign policy, is clearly circumscribed or curtailed by societal factors and internal factors, and a domestic political culture in which such a state is embedded. Needless to say, an overarching constraint on foreign policy is the external environment, which realists tend to overvalorize. Returning to Malayan foreign policy, we see that in the Tunku Abdul Rahman period, this external environment was the Cold War which defined the limits and limitations of foreign policy choices.

A summarized expression of the various sources of Malayan foreign policy is presented in Figure 3.1. In our interpretation, two antecedent historical factors are linked to a contested political culture which is anchored on ethnic politics of compromise and consociational accommodation, but with Malay predominance and high domestic agential power of the state, which is dominated by a ruling coalition of political parties under the aegis of the Alliance. The external agential power of the state is arguably much weaker given its low military capabilities and high dependence on British and Western linkages. Two historical factors which have had a lasting and profound impact on both domestic and foreign policy were British colonization and "The

Emergency". British rule provided Malaya with its political ethos of Western democratic norms and its politico-administrative infrastructure. The relatively peaceful transition to independence ensured a continuity of this political ethos after independence. The ten-year internal war with the communists, euphemistically called "The Emergency", is the other significant historical factor. Other factors such as geography, population, and culture have been excluded as they tend to be "constants" rather than variables. Often, they are better appreciated as indirectly relating to internal sources of policy.

Thus, Malaya's relatively small geographical size and population and its natural, or lack of natural, endowments could be seen as conditions resulting in various economic needs.

Similarly, geopolitical factors were perhaps of importance only in as far as they relate to the external environment of the Cold War. Malaya, falling within the British sphere of influence and being part of non-communist Southeast Asia, came within the orbit of the Western bloc. The most important external factor — and geopolitical factors are treated as such — was thus the Cold War which characterized the post-World War II international system. In Southeast Asia the emergence of the communist colossus of China and the onset of a spate of guerrilla wars in various Southeast Asian countries augmented the worldwide East-West conflict. As illustrated in Figure 3.1, British colonial rule, the Emergency, and the external Cold War environment combined to produce pro-West, anti-communist foreign policy postures in Malayan foreign policy in general, and particularly in matters of defence and security. In actions, this took the form of a defence pact with Britain and the many anti-communist pronouncements and acts described earlier.

However, these factors in and of themselves would not necessarily have resulted in the particular character assumed by Malayan foreign policy were it not for an elite ideology already predisposed towards certain values and norms. These values and norms were embedded in a conservatively biased elite ideology, marked by a strong predilection for Western democratic practices and values, as well as pragmatic norms nurtured in multicultural discourses and practices. It was the elite ideology that was largely responsible for the most characteristic features of Malayan foreign policy. This elite ideology was epitomized in the beliefs and attitudes of then Prime Minister Tunku Abdul Rahman and most, if not all, his cabinet colleagues. Indeed, there is strong evidence that it pervaded much of the top echelons of government and foreign service. In essence, the elite ideology was marked by a commitment to the Western form of democracy and its ideals, while its image of the international environment was that of the classic bipolar situation in which the so-called Free World faced the growing menace of a messianic world communism. In

FIGURE 3.1
Sources of Malayan Foreign Policy

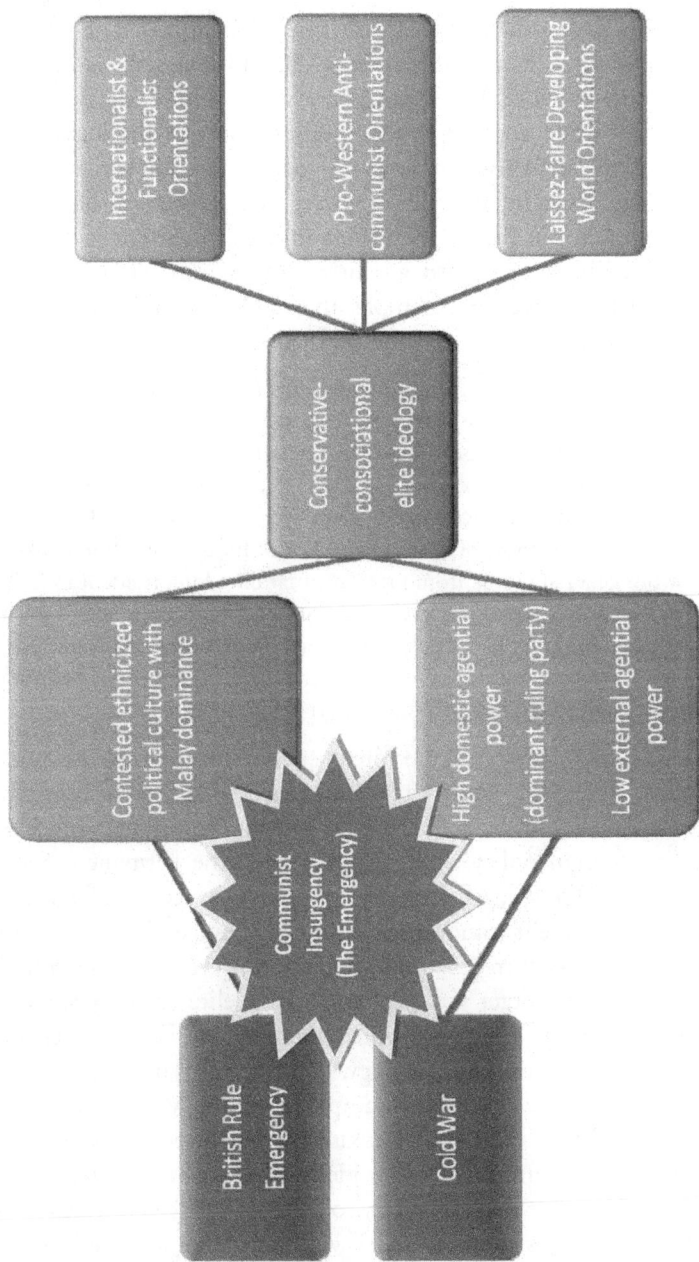

Source: Author's own illustration.

economic matters, this ideology extended to a commitment to free enterprise and capitalism.

There is little doubt that British rule itself provided the basis for the development of such an elite ideology. British colonialism had a durable and profound impact on Malayan political life. While Malayan politics are certainly no carbon copy of British politics, many of the ideals, traditions, and institutions of British parliamentary democracy still thrive here. Indeed, the politicians assuming the reins of government at the time of independence were schooled in the British tradition and it was their partiality to Western ideals that perhaps prompted an early and smooth handover of power.[24] Marvin Ott has noted, for example, that seldom could one find a greater degree of shared values than in the Malayan cabinet:

> The policy consensus in the cabinet reflected the stability and homogeneity of its membership. The men who counted — the Tunku, Tun Razak, Dr. Ismail, Tan Siew Sin, and Khir Johari — were colleagues in the independence movement and members of the cabinet throughout most of the post-independence period. They were all Westernized, pragmatic, conservative and most of them were Malays. Influential Chinese like Tan Siew Sin generally came from prominent families long resident in Malaya. The civil service, the upper levels of the armed forces and much of the local business community have also recruited men with these same characteristics. Policy differences within the cabinet were more a question of nuance and implementation than of substance. (Ott 1973, p. 22)

Ott goes on to suggest that the foreign policy formulating elite comprised only four or five men, namely the Tunku, who was *primus inter pares*, Tun Razak, Dr Ismail, Tan Siew Sin, the three most important cabinet ministers influencing foreign policy, and Ghazali Shafie, the Permanent Secretary to the Ministry of Foreign Affairs. Ott is probably correct insofar as these men represent the core elite among whom the highest level of decision making on foreign policy occurred. I would suggest, however, that this core elite was backed by a much larger group of supportive elite of party stalwarts, civil servants, and foreign service personnel, who, by and large, subscribed to the tenets of a well defined, elite ideology. For example, James C. Scott provides evidence from interviews with a sample of senior Malaysian civil servants that not only the political elite, but also the higher echelons of bureaucracy shared a strong commitment to an idealized model of Western democracy. Scott stressed the role that secondary socialization played towards inculcating Western values in his subjects, and I will quote him at some length:

> All the men with whom I spoke attended schools and universities patterned after the British model, where they followed curricula identical to those

in England and learned Anglo-Saxon practices and values. Later they were recruited by Englishmen to serve in a British style administration system. The standards and goals of this structure were, and still are in large measure, cast in an unmistakeably English mould. Both in school and in the civil service their success was gauged by how they had learned the lessons that England had sought to convey. Small wonder then that all of them came by their Western (British) orientation honestly. They are the more Western oriented since their English education and high administrative posts are what set them apart from the general population and confer on them their status and prestige. The maintenance of a western orientation among higher civil servants is further encouraged by a political elite that is itself largely pro-British and committed to liberal democratic ideals.[25]

There is little wonder then that Malayan foreign policy tended to lean heavily towards the West when senior bureaucrats exhibited strong affective orientation towards Western values and ideals.[26]

But perhaps it was the bitter war with the communists which left the greatest mark on Malaya's policymakers, supplying additional ballast to an already Western elite ideology. In particular, the Tunku's meeting with communist leaders Chin Peng in December 1956, just prior to independence, seemed to have hardened the premier's views on communism. The Tunku said after the abortive sessions in which Chin Peng refused to accept the amnesty terms offered:[27]

> Chin Peng really taught me what communism was. I had never really understood and appreciated its full meaning. When I was briefed in communism by the British experts I always felt they were interested in making a bad case against the communists. But there in that room in Baling, Chin Peng taught me something I shall not forget. He taught me that Malaya and communism can never co-exist.[28]

Thus, it was not until the Emergency was officially ended in 1960 that Malaya would vote for China's admission into the United Nations (but only on the basis of the two-China policy). Prior to this the newly independent country was not prepared even to discuss the China question. It has been pointed out that because the communist insurgency was largely (Malayan) Chinese in initiative and composition, the government could not afford overtures to China while the insurrection was still in progress. Indeed, it was the very conviction that the insurgency was China inspired and aided that caused Malaya to reinforce its internal policy of combating communism with an external posture of containing it.[29]

The external Cold War environment, with the events of Hungary, Cuba, Vietnam, Tibet, and the Sino-Indian conflict, tended, therefore, to augment the existing image of communism in the policymakers' minds. There is evidence that the existing elite world view represented something akin to Boulding's "national image" and Holsti's "belief system" that it "... is the last great stronghold of un-sophistication ... Nations are divided into "good" and "bad" — the enemy is all bad, one's own nation is of spotless virtue" and that "wars are either acts of God or acts of other nations, which always catch us completely by surprise".

The belief system, composed of a number of "images" of the past, present, and future, may be thought of as the set of lenses through which information concerning the physical and social environment is received. It orients the individual to his environment, defining it for him and identifying its salient characteristics. National images may be denoted as a subpart of the belief system. (Boulding 1969, p. 430). The Malayan elite ideology comprised a belief system which had its fundamental tenets in an adherence to Western democracy and its ideals. On this point, let me quote the Tunku:

> We have every reason to want to follow the Western (form of) democracy because it suits our people. We have had freedom to do what we like; to follow our own inclination, whereas with the communists, you've got to lead a regimented life, to follow whether you believe in it or not, what you are asked to do. Such a life would be foreign to our country and to our people, and so we naturally adhere to the Western form of democracy rather than follow communist ways. The Cabinet all along decided on this line.[30]

It had a national image in foreign policy matters of "good" and "bad" in which the actions of communist countries were invariably interpreted as bad, while the actions of Western or Western leaning allies were more often than not deemed to be good. The Tunku's statement above and the Malayan government's reaction to the events of Hungary, Cuba, Vietnam, Tibet, and the Sino-Indian conflict are good indicators of such a national image. Given such an image, Malaya found itself drawn willy-nilly into the Cold War arena, supporting the Western bloc in most questions of East-West conflict as its voting at the United Nations indicated.

Given the nature of the elite ideology, the impact of the Cold War was predictably in the direction of pro-Western, anti-communist policy outputs. Although defence and security needs existed by virtue of nationhood, British colonial rule and The Emergency tended to augment such needs. Little was done in the colonial era to provide an independent Malaya with adequate military capability to defend its borders in the event of external attack, while the internal war not only sapped already meagre capabilities, but also even after its official end, loomed large as a latent threat to national security.

Moreover, the perception on the part of the ruling elite that insurgency was externally fuelled added an international dimension to a strictly internal security question.

With Malaya's low military capability and its leaders' perception of external threat, AMDA (Anglo-Malayan Defence Agreement) seemed to be a logical step towards the fulfilment of the country's basic defence and security needs, at least in the eyes of the Tunku and his colleagues. National "needs" can be best appreciated as the obverse of "capabilities" — a well known concept in international relations literature. While it makes sense to talk of the capabilities of great powers, to speak in similar terms about small, developing countries would be somewhat inappropriate since these countries tend to have needs rather than capabilities. Yet there seems to be a woeful lack of foreign policy analysis of Third World countries from such a perspective.

The importance of national needs is even more evident in matters relating to economics. If Malaya was in a weak position with respect to defence and security, its weakness and vulnerability were all the more evident in matters of development and trade. I have stressed how Malaya, as an underdeveloped country with an economy dependent on rubber and tin, fought for international control of raw material prices while opposing all forms of protection and tariff barriers against Third World countries, in its pursuit of development goals. However, despite this developing world orientation in the question of international trade, Malaya neither espoused nor practised a policy of economic nationalism at home. Instead, it was committed to a *laissez-faire* policy which left its economy in foreign, largely British, control. This was again a product of the prevailing ideology which, apart from its Western-bloc orientation in matters of international security, also exhibited a capitalist economic philosophy. The basic tenets of this philosophy were a commitment to free enterprise and the belief that foreign investment provided the answer to economic stability and advancement. Minister of Commerce Tan Siew Sin, who later became the country's finance minister, enunciated such a philosophy as early as 1958 when speaking to Parliament in support of granting tax exemption to pioneer industries:

> It is frequently suggested that the amount of foreign capital coming into industry in this country should be limited, either by fixing a maximum percentage of the shares which may be held in any company by foreign capital, or in some other way. In view of the extremely large amounts of capital which will be required if we are to beat the unemployment menace this is a totally unrealistic approach to the problem. Limiting the amount of foreign capital in any enterprise is tantamount to linking the rate of industrial development in this country to the amount of capital which can

be raised locally… In other words, the need for capital is so great that there is room for all the local and foreign capital wishing to invest here, with plenty more room to spare. The danger of today and tomorrow is not a surplus of capital as rather a dearth of it. (Morais 1972, p. 115)

British colonial rule predisposed the Malayan economy to develop in the particular fashion on which I have already elaborated. Colonial rule was, therefore, the most significant factor determining the kinds of economic needs the new nation was to have.

Obviously, factors of climate and natural endowment are important in influencing the nature of economic needs, but the fact remains that colonialism skewed Malaya's economic development in particular directions.[31] This in turn resulted in two fairly stable foreign policy postures in the issue area: a developing world orientation which sprung directly from developmental needs, and a *laissez-faire* orientation towards foreign economic enterprise, which derived from the dominant elite ideology and its assessment of needs. A developing world posture led to the pursuit of two common LDC (Less Develoopment Country) objectives of promoting economic development (howsoever the government may choose to define this) and stabilizing commodity prices. This, in turn, resulted in the adoption of fairly standard economic strategies of supporting LDC trade groupings and negotiating trade agreements. Malaya's other posture on developmental and economic issues and the related strategy and actions were, however, more contrived, in that they arose from definite ideological tenets. Were Malaya's leaders to have adopted a socialist ideology, for example, the foreign policy posture *vis-à-vis* foreign enterprise would have probably taken a more "nationalistic" hue, with perhaps nationalization of major industries as its concomitant strategy. As it turned out, a *laissez-faire* orientation prompted the liberal strategy of providing fiscal and other incentives to foreign enterprise.

In the issue area of international cooperation, a prominent aspect of Malayan foreign policy was its pursuit of milieu or global goals. Malaya, despite being a small country, was rather active in its international relations. It showed considerable support for the United Nations and its functional activities, participated with keenness in the Commonwealth, and succeeded in forging a certain degree of regional cooperation among its more sympathetic neighbours. But for the most part, the pursuance of these milieu goals sprang from what we may term status needs. A new nation seeks recognition and acceptance from the international community, and the United Nations and other international forums are the most natural places to pursue these needs. As a Latin American scholar has stated:

[T]here are two types of sources of a nation's prestige: (1) those derived from institutional bases that make it possible for a nation to have high real status from the economic and military power point of view and (2) those derived from the nation's behaviour in the international system, whether this be to achieve a conformance with the value-orientations of this system or to obtain an influential position not related to its military might. (Lagos 1963, p. 132)

Since Malaya did not have the institutional bases of prestige, it had to depend on its foreign policy actions to boost its status. Malaya's contribution towards the Congo peacekeeping mission was perhaps geared, among other aims, towards establishing the new state's status in the world community. Status needs are based on the subjective evaluations of the ruling elite, as well as on objective domestic conditions, such as the presence or absence of a large military capability, great wealth, technology, and the like. In this sense, they are "internal" sources of foreign policy, like economic needs, but unlike the latter, are not solely based on objective factors. Status needs are real, nevertheless, and are reflective of the contemporary international system which operates on egalitarian principles at the formal level, but exhibits vast inequalities among states at the actual level. All states to some degree have status needs, but there is a greater tendency for states without the institutional bases of prestige to try and elevate their status by way of various diplomatic endeavours.

Although status needs dominated Malayan foreign policy in matters of international cooperation and diplomacy, it would be wrong to assert that such needs were the only sources of policy in the issue area. Foreign policy outputs are seldom single-purpose or unidirectional in intent. Thus developmental and even security needs indirectly impinged on policy outputs in the issue area. In particular, Malaya's functionalist orientation in supporting the specialized U.N. agencies and its support of U.N. collective security in general reflect the influence of these needs. As a former colony, Malaya also felt the obligation to press for self-determination of colonial territories and decolonization in general. Anti-colonialism as a foreign policy posture was, therefore, an almost automatic outcome of independence. As for Malaya's pursuit of regionalism, it was multidirectional in purpose, but for the most part of the period, the thrust was towards cultural and diplomatic exchanges among countries sharing a similar heritage. Finally, although the prevailing elite ideology had only minimal impact in this issue area, its pervasiveness was registered in such international issues as disarmament, East-West issues in general, and also with respect to the Congo question.

There is one aspect of the foreign policy formulation process that has not yet been discussed in explaining the emergent Malayan foreign policy:

to what extent did feedback effects emanating from the external and internal environment affect foreign policy? For the most part, Malaya's policymakers kept a tight rein on policy and postures, and objectives and strategies remained stable and coherent throughout the period. The events of the external environment — "aggressive" acts of the Eastern states and the friendly acts of the West — tended to reinforce positively the basic thrusts of its foreign policy. Given the elite ideology, the feedback was thus positively in the direction of continued anti-communist, pro-West postures, strategies and actions.

Internally, however, there was some indication of negative feedback towards certain aspects of foreign policy. In particular, opposition parliamentarians' criticisms and the UMNO backbench revolt against AMDA, put the government on the defensive in its first major foreign policy action. The Tunku was able, however, to summon his personal authority to stem rejection of AMDA, but we may attribute Malaya's softened pro-West line to these internal feedback effects. We can certainly attribute Malaya's absence from SEATO as an effect of the negative response to AMDA. The feedback sequence would be:

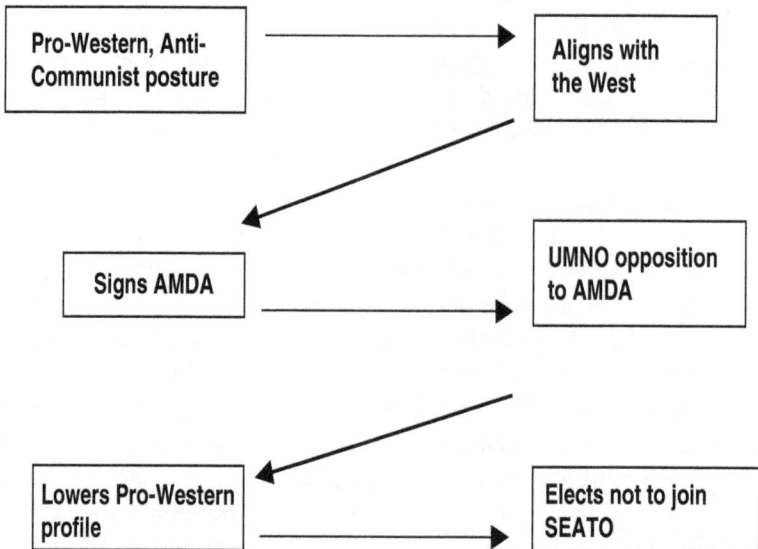

Pro-Western, Anti-Communist posture	⟶	Aligns with the West
Signs AMDA		UMNO opposition to AMDA
Lowers Pro-Western profile		Elects not to join SEATO

In issue areas other than defence and security, the influence of feedback on policy was negligible or non-existent. There was little or no opposition to economic policies, and the government was never seriously challenged on its policies in the third issue area. Externally, the environment more or less positively reinforced the government's policy outputs in these issue areas as well. In one instance, Indonesian hostility towards the Tunku's scheme for a regional organization resulted in the innocuous and ineffectual ASA and probably explains its non-political orientation. However, negative Indonesian reactions toward Malayan foreign policy in general probably confirmed existing images of Indonesia's pro-communist leanings, and therefore positively reinforced the prevailing foreign policy postures.

This study of the first period of foreign policy has revealed a remarkable stability and coherence in Malayan foreign policy. Notably, idiosyncratic or elite sources tended to account for the most characteristic aspects of foreign policy. In particular, the study shows that Malayan foreign policy was by and large underpinned by an ideology committed to certain Western values. It was this elite ideology that invariably gave the final expression to the more significant facets of foreign policy. However, particular historical experiences proved to be significant antecedent factors affecting policy, and the international environment tended to reinforce positively prevailing thrusts of foreign policy. In the next chapter we will review a turbulent period of external relations at the end of which a palpable shift to policies of neutralism became much more evident.

Appendix 3.1

ANGLO-MALAYSAN MUTUAL DEFENCE AGREEMENT, 1957

Agreement between the Government of the United Kingdom of Great Britain and Northern Ireland and The Government of the Federation of Malaya on External Defence and Mutual Assistance, Signed at Kuala Lumpur, on 12 October 1957.

Extracts

Article I
The Government of the United Kingdom undertakes to afford to the Government of the Federation of Malaya such assistance as the Government of the Federation of Malaya may require for the external defence of its territory.

Article II
The Government of the United Kingdom will furnish the Government of the Federation of Malaya with the assistance as may from time to time be agreed between the two governments for the training and development of the armed forces of the Federation.

Article III
The Government of the Federation of Malaya will afford to the Government of the United Kingdom the right to maintain in the Federation such naval, land and air forces including a Commonwealth Strategic Reserve as are agreed between the two Governments to be necessary for the purpose of Article I of this Agreement and for the fulfilment of Commonwealth and international obligations. It is agreed that the forces referred to in this Article may be accompanied by authorised service organisations, and civilian components (of such size as may be agreed between the two governments to be necessary) and dependants.

Article IV
The Government of the Federation of Malaya agrees that the Government of the United Kingdom may for the purposes of this Agreement have, maintain and use bases and facilities in the Federation and may establish, maintain and use such additional bases and facilities as may from time to time be agreed between the two Governments. The Government of the United Kingdom shall at the request of the Government of the Federation of Malaya vacate any base or any part thereof; in

such event the Government of the Federation of Malaya shall provide at its expense agreed alternative accommodation and facilities.

Article V

In the event of a threat of armed attack against any of the territories or forces of the Federation of Malaya or any of the territories or protectorates of the United Kingdom in the Far East or any of the forces of the United Kingdom within those territories or protectorates or within the Federation of Malaya, or other threat to the preservation of peace in the Far East, the Governments of the Federation of Malaya and of the United Kingdom will consult together on the measures to be taken jointly or separately to ensure the fullest co-operation between them for the purpose of meeting the situation effectively.

Article VI

In the event of an armed attack against any of the territories or forces of the Federation of Malaya or any of the territories or protectorates of the United Kingdom in the Far East or any of the forces of the United Kingdom within any of those territories or protectorates or within the Federation of Malaya, the Governments of the Federation of Malaya and of the United Kingdom undertake to co-operate with each other and will take such action as each considers necessary for the purpose of meeting the situation effectively.

Article VII

In the event of a threat to the preservation of peace or the outbreak of hostilities elsewhere than in the area covered by Articles V and VI the Government of the United Kingdom shall obtain the prior agreement of the Government of the Federation of Malaya before committing United Kingdom forces to active operations involving the use of bases in the Federation of Malaya; but this shall not affect the right of the Government of the United Kingdom to withdraw forces from the Federation of Malaya.

Article VIII

The Government of the United Kingdom will consult the Government of the Federation of Malaya when major changes in the character or deployment of the forces maintained in the Federation of Malaya as provided for in accordance with Article III are contemplated.

Article IX

The Government of the Federation of Malaya and the Government of the United Kingdom will afford each other an adequate opportunity for comment upon any major administrative or legislative proposals which may affect the operation of this Agreement.

Source: Saravanamuttu (1983), pp. 171–72.

NOTES

1. Agreement between the Government of the United Kingdom of Great Britain and Northern Ireland and the Government of the Federation of Malaya on External Defence and Mutual Assistance, Signed in Kuala Lumpur, on 12 October 1957 (Kuala Lumpur: Government Printer, 1957). See Appendix 3.1.
2. According to Jeshurun (1975, p. 5), the Malayan Armed Forces' strength in 1963 was 22,000. The army, known as the Royal Malay Regiment, consisted of seven infantry battalions, with one battalion each of Reconnaissance and Artillery. There were plans at that time for the setting up of the 4th Infantry Brigade in the Singapore area (Jeshurun 1975, p. 8).
3. Tun Abdul Razak, "Radio Malaya Talk on Defence Policy" (*Straits Times*, 4 October 1961).
4. For a sustained argument on why it was necessary on the British side to have AMDA, see Sharma (1993), pp. 34–54 who has consulted British sources to back this point. Sharma saw AMDA as a "convergence of mutual interests" and put down the Communist insurgency as a main factor for its signing. See also Chin (1983) for a similar argument from the Malaysian-Singapore perspective.
5. See Malaya. Legislative Council, Debates, 2 and 3 October 1957; Dalton (1967, pp. 67–69) and Harper (1999, p. 348).
6. See Malaya, Legislative Council, Debates, 2 and 3 October, 1957, cols. 3269ff and 31318ff.
7. Ibid., 2 October 1957, col. 3282.
8. The Tunku, in a personal communication, placed the utmost importance on the issue of military advantage. In reply to my question on why Malaya had a defence pact with Britain, but did not join SEATO, he said, "We had a defence pact with Britain under which Britain would come to our aid in the event of any aggression by a foreign power and we felt that was sufficient for our security and safety. SEATO is a pact between the countries which include America, Britain, Pakistan ... but there was no conclusive agreement to help one another in the event of war. There was no need for us to enter into any defence agreement with other countries as we felt our agreement with Britain was sufficient." (The Tunku, after meeting me in a brief interview, agreed to answer a schedule of questions, hereinafter cited as Tunku, June 1975: personal communication.)
9. See "Legislative Council Debates, 4 session, December 1958, col. 6029", cited in Boyce (1968, p. 42).
10. The government put out a list of eighty-seven countries which it recognized and listed six which it did not, namely, Communist China, Nationalist China, East Germany, North Korea, Outer Mongolia, and North Vietnam" (*Straits Times*, 7 November 1957). Although the government did not officially recognize Nationalist China (Taiwan), it showed its partiality by allowing the Taiwanese to set up a "consulate" in Kuala Lumpur, ostensibly to foster trade relations. See Parliamentary Debates, 15 and 16 December 1964, cols.75ff. and 4738ff., in which opposition members criticized the government for allowing this.

11. See Tilman (1969*b*, pp. 115–59), and Tilman (1969*a*, p. 37).
12. The Tunku, in reply to a question on whether policymakers thought in terms of goals and strategies, said, "a small country like Malaysia does not have to go into strategies and actions to formulate our foreign policy …", however, he stressed that foreign policy objectives were important, and considered defence a short range goal, and development, a long range goal (Tunku, June 1975: personal communication).
13. See Lim (1969, pp. 224–30), for a more detailed explanation of the import situation. However these details are not of great importance to the analysis here.
14. See Knorr (1945) and Saravanamuttu (1972), Chapter 2.
15. The importance of the United Nations was marked by the fact that the Tunku sent one of his most trusted ministers, Dr Ismail Abdul Rahman, to head its mission in the first year of Malaya's independence. To get the full falvour and significane of Ismail's year at the United Nations, see Tawfik and Ooi (2009) which compiles Ismail's set of reports and confidential notes to the Tunku.
16. *Straits Times*, 29 September 1960.
17. However, the Tunku's private attempts at mediating in the dispute were not appreciated by the Indonesians, who perhaps thought the Malayan premier presumptuous in undertaking the effort. In particular, a joint Malayan-Dutch-communiqué which alluded to the Tunku's secret plan for resolving the conflict was badly received in Indonesia (various reports, *Straits Times*, and *Malay Mail*, 26 November–3 December 1969).
18. Malaya's membership in international organizations by 1963 included: The International Labour Organization (ILO), the Food and Agriculture Organization (FAO), the U.N. Education, Scientific and Cultural Organization (UNESCO), the World Health Organization (WHO), the International Monetary Fund (IMF), the International Bank for Reconstruction and Development (IBRD). the International Development Association (IDA), the International Civil Aviation Organization (ICAO), the Universal Postal Union (UPU), the International Telecommunications Union (ITU), the World Meteorological Union (WMU), the U.N. Children's Fund (UNICEF), the International Tin Council (ITC), the International Rubber Study Group, the General Agreement on Trade and Tariffs (GATT), the Economic Commission for Asia and the Far East (ECAFE), and the Colombo Plan. See *Malaysia in Brief*, 1963, p. 106.
19. See reports in *Malay Mail*, 21 April 1958 and *Straits Times*, 18 April and 22 April 1958.
20. See *ASA: Report of the First Meeting of Foreign Ministers* (1961, pp. 13–14).
21. These were Tunku's views as expressed in his June 1975 personal communication.
22. See Ott (1973, p. 225). Ott nevertheless accepts the "salience" of certain historical experiences and the "geo-political milieu", including Malaya's strategic regional location, its vulnerable economy, and the impact of the Cold War. He also notes

the importance of the Ministry of Foreign Affairs. See his Ph.D. dissertation, John Hopkins University, 1971, p.19ff. and *passim*.

23. The notion is akin to Alexander George's concept of "operational code" although it would have a slightly wider meaning. According to George, " A political leader's beliefs about the nature of politics and political conflict, his views regarding the extent to which historical development can be shaped, and his notion of correct strategy and tactics — whether these beliefs be referred to as "operational code", "weltanschauung", "cognitive map", or an "elite political culture" — are among the factors influencing the actor's decisions (George 1969, p. 197).

24. The Alliance, led by the Tunku, in winning the 1955 general elections in resounding fashion (51 out of 52 seats) ensured that British traditions would be passed on after independence. The party has continued to dominate politics in Malaysia and its expanded version, the National Front, captured all but 20 of the 154 parliamentary seats and all states in the 1978 elections.

25. See Scott (1968, p. 202). Scott does note, however, that commitment to an idealized model of western democracy is coupled with a pessimistic outlook on its attainment in Malaysia. This nevertheless does not detract from the fact of that commitment and its prevalence among civil servants. See also Leo (1972, pp. 32–36).

26. While it is true that there was a dominant elite which largely supported the ideals and values of the power-wielders, evidence points to the existence of a latent or potential "counter-elite" within the ruling group, in particular, within UMNO. The brief but aggressive opposition to AMDA was proof of its existence. The leaders and members of the opposition parties can also be regarded as a "counter-elite", but their capacity to affect government decisions is very limited. In employing the notion of our elite ideology, one avoids having to define the size and the actual individuals that comprise the elite. It is the political beliefs and attitudes of the acknowledged policymakers rather than the policymakers themselves with which we are concerned.

27. This called for the dissolution of the Malayan Communist Party, which the communist leader found unacceptable.

28. See Miller (1959, pp. 192–93). The Tunku confirmed that "… to a large extent Malaysia's strong anti-communist policy was due to our trouble with the Malayan Communist Party at home and our knowledge of what was happening in countries around us, Vietnam, Cambodia, and one time, Indonesia" (Tunku, June 1975: personal communication).

29. For a brief period, Malaya appeared to have softened its line towards China when in 1960 after the official end of the Emergency, the Tunku said in various places such as the Netherlands and Washington, D.C., that China should be in the United Nations and Malaya would support its admission. When he returned to Kuala Lumpur, he announced this shift of policy towards China. The incident created a furore at home and led then Minister of Foreign Affairs, Dr Ismail to threaten to resign. The Tunku admits that Ismail thought "he had gone beyond

the agreed policy of China" (Tunku, June 1975 personal communications). This *faux pas* by Tunku is confirmed from Tun Ismail's account of the incident as narrated in his biography. Ismail did not resign because Tunku gave him no opportunity to deliver his letter (Ooi 2006, pp. 128–29). See also Dalton, "The Development of Malayan External Policy, 1957–1963" (Ph.D. thesis), pp. 96–98, and Saravanamuttu (2007, pp. 8–9).

30. Tunku, June 1975: personal communication.
31. When we look at Malaya's two major primary products, for instance, it is interesting to note that the rubber tree, while thrives in Malayan topography and climate, is not a "native" since it was introduced by the British from Brazil. Tin, on the other hand, is a natural endowment. The development of the two industries, however, was largely a function of colonialism, which expedited the large-scale emigration of Indian labour for the rubber industry, and Chinese labour for tin. See Lim (1967).

4

TRANSITION TO
NEUTRALISM 1964–69

KONFRONTASI

"Malaysia" became an international issue even before it actually came into being.[1] As early as January 1963, Indonesian Foreign Minister Dr Subandrio announced a policy of Confrontation (or *Konfrontasi*) against the Malaysia project, charging that it was "neo-colonialist" and "neo-imperialist". About the same time *Konfrontasi* was launched, the Philippines renewed their territorial claim on Sabah, the North Borneo territory that was to be included in the proposed new federation.[2] The Indonesian opposition was further fuelled by a revolt in Brunei under the leadership of the Brunei Party Rakyat leader, A.M. Azahari, who opposed the formation of Malaysia and put forward his own plan for the creation of an independent state consisting of the Sultanate of Brunei, North Borneo (Sabah), and Sarawak. Although it registered some initial success, the Azahari revolt was quickly suppressed by British troops at the request of the Brunei sultan. Thereafter, the Malaysia issue seemed to have subsided with the meeting of the Tunku, President Soekarno and President Macapagal in Manila in August 1963. The summit brought about the birth of MAPHILINDO — a vague scheme of cooperation among the three countries — amidst the showering of mutual compliments by the three leaders.[3] MAPHILINDO perished stillborn a little over a month after it was proposed. Following the proclamation of Malaysia on 16 September 1963, Malaysia broke off diplomatic ties with Indonesia and the Philippines.[4] Although the Indonesian Confrontation had not ceased after MAPHILINDO, it became more serious after Malaysia was officially declared. The Indonesian acts ranged from aggressive patrolling of the Malacca Strait, in which Malaysian fishermen were harassed, to border clashes involving members of the *Tentera Nasional*

Kalimantan (North Borneo National Army). By 1964, Indonesian troops had landed or were air dropped on Malayan coasts. *Konfrontasi* continued well into 1965, but began to simmer down after the September putsch of 1965 in Indonesia. There were various efforts of mediation between 1964–66, but it was only on 12 August 1966 that an accord was signed between Indonesia and Malaysia to cease all hostilities and renew diplomatic ties. (See Appendix 4.1 at the end of the chapter for a chronology of the main events and incidents from the outset of *Konfrontasi* till its termination).

Thus *Konfrontasi* and other developments arising from Malaysia's formation dominated Malaysian foreign policy in the issue area of defence and security for most of this period. The creation of Malaysia may be seen from one perspective as the pursuit of a possession goal, or an act of self-extension since it involved territorial expansion (Wolfers 1962, pp. 95–96). Foreign policy actions are seldom single-purpose in intent and the creation of Malaysia was clearly laden with multiple interpretations of the motives behind it.[5] A strong case can be made for the view that the Malaysia proposal grew out of a perceived security threat posed by communism to the Malaysia region.[6] The Tunku, who can be relied upon for his candidness, said soon after *Konfrontasi* was launched: "We have no territorial ambitions. All we want to do is try and save ourselves from the communists. Otherwise, I won't want Malaysia" (*Straits Times*, 8 February 1963). Indeed, the Malaysia idea arose in part from the Singapore Government's campaign for merger with Malaya to avert what the Singapore leaders saw as an imminent communist threat, if not its already disguised but widespread presence in Singapore.[7] The Tunku, who had previously rebuffed requests for merger found this argument sufficiently compelling, but not wanting to upset the delicate politico-racial balance in Malaya with Singapore's overwhelming Chinese population, conceived of bringing the Borneo territories into the new federation. On this point, R.S. Milne writes:

> The inclusion of the Borneo territories was not so urgent, but it did promise to solve two problems at once. To some degree the addition of the indigenous inhabitants would "balance" the Singapore Chinese majority. This argument should not be overstressed; the indigenous peoples were indeed more numerous than the Chinese in the Borneo territories, but the majority of them were neither Malays nor Muslims. However, the Malays in Malaya looked on the indigenous races as being their "brothers," and hoped that they could be persuaded to support Malaysia and also the Alliance Party. (Milne 1967, p. 63)[8]

One might add that the Tunku's perception of the internal security situation in the Borneo territories was probably also an important factor in prompting the rather hurried manner in which the new federation was created. As the Tunku told Parliament, "We cannot afford to wait so long (for Britain to grant the territories independence) without providing the communists with the weapons they require for subversion, infiltration and disruption with the ultimate objective of capturing these territories.... The important aspect of the Malaysian ideal, as I see it, is that it will enable the Borneo territories to transform their present colonial status to self-government for themselves and absolute independence in Malaysia simultaneously, and balk the communist attempt to capture these territories." (Gullick 1967, p. 41). Whatever the other motives for the Malaysia project, it would not be wrong to say that it carried undertones of anti-communism and reflected security considerations which were no doubt coloured by the prevailing elite ideology of the Malayan policymakers.[9]

The extent to which the Tunku and Malaysian policymakers had been influenced by a Western design perhaps still remains a moot point. Greg Poulgrain's 1998 study of *Konfrontasi* using declassified documents from U.S. sources clearly revealed an American hand in the episode which had hitherto been unexposed. The recent study by Tan (2008) on Malaysia's formation, drawing on declassified British records, reveals a British "grand design" and the "Ulster Model" for the merger of Malaya and Singapore. Such literature now perhaps provides a stronger case for the Indonesian position on the Malaysia plan as partly orchestrated by Western powers. It may be ironic that in some ways insider accounts such as that of Ghazali Shafie (1998, p. 27) who intimates that British old hands such as Malcolm MacDonald had long thought of a federation of Borneo territories, may also suggest that Malaysian policymakers were not totally innocent.

The immediate effect of *Konfrontasi* was to harden Malaysia's Western-world, anti-communist orientation. For one thing, it triggered into operation the Anglo-Malayan Defence Pact, thus resulting in a major Western power and two Commonwealth allies fighting on Malaysian soil. The Malaysian policymakers themselves tended to view *Konfrontasi* suspiciously as a communist, Parti Kommunis Indonesia (PKI)-inspired project, pointing to a Jakarta-Peking-Hanoi-Pyongyang axis, with Malaysia as the target of China's expansionism.[10] But oddly, it was *Konfrontasi* that brought about a softening of Malaysia's hard line anti-communist policy in the long run. The Indonesian military and diplomatic offensive prodded the hitherto cautious Malaysia into a concerted diplomatic drive to win friends in Afro-Asia, and later, Eastern Europe as well. Malaysia's failure to gain a seat at the Cairo non-aligned nations conference, largely because of Indonesian propaganda, sparked off a diplomatic counteroffensive which won Malaysia the recognition of a number of African and Asian countries and eventually support from twenty-eight countries to attend the following year's conference at Algiers (*Straits Times*, 23 June 1965). It was also at this time that the Tunku declared that Malaysia fulfilled the criteria of non-alignment, when in the past he had never failed to underscore Malaya's non-neutrality in East-West issues. The Tunku was also quick to endorse the Declaration of the Cairo conference on the principles of peaceful coexistence in a letter to President Nasser. Another spin-off from *Konfrontasi* was the first public review of Malaysian foreign policy by a Parliamentary group, albeit of only Alliance MPs, which while finding that "the present independent and non-aligned foreign policy was in conformity with the Alliance Party's principles", proposed "the widest diplomatic representation possible with countries irrespective of their ideologies" (*Straits Times* and *Malay Mail*, 9 August 1965). The government also received a fusillade of criticism from the opposition and certain public figures on its adamant, hard line anti-communist policy. In particular, the government was taken to task for its support of the American bombing of North Vietnam at a time when it was attempting to win Afro-Asian friends.[11] There is some indication of the ascendancy of a counterforce of Alliance and other politicians who were opposed to some of the views of the ruling group on foreign policy. An unofficial Malaysian delegation led by UMNO Member of Parliament Dr Mahathir[12] attended the Afro-Asian People's Solidarity Organization Conference at Winneba, Ghana, in May 1965, but its application to join the organization was rejected.[13] The Tunku commenting on the Winneba incident said he had "no knowledge" of the Malaysian mission and described the organization as a "communist setup ... financed by Russia and China". Nonetheless, it was in the wake of the Winneba episode that the Parliamentary group to review foreign policy was formed.

However, it was not until *Konfrontasi* actually ended that the rethinking in foreign policy took a more definite shape. The Tunku in a Malaysian Day broadcast in 1966 admitted to a shift in foreign policy "to keep pace with the trend of events in the world". Two months earlier, Tun Ismail, as foreign minister, had been more explicit in indicating the nature of the shift when speaking to the Foreign Correspondents' Association:

> We look forward to the day when outside powers both great and small will accept our right as a region (i.e. Southeast Asia) and as constituent nations of this region, to sustain our distinctive ways of life in freedom and prosperity, without interference... We do not oppose the communist system in mainland China so long as it confines itself within its own borders. But we call upon the People's Republic of China to keep its hands off our

region and to adopt a policy of peaceful co-existence towards its fellow Asians in Southeast Asia.

We look forward to a regional association embracing Thailand, Burma, Indonesia, Singapore, Malaysia, Philippines, Cambodia, Laos and Vietnam… Such a community would not be a military alliance. It would not be an anti-communist alliance. Nor, for that matter, would it be an anti-western alliance… I do not believe that military blocs and alliances by themselves can provide lasting solution to the problem of communist expansionism. I myself envisage an organization which would be first and last, pro-Southeast Asia, pro-development, pro-regional co-operation and pro-peace. (*Straits Times*, 24 June 1966)

It appeared that Malaysian foreign policy was shifting from a hard line, anti-communist, pro-West orientation towards some measure of neutralism. Foreign policy was at this stage still somewhat ambivalent and the policymakers themselves appeared to be a little confused as to whether Malaysia was non-aligned or neutral. For example, Tun Ismail in answering a parliamentary query said: "We are not committed to any power bloc and we crystalize our attitude on any issue strictly on its merits and in the light of our national interest. In that sense we are not aligned. We never claim to be neutral. We can never be neutral in the choice between right and wrong." It is perhaps more correct to say that Malaysia tried to be neutral with respect to particular international issues while being aligned de facto to the West by virtue of its military ties. Taking the cue from Premier Khrushchev on the other side, Malaysia had nevertheless transformed its hard line anti-communist posture into one of "peaceful co-existence". The general foreign policy strategy of the period was one of reaching out and diversifying diplomatic contact. While still relying on old allies, Malaysia went out of its way to win Afro-Asian supporters in the diplomatic war against Indonesia. Considerations of trade also prompted new ties with the Eastern European nations. In so doing, the contradictions in its foreign policy became more and more apparent, eventually necessitating a change in foreign policy posture.

By 1968, Tun Ismail, who had retired from the Cabinet six months earlier for health reasons, put forward as a backbencher in Parliament his seminal "Ismail Peace Plan".[14] He called for the neutralization of Southeast Asia guaranteed by the major powers, the signing of non-aggression pacts, and the declaration of a policy of coexistence:

The time is … ripe for the countries in the region to declare collectively the neutralization of Southeast Asia. To be effective, this must be guaranteed by the big-powers, including Communist China, Second, it is time that the countries in Southeast Asia signed non-aggression treaties with one another.

Now is also the time for the countries in Southeast Asia to declare a policy
of co-existence in the sense that the countries ... should not interfere in the
internal affairs of each other and to accept whatever form of government
a country chooses to elect or adopt...The alternative to the neutralization
of Southeast Asia guaranteed by the big powers ... is an open invitation
by the region to the current big powers to make it a pawn in big power
politics. The alternative to the signing of non-aggression treaties among the
countries in the region is an arms race among themselves which would be
detrimental to their economy. The alternative to the declaration of the policy
of co-existence is increased tension and subversion in the region.[15]

The Cabinet seemed to show mixed response to the Ismail suggestions. While
the Tunku said the neutralization idea was only "worth consideration", Razak
said Ismail's proposals had the full support of the government. There must
doubtless have been some differences of opinion on the Ismail proposals,
with the Tunku perhaps taking a more adamant stand than the other cabinet
members, but at any rate, the process of rethinking in foreign policy had
begun to affect the top policymakers.[16]

Coinciding with the end of *Konfrontasi*, a downturn in Anglo-Malaysian
relations developed. The deterioration of traditional ties exacerbated the
general turmoil of foreign policy in this period. It began with the separation
of Singapore from Malaysia of which Britain was apparently given very
little notice. Then came a cutback in British economic assistance, resulting
in a Malaysian request for $630 million in defence aid being turned down.
Relations reached their nadir when the Tunku uncharacteristically accused
Britain of talking with Indonesia about Malaysia behind its back. At about
the same time. Malaysia was also taking a second look at the Anglo-Malaysian
Defence Pact, as Britain, even before the Bangkok Peace Agreements of
1966, had announced in a White Paper its intentions to scale down troop
commitments and overall defence expenditures east of the Suez Canal. For
Malaysia, British withdrawal was to be effective by 1971 and completed by
the mid-1970s.[17] Thus in 1968, under the urgings of the Tunku, talks began
for a five-power defence arrangement among Malaysia, Singapore, Britain,
Australia, and New Zealand. This arrangement was to replace the Anglo-
Malaysian Defence Pact after Britain pulled out in 1971. In the course of
a series of talks in 1968 and 1969, the intricacies of the five-power defence
scheme were worked out. At one stage there were doubts expressed about
Australia's and New Zealand's participation after 1971, but by early 1970
an expensive ($15 million) military exercise over two months was carried
out to test the viability of the five-power defence arrangements.[18] Whatever
the merits of the scheme, it became increasingly evident to the Malaysian

leaders that they could no longer lean as heavily on Britain and other allies in matters of defence. Tun Ismail made his proposals in the backdrop of British withdrawal from the region.

Thus foreign policy in the issue area of defence and security throughout this period was in transition, if not turmoil. The previous rigidity of Malaya's foreign policy began to give way under the exigencies created by *Konfrontasi* and its related events. Therefore with the end of *Konfrontasi* also came a noticeable shift in foreign policy orientation and strategies, even if the latter at this stage were not particularly clear-cut. While Malaysia still hung on to its Western-world peggings, by the end of the period it had discarded its previously pronounced anti-communist posture for one of peaceful coexistence. This can perhaps be seen as an extension of the earlier posture of non-interference, but it would be difficult to deny a qualitative difference between the two concepts in terms of new foreign policy praxis.[19] Appendix 4.1 provides the reader with a chronology of *Konfrontasi* related events affecting Malaysian foreign policy.

DEVELOPMENTAL AND ECONOMIC CONCERNS

Although Malaysia's foreign relations in this period were dominated by *Konfrontasi* and security matters, there were at least two important events which related to economic policy, namely, the UNCTAD conferences of 1964 and 1968. At both these conferences, Malaysia joined the Group of 77 developing nations in espousing developmental issues, thus enhancing its developing world image. Thus Malaysia consciously aligned itself with the "South" in the "North-South" conflict between rich and poor nations. It was amongst the original "75" calling for UNCTAD I to be held in order to press a number of demands on the advanced, industrialized nations. The key demands, which were embodied in the historic "Prebish Report", were:

1. Creation of conditions for expansion trade between countries at a similar level of development, at different stages of development, or having different systems of social and economic organization.
2. Progressive reduction and early elimination of all barriers and restrictions impeding the exports of less developed countries (LDCs) without reciprocal concessions on their part.
3. Increase the volume of exports of developing countries in primary products, both raw and processed, to industrial countries and stabilization of prices at fair remunerative prices.
4. Provision of more adequate resources on favourable terms so as to

enable LDCs to increase their imports of capital goods and industrial raw materials essential for their economic development, and better coordination of trade and aid policies.

5.	Improvement of the invisible trade of developing countries, particularly by reducing their payments for freight and insurance, and the burden of their debt charges.

6.	Improvement of institutional arrangements, including, if necessary, the establishment of new machinery and methods for implementing the decisions made at UNCTAD I.[20]

UNCTAD I could boast of no immediate, concrete achievements, but the fact that it was convened represented a moral victory for the LDCs in the first few blows of North-South fisticuffs. Soon after UNCTAD I, Malaysia carried the North-South battle into the arena of tin conferences in bargaining for a higher price range for the 1965 Tin Agreement. Dissatisfied with the outcome of the negotiations, Malaysia, together with Bolivia, threatened withdrawal from the Agreement if a higher price range was not fixed. The threats were later withdrawn, but at a subsequent Tin Council meeting, the consuming countries conceded to a higher price range.[21] By the time of UNCTAD II in 1968, Malaysia was selected to serve on the Trade and Development Board. UNCTAD II's achievements included adoption of the International Development Strategy of the Second UN Development Decade, and a Generalized System of Preferences, both of which measures Malaysia strongly supported. In particular, the developed countries agreed in principle not to raise new tariff and non-tariff barriers or increase existing ones against imports of primary products of particular interest to developing countries. They also agreed to accord priority, by reducing or eliminating duties and other non-tariff barriers, to certain imports of primary products of export interest to developing countries. Thus in questions of development and trade, Malaysia's foreign policy became one which was marked by a greater commitment to its developing world posture, and thereby to its pursuit of developmental goals.

At the same time, however, Malaysia did not discard its *laissez-faire* orientation in respect to foreign enterprise. About the time when Anglo-Malaysian relations ebbed to a low point, Tun Razak toured the United States in late 1966, wooing American capital. In a speech made at the annual convention of Far East American Council of Commerce and Industry in New York, Tun Razak appeared eager to lay Malaysia bare to American enterprise:

> Malaysia is a peaceful and democratic country, politically and economically stable and friendly with the United States. We want to keep it that way. But

TABLE 4.1
Ownership of Assets in Modern Agriculture and Industry, Peninsular Malaysia, 1970*

| Ownership | Modern Agriculture¹ (Planted Acreage) | | | | Industry² (Fixed Assets) | | | |
| | Corporate Sector | | Non-corporate Sector | | Corporate Sector | | Non-corporate Sector | |
	(000 acres)	(%)	(000 acres)	(%)	($m)	(%)	($m)	(%)
Malay	5.0	0.3	349.3	47.1	11.2	0.9	3.9	2.3
Chinese	457.0	25.9	243.3	32.8	342.3	26.2	158.0	92.2
Indian	4.9	0.3	74.8	10.1	1.5	0.1	3.9	2.3
Others	48.1	2.7	13.2	1.8	187.2	14.3	1.4	0.8
Government³	–	–	17.0	2.3	17.5	1.3	–	–
Malaysian	515.0	29.2	697.6	94.1	559.7	42.8	167.2	97.6
Non-Malaysians	1249.6	70.8	44.0	5.9	747.3	57.2	4.1	2.4
Total	1764.6	100.0	741.6	100.0	1307.0	100.0	171.3	100.0
Percentage of Total	70.4		29.6		87.4		12.6	

Notes: *Although the figures are for 1970, they will probably not differ significantly from the data for the period under survey. Since no earlier data were available, I am compelled to use the more recent statistics.

1. Modern agriculture covers estate acreage under rubber, oil palm, coconut, and tea. Ownership is in terms of total planted acreage. Government FELDA schemes are included under this category in the non-corporate sector.

2. The industry sector covers manufacturing, construction, and mining. Ownership is in terms of fixed assets. Total excludes unallocatable assets amounting to $25.2 million.

3. Government ownership of 17,000 acres in modern agriculture is included in the non-corporate sector, while ownership of $17.5 million of fixed assets in industry is included in the corporate sector.

Source: Mid-term Review of the Second Malaysia Plan 1971–1975, p. 12.

it is sometimes difficult to understand why even though your government is so generous in providing assistance to so many other developing countries, it yet seems reluctant to give forthright and substantial aid to Malaysia... We are not looking for direct hand-outs. We are looking for people to have faith in us, and to invest in our country and to play a part in the development of industry and trade in our country. On the other hand, as hard-headed businessmen you are looking for opportunities of expansion of your enterprise, and my main message to you today is this. If you want to expand and invest and you look around the world for a suitable place to do this; then I suggest you look towards Malaysia where you will find the basic requirements you seek [-] political stability within a democratic framework and potential progress to mutual advantage of both our countries. (Morais 1965, p. 345)

The liberal attitude towards foreign enterprises in Malaysia had led to a staggering degree of foreign ownership and control of the Malaysian economy. Information released in 1973 showed that foreign ownership of fixed assets in the industrial sector in Peninsular Malaysia (that is, Malaya) was more than half of the total at 57.2 per cent (the Chinese share being 26.2 per cent) while it stood at an amazing 70.8 per cent in the modern agriculture sector, attesting the enduring impact of colonial rule despite more than a decade of independence. The foreign ownership in the non-corporate sectors was considerably less, but as the government itself put it:

The overall picture indicates that foreign corporate ownership of assets in Malaysia is substantial in agriculture, manufacturing and mining, though this is already declining in agriculture and mining. Further, ownership and control is largely in the hands of a relatively small number of multi-national foreign firms with diversified economic interests. Among Malaysians, Chinese won the highest shares in the corporate sector, while their share in the non-corporate sector of modern agriculture is more balanced ... (but) the value of assets accounted for by the non-corporate sector is small... In modern agriculture, (it only) comprised 29.6% of the total planted acreage. In industry, the non-corporate sector made up only 12.6% of the total value of fixed assets. (*Mid-Term Review of the Second Malaysia Plan 1971–1975*, p. 11)

The picture for the ownership of share capital in Malaysia was much the same, buttressing the already dominant position of foreign ownership in fixed assets:

The most significant feature is that foreign interests accounted for as much as 61 per cent of the total share capital invested in the corporate sector... Foreign participation is especially dominant in modern agriculture and mining while it amounts to about 50% to 60% of the total in manufacturing, commerce and finance.[22]

Towards the end of the period there were signs that Malaysia was beginning to temper its *laissez-faire* attitude towards foreign enterprise with a greater degree of governmental direction in the area of industrial development. The formation of the Federal Industrial Development Authority (FIDA) in 1968 was indicative of the slight shift in attitude. FIDA's main functions were to:

1. Undertake or direct economic feasibility studies of the range of industrial possibilities.
2. Undertake industrial promotion work in the country and abroad.
3. Facilitate exchange of information and coordination among institutions engaged in or connected with industrial development.
4. Recommend policy on industrial site development and, where necessary, undertake the development of such sites.
5. Evaluate applications for pioneer industries, which are entitled to tax relief ("pioneer status").
6. Report annually to the minister of trade and industry on the progress and problems of industrialization and to make the necessary recommendations.
7. Generally undertake such matters as may be incidental to, or consequential upon, the exercise of its powers or the discharge of its functions (under the Act of Parliament by which it was established).
8. Advise the government generally on measures for the protection and promotion of industries, including the imposition and alteration of, and exemption from, customs and other duties, and import and export licensing.[23]

Thus FIDA in general coordinated and systematized Malaysia's industrial development programme. Although the authority remained true to Malaysia's open door policy towards foreign enterprise, with its formation also came a shift from the promotion of import-substitution industries in the early years to a new emphasis on export-oriented industries towards the end of the period.

On the whole, Malaysia's basic foreign policy postures, goals, and strategies in the area of trade and development remained much the same for this period although there were signs of minor shifts. Its commitment to free enterprise did not stop Malaysia from seeking wider ties in the area of trade, particularly in responding to overtures from the Eastern European countries.

TABLE 4.2
Ownership of Share Capital of Limited Companies, by Race and Sector, Peninsular Malaysia, 1970

	Malay ($000)	%	Chinese ($000)	%	Indian ($000)	%	Foreign ($000)	%	Total ($000)
Agriculture, forestry and fisheries	13,274	0.9	177,438	22.4	16,191	0.1	1,070,714	75.3	1,432,400
Mining and quarrying	3,876	0.7	91,557	16.8	2,488	0.4	393,910	72.4	543,497
Manufacturing	33,650	2.5	296,363	22.0	8,880	0.7	804,282	59.6	1,348,245
Construction	1,258	2.2	30,855	52.8	447	0.8	19,937	24.1	58,419
Transport and communications	10,875	13.3	35,498	43.4	1,903	2.3	9,845	12.0	81,887
Commerce	4,715	0.8	184,461	30.4	4,711	0.7	384,549	63.5	605,164
Banking and insurance	21,164	3.3	155,581	24.3	4,434	0.6	332,790	52.2	636,850
Others	13,349	2.3	220,330	37.8	13,348	2.3	182,862	31.4	582,516
Total	102,611	1.9	1,192,083	22.5	52,402	1.0	3,207,889	60.7	5,288,978

The total includes share capital ownership by federal and state government and statutory bodies and other Malaysian residents (individual and nominee and locally controlled companies), amounting to about $734 million. In this table, the racial shares in each sector exclude these two groups.

Source: Mid-Term Review of the Second Malaysia Plan, 1971–1975, p. 83.

Thus in 1967, Malaysia signed a Trade Agreement with the U.S.S.R. — its first with a communist country — as a prelude to full diplomatic relations. About the same time, Anglo-Malaysian economic ties had also become relaxed. The Malaysian dollar was unpegged *vis-à-vis* the pound sterling and the Commonwealth trade preference was removed for certain commodities. The foreign policy of diversification, prompted by *Konfrontasi*, seemed to have spilled over to some extent into the development and trade issue area. The overall turbulence of the period generated a more moderate transition here in contrast to the more definite transition occurring in the issue area of defence and security.

INTERNATIONAL COOPERATION

This was a period of considerably increased international activity for Malaysia. I have already dwelt on its diplomatic drive to win friends and influence nations in a counteroffensive to Indonesian Confrontation. At the United Nations, Malaysia won something of a moral victory when a Norwegian resolution deploring the Indonesian landings on Malayan coasts received affirmative votes except from the Soviet Union and Czechoslovakia in an emergency Security Council session. However, it was not until *Konfrontasi* was well behind it that Malaysia's strenuous efforts in international diplomacy bore fruit. The resultant softening of its anti-communist line led to the historic establishment of diplomatic ties with the Eastern European countries. Admittedly, there were also pragmatic considerations of trade which spurred the détente. In August 1965, Malaysia's permanent representative to the United Nations, Ramani, said, "The central government's policy is to cultivate good trade relations with Russia since it is desirable that new markets be found for our rubber and tin… This dynamic business of political rethinking has been because of Russia's policy of peaceful co-existence which is also the central government's theme" (*The Straits Times*, 28 August 1965). Thus in April 1967, following the signing of a trade agreement after week-long discussions, Malaysia and the Soviet Union agreed to exchange diplomatic missions. Ties with Yugoslavia and Bulgaria were established by 1969.[24]

With the end of *Konfrontasi* also came a resuscitation of regional cooperation. Malaysia, in June 1966, was among the nine Asian and Pacific nations that agreed to set up the Asian and Pacific Council (ASPAC).[25] Although ASPAC had undertones of anti-communism, it was not formed as an anti-communist military pact. Khir Johari, the leader of Malaysia's delegation to the Seoul conference which set up ASPAC, was at pains to explain that Malaysia opposed a military pact of any sort: "It is not in line with our policy to be drawn into or encourage any military pacts, even if they are militantly anti-communist. We have steered clear of such pacts and will continue to do so... There are other more important things than military pacts. Regional development of cultural and economic ties is more vital in this region."[26]

As ASPAC foundered on its shaky beginnings, then Indonesian Foreign Minister, Adam Malik initiated moves for a "larger-than-ASA" regional Southeast Asian organization. Although the Tunku did not appear to be initially enthusiastic about replacing ASA, the Malaysian policymakers came around to accepting the need for a larger Southeast Asian organization which at least included Indonesia. Thus in August 1967 in Bangkok, after some quibbling over the name of new organization, the Association of Southeast Asian Nations (ASEAN) was born with Thailand, Indonesia, the Philippines, Malaysia, and Singapore as founder member countries. According to the Bangkok Declaration which established the regional organization, the goals of ASEAN were expressly socio-economic rather than political or military, and were not significantly different from those of its predecessor ASA. ASEAN's aims were declared as follows:

1. to accelerate the economic growth, social progress and cultural development in the region through joint endeavours....
2. to promote regional peace and stability through abiding respect for justice and the rule of law....
3. to promote active collaboration and mutual assistance... in the economic, social, cultural, technical, scientific and administrative fields.
4. to provide assistance to one another in the form of training and research facilities in the educational, professional, technical, and administrative spheres.
5. to collaborate ... for the greater utilization of their agriculture and industries, the expansion of their trade, ... improvement of their transportation and communication facilities and the raising of the living standards of their peoples.
6. to promote Southeast Asian studies.
7. to maintain close ... cooperation with existing international and regional organization.

As with ASA, membership to ASEAN was open to all states in the region "subscribing to the... aims, principles and purposes of the organization". Of particular interest was a reference to the temporary nature of foreign bases reminiscent of MAPHILINDO which affirmed that all foreign bases were temporary and remain only with the expressed concurrence of the countries concerned and were not intended to be used directly or indirectly to subvert the national independence and freedom of states in the area, or prejudice the orderly processes of their national development. This was the only ostensible reference to political cooperation, but it laid the ground for future collaboration in this area, as was enunciated nine years later in the Bali accords.

The machinery for carrying out the work of the regional body, as specified in the 1967 declaration, were as follows: (a) an annual foreign ministers meeting, (b) a standing committee with rotating chairmanship, sitting in the country of the foreign minister serving as chairman and comprising ambassadors of the other states, (c) *ad hoc* and permanent committees of specialists and other officials as needed, and (d) a national secretariat in each member country. Since 1976, the ASEAN structure has also incorporated summit meetings of heads of government as well as ministerial level meetings of economic, labour, social welfare, education, and information ministers and officials, whenever deemed necessary. Since 1976, too, a central ASEAN Secretariat was established in Jakarta with the secretary general appointed on a two-year, rotating basis. The committee system of the organization has also undergone some revamping.[27]

The immediate effect of ASEAN was to formalize the growing *entente* of the five Southeast Asian neighbours, thus marking the end of a period of turmoil in the region. However, towards the end of 1968, Malaysia-Philippines relations were again on the boil over the Sabah issue. A bill passed by the Philippine House of Representatives declared Sabah to be part of Philippine territory.[28] Malaysia responded by asking the Philippines to withdraw its diplomatic staff from Kuala Lumpur. However, mediation efforts by Thailand's Thanat Khoman led to a Philippine decision to observe a moratorium on the Sabah issue until after Malaysia's general election in May 1969. By the end of 1969, at the third ASEAN Foreign Ministers conference, it was announced that Malaysia and the Philippines would resume diplomatic relations. Held in the cool atmosphere of Malaysia's Cameron Highlands, the ministers approved all the ninety-eight recommendations put before them covering projects for cooperation in the areas of commerce and industry, tourism, shipping, civil aviation, air traffic services and meteorology, transportation and communication, food supply and production, fisheries, mass media, cultural activities, and finance. They also signed two agreements for the establishment of an ASEAN fund and for the promotion of cooperation in mass media and cultural activities.[29] It looked, therefore, like ASEAN had gained its credibility and was set on a definite course of fostering cooperation among its five member countries.

Konfrontasi aside, Malaysia continued to participate actively in the United Nations and the Commonwealth. We have already noted its election to the U.N. Security Council in 1965. At one point in September 1965 a furore resulted in which the Malaysian representative at the Security Council was alleged to have taken sides in the Indo-Pakistani clash over Kashmir.[30] Despite the Malaysian Government's assurance to Pakistan of its neutrality in the conflict, Pakistan severed diplomatic ties with Malaysia in October that year. On questions of decolonization, Malaysia continued to take a strong anti-colonial and anti-apartheid posture. The Rhodesia question was particularly prominent during this period. Apart from supporting all U.N. resolutions on Rhodesia, Malaysia adopted the following international measures against the rebel regime of Ian Smith: a total trade ban of imports and exports to and from Malaysia; non-recognition of passports and visas issued by the Smith government; a surcharge on any letters, parcels, or communications arriving by post in the same manner as items having no stamps; exchange control measures excluding Rhodesia from the Sterling Area, and restricting all payments and financial transactions of Rhodesian origin.

In summary, Malaysia's basic objectives, postures, and strategies on matters of international cooperation and diplomacy did not change appreciably over this period although the general strategy of external diversification tended to extend into this issue area as well. The most important development in this respect was the détente with Russia and the East European countries. The other important development of the period, although it did not reflect any change in foreign policy objectives, postures or strategies, was the resuscitation of regional cooperation in the formation of ASEAN, which succeeded the three-member ASA.

A TRANSITIONAL FOREIGN POLICY

The most striking feature about this study has been the general turmoil that engulfed Malaysia in these years. It is possible to identify two distinct phases in the transitional foreign policy of this period. In the first phase, the exigencies of *Konfrontasi* produced an even greater rigidity in previously held foreign policy postures. The prevailing pro-West, anti-communist elite ideology was reinforced. In the perception of the policymakers, *Konfrontasi* was communist inspired and ultimately linked to Peking. Malaysia, therefore, hardened its anti-China line. The support of the Russians and the Czechs for the Indonesians at the Security Council reaffirmed the existing image of *Konfrontasi* as a communist inspired project. The Philippines, with its claim on Sabah, was viewed as an opportunist, but its action at a time when

Malaysia was already pressured by Indonesia, made Malaysia more adamant about its position. The creation of Malaysia itself, as noted, grew partly out of the fear of a growing communist threat to the region, particularly in Singapore and Sarawak. The Indonesian reaction was thus not unexpected as, in the eyes of Malaysian policymakers, Indonesia had already moved towards Peking long before Malaysia was proposed. In addition, the unwillingness of Indonesia to join ASA on the grounds that it was "a tool of American imperialism" had also strained Malayan-Indonesian relations and established in the policymakers' minds Jakarta's leftist image. *Konfrontasi* confirmed the Malaysian policymakers' perception, so it seemed.

The initial hardening of foreign policy postures soon gave way to actions which turned towards identification with the Afro-Asian world. "Truth missions" were sent out to propagate Malaysia's position in the Indonesia-Malaysia conflict and, following Malaysia's failure to be seated for the Cairo Non-aligned Conference, to campaign for its recognition as a non-aligned country. These events also sparked considerable domestic debate on foreign policy. The government was taken to task on a number of foreign policy issues by the opposition and even members of its own party. Furthermore, a non-government group attempted to gain membership in the Afro-Asian People's Solidarity Organization at Winneba and failed. These events added to the growing public sentiment that Malaysia's foreign policy was inadequate in the light of British withdrawal. The Alliance Parliamentary Group was formed to review foreign policy. The government could not sit back and fail to take heed.

Thus began the second phase in this period of foreign policy — a phase of rethinking resulting in the eventual debunking of Malaysia's anti-communist posture for one of coexistence. The establishment of diplomatic ties with the Soviet Union and other Eastern European countries followed. Elite perceptions had undergone, or at any rate, were undergoing, a qualitative change. The Ismail Peace Plan, and the Tunku's and Razak's admissions of slight shifts in foreign policy were indications of the general change taking place. In all, this was a period of transition for Malaysian foreign policy. The diagram below illustrates the spillover effects of defence and security issues into the other issue areas.

Employing a constructivist perspective, one could say that ideas, norms, and interests underpinned by an elite ideology which remain stable and even became more rigid in the first phase of this period, underwent a fundamental reconstruction. These changes in some even prefigured the departure of first Prime Minister Tunku Abdul Rahman from the political stage. One hastens to add that domestic factors were mainly responsible for Tunku's departure, but

FIGURE 4.1

Spillover Effects of Defence and Security Issues into Other Issue Areas

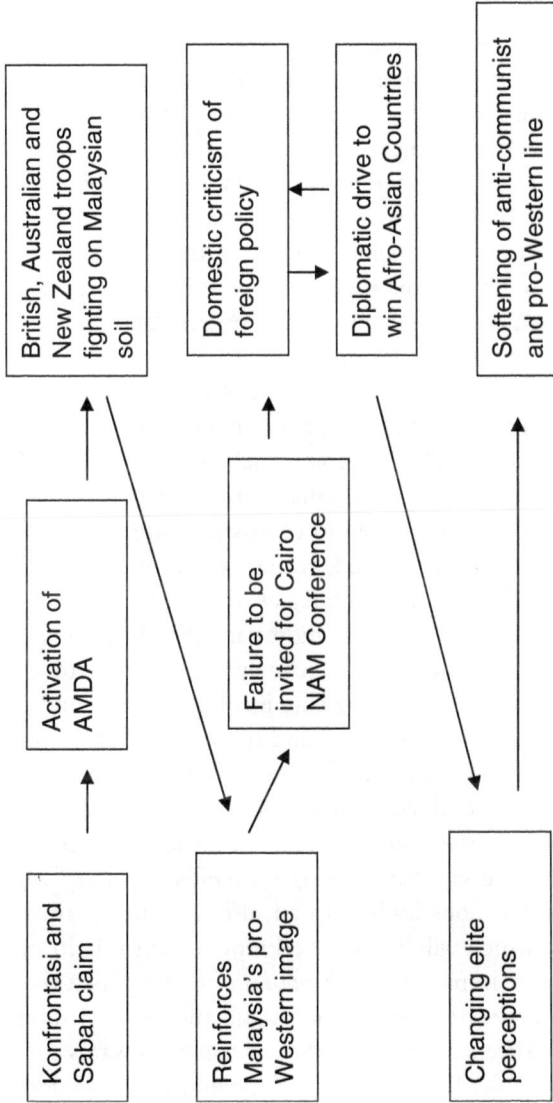

Konfrontasi and Sabah claim → Activation of AMDA → British, Australian and New Zealand troops fighting on Malaysian soil

Reinforces Malaysia's pro-Western image → Failure to be invited for Cairo NAM Conference → Domestic criticism of foreign policy ⇄ Diplomatic drive to win Afro-Asian Countries

Changing elite perceptions → Softening of anti-communist and pro-Western line

Source: Author's own illustration.

the linkage of the rise and role of young Turks such as Mahathir Mohamad and Musa Hitam to the overall change of political environment cannot be underestimated. In the event, new Prime Minister Tun Abdul Razak, who was acutely cognisant of the politics of the Young Turks, was himself quite clearly prepared to admit "new blood" into the first and second echelons of leadership. Many of these individuals were not subscribers to Tunku's more conservative and pro-Western foreign policy stances.[31] In an article on Tun Ismail's contribution to the changing policy (Saravanamuttu 2007), I have argued that the former foreign minister was beginning to infuse new ideas among the ruling group about foreign policy, premised on the changing global environment. While it is true that Ismail shared the old elite ideology of the Tunku's cabinet, he nevertheless recognized that changes were in order and was thus greatly responsible for the major shifts in foreign policy that Tun Razak implemented subsequent to Tun Ismail's death. We will follow up on this discussion in the next chapter.

The preponderance of external factors impinging on foreign policy, particularly during phase I of this period, is amply evident. All the significant factors — *Konfrontasi*, the Philippines' Sabah claim and communist support generally for *Konfrontasi* — emanated from the external environment. Their combined effect was thus to reinforce existing elite images. This in turn led to a continued adherence, indeed, greater commitment, to prevailing foreign policy postures, objectives, and strategies with their resultant actions as shown in the chart in Figure 4.1. For the most part, therefore, foreign policy during Phase I can be explained almost entirely by reference to external sources, given the thrust of the prevailing elite ideology. The second phase, however, shows the impact of both external and internal sources of foreign policy. In particular, it was the feedback effect of various external and internal events that led to a shift in Malaysia's foreign policy postures and strategies. It is not possible to show in the chart the constant feedback process affecting policy actions. Suffice it to say that the long-term effects of *Konfrontasi* was a series of actions and reactions leading to an ultimate change in the substance of foreign policy, which will be discussed more extensively in the next chapter. In addition to the impact of *Konfrontasi* on foreign policy, the general British policy of withdrawal east of the Suez, and the Soviet Union's new posture of peaceful coexistence, propelled the movement towards softened pro-West and anti-communist lines. Indeed, by the end of the period, Malaysia had largely dropped its anti-communist line for one of peaceful coexistence and was fast transforming its pro-West stance for one of neutralism.

There was also a tendency for the effects of changes in the defence and security issue area to spillover, as it were, into the other two issue areas. Thus

Malaysia responded positively towards Eastern European overtures to open trade and diplomatic ties. *Konfrontasi* also seemed to have shown Malaysian policymakers how few firm friends the country really had, and resulted in the general strategy of reaching out towards the Afro-Asian world and the setting up of diplomatic missions in many of those states. In all, it seemed to have been a good lesson in diplomacy for the new nation. Thus, while objectives, postures, and strategies did not change significantly in the issue areas of development and trade and in that of international cooperation and diplomacy, policy actions not only increased quantitatively in the two issue areas, but became more diversified in terms of their targets.

Thus this period of foreign policy demonstrates the importance of the feedback process in foreign policy formulation, and the manner in which this process affects shifts in foreign policy. In terms of constructivism, new norms and ideas began to percolate into the foreign policy decision-making processes and structures. Eventually this would lead to a new identity for the Malaysian social formation, seen in foreign policy terms. This is another way of saying that foreign policy is continually tailored to the existing needs of the nation as perceived by its policymakers, who constantly have to reappraise and adjust interests and policies to changing external and internal conditions. For Malaysia's policymakers, various events and conditions from the external environment signalled the need for an adjustment in foreign policy orientations so that the national goals could be better pursued. In particular, Malaysia found it necessary to adjust its posture and strategies in the pursuit of its core value goals in the aftermath of *Konfrontasi*, and in the wake of various changes in the international environment. At home, the general turmoil in foreign policy induced a spate of criticism which did not fail to have its effect on the policymakers either. In short, the elite ideology which had been rigidly adhered to was undergoing a revision. The previous "black-and-white" national image which sprung from a classic view of East-West struggle mellowed into recognition that coexistence was not only possible, but necessary. On the whole, idiosyncratic factors receded in importance or were overwhelmed in the face of strong external pressures and domestic demands for a shift in foreign policy. However, it is not until the next period of foreign policy that these incipient changes in foreign policy were consolidated and formalized.

Appendix 4.1

Chronology of Events from the
Outset of Konfrontasi till its Termination

Date	Event
1963	
20 January	Dr Subandrio, Indonesian foreign minister, announces a policy of "Confrontation" against Malaysia in a speech at Jogjakarta, denouncing the scheme as "neo-colonialist" and "neo-imperialist".
24 January	Tunku tells Indonesia to "keep your hands off", that "Malaysia" will go ahead as scheduled on 31 August.
28 January	Philippine-UK talks open in London. Philippines calls for "restoration" of Sabah to the Philippines in the interests of the security of the region.
13 February	President Soekarno declares at a mass rally that Indonesia now "officially" opposes Malaysia.
9 March	Tun Razak returns from Manila with "diplomatic triumph" after meeting President Macapagal who had earlier met with Dr Subandrio.
April—June	A series of meetings of representatives of Malaysia, Indonesia, and the Philippines, including a meeting of Sukarno and Tunku, in Tokyo on 30 May.
7–11 June	Tripartite Foreign Ministers Meeting in Manila in which accord is reached that the Philippines and Indonesia will drop their opposition to Malaysia on the understanding that there would be a United Nations assessment of the wishes of the Borneo people on Malaysia, and positive steps will be taken toward settling the Sabah claim.
30 July–5 August	Manila Summit Conference convened. The Manila Declaration is signed in which MAPHILINDO is proposed as a grouping of three nations bound together by "historical ties of race and culture", co-operating in the pursuit of common interests in the economic, social, and cultural fields and in the struggle against colonialism and imperialism. In a Joint Statement, the three leaders called upon the U.N. Secretary General to ascertain the wishes of the Borneo people by a "fresh approach", in particular, to verify whether Malaysia was a major, if not the main issue in the recent elections in the two territories; whether the elections were "free", and whether votes were properly polled and registers

properly compiled. The three heads of government further acknowledged that foreign bases were of a temporary nature and will not be used to subvert the national independence of any of the three countries and that they will each "abstain from the use of arrangements of collective defence to serve the particular interests of any of the big powers".

12 August	The United Nations names a nine-member mission to ascertain the wishes of the people of Sabah and Sarawak.
16 August	UN mission arrives in Sarawak, "greeted" by demonstrations against Malaysia.
22 August	Dispute over observers holds up U.N. assessment.
26 August	UN survey in Sarawak and Sabah begins with the Philippine and Indonesian observers still absent.
28 August	President Soekarno says in nation-wide radio talk, "We will have to bow our heads and obey" if the Borneo people want to join Malaysia.
29 August	Malaya announces that Malaysia will be formed on 16 September instead of 31 August as originally scheduled since the U.N. survey will not be completed until 14 September.
3 September	Indonesia sends protest to Malaya pointing to its "reckless and premature decision" to set formation of Malaysia on 16 September as a "unilateral act contravening the letter and spirit of the Manila Summit Agreements".
5 September	U.N. team completes work.
14 September	U.N. assessment is published. It finds that Malaysia was a major issue in the recent elections in Sabah and Sarawak, that the elections had been free, and that "a large majority of people favoured joining Malaysia".
15 September	Indonesian cabinet meets, decides Malaysia is illegal and cannot be recognized. Dr Subandrio says U.N. survey was not conducted in accord with the Manila agreement and was "hasty".
	Philippines informs Malaya it will defer recognition of Malaysia.
17 September	Malaysia severs diplomatic relations with Indonesia and the Philippines.
18 September	A Malaysian Defence Council is formed with power to call up reserves.
11 December	Tunku in report to Parliament on *Konfrontasi* says 66 "terrorists" were killed and 31 captured in 48 incursions since 12 April.

1964

7–11 January	President Soekarno and President Macapagal hold talks in Manila and issue statement saying, "they cherish the hope

that a tripartitie 'mushawarah' would be convened to resolve existing differences amongst the three signatories to the (Manila) agreements".

13 January	Tunku says that another summit meeting must be preceded by clarification of whether Indonesia and the Philippines recognize Malaysia as an independent sovereign state and whether Indonesia will withdraw its troops from Malaysian soil. The United States announces that Attorney-General Robert Kennedy will go to Japan to discuss Malaysia with Soekarno.
20 January	"Truth Mission" led by Singapore Premier Lee Kuan Yew is off to Africa to explain "Malaysia".
21 January	Tunku agrees to meet Macapagal in Cambodia after Prince Sihanouk arrives on a surprise visit to Kuala Lumpur.
22 January	Kennedy and Sihanouk, in Kuala Lumpur in mediation efforts, are hopeful of summit meeting.
23 January	Soekarno announces in Jakarta that Indonesia, Malaysia, and the Philippines have agreed on a truce and summit meeting. Tunku agrees to reciprocate.
25 January	Soekarno's ceasefire order comes into effect.
5–11 February	Tripartite foreign ministers' meeting in Bangkok. Agreement is reached to continue ceasefire, with Thailand supervising the truce with U.N. consent. Another foreign ministers' meeting is to be held within a month.
22 February	Malaysia protests six violations of ceasefire to Indonesia.
2–4 March	Resumed Bangkok ministerial talks break down on ceasefire question, with Malaysia insisting on the withdrawal of all Indonesian guerrillas from its territory if there were to be any settlement.
27 March	Malaysia informs U Thant of fifty incidents between 16 January and 27 March with Indonesia, requesting the Secretary General to take any initiative he deems desirable.
25 April	The Alliance in the general election wins 89 of West Malaysia's 104 seats, a gain of 15 seats.
3 May	Philippines and Malaysia issue joint communiqué that they have agreed to establish consular missions in both countries on 18 May.
18–19 June	Tripartite ministerial talks in Tokyo prepare agenda for summit meeting.
21 June	One-day summit conference of Soekarno, Tunku and Macapagal collapses on issue of guerrilla withdrawal; Indonesia says settlement should come first and there should be a fresh referendum in Sabah and Sarawak.
8–15 July	Commonwealth Prime Ministers Conference in London. Prime

	ministers in final communiqué express "sympathy and support" for Malaysia.
22–24 July	Riots involving Malays and Chinese break out in Singapore following a procession on the occasion of the Prophet Mohammed's birthday.
17 August	Malaysia reports Indonesian unit of forty armed raiders landing on west coast of Johore on Malayan mainland.
2 September	Indonesian aircraft flies over south Malaya, dropping around thirty armed paratroopers.
9–17 September	UN Security Council meets on Indonesia-Malaysia conflict. After six meetings, Norwegian draft resolution regretting and deploring Indonesian actions and calling on the parties "to refrain from all threat or use of force" receives nine votes in favour, with Czechoslovakia and the USSR voting against the resolution, the latter constituting a veto. Tunku claims moral victory.
25 September	Tunku appeals to heads of nations attending forthcoming non-aligned conference in Cairo to give Malaysia a fair hearing after Malaysia's failure to receive an invitation to the conference.
5–11 October	Heads of forty-seven non-aligned countries meet in Cairo. President Nkrumah of Ghana suggests mediation in the Indonesia-Malaysia conflict.
14 October	Tunku in a letter to President Nasser of UAR declares his support for the principles of coexistence expressed in the Declaration of the Cairo Conference.
11 November	Razak, enroute to Colombo Plan Conference in London, to meet African and Middle East leaders to canvass support for Malaysia.
26–29 November	Razak wins diplomatic recognition for Malaysia from Algeria, Morocco, and Tunisia.
30 December	UN General Assembly, under the formula of non-voting, elects Malaysia to serve on Security Council.
31 December	In Jakarta, Soekarno announces that Indonesia will withdraw from the United Nations in protest against Malaysia's seating in the Security Council.

1965

7 January	President Soekarno formally announces Indonesia's withdrawal from the United Nations at a mass rally in Jakarta.
January–March	Peace efforts by Pakistan and Thailand fail to produce any results.
16 March	Tun Razak off on a tour of North and East Africa (Sudan, Ethiopia, Kenya, Somalia, Malagasy, and Uganda).

15 April	Razak on return claims "95%" support for Malaysia in the countries visited.
17 April	Tunku in speech to the Alliance Party Convention says Malaysia supports all U.S. bombing of North Vietnam and speaks of the need for British bases in the country.
16 May	A Malaysian delegation's application for membership of the Afro-Asian People's Solidarity Organization is rejected at Winneba, Ghana. (China and Indonesia had threatened withdrawal if Malaysia gained membership.)
19 May	Tunku says the delegation to Winneba had no official sanction. Calls organization "a communist set-up" and is not surprised that the delegation failed to gain membership. The Tunku said, "But what I am surprised is why the Malaysians had gone there."
June	Goodwill missions by two ministers to West African and West Asian countries.
22 June	Report from Malaysian mission in Manila that a total of 28 nations would back Malaysia for the Algiers non-aligned conference this year, Malaysia's four sponsors being India, Nigeria, Ceylon, and Ethiopia.
28 June	Report that the Algiers conference is postponed till November. (The conference never came about as a result of a rebellion in Algeria which ousted President Ben Bella from power.)
8 August	An Alliance Parliamentary Group on Foreign Affairs, while expressing satisfaction with the present foreign policy, recommends "widest diplomatic representation possible with countries irrespective of their ideologies".
9 August	Singapore separates from Malaysia following an amendment to the Constitution approved by Parliament under a Certificate of Urgency.
30 September	Abortive pro-communist coup in Indonesia results in *de facto* military takeover.
5 October	Pakistan severs diplomatic relations with Malaysia over Malaysia allegedly taking sides with India at the United Nations in the Indo-Pakistan conflict.

1966

9 January	Report of Jakarta "peace feelers" from government and army officials.
31 May–1 June	Bangkok Peace Talks between Malaysia, Indonesia, and the Philippines, leading to Philippine recognition of Malaysia and rapprochement between Malaysia and Indonesia. Agreement is reached to submit proposals to end *Konfrontasi*.

3 June   Malaysia and the Philippines resume full diplomatic relations at
                     the ambassadorial level.
12 August   Malaysia and Indonesia reach accord to cease hostilities and
                     restore diplomatic relations.

Note: In three years of hostilities, 590 Indonesians were killed, 220 wounded, and 771 captured.
       Commonwealth casualties included 114 servicemen (64 British) and 36 civilians (mostly
       Malaysians) killed, while 118 servicemen and 53 civilians were wounded.
Source: Saravanamuttu (1983, pp. 64–70).

NOTES

1. The Tunku made the first public proposal for a federation of Malaya, Singapore, North Borneo (Sabah), and possibly, Brunei, as early as May 1961. There followed various phases in the Malaysia proposal thereafter. The project received official sanction and publicity after a series of Anglo-Malayan talks from 1961–62. See Milne (1967, pp. 60–73), for a succinct account of Malaysia's formation. For a more detailed account, see Sopiee (1974, pp. 125–82).

2. The claim was based essentially on the contention that the Sultan of Sulu had merely "leased" and not "ceded" the territory in 1878 to the predecessors of the British North Borneo Company from which it was passed onto the British Crown; that sovereignty could be transferred only to sovereigns; and that the Philippine Government was the heir to the Sultan of Sulu. See Milne (1967, pp. 187–88).

3. A sample of the outpouring of brotherly adulation is provided from the following statements of three leaders at the conclusion of the conference. From Macapagal: "I say that President Sukarno is a great leader and Tunku Abdul Rahman a great statesman."; From Sukarno: "The Tunku is a great statesman, and Macapagal a great leader of the people of Asia."; From *Tunku*: "President Macapagal and Sukarno are dynamic leaders who have fought colonialism and imperialism". (*Straits Times*, 6 August 1963)

4. A series of events prior to Malaysia's proclamation led to a total breakdown of relations among the three countries. Malaya had postponed the Malaysia formation from 31 August till 16 September to give enough time for the U.N. Secretary General's report to appear on 14 September. The Secretary General deplored the fact that the date was fixed before his conclusions were made known and so did Indonesia. After the report had been released and had shown that the majority of the Borneo people supported the project, Indonesia and the Philippines were still unwilling to accept the U.N. team's conclusions.

5. For a thorough and detailed examination of the motives and reasons behind Malaysia's formation, see Sopiee (1974, pp. 43–145).

6. See the memoir of Ghazali Shafie (1998) who, as Permanent Secretary to the Foreign Ministry, was given the job to set up a task force to travel to Sabah and Sarawak to convince its leaders and its communities to be part of Malaysia. Ghazali was himself persuaded that were it not for the formation of Malaysia, the region would have come under the hegemony of Communist China and Soekarno's Indonesia (pp. 21–22). Ghazali was later appointed to the Cobbold Commission set up to assess the inclination of the British Borneo territories to join Malaysia. Ghazali's interesting detailed account shows how he was personally involved in the intricate negotiations with internal parties (Sarawak and Sabah politicians) and external individuals (British, the United Nations, Indonesian leaders).

7. In a series of twelve radio talks called "The Battle for Merger", Singapore Premier Lee Kuan Yew spelled out the nature of the communist threat to Singapore and the Malaysia region in general. See Lee (1961).

8. See also Sopiee (1974, pp. 144–45).

9. The Tunku denied the importance of the communist threat in the formation of Malaysia, but agreed that the racial balance theory has "some truth". He insisted that "the truth of the matter...was that the people living under the same form of administration previously (that is, British rule) would naturally want to live again under the same form of administration in independent Malaysia" (*Tunku*, June 1975 personal communication). The same administration nevertheless implied to me, a pro-Western, anti-communist political framework.

10. Cf. Tilman (1969*a*, pp. 47–48). Former Permanent Secretary to the Ministry of Foreign Affairs, Tan Sri Ghazali Shafie also indicates this perception of *Konfrontasi*. See his "Neutralisation in Southeast Asia", *Foreign Affairs Malaysia* 4 (1971): 49.

11. See *Straits Times*, 28 May 1965, in which the Socialist Front MP, Dr Tan Chee Khoon, queries the Tunku on the issue in a House debate. A PAP opposition member, Devan Nair, wrote pointedly in a letter to *The Straits Times*, "We do not advance our cause in Afro-Asia by doing an ecstatic jig round the American totem" (*Straits Times*, 5 June 1965).

12. Other members of the delegation were Lee San Choon, Alliance MP, Abdullah Ahmad, political secretary to the deputy prime minister; Musa Hitam, political secretary to the Minister of transport; Wong Leng Ken, PAP leader; Devan Nair, PAP MP; James Puthucheary, lawyer; Samad Ismail, journalist. These individuals comprised a "National Committee" according to PAP MP Devan Nair. See *Straits Times*, 20 May 1965; and *Parliamentary Debates*, 26 May 1965, col. 124.

13. Malaysia's support of the U.S. bombing of North Vietnam was apparently the major obstacle to the delegation's acceptance. There was also an element of interparty competition involved as Malaysia's socialist parties, the Labour Party, Party Rakyat and the Barisan Socialis of Singapore, had been sponsored for membership by Indonesia although these parties did not send any delegation to the Conference. (Interview with Encik Samad Ismail, *New Straits Times*, 19 May 1975; and Malaysia. Parliament, 2d. (Dewan Ra'ayat). *Parliamentary Debates*, 26 May 1965, cols. 123–26.)

14. Tun Ismail said he had not discussed his proposals with the prime minister or any of his former cabinet colleagues (*Straits Times*, 24 January 1968).

15. See *Parliamentary Debates*, 23 January 1968, cols. 1615–16.

16. Opposition party leader, Dr Tan Chee Khoon, alleged that Tun Ismail resigned from the cabinet not only for health reasons but because he had differences with the Tunku on foreign policy matters. Dr Tan also alleged that Ismail wanted to hold the Ministry of Foreign Affairs, but the Tunku was adamant in not giving up the portfolio. The Tunku-Ismail differences dated back to the early years of independence and seems to have an ideological edge to it. Ismail in the later

years appeared to have changed his hard line anti-communist position, but the Tunku had remained uncompromising in his attitude toward communism and communist countries, especially China (interview with Dr Tan Chee Khoon, 22 May 1975; and Tunku, June, 1975 personal communication).

17. The British pull-out plans announced were as follows: Phase I: withdrawal of 10,000 men by April 1968; Phase 2: Withdrawal of a further 20,000 men by 1970–71, reducing the size of British forces to about half the pre-Confrontation level of 60,000; Phase 3: Total withdrawal by about the mid-1970s (*Sunday Times*, 14 January 1968).

18. The widely publicized "Bersatu Padu" involved the deployment of 4,000 men, 500 aircraft and 50 ships (*Malaya Mail*, 10 April 1970). It was not until April 1972, after a ministerial meeting in London that the five-power arrangement was finally formalized in a joint communiqué issued by the five governments. It is, however, not equivalent to a military pact despite its expressed purpose of replacing AMDA which was terminated in November 1971.

19. The then Permanent Secretary to the Ministry of Foreign Affairs stated that "We have steadfastly maintained these principles (of peaceful coexistence) ever since our independence and mostly recently they have borne fruit in the exchange of diplomatic missions between the Soviet Union and Malaysia It is not that the principles of co-existence have changed; it is rather that these principles …which we …have long espoused have won gradual acceptance" (Ghazali Shafie 1969, pp 12–13). Tan Sri Ghazali, in an interview, maintained that it was the communist countries that had changed rather than Malaysia (Interview with Tan Sri Ghazali Shafie, 30 October 1975).

20. The original demands of the developing countries were contained in "The Joint Declaration of the Developing Countries made at the Eighteenth Session of the General Assembly" (General Assembly Resolution 1897 (xviii), 11 November 1963).

21. If both Malaysia and Bolivia had withdrawn from the Agreement, it would have collapsed since Malaysia was the leading tin producer and Bolivia was second in line. See "Storm in a Tin Cup". *Far Eastern Economic Review*, 20 January 1966, pp. 90–91.

22. Ibid., p. 81.

23. See *Malaysia Year Book 1973–74*, pp. 320–30.

24. Czechoslovakia, Poland, and Rumania were at this time also reportedly seeking ties with Malaysia. See *Malay Mail*, 25 July 1967 and *Straits Times*, 3 January 1969.

25. The other ASPAC countries were: Australia, Taiwan, Japan, New Zealand, the Philippines, South Vietnam, Thailand and South Korea.

26. See *Straits Times*, 12 June 1966. The purported aim of the organization was co-operation in the economic and cultural fields, Malaysia and Japan, having reportedly blocked moves to mould the organization as an anti-communist front. On the whole, Malaysia was not particularly enthusiastic about ASPAC.

27. The ASEAN Committees as of 1977 comprised the following:
    Permanent Committees
    1. Food and Agriculture
    2. Shipping
    3. Civil Air Transportation
    4. Communication/ Air Traffic Services/Meteorology
    5. Finance
    6. Commerce and Industry
    7. Transportation and Telecommunication
    8. Tourism
    9. Science and Technology
    10. Socio-Cultural Activities
    11. Mass Media

    Special Committees
    1. Special Coordinating Committee of ASEAN Nations (SCCAN), assisted by ASEAN Brussels Committee (ABC)
    2. Special Coordinating Committee of ASEAN Central Banks and Monetary Authorities

    Ad Hoc Committees
    1. ASEAN Coordinating Committee for the Reconstruction and Rehabilitation of Indochina States (ACCRIS)
    2. ASEAN Senior Officials on Synthetic Rubber
    3. ASEAN Senior Officials on Sugar
    4. ASEAN Senior Trade Officials on the Multilateral Trade Negotiations and the General Agreement on Tariffs and Trade, assisted by ASEAN Geneva Committee
28. See Chapter 10 for more details of the Sabah claim issue.
29. "The ASEAN Fund was to have an initial grant of $15 million, that is, a contribution of $3 million per member state" (*Straits Times*, 18 December 1969).
30. The Malaysian representative, Ramani, indicated that he would support a resolution calling only on Pakistan to implement ceasefire since, he said, India had already indicated it would accept the ceasefire unconditionally. The Tunku, in defending Ramani, said that Malaysia's international ties were more important than its religious ties (*Straits Times*, 21 and 27 September 1965).
31. Among such second echelon leaders were Abdullah Ahmad and Abdullah Majid. Further discussion of this follows in the next chapter.

5

CONSTITUTING CHANGE WITH INNOVATION 1970–75

THE SHIFT FROM DEFENCE TO SECURITY

With the turmoil of the 1960s behind it, Malaysia moved towards consolidation of regional relationships in the 1970s, putting the final touches to its rapprochement with Indonesia by signing with it in March 1970 a Friendship Treaty and a Delimitation of Territorial Seas Treaty. The Friendship Treaty was a renewal of a similar treaty signed in 1959, the only such treaty Malaysia has signed with any country. The 1970 treaty has the aura of a non-aggression pact. Article 3 states that "the two High Contracting Parties undertake that in case any dispute on matters directly affecting them should arise they will not resort to the threat or use of force and shall at all times endeavour to settle such a dispute through the usual diplomatic channels in the true spirit of friendship and goodwill between good neighbours".[1] In the 1959 treaty, a similar article stated merely that the parties "shall endeavour" to settle a dispute through peaceful means. The Delimitation of Territorial Seas Treaty had international ramifications and sprung from Malaysia's and Indonesia's claim of twelve-mile territorial waters instead of the traditional three miles.[2] The treaty related in particular to the Strait of Malacca, which being less than 24 miles wide in places, meant that the two countries did not consider the strait to be international waters.

In December 1971, Malaysia and Indonesia, after tripartite consultations with Singapore, announced that "the Straits of Malacca and Singapore are not international straits, while fully recognising their use for international shipping in accordance with the principles of innocent passage".[3] Singapore, while not holding this position, agreed with Malaysia and Indonesia that the safety of navigation was the responsibility of the littoral states and that there was a need for tripartite cooperation on the question. Singapore's position is understandable because of its international status as an entrepôt and commercial centre. The Malaysian-Indonesian position, however, arose from a wish to assert national sovereignty over the Malacca Strait for a number of reasons. While the two countries claimed navigational safety and pollution to be the most compelling reasons for controlling the Strait, the obviously important strategic implications of the move cannot be denied. At one point, Tengku Razaleigh, speaking as president of the Associated Malay Chamber of Commerce, proposed that the Malacca Strait be turned into "the Suez Canal of Southeast Asia" and a shipping levy be imposed on all vessels passing through it. The scheme received no official endorsement, however. The official view on the extension to twelve miles of territorial seas is that it was necessary for the day to day administration of defence and commercial security and that Malaysia was merely "falling in line with the large majority of nations".[4]

In May 1970, Malaysia served on the three-nation mediation task force (Indonesia and Japan were the other two countries) which was appointed by a Jakarta conference to look into the deteriorating war situation in Cambodia.[5] Towards the year's end, Malaysia attended its first non-aligned nations conference at Lusaka. The event marked Malaysia's acceptance as a "non-aligned" nation. Malaysia's delegation to Lusaka was led by then Deputy Prime Minister Tun Abdul Razak shortly before his succession as the nation's prime minister.[6] In his speech to the conference, Razak spoke in glowing terms of non-alignment and identified Malaysia's foreign policy goals as consonant with its principles:

> [T]oday with the détente between the two power blocs, it is an important responsibility of the Non-aligned Group to ensure that the interests of the big powers do not converge at the expense of the medium and small powers. The hegemonistic tendencies on the part of the major powers which appear to be under various guises and with various justifications must be resisted. Furthermore, the world today is no longer bipolar. It is at least tri-polar with the emergence of China and her legitimate role in the world cannot be simply washed away by those who are opposed to her. At the same time, it is a fact which also cannot be washed away that the relations between China and a number of countries remain unsatisfactory. I submit that here the non-aligned countries have an extremely important role to play and have a unique duty to discharge if we are to remain loyal to the principles of co-existence and to our basic tenets of non- alignment in our efforts to bring about a harmonisation of international relations on the basis of respect for independence and integrity of states.[7]

It was also at the Lusaka Conference that Razak for the first time sought endorsement at an international forum for Malaysia's proposal for the neutralization of Southeast Asia. Although the scheme received only partial endorsement at Lusaka, Malaysia continued to air it at various international conferences, notably, the commemorative session of the twenty-fifth anniversary of the United Nations in December 1970, and then at the 1971 Commonwealth Conference at Singapore. Razak in his speech to the Commonwealth summit called for restraint and consideration from the big powers in their actions and decisions affecting smaller countries. He called for the neutralization of Southeast Asia which would include Vietnam, Laos and Cambodia and which necessitated the endorsement and guarantee of the United States, USSR (the United Soviet Socialist Republics) also known as Soviet Union, and China of the scheme.[8]

Malaysia's neutralization proposal was no doubt based on the 1968 "Ismail Peace Plan". However, it was not until two years after Tun Ismail had presented his proposals to Parliament that they were formalized as part of Malaysia's foreign policy. Initially, the proposal, as explained by party ideologue Tan Sri Ghazali Shafie, involved "two levels" of policy options: On the first level, the countries of Southeast Asia should get together and clearly view their present situations and agree on the following:

• individual countries in the region must respect one another's sovereignty and territorial integrity, and not participate in activities likely to directly or indirectly threaten the security of another. This is an essential requirement. Non-interference and non-aggression are basic principles which Southeast Asian countries must unequivocally accept before any further steps can be taken.
• all foreign powers should be excluded from the region.
• they should devise ways and means of, and undertake the responsibility for, ensuring peace among member states.
• they should present a collective view before the major powers on vital issues of security.
• they should promote regional cooperation.

On the next level, the major powers (the United States, Russia, and China) are expected to agree on the following:

• Southeast Asia should be an area of neutrality.
• the powers undertake to exclude countries in the region from power struggle among themselves.

- the powers devise the supervisory means of guaranteeing Southeast Asia's neutrality in the international power struggle.[9]

The scheme, while ambitious, was based on a pragmatic appreciation of the Southeast Asian situation. It became the most important of Malaysia's foreign policy strategies in the area of defence and security. By November 1971, Malaysia had partially achieved the first step of the plan in persuading the four other ASEAN members to endorse the scheme. In the historic Kuala Lumpur Declaration, the ASEAN countries, "agreeing that the neutralization of Southeast Asia is a desirable objective and that we should explore ways and means of bringing about its realization", stated further that:

a) "Indonesia, Malaysia, the Philippines, Singapore and Thailand are determined to exert initially necessary efforts to secure the recognition of and respect for, Southeast Asia as a Zone of Peace, Freedom and Neutrality, free from any form or manner of interference by outside powers" [and]

b) "Southeast Asian countries should make concerted efforts to broaden the areas of co-operation which contribute to their strength, solidarity and closer relationship".[10]

The neutralization scheme was subsequently also endorsed in principle by the Commonwealth Conference of Ottawa in August 1973, and the Fourth Non-aligned Summit Conference in Algiers in September 1973. Support is, of course, a far cry from implementation. The big two, the United States and Soviet Union, did not respond officially to the scheme, while China verbally expressed support for the idea. The slowness of big-power response and the feedback from other countries, particularly the ASEAN countries, led to a slight shift of emphasis in the foreign policy strategy. Increasingly the term "neutralization" was dropped in favour of the expression "Zone of Peace, Freedom and Neutrality", or ZOPFAN, its acronym.

The emphasis appeared to have shifted from big-power guarantee for neutralization, to an ASEAN or Southeast Asian initiative in fostering neutrality. The concept of neutralization implies big-power participation, or at any rate, control, and this did not sit well with some ASEAN countries that would rather prefer to see big-power disengagement from the area or, alternatively, some balance of power system. The scheme made baby steps of progress after the Kuala Lumpur Declaration of 1971. By May 1975, during the ASEAN Ministerial Conference in Kuala Lumpur, it was publicly announced that a "Blueprint for the Zone of Peace, Freedom and Neutrality" was in the process of being mooted and formulated by senior ASEAN officials. Razak underscored the change of emphasis from big-power guarantee to national and regional initiative in his speech to the ASEAN ministers:

> The premise of the neutralisation proposal is regional and national resilience. Southeast Asia must stand on its own feet. We — individual countries as well as the region as a whole — must be self-reliant if we wish to survive. If a country or a people values its way of life, it must be prepared to defend it against any form of external encroachment. If a people are not prepared to fight in the defence of its sovereignty and its values, it will not survive — indeed it does not deserve to survive. The best defence lies in the people themselves — in their commitment, their will and capacity. This is the premise of the neutrality system as it applies both to individual countries and to the region as a whole. It is not premised on vague hopes and euphoric dreams. It is premised on friendship and goodwill, on all open-minded readiness to co-operate, and patience and perseverance in working out detailed arrangements — and equally on national resilience, on our readiness to fight and defend our values and way of life…This is the meaning of and thrust of the neutrality system… The key to our future security and stability lies not in outdated and irrelevant attitudes of the Cold War, but in imaginative and constructive response to the new realities of today.[11]

This shift in the neutralization strategy was explained in a more comprehensive fashion by foreign policy troubleshooter and Home Affairs Minister Tan Sri Ghazali Shafie. In a talk on regional security to the Centre for Strategic and International Studies in Jakarta, Ghazali spelled out three security issues areas, namely, internal security issues that arose from internal conflict situations; intraregional security issues that arose out of intraregional (Southeast Asian) conflict situations; and external security issues that arose out of extraregional conflict situations.[12] He argued that these conflict situations could be alleviated by a "Southeast Asian Neutrality System" which would entail the pursuit of three "essential elements", namely (a) national cohesiveness and resiliency, (b) regional cohesiveness and resiliency, and (c) the observance of a policy of equidistance by Southeast Asian states vis-à-vis the major powers. National resilience refers to a state's "capacity to mobilize (its) population for nation-building and rapid economic development…" A state is said to be resilient if "its socio-political system is nationally accepted and has the inherent ability to meet the heightened expectations for greater prosperity and social justice of its population".

The second element, regional resilience, was more than a mere extension of the national concept and appeared to incorporate some notion of regional integration: Ghazali defined it as the ability of each state in the region to be fully committed to its organized international relatedness and interdependence as the first principle of foreign policy. ASEAN was a step in the right direction. It focused interest on the real possibility of accelerating economic development through increased intraregional trade, improvement of collective extraregional trade terms, sectoral plan harmonization, as well as collective utilization of a larger volume of external resources through joint regional projects.

The third element, equidistance, was taken to mean a policy of maintaining non-involved, and, more or less, impartial or neutral relationships with the great powers. As Ghazali put it, "In the short term, equidistance reinforces the adoption of a neutral, non-aligned policy stance, which in turn reinforces accommodation between external powers. In the long term, equidistance will entrench a regional policy of neutrality and non-alignment that will facilitate and perpetuate great power disengagement from Southeast Asia." He suggested that none of these policy trends was fundamentally unacceptable to any Southeast Asian state. The elements necessary for a neutrality system were mutually reinforcing, such that once firmly established, would provide the dynamics for spontaneous institutionalization through collective agreement.

Because of the changing nature of the neutrality proposal, some confusion was generated over its precise meaning and doubts had arisen with respect to its practicality. As one foreign policy analyst put it:

> The (neutralization) proposal may not be practical; indeed, may be utopian as many of the critics have argued. Quite realistically, Southeast Asia is not likely to develop into a Zone of Peace, Freedom and Neutrality soon. Yet it is important to distinguish between neutralisation as an end or as a goal, and as a means, or more particularly, a theoretical framework — a process of thinking, articulation and formulation of individual and collective policies. (Chee 1974, p. 49)

Seen from the perspective of Malaysian foreign policy, the neutralization scheme could be viewed simply as a foreign policy strategy grounded on a number of foreign policy objectives and springing from a foreign policy posture of non-alignment or "neutralism" as I would prefer to call it. It wasn't necessarily a concrete or even immediately practicable proposal. Malaysia's claim to neutrality was dubious as long as the Five-Power Defence Arrangement, however loosely, remained in force. The proposal for a neutral Southeast Asian zone was also hardly in the tradition of non-alignment, having perhaps greater affinity to European neutrality. The change of emphasis in the foreign policy strategy reflected a continual adjustment towards external developments and, to some extent, domestic events. Although the strategy is flexible, Malaysia's basic posture of neutralism was a stable facet of foreign policy for this whole period. The neutralization scheme, because it specifies clear-cut lines of action and is based on a particular ideological or political position, may also be looked upon as a "doctrine". A Foreign Ministry official stressed, for example, that it was a "total concept" on which all foreign policy actions were "tested" so that they conformed to its premises. However, I would use the terminology of "constructivist strategising" to describe the concept, in keeping with the theoretical thrust of this book. Neutralization was an enabling construct for a particular political conjuncture which sat well with a newer set of interests, norms, and ideas nested within the Malaysian political class. By the end of the period, Malaysia had initiated, under ASEAN auspices, a "blueprint" for Southeast Asian neutrality, which, according to a Wisma Putra official, enjoyed "90 per cent support" of the other ASEAN countries.[13]

Malaysia's most important step towards neutralism actually came with the recognition and establishment of diplomatic relations with the People's Republic of China. While the move was strictly a diplomatic move, its implications for Malaysia's national defence and general security will become obvious in the course of my account. Overtures of rapprochement with China became evident when Malaysia began to soften its China line soon after the termination of *Konfrontasi*. At various points, Malaysian spokesmen publicly lamented the absence of China from the United Nations, although they invariably defended the rights of Taiwan. Tun Razak in 1966 called this position the "One China, one Formosa" policy, not wishing to be identified with the "two-China" policy. Until 1970, Malaysia held this position. Thus Tun Ismail told the U.N. General Assembly in December that year that, in his view, the world today was no longer bipolar, and if not multipolar, at least tripolar. Referring to the People's Republic of China, whose absence from the United Nations reflected a serious shortcoming, he said the denial to a big power of its proper role cannot be conducive to the establishment of a stable and harmonious world order. Hedging on Taiwan, he then stated that, while taking into account the rights of the people of Taiwan to self-determination, China should be properly and fully represented in the United Nations.[14]

By 1971, the Malaysian position on China and Taiwan had become more definite. In a briefing to the Commonwealth Parliamentary Association, Tan Sri Zaiton, the Permanent Secretary to the Ministry of External Affairs, said:

> Malaysia's policy on China is this: We subscribe not to a two-China policy or one China one Taiwan policy but rather, I say this quite categorically, to a one China policy, but the problem of Taiwan remains a difficult issue. The fact has to be accepted that a *de facto* government exists on this island,

based on an ideology different from that existing on the mainland. On the other hand, for centuries it has been accepted that Taiwan is part of China. The problem is well-nigh impossible to resolve unless there is a spirit of give and take on both sides. It is for this reason we say that, while the problem is essentially one for the Chinese people to decide, in considering its solution, we urge that cognizance be taken of the principle of self-determination to assess the wishes of the twelve million or so people inhabiting the island of Taiwan…We do not seek to involve ourselves in the minutiae of the Chinese problem. (Noordin Sopiee 1974, pp. 52–53)

Thus in the 1971 U.N. General Assembly, Malaysia voted for the Albanian resolution which allowed for the seating of China and, consequently, Taiwan's expulsion. There followed in October 1971 a nineteen-man trade mission to China, led by Pernas chairman, Tengku Razaleigh, to establish direct trade links with the People's Republic. Subsequent missions followed, paving the way for unofficial negotiations on recognition and diplomatic ties. The most important of these negotiations were carried out, it was revealed later, in secret meetings between the Malaysian U.N. representative in New York, Zakaria Mohd Ali, and his Chinese counterpart, Huang Hua. The two men had first met in Ottawa when they were ambassadors to Canada. Initial contacts over the question were made in New York in June 1973 as revealed recently by the Malaysian diplomat recently (Zakaria Mohd Ali 2006, p. 125). The Malaysian delegation to the secret meetings included senior officials from Kuala Lumpur, namely, Zain Azraai, then with the Prime Minister Office, Khor Eng Hee, from Wisma Putra, and Zakaria's deputy, Ahmad Kamil. The negotiations spread over nearly a year and revolved around the issues of cessation of support for the Malayan Communist Party and Chinese citizenship.

The Chinese position at these meetings was that diplomatic relations should come first while Malaysia wanted the outstanding issues settled before ties could be formalized (Noordin Sopiee 1974, p. 50, Zakari Mohd Ali 2006, pp. 126–27). From the Malaysian perspective, there were three main issues: (a) China's support for the Malayan Communist Party (MCP), (b) the related question of "Suara Revolusi Malaya" (Malayan Voice of Revolution) radio broadcasts which emanated from China, and (c) the status of the 220,000 stateless Chinese in Malaysia. China, apparently after a little hesitation, agreed to discuss these and other issues and by December's end, agreement had been reached on the entire range of questions. As a prelude to the China ties, Malaysia had recognized without much fanfare the Mongolian Republic, North Vietnam, North Korea, and East Germany between 1972–73.

Then, on 27 May 1974, a Malaysian entourage, led by Prime Minister Tun Abdul Razak, left for the People's Republic of China in the first high-level official contact of the two governments since Malaya's independence in 1957. On 31 May, Malaysia and China announced the normalization of relations to be followed by an exchange of ambassadors. At the same time, Malaysia terminated diplomatic (consular) relations with Taiwan. In the joint communiqué announcing the normalization of relations, the two governments agreed on the following chief points:

> [T]hat although the social systems of the People's Republic of China and Malaysia are different, this should not constitute an obstacle to the two Governments and people in establishing and developing peaceful and friendly relations between the two countries on the basis of the principles of mutual respect for sovereignty and territorial integrity, mutual non-aggression, non-interference in each other's internal affairs, equality and mutual benefit, and peaceful co-existence. The two Governments consider all foreign aggression, interference, control and subversion to be impermissible. They hold that the social system of a country should be chosen and decided by its own people. They are opposed to any attempt by any country or group or countries to establish hegemony or create spheres of influence in any part of the world.[15]

Specifically, Malaysia stated that it recognizes "the Government of the People's Republic of China as the sole legal Government of China and acknowledges the position of the Chinese Government that Taiwan is an inalienable part of the territory of the People's Republic of China". The Chinese Government, on its part, took note of the fact that Malaysia was a multiracial country with people of Malay, Chinese, and other ethnic origins and rejected dual nationality. Proceeding from this principle, the Chinese Government considered anyone of Chinese origin who had taken up of his own will, or acquiring Malaysian nationality, as automatically forfeiting Chinese nationality. As for those residents who retain Chinese nationality of their own will, the Chinese Government, acting in accordance with its consistent policy, enjoined them to abide by the law of the Government of Malaysia, respect the customs and habits of the people there, and live in amity with them. Although not specifically mentioned in the joint communiqué, it seemed that China was prepared to stop actively supporting the MCP and base its relations with Malaysia on the five Bandung principles of coexistence. At any rate, it appeared to be the Malaysian Government's understanding that "non-interference" in internal affairs was a reference to the MCP issue. Thus the Malaysian prime minister said on his return that he had received assurances in private talks with both Chairman Mao and Premier Chou that the MCP was Malaysia's "internal problem".[16]

China also accepted Malaysia's position on the issue of overseas Chinese (*hua chiao*), which is based on the principles of *jus soli*. In the past, China applied the principle of *jus sanguinis* in the fear that Taiwan would absorb the *hua chiao* if the local societies rejected them. As a *quid pro quo* to the concessions made by China, Malaysia discarded its ambivalent stand on Taiwan in stating plainly that the island was an inalienable part of the People's Republic of China, and in so doing, also breaking off ties with the island republic. Premier Chou also spoke favourably, if only generally, of the Malaysian-ASEAN scheme for the neutralization of Southeast Asia. In his words, "[T]he Malaysian Government's position for the establishment of a Zone of Peace and Neutrality in Southeast Asia gives expression to the desire of the Southeast Asian People to shake off foreign interference and control (and) has won support from many Third World countries." The China visit represented a diplomatic breakthrough for Malaysia and a personal triumph for Tun Razak. On his return from the historic trip, the Malaysian premier said with considerable truth that the prestige of Malaysia had never been higher, that every major power in the world could without equivocation support Malaysia's policy of friendship because it was directed against no one, was fair and objective, and that its strong commitment to regionalism was constructive, and its pursuit of regional neutrality would bring and build peace.[17]

Thus with the establishment of diplomatic ties with the People's Republic of China, Malaysia's foreign diplomacy had more or less come full circle. It could now claim with greater credibility to have a non-aligned foreign policy and thereby pursue a policy of equidistance *vis-à-vis* the major powers. As long as it did not recognize China and China did not recognize Malaysia, such a strategy of equidistance, *ipso facto*, could not be pursued.

A little under a year after Malaysia's rapprochement with China came a dramatic turn of events in Indo-China in April 1975. In unprecedented and relentless military offensives, the revolutionary movements of South Vietnam and Cambodia — admittedly with generous support and participation from Hanoi — overwhelmed the non-communist regimes of Thieu and Lon Nol within a matter of months. The communist victories led to the establishment of communist governments in South Vietnam and Cambodia under the National Liberation Front and the Khmer Rouge respectively. Malaysia extended recognition to the two new Indo-China governments and took a positive attitude to the events in Indo-China. This was concomitant on its adherence to a neutralist foreign policy. Then Prime Minister Tun Razak, speaking to the ASEAN Foreign Ministers in Kuala Lumpur in May 1975 said:

We meet today at a historic moment in Southeast Asia. Only days ago, we have seen the emergence of new governments in Cambodia and South Vietnam, born out of the turmoil of a protracted war and extraordinary and untold human sufferings ... Southeast Asia today is a different place from what it was only a few weeks ago. Peace, for the most part, has come to this region. This must indeed be a decisive moment in our history. Never before in the history of this region have we the opportunity to create and establish for ourselves a new world of Southeast Asia — a world at peace and free from foreign domination and influence — a world in which the countries of the region can co-operate with one another for the common good ... We are now at the threshold of exciting possibilities. This is the challenge which faces us in Southeast Asia today. This challenge brings new opportunities for peace, friendship and co-operation for us to grasp... Which path shall we follow? The path of unity or the path of division? The path of co-operation or of confrontation? ... It is a[n] historic choice — a[n] historic opportunity — a[n] historic responsibility which will determine the future of our region and of our people. As brother Southeast Asians, we in Malaysia are happy the guns of war in the countries of Indo-China have at last been muted... We extend our friendship and goodwill to the governments and people of the Indo-China states with whom it is our earnest desire to have friendly and neighbourly relations. Basic to our thinking about the future is our commitment to do our utmost to ensure that the countries of Southeast Asia irrespective of political ideology or social system — can co-operate together in ensuring peace and prosperity for all our peoples.[18]

Malaysia's policymakers made it absolutely clear that they did not subscribe to the so-called "Domino Theory". Party theoretician Ghazali Shafie went on *Radio-Television Malaysia* to explain what he called "The Great Domino Fallacy". Ghazali submitted that the two simplistic assumptions of the theory were untenable, namely, the inevitability of communist victory, that is, that it would spread from country to country, and the assumption of the uniformity of Southeast Asian countries. In short, he argued that the fall of "American dominos" did not necessarily presage the fall of other states, which may not even be "dominos", that in theoretical, as well as practical terms, the domino theory had little relevance to the states of Southeast Asia. The collapse of American policy in Indo-China did not determine the internal order of these states, unless their internal order happened to be a function of American support, and that they depend on the United States for the maintenance of their internal political system: "Whether or not a country goes communist depends on the success of the internal and external policies of that country itself ... In the years ahead the Domino Theory will come to be regarded as being increasingly irrelevant even by the United States," Ghazail said. If the Americans could begin to grasp the reality that their global security links were actually premised on political socio-economic and not military efficacy, there would be no cause for them to hold on to the myth of the domino theory (Ghazali Shafie 1975).

In constructivist terms, Malaysia's general strategy of the period appeared to be a shift from the pursuit of "defence" to that of "security", a sort of shift in ideas, which in more recent theoretical parlance, would be considered a movement from notions of "hard' power to notions of "soft" power. "Defence" implies a definite military strategy of a state protecting its borders, usually by means of a military pact where its own military capabilities are thought to be inadequate. "Security", on the other hand, suggests a more general conceptual orientation, both political and military, towards minimizing threats to a state's territorial integrity, using alliances and less formal linkages and relationships. In Malaysia's case, the emphasis on defence in the first period was manifested in the Anglo-Malayan defence pact, while the new emphasis on security in the third period is reflected in its pursuit of regional neutrality. For the most part then, the pursuit of national security initially was the Swiss-style proposal for the neutralization of Southeast Asia to be guaranteed by the major powers. The strategy evidently underwent a slight modification and became the promotion of a Zone of Peace, Freedom, and Neutrality in Southeast Asia, a concept which was duly endorsed by all the ASEAN countries in 1971. There subsequently appeared another package of strategies consisting of the promotion of national and regional "resilience" and a policy of "equidistance" *vis-à-vis* the major powers. But these more general strategies are no doubt tied to the promotion of a zonal neutrality system, which for the most part, had been the cornerstone of Malaysia's foreign policy for the whole period.

A summary of the main foreign policy objectives, postures, strategies, and actions for the period in the defence and security issue-area appears in Table 5.1.

THE SWITCH TO A POLITICAL ECONOMY APPROACH

There was some indication of a change in posture and strategies in economic matters although Malaysia's economic policies in broad terms, particularly its objectives, did not change fundamentally. Notably, Malaysia's developing world posture took on a more forceful or even radical orientation, perhaps what may be termed a more self-conscious political economy approach in issues of development and trade. Malaysian spokesmen began to stress more

TABLE 5.1
Policy Outputs in Security Issue Area, 1970–75

Objectives	Postures	Strategies	Actions
Maintaining political independence	*Neutralism* – orientation of neutrality *vis-à-vis* major powers and Cold War issues	Seeking security rather than defence 1. Promoting the neutralization of Southeast Asia through big power guarantees (ZOPFAN)	Signing Friendship and Delimitation of Territorial Seas Treaty with Indonesia (1970)
Protecting territorial integrity			Attending fist NAM conference in Lusaka (1970)
	Non-interference – respecting territorial integrity and political sovereignty of other states	2. Promoting national resilience, regional resilience and equidistance with major powers	Initiating and signing with ASEAN states KL Declaration of ZOPFAN
			Voting for China's admission into the United Nations (1971)
			Establishing diplomatic ties with Mongolian Republic, North Vietnam, and East Germany (1972–73)
			China visit and diplomatic recognition of China (1974)
			Recognition of new communist governments of South Vietnam and Cambodia (1975)
			Formulating with ASEAN states a "blueprint" for ZOPFAN

Source: Author's own compilation.

persistently the need to institutionalize various measures aimed at alleviating price fluctuations in primary commodities of developing countries, and measures generally aimed at a more equitable distribution of world wealth. For example, at the Third UNCTAD Conference at Santiago in April 1971, Malaysia's chief delegate, in complaining of the slow advancement of UNCTAD goals, said:

> The debate and discussions in UNCTAD and other forums of the UN have certainly added to our understanding of the problems of developing countries, but positive action has not matched the pace of rhetoric and we have so far failed to achieve a truly interdependent and integrated world economy ... The terms of trade of the developing countries continue to grow worse. Their share of world trade and share of their carriage of sea borne trade has persistently declined. The flow of resources from developing countries to developing countries has not been commensurate with the development needs of developing countries. Debt servicing has become an acute problem for developing countries and there is clear danger that the inflow of development resources into developing countries would be nullified by the outflow of capital from developing countries. On the top of all these problems, we are saddled with the ailments of the wealthy nations.[19]

The last remark was in reference to the international monetary crisis, and specifically with respect to the realignment of currencies among the major developed countries — the group of ten — which prompted the developing countries to form its own Inter-Governmental Group of twenty-four to look into monetary issues. The international monetary situation did little to ameliorate North-South relations and the lack of progress of UNCTAD III reflected this poor state of affairs. The impending World Multilateral Trade Negotiations to liberalize trade scheduled for Tokyo in 1973 tended to prompt the developed countries to put things off. There were, nevertheless, several minor achievements at UNCTAD III. These, in brief, were (a) recognition of the pollution hazards in the production of synthetics and substitutes, (b) a decision to carry out a series of studies on the marketing and distribution system of commodities of special interest to developing countries, (c) agreement in respect to shipping and freight that liner conferences should be given adequate notice, and that consultation precede any freight increases and particular account be taken on the effects of such increases on commodities of importance to developing countries, (d) agreement on the need for a code of conduct for liner conferences, and (e) a decision to invite the IMF to consider establishing a committee of twenty Central Bank governors in the Fund to advise it on reform of the international monetary system. As for Malaysia's private achievements, it was re-elected to serve on the Trade and

Development Board, which is the governing body of UNCTAD, and the leader of the Malaysian delegation also served as a vice-president of the Conference. This was testimony that Malaysia had become increasingly recognized as a champion of southern causes, while at the same time being more acceptable to the industrialized countries than perhaps some of the more radical African and Latin American countries.

The more aggressive tone of Malaysia's orientation towards North-South issues was also evident from Malaysia's participation in other U.N. bodies. The Malaysian finance minister, speaking at the annual meeting of the IMF and IBRD in 1970, said, "[I]t is clear that the developing world must re-appraise its basic financial and economic policies. The countries in this category must attain industrial self-sufficiency at whatever cost. Whatever the sacrifices needed, we must reduce our imports of manufactured goods from the highly industrialised countries — and we must do this as quickly as possible. We must form trading blocs which would be in a position to compete on more equal terms with the developed world." The two notions or economic strategies of "industrial self-sufficiency at whatever cost" and that of "forming trading blocs" were voiced openly at an international forum for the first time. In the past, Malaysia's spokesmen had been content to speak mostly in general terms of industrial development and support for price fixing schemes, such as that of tin. Malaysia also began to throw its support behind the call for a "new economic world order", a concept originally attributed to President Boumediene of Algeria, based on the premises that (a) producer countries should have absolute control over their own natural resources, (b) primary producing countries should have remunerative returns for their primary produces, and (c) prices of primary products should be tied to the price trends of manufactures. On questions of aid, Malaysia's attitude seemed to have become one of cynicism with regard to its efficacy. Again let me quote the then finance minister:

> If I may say so, much of the so-called aid being given can hardly be called aid because it is tied to the exports of the donor country. Malaysia has experienced great difficulty in utilising such so-called aid which is really nothing more than export promotion on the part of the developed country. This is fair enough, because even developed countries have a right to sell as much of their goods as possible but let us be honest about it and not call it aid. All that this exercise does is to force the recipient of such credits to buy from this donor country at inflated prices. In the last analysis, this form of aid could benefit the donor more than the recipient, particularly when the latter has managed its finances well and is not short of foreign exchange. Malaysia is one of those countries in this (dubiously) happy position.[20]

In general, then, Malaysia's foreign policy posture towards the developed
or industrialized countries during this period became more radicalized and
aggressive, even if in the broad context of Third World politics, Malaysia
was by no means regarded as a "radical". It nevertheless appeared to have
gained acceptance and even esteem among the large majority of Third
World states.

Before we discuss Malaysia's policies towards other economic issues, it
may be useful at this juncture to re-examine the nature, composition, and
direction of Malaysia's trade and compare this with the trade statistics of the
first years of independence, in keeping with the dynamic approach employed
in this book. From the table on exports (Table 5.2), it is evident that although
there has been some degree of export diversification, Malaysia in 1974 was
still heavily dependent on primary commodities for nearly 70 per cent of
the value of its exports (excluding petroleum and petroleum products). The
share of manufactured goods, included under "others", however, increased
from a small 5 per cent in 1961 to a significant 16 per cent with the value
of $1,530 million by 1974.[21] As for the direction of Malaysian trade, this
did not change significantly since the early years of independence (see chart
in Figure 5.1). Japan maintained its position as the single most important
buyer of Malaysian exports, with its share increased to 18 per cent in 1974
compared with 15 per cent in 1963. The overall picture was still one in which
Malaysia's major customers were the industrialized countries and Singapore
acted as a purveyor of Malaysian goods to the Southeast Asian countries.

TABLE 5.2
Breakdown of Exports by Major Commodities

Commodities	1974		1961	
	RM	%	RM	%
Rubber	2,882	30	1,567	48
Timber	1,272	13	185	6
Tin	1,408	15	553	17
Palm oil	1,022	11	61	2
Petroleum and petroleum product	940	10	212	7
Others	2,056	21	660	20
Total	9,580	100	3,238	100

Source: *Malaysia Treasury, Economic Report 1971–75* (Kuala Lumpur: Government of Malaysia, 1974),
p. 22.

FIGURE 5.1
Exports by Destination

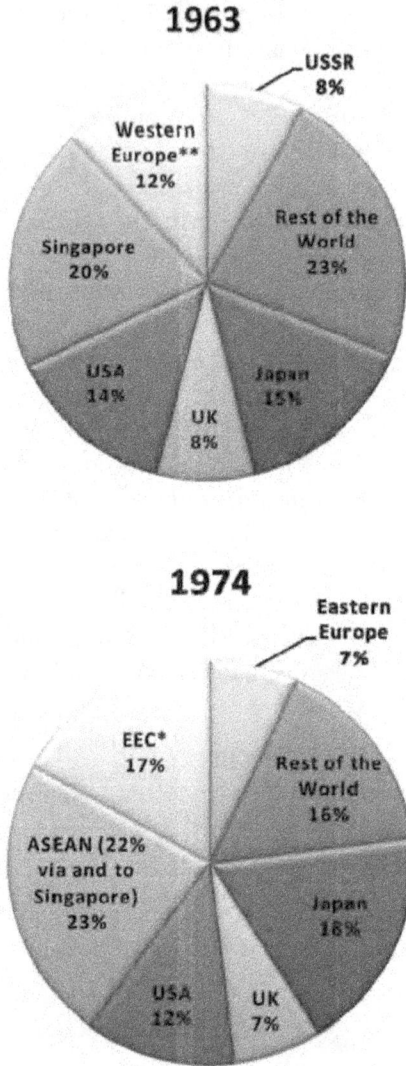

1963

USSR
8%

Western
Europe**
12%

Rest of the
World
23%

Singapore
20%

USA
14%

Japan
15%

UK
8%

1974

Eastern
Europe
7%

EEC*
17%

Rest of the
World
16%

ASEAN (22%
via and to
Singapore)
23%

Japan
18%

USA
12%

UK
7%

Source: Malaysia Treasury, 1974, *Economic Report, 1974–75*, p. 19, and Table 4, *supra*. The statistics do not allow for perfect comparability in some instances (such as EEC and Western Europe).

The composition of imports showed a continuation of the heavy buying of manufactured and capital goods (Figure 5.2). In fact, this increased over the decade by 16 per cent. The largest import items in 1974 were machinery and transport equipment, comprising 31 per cent of total imports. It would appear therefore that a major portion of Malaysia's foreign exchange earnings went into the purchase of such capital goods which were no doubt necessary for industrial development. This made Malaysia doubly dependent on the industrialized countries, as we shall see from the following discussion on Malaysia's major suppliers. The sources of Malaysian imports (Figure 5.3) provide an interesting picture of change in the decade under consideration. The most outstanding fact was Japan's rise as Malaysia's single most important supplier, with a startling share of 26 per cent of total imports. Compare this with its figure of 10 per cent in 1963. Together with Japan's rise and concomitant upon it was Britain's plunge from major supplier in 1963 with 21 per cent share, to a comparatively small 9 per cent in 1974. Another interesting change was the declining imports from Malaysia's Southeast Asian neighbours. While Thailand, Singapore, and Indonesia supplied a substantial 28 per cent of Malaysia's imports in 1963, ASEAN nations contributed only a 14 per cent share of its imports in 1974.

The foregoing discussion on Malaysia's external trade has underlined the continued importance of the industrialized countries to Malaysia's economic well-being. Japan emerged as Malaysia's single most important trading partner, buying 18 per cent of Malaysia's exports and supplying 26 per cent of its imports. Malaysia continued to be heavily dependent on several major primary commodities for external revenue although there was some indication of export diversification. In particular, the export of manufactures showed impressive progress. Since Malaysia's major buyers and suppliers were still the industrialized countries it was doubly dependent on these countries and its economy remained vulnerable to the vicissitudes of external economic forces (see Figure 5.3). In the circumstances, it is understandable that Malaysia's finance minister called for the pursuit of "industrial self-sufficiency at whatever cost" and the formation of trading blocs. It reflected a frustration with the persistence of the status quo in the world economic order despite more than a decade of the promotion of developmental goals in many international organizations. As the finance minister said in his major policy speech to the World Bank and International Monetary Fund:

> I now come to the most important problem of all, and that is the trading relationship between the developed and developing world. Broadly speaking, we in the developing world buy manufactured goods from the developed world and pay for them with the proceeds of sale of our primary commodities.

FIGURE 5.2
Composition of Imports

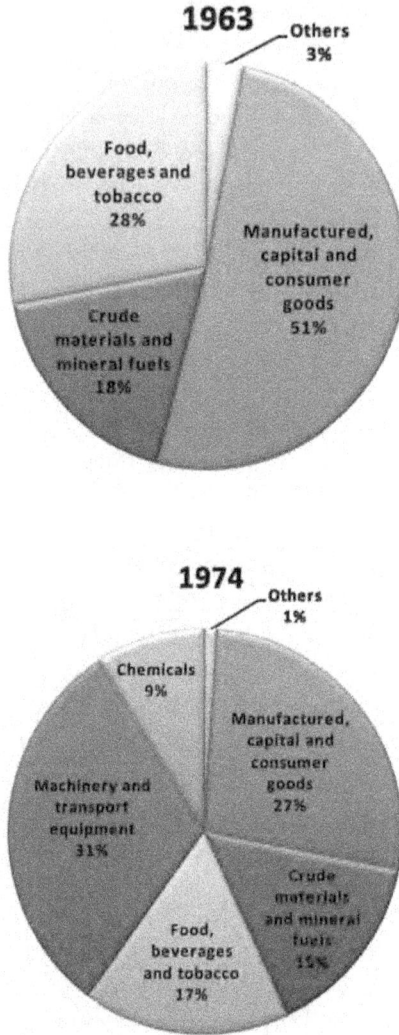

1963

Others
3%

Food,
beverages and
tobacco
28%

Manufactured,
capital and
consumer
goods
51%

Crude
materials and
mineral fuels
18%

1974

Others
1%

Chemicals
9%

Manufactured,
capital and
consumer
goods
27%

Machinery and
transport
equipment
31%

Crude
materials
and mineral
fuels
15%

Food,
beverages
and tobacco
17%

Source: Malaysia Treasury, 1974, *Economic Report, 1974–75*, p. 71, and Table 5, *supra*.

FIGURE 5.3
Imports by Major Countries of Origin

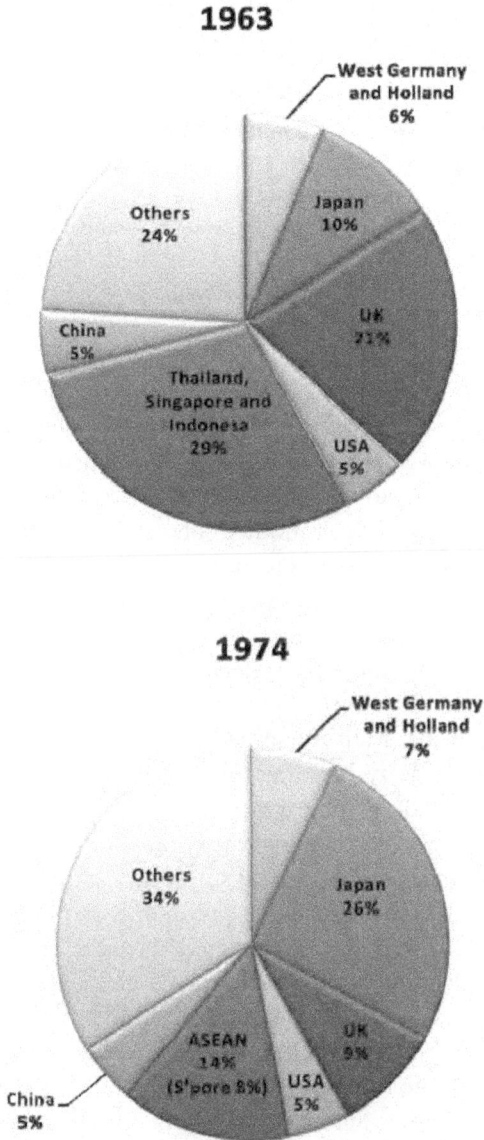

1963

West Germany and Holland 6%
Japan 10%
Others 24%
UK 21%
China 5%
Thailand, Singapore and Indonesia 29%
USA 5%

1974

West Germany and Holland 7%
Japan 26%
Others 34%
UK 9%
ASEAN 14% (S'pore 8%)
USA 5%
China 5%

Source: Malaysia Treasury, 1974, *Economic Report, 1974–75*, p. 71, and Table 6, *supra*.

As is well known, the prices of manufactured goods, compared with pre-war prices, have risen much faster than the prices of primary commodities in the post-war period. Broadly speaking, therefore, we have to pay more and more for what we buy from the developed world which continues to pay less and less for what we sell to them. On this basis, no developing country can be economically viable for reasons which are painfully obvious. Even if we adopt the most prudent and sensible policies and execute them with maximum efficiency, we would still be in the red because no amount of prudence, good sense and efficiency can overcome such overwhelming odds. The terms of trade which are so overwhelmingly loaded against the developing world will continue to impoverish them whatever the beautiful things are said in this ... assembly and outside it. We in the developing world do not want charity or even aid from the developed world. All we want is fair terms of trade, a square deal.

In 1973, a group of thirteen developing countries, the Organization of Petroleum Exporting Countries (OPEC) demonstrated that it could turn the tables on the industrialized countries with devastating effect. But this is only a small group of countries operating as a cartel with an essential, and up till now, indispensable commodity. The bulk of developing countries are not in this happy position, and indeed, the very action of the OPEC countries in quadrupling oil prices was not without its adverse effects on the developing, especially the very poor countries.[22] As such, Malaysia's finance minister's observations holds true in large measure for the great bulk of developing countries. It is in the light of the perception of the international economic situation that Malaysia joined the call for a new economic world order. Accordingly, Malaysia noticeably modified its economic strategies in pursuing its economic objectives at the international level. Rather than use the existing traditional frameworks and institutions, there was a greater inclination to seek out new steps, or at any rate, to reshape the old frameworks in order to change the economic status quo. For example, Malaysia during this period took unilateral steps to stabilize the price of rubber. According to a senior official of the Ministry of Trade and Industry, the government had been operating a "mini buffer stock scheme" on its own for some time by buying when the price was low and selling when it went up.[23] This scheme received official sanction in July 1975 through the introduction of a Rubber Stabilization Bill in Parliament, allowing for the establishment of a national advisory council for rubber stabilization and establishment of a rubber stock.

However, it was in relation to the question of foreign investment that Malaysia's economic postures and strategies saw the greater change. The government's New Economic Policy (NEP), which formed the basis for the Second Malaysia Plan, 1971–75, provided the point of departure for the general change in economic posture. The most important concept in the NEP in this respect was the notion of "economic balance". Although the main emphasis appeared to be the balance between Malay and non-Malay participation in the economy, the concept undoubtedly had an external dimension, given the predominant role of foreign capital in the country. I quote from the Second Malaysia Plan:

> Economic balance, in a growing and dynamic economy, refers to the equitable and legitimate sharing of the rewards and responsibilities of economic development. The principal reward of economic development — the growing income generated by the national economy — must be equitably distributed ... Balance also refers to racial shares in management and ownership and in employment in the various sectors of the economy. At present, non-Malays and foreigners dominate the manufacturing and commercial sectors.... The Government has set a target that within a period of 20 years, Malays and other indigenous people will manage and own at least 30% of the total commercial and industrial activities in all categories and scales of operation.[24]

In 1973, the mid-term review of the plan recognized in clear terms that the goal of economic balance necessarily entails the reduction of the share of foreign interests in the Malaysian economy:

> [T]he attainment of the growth targets of the Perspective Plan (1970–90) will enable non-Malay ownership of share capital to expand by nearly 12% per year and to increase its share of the total to over 40% by 1990, nine times more than the 1970 level in absolute terms. There will also be ample opportunities for ownership by foreign interests to increase by about 8% per year during the same period. In relation to total share capital, however, the expansion of the share of Malays and other indigenous people from under 2% in 1970 to 30% in 1990 will involve a sizable decline in the share of foreign interests from 61% to about 30% during the period.[25]

In general, however, Malaysia's orientation towards foreign enterprise continued to be one of welcome although one would be wrong to call this is a *laissez-faire* posture. There was an increasing sense that foreign economic participation must be trimmed to the pursuit of national goals. But the prevailing attitude remained that foreign capital was necessary for Malaysia's development and that the transfer of professional and technical know-how, as well as the job creation function of foreign enterprise, outweighed the effects of foreign economic control. To quote FIDA on this point:

> The Malaysian Government's policy towards new industrial investments
> and ... foreign capital inflow is one of welcome. Malaysia still lacks the
> necessary expertise and know how in many fields but it has rich investment
> opportunities to offer ... the Malaysian Government encourages foreign
> investments in the form of joint-ventures where Malaysian capital and
> resources (are) combined with foreign technical know-how, management,
> international marketing expertise and to some extent capita[l].[26]

Thus attractive fiscal incentives continued to be granted to foreign investors.
There are four major investment incentives:[27]

1. Pioneer status
2. Investment tax credit
3. Labour utilization relief
4. Export incentives

Under pioneer status, incentives include total exemption from income tax
for a period ranging from two to five years, depending on the level of fixed
capital investment; extension of relief for up to another five years for additional
investment,[28] and further extension for a year if the company met certain
other conditions.[29] The investment tax credit allowed for the deduction from
a company's taxable income of at least 25 per cent of its expenditure on fixed
assets, and an additional 5 per cent for meeting conditions of "location",
"priority product", and "Malaysian content". The labour utilization relief
incentive refers to the exemption from income tax from two to five years,
depending on the number of employees engaged.[30] Export incentives are the
various tax rebates and deductions for companies manufacturing products
mainly for export, and particularly of Malaysian-based products.

It became evident, towards the end of the period, that Malaysia would
find it hard to achieve the rather ambitious goals of the New Economic
Policy, particularly those of the Perspective Plan, which targeted increases
of Malay participation and ownership in the economy to reach 30 per cent
level by 1990. If these targets were to be attained, it seemed therefore that
some drastic measures had to be taken in the economic sphere. Thus towards
the end of 1974, Malaysia had edged towards a new economic posture. The
prime minister in September that year told a conference on Southeast Asia's
Natural Resources and the World Economy that Malaysia believed in the
concept of "economic nationalism", which could be said to be at the heart
of its new political economy approach:

> We in Malaysia believe in economic nationalism in guiding the exploitation
> of our natural resources in such a way that our people and country will

obtain the greatest benefit. We believe that private enterprise, whether domestic or foreign has an important role to play in our development. Our objective is to bring about an effective and equitable mixture of domestic and foreign enterprise on the one hand, and private and public enterprise on the other, so that our national interest can be advanced to the context of an expanding, stable and equitable world economic order. (*New Straits Times*, 18 September 1974)

Tun Razak went on to explain why the government set up a National Petroleum Corporation (Petronas) under the Petroleum Development Act, 1974. The reason was to ensure that Malaysians would reap the major benefits from this vital resource. Accordingly, Petronas has been given exclusive rights in the exploration and exploitation of oil in Malaysia.[31] In practice, this has meant a policy of signing exploration and production sharing agreements with oil companies operating in Malaysia. Under the aggressive, and some would contend, ruthless, direction and chairmanship of Tengku Razaleigh Hamzah, Petronas was to be conferred with further powers in 1975 to acquire an apparently innocuous one per cent "management shares" in foreign oil companies, which effectively allowed it to control the oil companies' policies through a mechanism of weighted votes.[32] This led to the charge in business circles that the government, in particular Petronas, was pursuing a policy of "nationalization without compensation".[33] The upshot was the "temporary" pull-out of Exxon from oil prospecting off the east coast of Peninsular Malaysia, presumably as a protest against the sweeping powers of Petronas. At one point, Tengku Razaleigh accused "several companies" of "trying to blackmail" the government and of launching a campaign against Petronas. Government officials denied that holding management shares was tantamount to nationalization or quasi-nationalization, pointing out that Malaysia has a number of investment guarantee agreements with the major Western countries, thereby foreclosing any possibility of nationalization without compensation of companies based in these countries.[34] They contended that the provision for management shares is merely a "contingency plan" to protect a very vital resource. In the end, the controversial management shares idea was shelved, although according to the Act, it was to be carried out "as soon as practicable".

The changing posture and strategies in Malaysia's pursuit of economic objectives was evident as well in areas other than oil. Working within the framework of the free enterprise system, Tengku Razaleigh in his capacity as the chairman of PERNAS, Malaysia's government-funded corporation for the promotion of Bumiputera interests, proceeded to acquire for the corporation major interests in a number of foreign and local companies.[35] These moves were in accordance with the New Economic Policy of "economic balance" and promoting greater Bumiputera participation in the economy. Thus by a strategy of state capitalism, Pernas Securities, a PERNAS subsidiary, succeeded by 1975 in acquiring, *inter alia*, a 19 per cent holding in Island and Peninsular Development, a 20 per cent holding in London Tin Corporation, and a 10 per cent share in Sime Darby, all large companies with major interests in Malaysia's economy.[36] In a yet more ambitious but abortive project, Pernas Securities announced in July 1975 its plan to acquire a controlling interest (40 per cent) in Haw Par Brothers International, a Singapore-based company with various interests in Malaysia and abroad.[37] At the height of the episode, Razaleigh said that the government would continue to employ the technique of takeovers and swaps until the NEP target of 30 per cent Bumiputera participation was achieved. However, following the failure of the Haw Par deal, no new ventures had been undertaken by the end of the year. The various initiatives and acts of Tengku Razaleigh ensured his retention of a vice-president post in UMNO during the 1975 General Assembly[38] and won him the title of "*Bapa Ekonomi* Malaysia" (Father of Malaysia's Economy), conferred by the Malay Chamber of Commerce of which Tengku Razaleigh was the president. In his speech to the chamber, Tengku Razaleigh castigated foreign firms for not being responsive to Malaysia's national needs and stressed his chamber's support for "economic nationalism", arguing that "[i]f other countries have legislation and regulations to ensure that their economies do not fall into the hands of others, the time has come for Malaysians themselves to control the nation's resources".[39]

The increasing concern over foreign ownership in Malaysia's economy led to the setting up in February 1974 of a Foreign Investment Committee (FIC) which has its secretariat with the Economic Planning Unit of the Prime Minister's Department. The FIC has been charged with formulating guidelines on foreign investment in all sectors of the economy in accordance with the NEP, and to supervise and advise all the pertinent Ministries and government agencies on all matters concerning foreign investment.[40] Its first act was the formulation of guidelines for the regulation of acquisition of assets, mergers, and take-overs with a view towards ensuring that such actions "should result directly or indirectly in a more balanced Malaysian participation in ownership and control", among other things.[41]

By the end of the period, however, Malaysia had begun to soft-pedal its economic nationalism posture, but without really discarding it. In a "Malaysian Investment Seminar" held in Kuala Lumpur in October 1975, various cabinet members made speeches assuring foreign investors of the government's continued adherence to a private enterprise-oriented economic system. The prime minister, in his address, admitted that there were recent "uneasy comments" and "misgivings" in the foreign media about Malaysia's investment climate, but he tried to dispel any idea that Malaysia either did not want or need foreign investment:

> A major misinterpretation of the New Economic Policy concerns the government's attitude towards the private enterprise system generally and the private sector in particular. Let me reiterate our position once more. The Malaysian economy has prospered because of the open nature of the economy and the initiative of its private sector ... The Government therefore realizes that it has a major responsibility to assist the private sector to play its proper role in the structural transformation of the economy. We are only too aware that all this implies the need for pragmatism in our economic policies and the maintenance of a healthy climate for investment and business in the country. (*New Straits Times*, 28 October 1975)

On the Petroleum Development Act(s), the prime minister explained that because oil was a vital resource, the special legislation was necessary to control its depletion, but he ensured investors that "this law will be implemented fairly and equitably and in a manner that will not affect adversely Malaysia's investment climate and our unblemished record of fair treatment to all investors". He ensured investors that the other sectors of the economy will continue to operate "within the framework of normal and established practice".

In summary, Malaysia's foreign policy in the area of developmental and economic concerns saw fundamental shifts during this period. In particular, its developing world posture took on a more forceful political economy thrust and Malaysia appeared ready to adopt more radical measures in its pursuit of its Third-World economic goals in general, and its own developmental objectives in particular. However, the most significant shift occurred with respect to the issue of foreign participation and investment in the country's economy. The adoption of the New Economic Policy led to policies which were geared towards a reduction, if not of the role, at least of the share, of foreign participation in the economy. However, Malaysia's attitude towards foreign investment remained one of "welcome", but it by and large dropped its *laissez-faire* economic posture for one which its policymakers call "economic nationalism". The summary of Malaysia's main postures, objectives, strategies, and actions in this issue area for the period studied is shown in Table 5.3.

INTERNATIONAL COOPERATION

For most of this period, issues of international cooperation and diplomacy tied in closely with issues of national and regional security. Malaysia by and

TABLE 5.3
Policy Outputs in Economic Issue-Areas

Objectives	Postures	Strategies	Actions	
Promoting economic development	*Developing World Orientation* — supporting policies and measures aimed at raising the lot of LDCs	Promoting and participating in trade groupings and price stabilization schemes of LDCs	Adopting New Economic Policy as basis of Second 5-Yr Plan, 1971–75	Establishing national oil corporation, Petronas, with Petroleum Development Act (1974)
Stabilizing prices of primary commodities		Operating unilateral stabilization schemes (rubber)	Attending UNCTAD III, supporting developmental issues and measures (1971)	Passing Petroleum Development (Amendment) Act (1975)
	Economic Nationalism — seeking national control of resources and economy	Pursuing industrial self-sufficiency by encouraging particular kinds of direct foreign investment	Calling for a "New Economic World Order" at various global forums with other LDCs at various global forums	Acquiring controlling interests in various companies through the parastatal company Pernas
		Employing tactic of state nationalism to gain control of the economy	Participating in Multilateral Trade Negotiations, Tokyo (1973–75)	Passing guidelines for acquisition of assets, mergers, and takeovers under Foreign Investment Committee (1974)
			Operating rubber price stabilization scheme	Joining International Tin Agreement (1975)
			Opting out of the Sterling Area and floating Malaysian dollar (1972)	Holding investment seminar in Kuala Lumpur (1975)
			Joining International Sugar Agreement (1973)	

large paid less attention to long-range milieu goals and concentrated on the medium-range goals of regional security, which dovetailed nicely with its pursuit of national security. While there was recognition that defence was strictly a national matter, security was seen more and more in regional terms. It was in this sense that a Wisma Putra official spoke of neutralization as a "total concept" and that all foreign policy moves and actions must be consistent with the concept. Thus Malaysia throughout the period was promoting its neutralization scheme at various international forums, notably at the Lusaka and Commonwealth Conferences, and diplomacy at this level became linked to the general pursuit of security. At the regional level, the process was carried out with even greater vigour, most importantly through the declaration of an ASEAN Zone of Peace, Freedom, and Neutrality, and the active pursuit of a "blueprint" for ZOPFAN. The détente with the communist countries, in particular the establishment of diplomatic relations with China, should also be appreciated in the light of the search for and pursuit of security through the avenue of international diplomacy.

However, milieu goals were not totally ignored or discarded. Malaysia continued to support or pay lip service to the many United Nations ideals and still pursued, for example, anti-colonial causes. It also began to develop ties with the Muslim world. What was evident, however, was that much more emphasis was given to regional (Southeast Asian) cooperation, when in the other two periods, the United Nations and the Commonwealth took precedence over ASA. A Foreign Ministry official suggested that Malaysia's pursuit of "international" goals can be appreciated in terms of concentric circles, at the centre of which is ASEAN, extending to Asia in the next circle and so forth to the rest of the world. ASEAN had indeed grown in importance and had become the chief avenue of Malaysia's efforts at international cooperation. In his speech to the 1975 UMNO General Assembly, Tun Razak spoke glowingly of ASEAN having "reached maturity" and accorded a status similar to that of an organization such as the Organization of African Unity (OAU). The prime minister also thought that ASEAN was ready to extend to the rest of Southeast Asia, following the cessation of war in Indo-China. Emphasizing its non-ideological nature, he told ASEAN foreign ministers in May 1975:

> Some eight years ago, even as the war in Indo-China was raging, we five countries in Southeast Asia, established ASEAN and began nurturing a structure of regional co-operation which over the years has proved itself constructive in promoting regional understanding and friendship ... The growth of ASEAN has been nurtured with care to maintain its non-antagonistic, non-military and non-ideological character. I think today we can truly say that ASEAN's independent and progressive nature has won

> admiration from many quarters - large and small powers alike … At this juncture, when the war in Indo-China has ended, the countries of Southeast Asia have the opportunity to extend the scope of regional co-operation throughout Southeast Asia. I think I can say for the other ASEAN countries that ASEAN is ready to co-operate with the new Governments of Indo-China and to offer its hand of friendship … to them.[42]

Towards the end of the year, the newly appointed Malaysian foreign minister, Tengku Ahmad Rithaudeen, made further overtures at the United Nations to non-ASEAN Southeast Asian countries to join the organization, reiterating the ASEAN goal of zonal neutrality.

Despite the emphasis placed on regional cooperation during this period, Malaysia had to contend with a major area of global cooperation (and controversy) at the Law of the Sea Conference in 1974, which had important ramifications for its stand on the Strait of Malacca. At the Caracas Conference, the attorney general and minister of law explained that Malaysia's position on the Malacca Strait was based on the following points: that while the strait was a major waterway for internal shipping, the coastal states were burdened with the sole responsibility of maintaining and cleaning up the strait; that the heavy usage of the strait would inevitably lead to damage of the marine environment by pollution and accident; and that under the guise of commercial shipping, military vessels may use the strait with strategic intentions:

> What we would like … therefore, to see is a greater appreciation of our legitimate interests and a clearer enunciation of the responsibilities of the international maritime community to be embodied in the Convention that would emerge from this Conference. Among other things, the Convention should contain regulations to ensure unhindered passage for commercial shipping, adequate safety for pollution prevention standards, liability and compensation for damage and passage for military vessels.[43]

In addition, Malaysia supported the call by the bulk of Third World countries for all economic zones to extend 200 nautical miles, and for an international machinery to regulate exploitation of seabed resources in accordance with the interests of developing countries. Little was decided at Caracas and most of the Law of Sea issues remain unresolved in this first round of negotiations. Malaysia's positioning for the most part was based simply on the pursuit of self-interest although it tended in general to support issues propagated by the Third World countries.

An area of international cooperation and diplomacy which gained prominence during this period was Malaysia's relations with the Muslim world. Although it was known to be an Islamic country by virtue of its predominant

Muslim population, Malaysia had, on the whole, maintained a low profile in Islamic affairs as reflected in its token non-recognition of Israel, general support for Muslim causes, and participation in the first Islamic summit conference in Rabat in 1969, held as a response to the Israeli burning the Al-Aqsa Mosque, and in the subsequent conferences. However, in June 1974, amidst considerable fanfare, Malaysia hosted the Islamic Summit in Kuala Lumpur and Tun Razak spoke in grandiose terms of Islamic solidarity and identified Malaysia with the Arab and Palestinian cause in the Middle East:

> Since the historic First Islamic Summit in Rabat in 1969, we can find satisfaction in the knowledge that we have laid a strong foundation for mutual co-operation. But we cannot sit back on the progress we have made, encouraging though it has been[.] The Islamic Conference must now enter a new phase in its history. The concept of unity and co-operation has been effectively worked out; we must now give it the necessary content and substance. We must enter a period of imaginative consolidation, of building on the foundation already laid, by implementing concrete measures, programmes and projects which will make our aim of Islamic unit a reality.
>
> Today, as our Arab brothers embark on the road of negotiations to seek peace and justice, we in this Conference must, more than ever, remain solid and united. We must not allow ourselves to become complacent by the current mode of expectancy or to be confused by the machinations of Zionism. Our unity through this organization must be clearly demonstrated so that the world will know that we will not weaken and we will not be divided... Let our voices ring clear and loud in total and united support for the Arab and the Islamic cause in West Asia.[44]

As a measure of this support, a representative of the Palestinian Liberation Organization was seated at the Conference.

One suspects, however, that Malaysia's Muslim ties served medium-range pragmatic goals rather than long-term interests. For Malaysia then, the goals of Muslim solidarity were still vague and distant, augmented by Malaysia's geographical distance from the hub of Muslim activity in the Middle East. Nevertheless, because of its good relations with the Arab countries, Malaysia was among the ten most favoured nations exempted from oil cutbacks in the 1973 "energy crisis". Domestically, there was political mileage to gain from Malaysia's international Muslim ties, considering its predominantly Muslim population. Thus the 1974 Islamic Conference in Kuala Lumpur was nicely timed just before the general election. A Foreign Ministry official I spoke with thought that this event had an even greater impact on the elections than the prime minister's China visit. He would be right on strictly arithmetic terms since Malaysia has more Malays than it has Chinese, although one would be foolish to deny the dramatic impact of the rapprochement with China. By 1975, Malaysia began to cash in on its Arab ties by concluding a number of cultural, scientific, technical, and economic agreements with several oil-rich countries. On a tour of these countries in January and February, the prime minister signed six such agreements with Kuwait, Oman, Qatar, United Arab Emirates, Bahrain, and Saudi Arabia.

In ongoing efforts — ever since *Konfrontasi* — to forge a plurality of diplomatic connections while maintaining old ones, the Malaysian prime minister toward the end of 1975 paid courtesy state visits to Australia and New Zealand, two long-standing Commonwealth allies. A cultural agreement with Australia resulted with broad aims for cooperation in the fields of the arts, education, science, technology, the media, sports, youth activities, and academic exchanges. New Zealand was content to issue a joint communiqué reaffirming basic mutual interests. One of the motives of the visits concerned the position and interests of some 2,000 and 6,000 Malaysian students in New Zealand and Australia respectively. The students themselves advertised their presence when some of them, along with Australians and New Zealanders, demonstrated against various "repressive" measures in Malaysia, such as the Internal Security Act and the University and Colleges (Amendment) Act. The Australian-New Zealand visits concluded Malaysia's diplomatic activities for the period and, as it turned out, were the last external official acts of Prime Minister Tun Razak before he passed away in January 1976.

In summary then, Malaysia's foreign policy orientation in matters of international cooperation underwent little fundamental change during the third period although it became increasingly evident that "international" goals were being pursued in greater unison with matters of national security. Thus the détente with the communist countries, the ZOPFAN proposal and regional cooperation in ASEAN, and overtures towards the new Indo-China states, all converged as part of Malaysia's broad plan for national and regional security. Pragmatism seemed to be the philosophy of the day as even Malaysia's Muslim ties seemed calculated to reap real benefits. The shift in emphasis seemed to be concomitant with a shift towards the pursuit of medium-range goals instead of the more distant long-range goals. A senior Foreign Ministry official attributed the change to Malaysia's wide acceptance among the community of nations and the fact that it did not have to prove its mettle internationally anymore as it did in its early years as a newly independent nation. In Table 5.4, I summarize the major postures, objectives, strategies, and actions of Malaysia's foreign policy in this issue area during the period surveyed.

TABLE 5.4
Policy Outputs in International Cooperation

Objectives	Postures	Strategies	Actions
Promoting regional cooperation and regional security	*Regionalism* – enhancing Southeast Asian solidarity	Promoting goals of general and specific purpose international organizations	Participating in ASEAN activities Participating in U.N. specialized agencies and their work
Promoting international Muslim causes	*Muslim Solidarity* – supporting international Muslim causes	Promoting and enlarging role of regional organizations	Supporting Arab and Palestinian cause Hosting 5th Islamic Foreign Ministers' Conference in Kuala Lumpur (1974)
Promoting U.N. ideals	*Internationalist Functionalist Orientations* – believing in the usefulness of IGOs *Anti-Colonialism* – supporting self-determination and human rights in the Third World		Attending Law of the Sea Conferences and voting generally with Third World (1971, 1975) Overtures to Indo-china governments via ASEAN Concluding cultural, scientific, technical and economic agreements with Kuwait, Oman, Qatar, UAE, Saudi Arabia, and Bahrain (1975) State visits to Australia and New Zealand (1975)

Source: Author's own compilation.

CONSTITUTING CHANGE AND INNOVATION WITH NEW POLICY DIRECTIONS

The most prominent feature of the study of this period of foreign policy has been the new directions to which the Malaysian policymakers had steered the nation's foreign policy. The primary changes occurred in the issue area of defence and security. Signs of détente with the communist countries became increasingly evident and culminated in Malaysia's rapprochement with China in May 1974, Malaysia also began publicly to profess its non-aligned status, pursue a posture of equidistance, and promote its concept of Southeast Asian neutrality. The strategy of promoting a Zone of Peace, Freedom, and Neutrality in the region became the cornerstone of Malaysia's foreign policy in matters of defence and security in much the same manner as AMDA provided the anchor to foreign policy for the greater part of the first two periods. There was also a tendency for the more internationally-oriented goals to be sought in unison with the medium-range goals of security, thus boosting the role of ASEAN as an avenue for international cooperation and the pursuit of security goals. In matters of development and trade, while objectives remained fundamentally unaltered, a more thoroughgoing posture and a willingness to employ more radical strategies were evinced.

In my view, the changes in foreign policy reflected a change in the elite ideology, which arose out of a new appreciation of the nature of Malaysia's national needs and interests, and of the nature of the international environment. The new elite ideology took its underpinnings from the tenets of non-alignment, or preferably, neutralism, but in large part was also based on hard-nosed pragmatism. A number of developments brought about the change in the elite ideology, but these factors can be subsumed under two broad categories: (a) domestic events, and (b) the changing international environment.

A domestic event that had a profound impact on Malaysian political life in general and which indirectly influenced the course of foreign policy was the 1969 May 13 racial riots in Kuala Lumpur and other major towns. We need not concern ourselves here with the details of 13 May, but suffice it to say that the aftermath brought about a crisis of leadership in the ruling coalition, particularly within UMNO. In the end, it resulted in the retirement of the Tunku from politics, just over a year after the crisis, in September 1970. Soon after the riots, the Tunku came under mounting pressure from the UMNO rank and file and students to resign. In a rash of student demonstrations at the University of Malaya and the MARA Institute of Technology, the Young Turks or "ultras",[45] as they became known, attacked the Tunku on his poker playing and horse racing habits and his lack of dynamic leadership. A member of the UMNO Executive Council, Dr Mahathir Mohamad, fuelled the anti-Tunku campaign with a scathing letter which he wrote to the Tunku and which was widely circulated among civil servants and the Malays generally. Although Mahathir was later dismissed from the Executive Council and from UMNO, the leadership crisis had set in and the stage was set for easing the Tunku out of politics. The Tunku has himself written of this "power struggle" within the UMNO following the events of 13 May:

> There is no denying that there is struggle for power going on inside UMNO as between those who built the party and helped in our independence and the new elements, the "ultras". In fact this struggle started two years ago, even longer back than that. The truly loyal supporters of the party were able to keep the "ultras" in check because UMNO was strong, and had the full support of all who belonged to it, from the top level right down to the lowest rung. As a result of this the so-called "ultras" have generally kept quiet although they have never ceased to be active; carrying out an intense underground campaign among the younger generation, the so-called "Intellectuals".[46]

The Tunku also illuminated on the goals of the "ultras":

> One might well ask what it is that they are after. Inquiring through other people, I have tried to find out from some of these "ultras" what the answer is, and as far as I know they want to establish a new order of things inside the UMNO and the country. For instance, they consider our political thinking is outdated and out of line with Afro-Asian policies. Among the ideas they have in mind are probably to remove the constitutional monarchy and to set up Malaysia as a republic. I suppose that, having proclaimed a Republic, they will probably change our foreign policy to bring us closer to the Afro-Asian group. (Tunku Abdul Rahman 1969, p. 136)

Indeed, the "ultras" were elements of the same group of counter-elite within the UMNO rank and file to which I have alluded earlier. Very possibly, these "counter-elite" had their origins in the group that rose up in opposition to AMDA as far back as 1957, and their continued presence was felt, as the Tunku noted, in the latter part of the 1960's. In the aftermath of *Konfrontasi*, this group organized an unofficial delegation to the Afro-Asian Solidarity People's Organization at Winneba in 1965. It is no coincidence that both Dr Mahathir and Datuk Musa were members of the Winneba delegation. The events of 13 May provided this group with the justification to oust the Tunku from power, but the Tunku survived the first onslaught which was marked by the expulsion of Mahathir from the UMNO Executive Council and Musa's removal as secretary general of the party. There was little doubt, however, that the Tunku would in time relinquish his leadership of UMNO as his image was already tarnished in the eyes of the large majority of the Malays. Thus it was Tun Razak who assumed control as director of the National Operations Council in the Emergency following 13 May. With the assumption of Tun Razak as prime minister, Mahathir and Musa soon became cabinet ministers.[47] Again this is no coincidence, but rather indicates the ascendancy of the "counter-elite" in the UMNO leadership.[48] These various domestic developments were perhaps more symptomatic of the Tunku's exit than of direct consequence to foreign policy, but they nevertheless set the stage for the change in the elite perceptions with respect to foreign policy. The ascension of Tun Razak to power was the domestic impetus to such a change as he had always shown a tendency to move towards the Afro-Asian bloc of countries even as deputy prime minister to the Tunku.[49] Indeed, Tun Razak apparently considered the various moves in foreign policy to be his personal initiatives. Nonetheless, one suspects it was Razak's pragmatism rather than his ideological fervour that engendered the change in elite ideology, just as it was the Tunku's adamance that probably postponed it.

One should however not forget the importance of Tun Ismail's role in changing the character of Malaysian foreign policy, to which we have already alluded in the previous chapter. Based on his biography by Ooi Kee Beng (2006) and Ismail's own memoirs,[50] I drew the conclusion that Ismail not only was greatly responsible for formulating the definitive aspects of foreign policy in the early independent years but, rather more interestingly, was also responsible for its shift to non-alignment in the late 1960s and early 1970s. This isn't gainsaying the fact that Tun Razak, with whom Ismail was particularly intimate, was in agreement with many of Tun Ismail's ideas. Indeed, much of what Tun Ismail propounded in his years at the United Nations and also later as acting foreign minister followed very much what may be considered the established foreign policy of Malaya; its anti-communism and pro-Western policies. In the later years, however, it could well be said that Tun Ismail was the "early architect" of the palpable shift of Malaysian foreign policy towards non-alignment that was clearly pivotal to his notion of the neutralization of Southeast Asia, which he was first to propound (Saravanamuttu 2007).

If domestic events provided the impetus for change, it was the international environment that precipitated it. At the very least, the changing international environment made the transition smoother and acceptance easier, especially for the old guard elements in the ruling party. Tun Razak aired the new elite perception of the international environment at the 1970 Lusaka Conference by his observations on the East-West détente and the increasing multipolarity in the international system:

> Today with détente between the two power blocs, it is an important responsibility of the Non-aligned Group to ensure that the interests of the Big Powers do not converge at the expense of the medium and small powers. The hegemonist tendencies on the part of the major powers which appear under various guises and with various justifications must be resisted. Furthermore, the world today is no longer bipolar. It is at least tri-polar with the emergence of China onto the international stage. The fact of China and her legitimate role in the world cannot be simply washed away by those who are opposed to her. (*Foreign Affairs Malaysia* 3, 1971, p. 15)

It may seem therefore that the changing international environment is largely responsible for Malaysia's shift in foreign policy. A Foreign Ministry official was convinced that even if the Tunku had remained in power, it would have been only a matter of time before he too would have yielded to the overwhelming weight of external factors. However, I would argue that internal developments within Malaysia were equally crucial as shown earlier. Thus out of the changing domestic and international scenes sprung a neutralist elite ideology which provided the basis for the new foreign policy positions. The new elite ideology comprised a belief system which was premised on the coexistence of the non-communist and communist ideologies, buttressed by a national image of a multipolar international system in which a balance of power largely existed among the major ideological blocs and in which Malaysia's national interests were tied with those of the Third World bloc of nations. In economic matters, this ideology exhibited a form of economic nationalism within the bounds of a capitalist philosophy. It may be appropriate at this juncture to present in diagrammatic style (Figure 5.4) my analysis of the sources of the third period of Malaysian foreign policy.

The historical factors of British and Commonwealth links remained important, if less so, during this period of foreign policy. Indications of this are the persistence of the Five-Power Defence Arrangements, however loose, Malaysia's wariness in its relations with communist countries, and the continued national alertness with respect to communist insurgency in the country. Indeed, its strategy of "national resilience" was in direct response to a spate of insurgent activity in the country.[51] One other historical factor has been added namely, *Konfrontasi*, which during the second period, acted as a catalyst for shifts and changes in the Malaysian foreign policy and remained as a reminder of Malaysia's defence and security needs, prompting its policymakers to maintain good regional relations and wide-ranging ties with the outside world generally.

FIGURE 5.4
Malaysian Foreign Policy, 1970–75: Change with Innovation

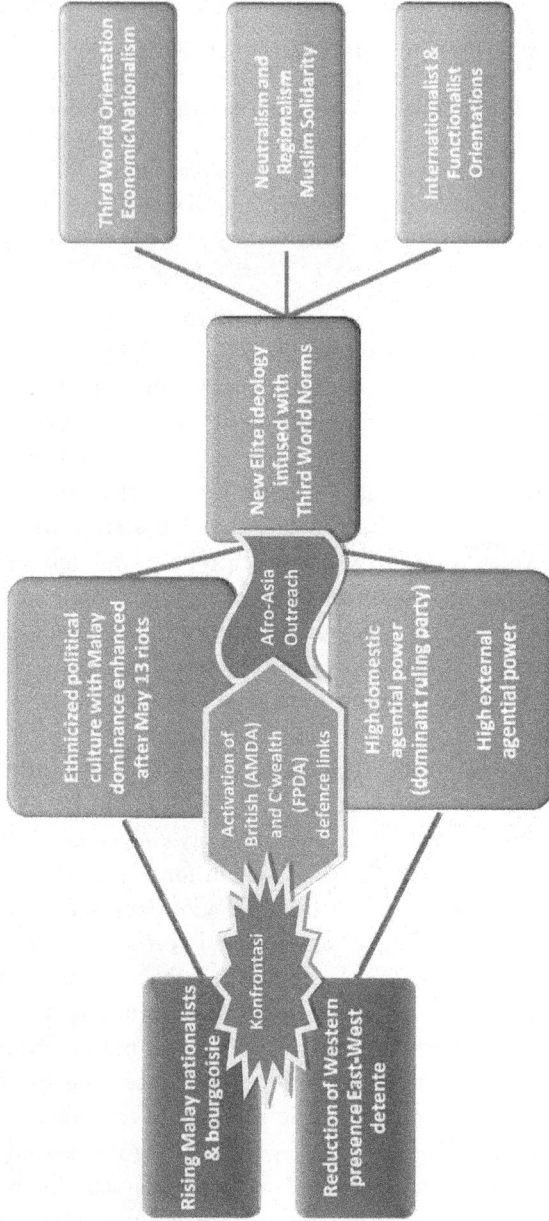

Among the most important variables in the external environment that affected the course and content of Malaysian foreign policy was the general reduction of Western presence in Southeast Asia, marked by the British east of Suez pull-out and the U.S. exit from Vietnam. I have already touched on the East-West thaw and the increasing multipolarity in the international system. According to a Foreign Ministry official, these various developments in the international environment reinforced the belief that Malaysia "made steps in the right direction" when it opted for a neutralist foreign policy despite cautioning by its allies and neighbours.

The most important domestic developments affecting the direction of foreign policy were the events arising out of the May 13 incident as this resulted in a leadership shift. More importantly, this led to the entrenchment of a more dominant Malay leadership with high agential power in domestic as well as foreign affairs. Admittedly, the process of foreign policy rethinking had already begun in the aftermath of *Konfrontasi*, as noted in the previous chapter. However, it was really the May 13 events with its resultant leadership changes that brought about the final crystallization of the inchoate foreign policy changes of the second period. May 13 notwithstanding, the inherently "stable" internal sources remained as important determinants of foreign policy. Under the existing state-centric world order, security needs would continue to demand attention although Malaysia in this period was able to pursue an imaginative strategy of regional security with minimal emphasis on defence to fulfil these needs. Despite this, expenditure on security (including that on internal security) ran at a 17 per cent share of the Federal Budget (*Economic Report* 1974–75, p. 3). Similarly, developmental needs continued to dominate Malaysia's economic policies although a number of domestic events and developments — on which I shall elaborate later — changed to some extent the character or definition of such needs. Status needs, while always present, may have receded in importance by the end of the period, following Malaysia's acceptance as a full-fledged member of the NAM group of nations.

Finally, at the elite level of foreign policy determinants, using a constructivist approach, one could say that the new elite ideology with a new set of interests, norms, and ideas, developed largely out of a leadership shift in the ruling party. The new elite ideology reflected the ascendancy of a younger (or newer) crop of UMNO leaders under a prime minister who was generally receptive to new ideas. As subsequent events proved, the top echelons of the newer group drew its support from a larger supportive core of UMNO rank and file who had been dissatisfied with the policies of the Tunku era. In foreign policy matters, the new elite ideology took its theoretical underpinnings from the tenets of "Third Worldism" and economic nationalism which was discussed earlier.

In my analysis then, the new elite ideology acted as the phenomenological filter for all the other various sources of foreign policy, rendering them into a new set of foreign policy objectives, postures, strategies, and actions. This was especially evident in the issue area of policy outputs in the security and economic issue areas. The elite ideology dominated almost all the important actions in these issue areas via its foreign policy postures of economic nationalism and neutralism, and its central strategy of promoting a zone of neutrality in Southeast Asia. Towards the end of the period, there was some indication that the creative phase of foreign policy initiatives was replaced by a phase in which actions flowed almost automatically from the prevailing elite ideology. The almost automatic recognition of the new Indo-china governments is indicative of this routinization of foreign policy. But more significantly, the elevation of Special Functions Minister Tengku Rithauddeen to foreign minister in August 1975 showed that foreign policy had become perhaps sufficiently clear-cut for another man other than the premier to hold the portfolio.[52] Tengku Rithauddeen was thus the third person other than the prime minister to hold the foreign minister's portfolio ever since the late Dr Ismail relinquished it after holding it briefly in 1960.

In Chapter 4, we demonstrated the importance of the feedback process in affecting the course of Malaysian foreign policy. The impact of *Konfrontasi* with its train of developments was especially important. While in that period there was a preponderance of negative feedback effects, in the third period, feedback from both the internal and external environment tended to be positive. The shift in foreign policy under Tun Razak was well taken at home as even opposition members of Parliament supported the new policy thrusts.[53] Abroad, Malaysia's new posture of neutralism was generally well received and finally won it a place in the NAM group of nations. As for its neutralization strategy, there appeared to be no adverse reactions to the proposal although the virtual lack of response from the great powers and varying enthusiasm among Malaysia's Asian and ASEAN neighbours prompted slight shifts in the strategy. The feedback on the scheme has never been severely negative, but the changing nature of the proposal does suggest that Malaysia was responding to the varying feedback on the scheme. The scheme had its roots in the Ismail proposals of 1968, but was officially publicized only in 1970 in Lusaka as a European-styled neutralization of Southeast Asia with great power guarantee. The emphasis then shifted to the ASEAN-initiated proposal of ZOPFAN or for some form of a "neutrality system".

Two main factors affected the change of emphasis in the scheme. The first was the lack of great power response, except fir China's verbal assurance that it supported the scheme.[54] More importantly, Malaysia's Southeast-East Asian, particularly, ASEAN, neighbours showed a varied response to the original scheme and were not equally enthusiastic about the plan for zonal neutrality. Singapore, for example, was known to prefer some form of great power participation in the region in some kind of counterweight or balance of power system. This could presumably occur within a neutrality system which allows access to major powers. Thailand and Indonesia were perhaps closer to Malaysia in wanting great power disengagement from the area, while the Philippines did not indicate its intention to ask the United States to withdraw from its military bases. The other countries of Southeast Asia, Burma and the Indo-China states, would clearly not have participated in any neutrality system without total great power disengagement from the area. It seemed therefore that Malaysia's neutralization strategy had to remain flexible and subject to minor adjustments, depending on political developments in the region. The evolution of the neutralization scheme indicates therefore the importance of the feedback process on foreign policy which can be briefly traced in Figure 5.4 mentioned above. In the economic issue areas, the elite ideology with its new emphasis on economic nationalism led to more radical, or at any rate, aggressive strategies and actions in the pursuit of economic objectives. For the most part domestic factors caused the change in policy. As indicated in Figure 5.5 and in Figure 5.4, the changes in policy may be seen as internal long-term feedback effects.

Malaysia's *laissez-faire* policies in the previous periods (particularly during the first) led to a high level of foreign ownership and control of the economy. This resulted in a redefinition of economic needs with the New Economic Policy as a direct response. However, many of the major tenets of the NEP reflect purely political inputs. They nevertheless indirectly relate to the question of foreign ownership. This is true, for example, for the 30 per cent targets of Bumiputera wealth, ownership, and management, the achievement of which would *ipso facto* result in a lower percentage in the level of foreign capital. The transformation in elite ideology (in economic matters) from the pristine capitalist-free enterprise variety of the first period to a capitalist-interventionist kind provided a further impetus for the new directions in economic policies. The end result of all the various domestic inputs and their interaction thereof, as shown in Figure 5.4, was the shift in economic posture. While Malaysia's new posture of economic nationalism sprung from the domestic processes just discussed, its developing-world orientation continued to be a direct function of its developmental needs, on which I have already elaborated. Malaysia's

FIGURE 5.5
Neutralization Policy

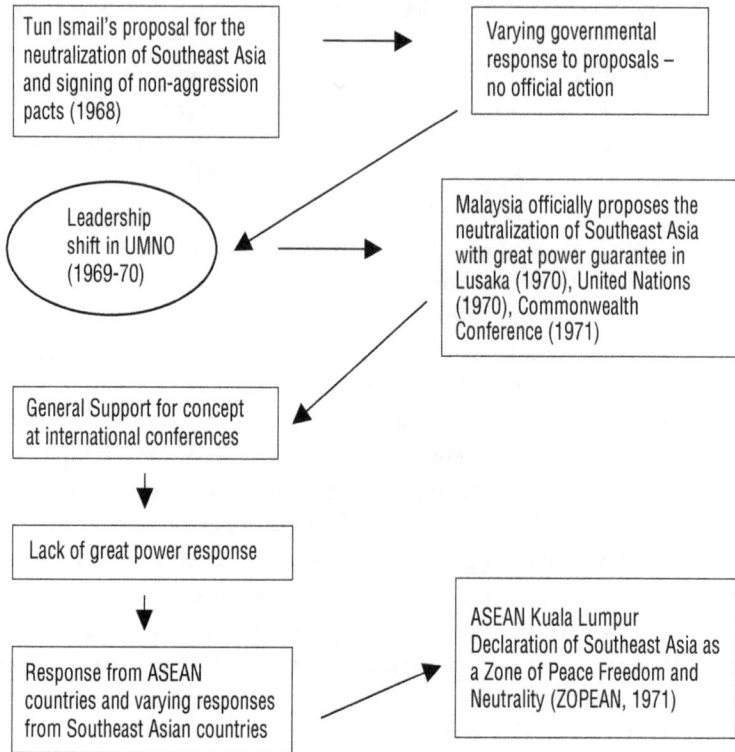

| Tun Ismail's proposal for the neutralization of Southeast Asia and signing of non-aggression pacts (1968) | → | Varying governmental response to proposals – no official action |

Leadership shift in UMNO (1969-70)

Malaysia officially proposes the neutralization of Southeast Asia with great power guarantee in Lusaka (1970), United Nations (1970), Commonwealth Conference (1971)

General Support for concept at international conferences

Lack of great power response

Response from ASEAN countries and varying responses from Southeast Asian countries

ASEAN Kuala Lumpur Declaration of Southeast Asia as a Zone of Peace Freedom and Neutrality (ZOPEAN, 1971)

Source: Author's own illustration.

economic objectives were in turn a function of the nation's developing world orientation, but the manner in which these objectives were sought was clearly affected by its posture of economic nationalism.

There was also some indication of external feedback effects on Malaysia's new economic nationalism posture and some of its resultant policies by the end of the period. Cases in point were the negative reactions to the Petronas Development (Amendment) Act and the various actions of Petronas and Pernas Securities Chairman Tengku Razaleigh. The most severe reaction was the withdrawal of Exxon from prospecting for oil off the east coast of Peninsula Malaysia. By the end of 1975, Malaysian spokesmen, including the prime minister, had begun ensuring investors of Malaysia's continued policy of welcome towards foreign investment. The slight backtracking did not, however, amount to a renunciation of the posture of economic nationalism although it was clear that Malaysian spokesmen would in future probably be less aggressive or antagonistic towards foreign enterprise. It was common knowledge that the various moves and pronouncements of Tengku Razaleigh were calculated with specific political ends in view, earning him, in particular, a vice-president's post in UMNO, and the "*Bapa Ekonomi* Malaysia" title. Discussions with various government and public persons gave indication that Tengku Razaleigh's actions were not altogether well received in many government agencies and Ministries.[55] It was therefore not entirely unexpected that Malaysia would eventually soften what appeared to have become a hard line nationalistic economic posture.

In the issue area of international cooperation, the most significant change here was that the various policy outputs became more closely identified with those of the defence and security issue area. This largely reflected a shift in the perception of the policymakers in which the pursuit of international cooperation and peace was seen to be closely related to the pursuit of security, particularly regional security. Thus while in the one case, the short-range goals of defence receded into the background in favour of the medium-range goals of security, in the other case, the more distant goals of global collective security, for example, made way for what was thought to be the more attainable goal of regional security via zonal neutrality. In discussions with Wisma Putra officials, I was given to understand that the main thrust of Malaysian foreign policy was towards regional security and ASEAN was the avenue through which this could most reasonably be attained. In general, the Foreign Ministry had become less idealistic about the more distant international institutions, including the United Nations and its agencies. Under the organizational structure of the Ministry of Foreign Affairs in 1975, the United Nations was put together with "Non-aligned Conferences, Americas and Africa, South of Sahara". In 1958, the corresponding desk was "U.N. and International Institutions". In 1958, there was also no special desk for Southeast Asia, the overall desk being "Asia, Australia and Africa". In 1975, there were two Southeast Asia desks, one for ASEAN members, and one for non-ASEAN members and there was an undersecretary for economics who was also secretary general for ASEAN.[56]

Malaysia also began to highlight its ties with the Muslim world and here ideological and cultural compatibility were perhaps exploited with an eye towards economic and other real gains. Pragmatism became the order of the day as the significance of status needs, assiduously pursued in the first period, receded as sources of foreign policy. Figure 5.4 provides a charting of the various sources of policy in this issue area as they relate to the policy outputs.

Appendix 5.1

FIVE POWER DEFENCE ARRANGEMENT, 1971

Comununiqué issued at the Conclusion of the Five-Power Ministerial Meeting on the External Defence of Malaysia and Singapore, London, 15–16 April 1971

1. Ministers of the Government of Australia, Malaysia, New Zealand, Singapore and the United Kingdom met in London on 15th and 16th April 1971, in order to consider matters of common interest to all five Governments relating to the external defence of Malaysia and Singapore.

2. The Ministers of the five Governments affirmed, as the basic principles of their discussions, their continuing determination to work together for peace and stability, their respect for the sovereignty, political independence and territorial integrity of all countries, and their belief in the settlement of all international disputes by peaceful means in accordance with the principles of the United Nations Charter.

3. In the context of their Governments' determination to continue to co-operate closely in defence arrangements which are based on the need to regard the defence of Malaysia and Singapore as indivisible, the Ministers noted with gratification on the development of the defence capability of Malaysia and Singapore, to which the other three Governments had given assistance, and the decisions of the Governments of Australia, New Zealand and the United Kingdom, which had been welcomed by the other two Governments, to continue to station forces there after the end of 1971.

4. In discussing the contribution which each of the five Governments would make to defence arrangements in Malaysia and Singapore, the Ministers noted the view of the United Kingdom Government that the nature of its commitment under the Anglo-Malaysian Defence Agreement required review and that the Agreement should be replaced by new political arrangements. They declared that their Governments would continue to co-operate, in accordance with their respective policies, in the field of defence after the termination of the Agreement on 1st November 1971.

5. The Ministers also declared, in relation to the external defence of Malaysia and Singapore, that in the event of any form of armed attack externally organised or supported or the threat of such attack against Malaysia and Singapore, their Governments would immediately consult together for the purpose of deciding

what measures should be taken jointly or separately in relation to such attack or threat.

6. The Ministers reviewed the progress made regarding the establishment of the new defence arrangements. In particular:

- They welcomed the practical steps being taken to establish the Integrated Air Defence System for Malaysia and Singapore on Ist September 1971.
- They agreed to establish an Air Defence Council, comprising one senior representative of each of the five nations, to be responsible for the functioning of the Integrated Air Defence System, and to provide direction to the Commander of the Integrated Air Defence System on matters affecting the organization, training and development and operational readiness of the system.
- They noted the progress made by the Five Power Naval Advisory Working Group.
- They decided to set up a Joint Consultative Council to provide a forum for regular consultation at the senior official level on matters relating to the defence arrangements.

Ministers also noted that further discussion would take place between Governments on the practical arrangements required for the accommodation and facilities for the ANZUK forces to be stationed in the area. They looked forward to the early and successful conclusion of these discussions as an essential basis for the completion of plans for the new defence arrangements.

7. The Ministers agreed that from time to time it might be appropriate for them to meet to discuss their common interests. It would also be open to any of them, the participating Governments to request at any time, with due notice, a meeting to review these defence arrangements.

Source: Saravanamuttu (1983, pp. 176–77).

Appendix 5.2

KUALA LUMPUR DECLARATION, 1971

Kuala Lumpur Declaration by ASEAN Foreign Ministers of Southeast Asia as a Zone of Peace, Freedom and Neutrality, 27 November 1971

WE the Foreign Ministers of Indonesia, Malaysia, the Philippines, Singapore and the Special Envoy of the National Executive Council of Thailand:

Firmly believing in the merits of regional co-operation which has drawn our countries to co-operate together in the economic, social and cultural fields in the Association of Southeast Asian Nations.

Desirous of bringing about a relaxation of international tension and of achieving a lasting peace in Southeast Asia.

Inspired by the worthy aims and objectives of the United Nations, in particular by the principles of respect for the sovereignty and territorial integrity of all States, abstention from the threat or use of force, peaceful settlement of international disputes, equal rights and self-determination and non-interference in the internal affairs of States.

Believing in the continuing validity of the "Declaration on the Promotion of World Peace and Co-operation" of the Bandung Conference of 1955, which, among others, enunciates the principles by which States may co-exist peacefully.

Recognising the right of every State, large or small, to lead its national existence free from outside interference in its internal affairs as this interference will adversely affect its freedom, independence and integrity.

Dedicated to the maintenance of peace, freedom and independence unimpaired.

Believing in the need to meet challenges and new developments by co-operating with all peace and freedom loving nations, both within and outside the region, in the furtherance of world peace, stability and harmony.

Cognizant of the significant trend towards establishing nuclear-free zones, as in the "Treaty for the Prohibition of Nuclear Weapons in Latin America" and the Lusaka Declaration proclaiming Africa a nuclear-free zone, for the purpose of promoting world peace and security by reducing the areas of international conflicts and tensions.

Reiterating our commitment to the principle in the Bangkok Declaration which established ASEAN in 1967, "that the countries of Southeast Asia share a primary responsibility for strengthening the economic and social stability of the region and ensuring their peaceful and progressive national development, and that they are determined to ensure their stability and security from external interference in any form or manifestation in order to preserve their national identities in accordance with the ideals and aspirations of their people."

Agreeing that the neutralization of Southeast Asia is a desirable objective and that we should explore ways and means of bringing about its realization, and

Convinced that the time is propitious for joint action to give effective expression to the deeply desire of the peoples of Southeast Asia to ensure the conditions of peace and stability indispensable to their independence and their economic and social well-being:

Do hereby state:

1. That Indonesia, Malaysia, the Philippines, Singapore and Thailand are determined to exert initially necessary efforts to secure the recognition of, and respect for, Southeast Asia as Zone of Peace, Freedom and Neutrality, free from any form or manner of interference by outside Powers.

2. That Southeast Asia countries should make concerted efforts to broaden the areas of co-operation which would contribute to their strength, solidarity and closer relationship.

Source: Saravanamuttu (1983, pp. 178–79).

NOTES

1. The points mentioned here are taken from the two following documents: Treaty of Friendship between the Federation of Malaya and the Republic of Indonesia (1959) and Treaty of Friendship between the Government of Malaysia and the Republic of Indonesia (1970) in *Perjanjian Kerajaan Malaysia dengan Kerajaan Asing* (1973).
2. See Pathmanathan (1973, pp. 189–90), who points out that Malaysia had in 1969 unilaterally declared the extension of its territorial waters to 12 miles under the Emergency (Essential Powers) Ordinance, No. 7.
3. See "Straits of Malacca and Singapore -Joint Statement", *Foreign Affairs Malaysia* 4 (1971): 54.
4. Interview with L.C. Vohra, head, International Law Division, Ministry of Law and Attorney-General Chambers, 21 May 1975.
5. The participating countries were Australia, Indonesia, Japan, Republic of Korea, Laos, Malaysia, the Philippines, Singapore, Thailand, and the Republic of Vietnam, *Foreign Affairs Malaysia* 5 (1970): 52.
6. The Lusaka Conference was held from 8–10 September. Tun Razak returned to Malaysia and assumed the prime ministership on 22 September.
7. Retrieved from *Foreign Affairs Malaysia* 3 (1970): 16.
8. Ibid., p. 14.
9. See Ghazali Shafie 1971, pp. 51–52.
10. Retrieved from *Foreign Affairs Malaysia* 4 (1971): 58.
11. Address by prime minister, Tun Abdul Razak at the opening of the Eighth ASEAN Ministerial Meeting, 13 May 1975, *Siaran Akhbar* (Kuala Lumpur: Jabatan Penerangan).
12. The points discussed here are taken from Ghazali Shafie (1974).
13. Interview with Encik Yusof Hitam, undersecretary III, Southeast Asia, Ministry of Foreign Affairs, 27 June 1975.
14. Speech retrieved from *Foreign Affairs Malaysia* 3 (1970): 57.
15. Retrieved from *Foreign Affairs Malaysia* 7 (1974): 52–53.
16. See ibid., pp. 56–57. These "assurances" did not, however, prevent the People's Republic from sending a congratulatory message to the MCP in April 1975, a little over a year after the establishment of diplomatic relations. Malaysia protested the Chinese action and said that relations would not remain as "cordial" if the practice continued. The episode did not however, trigger a serious strain in ties, the Chinese action being probably routine rather that premeditated.
17. Address by the prime minister at the opening of the Eight ASEAN Ministerial Meeting 13 May 1975.
18. Ibid.
19. Retrieved from *Foreign Affairs Malaysia* 5 (1971): 38.
20. Retrieved from *Foreign Affairs Malaysia* 3 (1970): 43.
21. Statistics drawn from *Economic Report 1974–75*, p. 26.

22. While oil revenues are recycled into industrial countries, the LDCs which have little to sell are left out of the cycle. Moreover, they are saddled with the higher oil prices.

23. Interview with Yee Che Fong, Deputy Director, International Trade Division, Ministry of Trade and Industry, 31 May 1975.

24. See *Second Malaysian Plan 1971–1975* (Kuala Lumpur: Government Printer, 1971), pp. 41–42.

25. See *Mid-Term Review of the Second Malaysia Plan, 1971–1975*, p. 85.

26. See *Malaysia Industrial Digest* 8 (1975): 5.

27. See *Economic Report 1974–75*, p. 111. See also "Industrial Development in Malaysia and Incentives for Investment" (Speech by J. Jegathesan, director, Investment Promotion, FIDA, given at the Malaysia Investment Conference, London, May 1975). Mimeographed.

28. Less than $250,000 — two years; more than $250,000 — three years; more than $500,000 — four years; and more than $1 million — five years (*Economic Report 1974–75*, p. 111).

29. These were (a) the location of a factory in a development area (b) if the product was a priority product and (c) if the required percentage of Malaysian content in the employment of resources was attained (ibid.).

30. From 51–100 employees, two years; 101–200, three years; 201–350, four years; 350 and above, five years (ibid., p. 112).

31. Malaysia, *Petroleum Development Act*, 1974.

32. Malaysia, *Petroleum Development (Amendment) Act*, 1975. According to the Act, "the holder of management shares of a relevant company shall be entitled either on a poll or by a show of hands to five hundred votes for each management share held by him upon any resolution relating to the appointment or dismissal of a director or any member of the staff of the relevant company" (ibid., p. 6). Since each management share is equivalent to 500 ordinary shares, the government's 1 per cent will give it more than five times the number of shares held by other shareholders. In fact, it needed hold only 0.2 per cent of management shares to have a slight edge over the other shareholders. (If x represents shares, 0.2 per cent of management shares is equal to $0.2 \times 500x = 100x$, whereas 99.8 per cent of ordinary shares is equal to only 99.8x).

33. Informal discussions with a senior oil company executive, various journalists, and government officials. See also *New Straits Times*, 26 May 1975, in which the Chairman of the Chinese Chamber of Commerce calls on the government not to "deviate from the principle of the free economic system" and adopt quasi-nationalization policies.

34. Interview with M. Shanmughalingam, deputy undersecretary, Economic Division, Treasury, 19 May 1975.

35. Perbadanan Nasional (National Corporation), or PERNAS, was formed in September 1969, roughly coinciding with the enunciation of the NEP. "Pernas Securities" is a wholly-owned subsidiary of PERNAS, and operates in the

commercial sector like any private company. Razaleigh subsequently became chairman of Pernas Securities after relinquishing chairmanship of PERNAS.

36. Island and Peninsula Development is one of the largest housing developers in Malaysia and Singapore, with interests in tin, rubber, and oil palm. London Tin Corporation is a Britain-based company with major shares in twelve tin mining companies in Malaysia, Thailand, and Nigeria, and Sime Darby is a Malaysia-based company with interests in rubber, tin, and various industries. See *Far Eastern Economic Review*, 13 June 1975, pp. 55–56.

37. The deal initially appeared to be a cleverly manoeuvred "reverse swop" whereby Pernas Securities was to surrender all its holdings to Haw Par for its controlling 40670 stake in the company which would then have controlling interests in Island and Peninsular and London Tin Corporation. The deal was abandoned when Haw Par was suspended by the Singapore government, which subsequently authorized an investigation into the company's alleged mismanagement. See *Far Eastern Economic Review*, 13 June 1975, pp. 55–56; *New Straits Times*, 23 July 1975.

38. In a hotly contested race, Razaleigh emerged with the second highest number of votes for the three vice-president posts up for election (*New Straits Times*, 22 June 1975).

39. *New Straits Times*, 7 July 1975. Following Tun Razak's death in 1976, Razaleigh became finance minister in Prime Minister Hussein Onn's Cabinet.

40. Interview with Zainal Aznam, deputy secretary, Foreign Investment Committee, Economic Planning Unit, Prime Minister's Department, 29 May 1975.

41. The other stipulations were that such mergers and takeovers should lead directly or indirectly to net economic benefits in the extent of Malaysian, especially *Bumiputera*, participation, ownership and management, income redistribution, growth, employment, exports, quality range of products and services, economic diversification, processing and upgrading of local raw materials, training, efficiency, and research and development. See *Guidelines for the Regulation of Acquisition of Assets, Mergers and Takeovers*, 1974, pp. 2–3.

42. Address by Prime Minister Tun Abdul Razak to the Eighth ASEAN Ministerial Meeting 13 May 1975.

43. Statement by Tan Sri Dato Haji Abdul Kadir bin Yusof, attorney general of Malaysia to the Plenary Session of the Third United Nations Conference on the Law of the Sea, Caracas, 10 July 1975.

44. Address by Prime Minister Tun Abdul Razak at the opening ceremony of the Fifth Islamic Conference of Foreign Ministers, 21 June 1974, Kuala Lumpur (*Foreign Affairs Malaysia* 7 (1974): 65 and 67).

45. The term was used to describe the extremist elements in regard to Malay demands within UMNO and the Malay community at large. In Tunku's book, among such "ultras" were Dr Mahathir and Datuk Musa Hitam who later rose to prominence in Tun Razak's tenure. They became even more prominent subsequently.

46. The Tunku is referring here to the furore arising from the controversial National

Language Bill of 1967, the upshot of which the director of the Dewan Bahasa dan Pustaka (Language and Literary Institute), Syed Nasir, an acknowledged ultra, was sacked from the UMNO Executive Council for agitating against the slowness of implementing Malay as the sole official language. See Roff (1967, pp. 316–28).

47. Seven years after 13 May, Mahathir became the surprise choice of Premier Hussein Onn for deputy prime minister. See *New Straits Times*, 2 March 1976.

48. A more radical thesis has been propounded by Kua (2007) that May 13 was an event orchestrated by "Malay state capitalists" to oust the Tunku. This corresponds with my idea of the emergence of a "counter-elite", whether May 13 was planned or not. Kua used declassified documents from the British Public Records Office to make his case. I find that too much of Kua's argument is *ex post facto* reasoning and the documents consulted are from British diplomats and foreign correspondents, which provide no unassailable proof for Kua's thesis. However, I do take the well known point that the anti-Tunku forces within UMNO was out to remove him. This said, the persons who took the helm after 13 May were Razak and Ismail, close associates of the Tunku, who clearly tried to accommodate these forces.

49. According to a close aide, none of Razak's speeches, even when he was the Tunku's deputy, could be said to be blatantly anti-communist or pro-West and he (Razak) had always put a premium on Afro-Asian relations. (Interview with Zain Azraai, special principal assistant secretary to the prime minister, 1 November 1975.)

50. The memoirs are in part contained in *Tun Ismail Papers*, Folio 5 (1 & 2), *Notes by the Ambassador*.

51. In line with this strategy, the government launched the *Rukun Tetangga* (Community Self-Reliance) scheme, which calls for the citizenry to participate in community security.

52. In the light of revelations about Tun Razak's failing health, this factor may have prompted the prime minister to give up the portfolio a little earlier than he had intended.

53. Interviews with Dr Tan Chee Khoon, MP, chairman Pekemas, 22 May 1975; Lim Kit Siang, MP, chairman DAP, 10 July 1975; and Fan Yew Teng, MP, DAP, 9 July 1975.

54. The Soviet Union has itself made a vague proposal for an Asian Collective Security System. See Simon (1975, pp. 64–74).

55. Interviews with various government officials and journalists who prefer to remain anonymous.

56. See Chapter 2 for a discussion of the expansion of ASEAN desks in the MFA.

6

CONSOLIDATING REGIONALISM IN A CHANGING WORLD, 1976–77

NEW SECURITY ISSUES

The ascendance of Datuk Hussein Onn as prime minister following the unexpected death of Tun Razak did not appear to affect foreign policy in fundamentals. Although the prime minister lost little time in familiarizing himself with foreign relations in Southeast Asia, making official visits to Singapore, Jakarta, and Bangkok within two weeks in power, Hussein's relative inexperience in foreign policy matters meant that newly appointed Foreign Minister Tengku Rithaudeen would, by and large, follow through the initiatives and maintain positions enunciated in the Razak period.[1] By now foreign policy had become fairly stabilized in that actions flowed logically, if not almost automatically, from established postures and strategies which became familiar positions at international forums or conferences. The fundamental posture in the security issue area was neutralism or non-alignment and the chief strategy remained the promotion of a neutral zone in Southeast Asia.

However, there was clearly a major disruption in the regional politics of Southeast Asia stemming from the aftermath of the Vietnam War. Developments towards the end of the period strained the incipient moves of rapprochement between ASEAN and the Indo-China states, in which Malaysia played a significant part. The massive exodus of "boat people" from Vietnam and the intractable "Kampuchea" problem were the two major issues leading to a political impasse and stalemate. Even before Hussein Onn assumed the levers of government, hundreds of "boat people" began to land on Malaysian shores after Saigon's surrender in April 1975 to North Vietnam. The first wave of refugees was thought to be Catholics and later, thousands of urban Chinese landed on Malaysian beaches (Means 1991, p. 75). Then the Vietnamese invasion of Cambodia in April 1976 sparked a second wave, creating a huge refugee problem which, while mainly affecting Thailand, saw many more refugees coming to Malaysia. The third wave of refugees came after China's short and intensive "teach-Vietnam-a lesson" war of February and March 1979. Those escaping Vietnam were mainly Chinese from the North and South who feared reprisals from the Vietnamese. By 1978, 64,328 refugees had landed in Malaysia, and by 1979, some 166,709 found their way there. According to Gordon Means, "Since those who came from Vietnam were 70–80 per cent Chinese, the Malaysian authorities were distressed not only by the numbers but by the fear that the new refugees would 'upset Malaysia's racial balance'" (Means 1991, p. 75). The upshot was Deputy Prime Minister and Home Minister Mahathir Mohamad announcing on 15 June 1979 that refugees landing on Malaysian shores would be shot, which then sparked an international controversy.[2] According to Wain (1998, p. 275), Mahathir never denied the statement, saying merely that he was misunderstood, volunteering to a U.S. congressional delegation that he said, "we will do everything short of shooting them for which we would need the approval of Parliament". Foreign Minister Ghazali Shafie weighed in to say that what was meant was "shoo on sight". Prime Minister Hussein Onn denied there would be action such as shooting although it was official policy to refuse asylum from that date. Although no refugees were shot, the public outcry ironically accelerated the repatriation of the refugees to third countries. Malaysia, on its part, had "processed" more than 80,000 boat refugees who had landed on its shores and with ASEAN support had succeeded in reducing the refugee problem to manageable proportions, after urging for the convening of a Geneva Conference in July 1979. Malaysia's handling of what is one of the most tragic humanitarian episodes of modern history, will, at the end of the day go on record as a triumph for sanity, even if at points its actions and policies verged on the limit of callousness.[3]

Thus one could say that the Hussein Onn government was partly blessed by a stable foreign policy laid down by Tun Abdul Razak, but this did not absolve his government from dealing with new, complex regional development, emanating especially from the Indo-China states of Southeast Asia. Early indications of the imperative to address the situation came in the somewhat rapid fire recognition of the Provisional Revolutionary Government of South Vietnam (subsequently, the reunified Socialist Republic of Vietnam), Democratic Kampuchea, and the People's Democratic Republic of Laos, and the establishment of diplomatic relations at the ambassadorial level with the new Indo-China governments by 1976. While it may be true that foreign policy in fundamentals had become stabilized, it would be a mistake to suggest Malaysia undertook no new foreign policy initiatives. Indeed the external, in particular Southeast Asian environment, as mentioned above, had by no means remained unchanged. The new Indo-China situation demanded more than just standard responses to the question of defence and security for non-communist Southeast Asia. It was this situation that perhaps prompted Malaysia and its ASEAN partners into holding the first meeting of ASEAN heads of government in Bali in February 1976 after eight years of ASEAN's existence. The historic Bali summit produced two important documents — the Declaration of ASEAN Concord and the Treaty of Amity and Cooperation.

The treaties, however, were somewhat predictable. In Malaysia, the late prime minister, the foreign minister, and Wisma Putra officials had alluded fairly often to a so-called "blueprint" for the region's neutralization on which senior ASEAN officials had been working for some time. The Bali agreements were evidently the products of these earlier efforts. The treaties, however, fell short of any concept of neutralization, but may provide a useful construct along with the Kuala Lumpur Declaration of 1971, for what Malaysia hopes will eventually result in some form of a neutrality system in the region. The Bali accords do in themselves represent the most significant self-reflexive Southeast Asian multilateral agreements to emerge out of the political cauldron of a turbulent region. They thus merit our consideration, particularly in terms of their implications for Malaysia's foreign policy in the security issue area.

The ASEAN Declaration of Concord reaffirmed the declarations of Bandung, Bangkok, and Kuala Lumpur, and the U.N. Charter and went on to specify the following broad objectives and principles in pursuit of regional cooperation:

- Resolving to eliminate subversive threats to stability through national and ASEAN resilience, resolving to individually and collectively pursue actively the early establishment of a zone of peace, freedom, and neutrality.
- Intensifying cooperative efforts to eliminate poverty, hunger, disease, and illiteracy in ASEAN states.
- Assisting and relieving member states in distress in the event of natural disasters and other major calamities.
- Cooperating in the harmonization of national and regional development programmes to complement each other's economies.
- Relying exclusively on pacific processes in the settlement of intraregional differences.
- Developing vigorously an awareness of regional identity and creating a strong ASEAN community based on mutually advantageous relationships

and the principles of self-determination, sovereignty, equality, and non-interference in internal affairs of other states.

While the Declaration of ASEAN Concord emphasized the more general areas of cooperation, the Treaty of Amity and Cooperation specified the manner in which political cooperation was to take place. In fact, it was political consensus that saved the day at Bali given that the Singapore-Philippine lobby for a free trade zone or customs union fell through on account of an Indonesian damper on the proposal. Malaysia lobbied strongest for the amity treaty which Hussein Onn described as "the first wholly indigenous multilateral treaty in the entire history of Southeast Asia" (*New Straits Times*, 1 March 1976). The ASEAN leaders went to great lengths to disclaim any military provisions in the treaty in anticipation of adverse reactions from the Indo-China states. The treaty, while certainly not a military pact, is perhaps superior to a friendship treaty or non-aggression pact in that it included mechanisms for the pacific settlement of conflict. (Rao and Rosss-Larson 1977, p. 182). Among its major provisions were:

- That establishment of a Ministerial High Council which can provide good offices, enquire into, mediate, and conciliate disputes referred to it by the signatories (Article 15). [The proviso is that the parties to the dispute must agree to such action after direct negotiations between them offers no solution].
- That the signatories should refrain from the use of threat or force and that disputes should at all times be settled through friendly negotiations (Article 13).
- That the signatories should exhaust the regional pacific settlement machinery before resorting to U.N. Charter procedures (Article 17).
- That the signatories should endeavour to cooperate in all fields for the promotion of regional resilience, based on the principles of self-confidence, self-resilience, mutual respect, cooperation, and solidarity (Article 12).
- That the treaty be open for accession by other states in Southeast Asia (Article 18).

The last mentioned provision and the persistent references to its non-military character by the ASEAN heads were obviously in response to the Indo-China states, in particular, the Socialist Republic of Vietnam (SRV or North Vietnam), which on the eve of the Bali Meeting, launched a scathing attack on ASEAN as an American-inspired bloc used "to carry out US neo-colonialist policy to oppose the patriotic and progressive movements in

Southeast Asia" (Chan 1977, p. 18). The ASEAN leaders' tactic of leaving the treaty open for accession by all Southeast Asian states was aimed both at defusing the Indochina criticism of ASEAN, and also as a positive peace overture to these countries.

The Bali overture appeared to have had some effect on the Vietnamese, who sent their deputy foreign minister, Phan Hien, on a swing through the ASEAN countries (Thailand excepted) after Foreign Affairs Minister Nguyen Duy Trinh had proclaimed as Hanoi's policy, the five peaceful coexistence principles, and made reference to the peaceful settlement of disputes through negotiations and the building of prosperity in keeping with genuine neutrality (Rao and Ross-Larson 1977, p. 19). Phan Hien, for his part, officially relayed Hanoi's conciliatory attitude towards ASEAN and was warmly, if not enthusiastically, received in Malaysia where he was reportedly alleged to have supported ZOPFAN and even hinted at the SRV's possible entry into ASEAN (*Asia 1977 Yearbook*, p. 230).

The euphoria of Wisma Putra towards Hanoi's moves was short-circuited by the turn of events at the Non-aligned Nations Conference in Colombo in August that year. Amidst suggestions of a superpower plot, Laos, with Vietnamese support, blocked Malaysia's efforts to seek a reaffirmation of the K.L. Declaration. The Laotians found the proposal unacceptable on the rather predictable stance that:

> The KL Declaration was issued at the time when the US was intensifying their war of aggression in Indochina in order to cover up the participation of the ASEAN countries in the US war of aggression in Laos, Vietnam and Cambodia and to fool world public opinion into thinking that ASEAN countries had good intentions. (Chan 1977, p. 20)

While Hussein and Rithaudeen returned to Kuala Lumpur visibly annoyed at what Wisma Putra officials called an "absurd show", these negative inputs failed to ruffle the Malaysian foreign minister who reportedly said a few days later:

> Through our new ambassador (to Vietnam) Yusof Hitam, we will pursue through the new closer contact our foremost foreign policy objective of promoting a zone of peace, freedom and neutrality in our region ... It will take time ... We need peace, freedom and neutrality to prosper, and we are prepared to work, understand other points of view and consider other aspirations to this end, so long as our views, hope and aspirations are equally understood and sympathized with. (Asia 1977 Yearbook, p. 230)

It is evident from Rithaudeen's statement that Malaysia was not prepared to budge from its neutralization proposal and considered the Laotian rebuff no more than a minor setback for what was clearly considered the most significant plank of Malaysia's security policy. Instead, Malaysia sought the support of major powers. Deng Xiaoping, China's then vice-premier, visited Malaysia in 1979 in the midst of its war with Vietnam, and although Malaysia was unable to get China to cut its symbolic links with the MCP, both sides agreed to checking Soviet and Vietnamese expansionism in the region. Moreover, in September 1979, Hussein visited the Soviet Union, Vietnam's ally, and secured from President Brezhnev, "a guarantee of non-aggression by Vietnam" (Means 1991, p. 77).

On the border and home fronts, security also took a couple of hard knocks in 1976. These came in the form of a temporary stoppage of cooperation with Thailand, following the Betong demonstrations by 10,000 of the Thai Sovereignty League in May. The development caused the home minister, Ghazali Shafie, to make the gloomy pronouncement that the Betong salient would be completely dominated by communists and that "to protect our national interest and survival we will have to regard that part of Thailand as hostile territory and the ramifications of such an attitude must not only be understood but also accepted by all" (Means 1991, p. 229). The matter was only partially resolved after a meeting of Hussein and Seni Pramoj, but subsequently virtual *carte blanche* was given for the "hot pursuit" of terrorists in Thai territory under the new right wing government of Thanin Kraivichien. By July 1977, Malaysian and Thai forces had launched a massive joint operation, "Cahaya Bena", involving some 10,000 troops, as well as air strikes in the Betong and Weang salients, Yala, and other known terrorist border areas, to demonstrate their cooperation on this issue.

Closer to home, politics was on the brew. Amidst charges of communist plot and conspiracy, levelled by the UMNO old guard and pro-Harun Idris elements, two deputy ministers and two journalists with evidently strong government connections were arrested and detained under the Internal Security Act (ISA). The Abdullah Ahmad-Abdullah Majid, Samad Ismail-Samani Amin arrests were seen as politically expedient, both to defuse old guard criticism of the government and a volatile internal security situation, but despite the obvious innuendo to discredit Tun Abdul Razak's government in the old guard attack, Prime Minister Hussein Onn allowed none of these domestic developments to affect materially the Razak's basic thrusts in foreign policy. Indeed the continued maintenance of neutralism in external security matters and the Indo-China overtures indicated that foreign policy remained fundamentally unshaken in a time of considerable domestic turbulence in the ruling Malay party.

The continued stability of policy was evident throughout 1977. In spite of the high expectations of the second ASEAN summit held in Kuala Lumpur, no new paths in policy were charted for the regional body or for its individual members. The only drama of the summit was President Marcos' announcement of dropping the fourteen-year old Sabah claim, later modified as an intention of making "definite steps" to eliminate the claim.[4] The 1977 summit came too close on the heels of Bali to be of any real significance. The presence of the Japanese, Australian, and New Zealand premiers suggested that the thrust of the summit was to be economics rather than politics. As it turned out, the ASEAN leaders merely reaffirmed an "offer of peace" to the Indo-China states, the final communiqué stressing ASEAN's desire to develop "peaceful and mutually beneficial relations with all countries in the region, including Kampuchea, Laos and Vietnam" (*Far Eastern Economic Review*, 19 August 1977). This emphasis on peace overtures to the Indo-China states was preceded by Malaysia's own unilateral diplomatic initiatives in forging bilateral links with Vietnam, including the proffering of technical assistance to help reconstruct Vietnam's battle-worn economy in matters ranging from rubber, palm oil, medical aid, port building, and road construction to telecommunications. Foreign Minister Tengku Rithaudeen on his two-leg tour of Hanoi and Vientiane made these offers three months before the KL summit.[5]

In the economic sphere, the KL summit reaffirmed the five regional industrialization projects of urea plants in Malaysia and Indonesia, Soda Ash in Thailand, diesel engines in Singapore and phosphate fertilizer in the Philippines, first proposed at Bali the year before. The ASEAN leaders were able to extract from Japan a pledge of US$5 million for the projects on the condition that "each is established as an ASEAN project". The Australians on their part pledged an increase of aid from A$90 million to A$250 million (Asia *1978 Yearbook*, p. 347).

In security matters, it was clear that Malaysia, on its own and through ASEAN, was determined to follow through its peace initiatives to Indo-China with a view to breaking down suspicions and forestalling a possible polarization of the region into non-communist ASEAN and communist (Indo-China) blocs. This general strategy of rapprochement with the communist states had been a stable post-Vietnam War strategy of Malaysia's foreign policy, in keeping with its professed non-aligned status and has characterized policy in the security issue area under the leadership of Datuk Hussein Onn and his Foreign Minister Tengku Rithaudeen. The general thrust of the strategy was already clearly suggested by Tun Razak in the wake of the communist victory in Indo-China. However, it was left largely to the

Hussein-Rithaudeen team to operationalize or concretize the strategy in terms of actual foreign policy actions. In particular, the Hussein government and its fellow ASEAN governments had to deal with the complex and thorny issue of Cambodia or Kampuchea. The tragic Cambodian conflict put Malaysia and ASEAN into a quandary when Vietnam sent some ten divisions of troops (200,000) into Democratic Kampuchea to topple the Pol Pot regime (largely acknowledged to have been responsible for the death of some one million Cambodians in the infamous "killing fields") in December 1978.[6] This was followed by a twenty-seven-day war of China with Vietnam in February and March 1979 (mentioned earlier), which plunged the region into a state of disequilibrium. These events may be said to have sparked the "Second Cold War" in the region as it did across the globe, given that the Indo-China-Soviet Union alliance began to materialize while the ASEAN states found themselves willy-nilly encamped on the side of the Americans and China.

It was around this time then that Malaysia and Indonesia took the initiative to propound and proclaim the so-called "Kuantan Doctrine". Believing that the Vietnamese action was in part motivated by its mistrust of China, President Soeharto and Premier Hussein Onn met in March 1980 at Kuantan, Pahang, and put forward a proposal which called for Vietnam to move to a position of neutrality between China and the Soviet Union. It was assumed at that time that this was an attempt by Malaysia and Indonesia to find a way out of the Cambodian impasse (Gyngell 1982, p. 133). The Kuantan declaration was followed by a call to form a U.N. peacekeeping force. The fact that Malaysia and Indonesia had to go it alone on this issue was indicative of splits within ASEAN over the Cambodia question, and views towards Indo-China in general. However, given Vietnam's commitment to the Heng Samrin regime and ASEAN's already established support for the exiled Coalition Government of Democratic Kumpuchea (CGDK), the Kuantan principle could be said to have expired stillborn. In the communiqué issued after the ASEAN Foreign Ministers' Meeting in Kuala Lumpur, three days after the Suharto-Hussein Onn meeting, ASEAN's broad policy was reiterated, namely that it:

> [S]trongly reaffirmed the solidarity of ASEAN member countries in, and their continued total commitment to, their position on the Kampuchea conflict, particularly on the fundamental issues of total withdrawal of Vietnamese forces from Kampuchea, the exercise of the right to self-determination of the Kampuchea people, free from outside interference, subversion and coercion and non-interference in the internal affairs of the states of Southeast Asia. (Gyngell, 1982, p. 134)

Malaysian foreign policy discourse and practice during this period had already been set on an even keel by the various Tun Razak initiatives. The underlying posture and policy of non-alignment and dependence on, as well as the use of, ASEAN to achieve its immediate and medium-range objectives associated with this broad foreign policy orientation was clearly evident. The Bali accords were the prime examples by which the Malaysian goal for neutralization of Southeast Asia saw a partial fulfilment, while its various attempts of overtures to the Indo-China states to become constructively engaged with ASEAN were perhaps more autonomous efforts made in the same general direction. These efforts were, however, rebuffed by the actual developments in Indo-China and, more broadly, by the general slide of world politics into the Second Cold War. The attempt by Malaysia and Indonesia to enunciate the stillborn Kuantan doctrine did, nonetheless, indicate that both these states were still more prepared to maintain non-alignment principles than were other ASEAN members. In the event, the two had to close ranks and toe the overall ASEAN line on Kampuchea. In one assessment, Malaysian and Indonesia constitute "the core of ASEAN".[7] Given that ASEAN's formation could not have come about had it not been for the Malaysian-Indonesian rapprochement in 1966, there is some truth to this assertion. It was also clear that in the formative years of ASEAN, the two countries had tended to initiate most of ASEAN's definitive agendas. On the Kampuchea question, however, it was obvious that Thailand was the so-called "frontline state" and its views became critical on most ASEAN matters regarding the conflict. ASEAN's growth over the years would make it more problematic to talk of core and non-core states, particularly when consensual decision making remains as its dominant policymaking practice. Towards the end of the Hussein Onn period in October 1980, Malaysia announced that it would provide aid to Thailand if it were threatened with military attacks. Malaysia at the same time increased its military expenditure by 56 per cent and arranged for the acquisition of eighty additional Sykhawk planes and an increase in its armed forces (Means 1991, p. 77). This indicated succinctly that in terms of Malaysian foreign policy, it was now necessary for ASEAN to close ranks on the Indo-China situation.

ECONOMIC CONCERNS

On the economic front, Malaysia's orientation remained closely aligned to Third World or Southern positions. In particular it adhered firmly to the growing Southern chorus for a New International Economic Order (NIEO), which was a refurbished version of the "New Economic World Order". As proof of Malaysia's earnestness, on the urging of the prime minister's cabinet colleagues, a national seminar was held towards the end of 1975 on "The New International Economic Order and UNCTAD IV". Policy in the economic issue area had become stabilized even much earlier than that in the political issue area. However, this did not necessarily preclude taking initiatives and carrying out actions consistent with existing postures, objectives, and strategies. In its pursuance of economic objectives, however, there was an increasing sense of moderation or realism. As then Primary Industries Minister Musa Hitam put it with respect to the NIEO:

> In its efforts to seek solutions to these problems Malaysia believes in a multi-pronged approach ... We believe that the UNCTAD mechanism holds special promise for developing countries. As you are all aware, in the UNCTAD mechanism, developing countries have managed to achieve some measure of solidarity as the Group of 77, thereby obtaining leverage necessary to reconcile competing goals with the developed countries on a co-operative basis ... Now that we have a more balanced negotiating strength, it is possible to achieve results faster through constructive negotiations and not negative confrontation if developed countries are more co-ordinated in their response. We believe in this approach because no nation or economic grouping, I really mean no one, has anything to gain from the confrontation tactics that can so easily lead to a prolonging and worsening of the depressing atmosphere that afflicts the world economy today.[8]

Malaysia's Minister of Trade and Industry Hamzah Abu Samah in his speech to UNCTAD IV in May 1976 in Nairobi, explained what this "multi-pronged approach" entailed:

> Malaysia believes in a multi-pronged approach towards solving commodity problems. In this regard the proposal for an Integrated Programme for Commodities has great significance ... The Integrated Programme does not mean a multi-commodity agreement. What it means is an approach to commodity policies and questions that are both integrated and comprehensive. This is certainly compatible with the commodity-by-commodity approach. As a major producer of raw materials...Malaysia too believes in the merits of treating commodity questions on a commodity-by-commodity basis but never in the narrow and strict sense that some would wish us to believe. In fact, we in Malaysia are going ahead with seeking solutions to the problems of individual commodities, and will, necessarily dovetail all these efforts into the Integrated Programme at some future date.[9]

The multipronged approach did not alter Malaysia's basic strategies of using general-purpose IGOs such as UNCTAD and specific-purpose instruments such as the Tin Agreements to overcome problems relating to commodity trade.

The latter strategy was manifested in Malaysia's leadership role in concluding the Fifth International Tin Agreement, to which the United States finally acceded, and its initiatives in promoting dialogue among the Association of Natural Rubber Producing Countries (NRPC). The more general measures which Malaysia supported in relation to the creation of the NIEO included compensatory financing such as that for the Lomé group of countries, while it demonstrated a cautionary attitude towards the indexation approach to commodity problems.[10]

The general inconclusiveness of UNCTAD IV and lack of agreement on the Integrated Programme further augmented the air of realism towards economic problems, which was increasingly demonstrated in Malaysia's push for national self-reliance or *berdikari*, and a shift of emphasis from the use of large-scale forums to regional instrumentalities for resolving its trade problems. The go-it-alone attitude is evident from Malaysia's own national rubber buffer stock programme in operation since 1974. However, the shift to "regional *berdikari*" (self-reliance) became particularly evident during this period. This was achieved via ASEAN. In pursuance of this shift in strategy growing out of the increased reliance on ASEAN, Malaysia has supported economic initiatives through various ASEAN *ad hoc* committees viz:

- Special Coordinating Committee of ASEAN Nations (SCCAN) — responsible for negotiating better terms of trade with the EEC.
- ASEAN Brussels Committee (ABC) — assists SCCAN and is composed of the five ASEAN ambassadors accredited to the EEC.
- Senior officials on sugar (not particularly important to Malaysia).
- Senior trade officials on General Agreement on Tariffs and Trade —Multilateral Trade Negotiations (GATT-MTN).
- ASEAN Geneva Committee — assisting trade officials on GATT-MTN.

Since their formation in 1972, SCCAN and ABC had been instrumental in negotiating better terms for ASEAN products and securing access to the EEC under the Generalized System of Preference (GSP). With the view of establishing a Lomé-type arrangement, ABC had initiated a dialogue with the EEC and set up the Joint Study Group (JSG), which held its inaugural meeting in June 1975.[11] Although the JSG achieved little by way of concrete results, it nonetheless provided an institutionalized framework for continuing ASEAN-EEC dialogue.[12]

Perhaps more important than its European dialogue is that with Japan, by far, the region's foremost trading partner. Malaysia and its ASEAN partners would probably have liked a Lomé arrangement with Japan, but the Japanese continued to follow heavily protectionist trade practices and preferred to rely on the GATT-MTN machinery to counter LDC offensives rather than negotiate with regional groups such as ASEAN. ASEAN's relations with Japan hinged on aid and investment as demonstrated by its support for the regional industrialization programme. The ASEAN group had also begun a dialogue with the United States since mid-1977 on a range of politico-economic issues. In mid-1978, a two-day meeting of ASEAN foreign and finance ministers with President Carter had produced a number of broad US pledges on ASEAN goals and aspirations (*New Straits Times*, 5 August 1978).

Malaysia's orientation towards foreign investment continued to be rooted in its basic posture of economic nationalism of controlling vital natural resources while at the same time extending a liberal hand towards would-be investors. As a token of its sincerity in attracting foreign enterprise, the nationalistic Petroleum Development Act (Amendment) 1975 was dropped and the implementation of the Industrial Coordination Act (which allowed for *Bumiputera* quotas in jobs) was slowed down, if not altogether forgotten. The level of foreign investment and ownership of capital continued to rise appreciably although the foreign share was progressively reduced. For example, foreign ownership of share capital of $3,377.1 million in 1970 increased to $4,813.0 million in 1973 and to $5,434.0 million in 1975, these figures representing a percentage share of 63.3, 58.1 and 54.9 respectively. The anticipated figure for the foreign share by 1980 was to be 43.6 per cent.[13] While these figures do indicate the earnestness in reducing foreign control, it is clear that the level of foreign investment would continue to rise based on the attractive incentives that it continued to receive in Malaysia.

INTERNATIONAL COOPERATION

The dovetailing of milieu goals with the medium-range objectives of security and development provided the dominant theme of Malaysia's foreign policy in this issue area under Hussein Onn's prime ministership. As in the other two issue areas, policy in this period manifested little or no change in terms of fundamental postures, objectives, and strategies. Clearly the foremost vehicle for Malaysia's policies in matters of international cooperation and diplomacy was ASEAN, and the continued and increased use of the regional body to pursue global goals was becoming more evident as it grew in the scope and range of its undertakings, and concomitantly, in prestige and recognition. I have already touched on the ASEAN members' commitment to joint responses and actions *vis-à-vis* other actors as embodied in the Declaration of ASEAN

Concord, while intraregional cooperation attained a hitherto unachieved level with the signing of the Treaty of Amity and Cooperation. Indeed, Malaysia's strong orientation towards regional international cooperation and diplomacy can be said to be the central theme of foreign policy in these first two years of the Hussein government.

In some areas of diplomatic activity Malaysia nevertheless did go it alone where ASEAN consensus seemed to be lacking. In these instances Malaysia did not see itself as breaking ranks with ASEAN, but rather saw its role as representing the leading edge of ASEAN aspirations. Such were its peace overtures and diplomatic thrusts towards the new Indo-China governments to which I already alluded from the security perspective. Thus Malaysia was the first ASEAN country to establish diplomatic ties with the SRV, Laos, and Kampuchea. The Malaysian foreign minister furthermore lost little time in visiting and playing host to all three countries in the course of 1976 through to early 1978. Along with the diplomatic offensive, Malaysia extended economic and technical assistance to Indo-China. Diplomacy in this case tied in nicely with the general strategy of reducing the charged atmosphere of tension in the aftermath of Vietnam between the non-communist ASEAN and communist (Indo-China) states, with the goal of avoiding polarization of the region along Cold War lines. Wisma Putra persisted in its Indo-China overtures at times in the face of Vietnamese and Laotian attacks on ASEAN as a U.S.-sponsored military bloc, perhaps with the hope that this persistence would encourage the two countries to warm up relations with non-communist Southeast Asia eventually. However, it should be noted that in 1978 and 1979, during which years the Vietnamese appeared to have further exacerbated their relations with the ASEAN countries, Malaysia visibly hardened its posture while maintaining healthy diplomatic contact with the SRV. Along with the other ASEAN countries, it condemned Vietnamese actions in respect of boat refugees and the ousting of the Pol Pot regime in Kampuchea, remaining adamant about possible recognition of the Vietnamese backed Heng Samrin regime. In all these matters, Malaysia, nevertheless, assiduously professed a non-aligned position and its ZOPFAN principles and did not foreclose dialogue with the Vietnamese.

It was mostly in ASEAN and with ASEAN states that Malaysia mounted the bulk of its diplomatic activity. This grew out of a recognition that ASEAN was the most logical instrumentality for the pursuance of national-cum-regional objectives, be they of the security-oriented or developmental-economic variety. This is not to say that the organization faced no problems at that point of time. There was the criticism that a proliferation of diplomatic and bureaucratic activity did not necessarily produce commensurate results in real terms. Singapore's outspoken Foreign Minister S. Rajaratnam noted a lack of "political will" on the part of the regional body to follow through its programmes. Referring to the five regional industrialization projects, he opined:

> It is two years since Bali but these projects have not yet been tied up. We are still in the process of feasibility studies or details of implementation. To that extent we are frittering away valuable time. What we should be doing now is looking ahead to five more projects. The vigour of ASEAN has been focussed on these five projects ... if these are the test, then this is a disappointment. (*Far Eastern Economic Review*, 9 June 1978)

The minister's words had a ring of realism in contrast to the often euphoric pronouncements of ASEAN summitry. The criticism was admittedly a little harsh for a fledgling regional body, which while not often matching commitment with action, had demonstrated a level of international cooperation hitherto unachieved in the region. ASEAN intraregional cooperation was at that point on the threshold between institutionalization and action-oriented programmes. The organizational structure of the Annual Foreign Ministers Meeting, Economic Ministers Meeting, the ASEAN Secretariat, Standing Committee, permanent and *ad hoc* committees, provided the formal structure for the bulk of intraregional cooperation as well as extraregional activity. Whether they are used fruitfully depended on the members themselves.

It was mostly in the realm of extraregional relations that ASEAN has proved particularly advantageous to Malaysia and its other member states. Malaysia thus took advantage of the multilateral ASEAN approach to press for certain national objectives. In the economic sphere, the initiation of the various dialogues with the EEC, Japan, Australia-New Zealand, and the United States are cases in point. Thus for Malaysia, ASEAN provided an additional instrumentality to bilateral actions. ASEAN provided a sense of solidarity for a set of largely like-minded states with similar goals that together could achieve somewhat more than if they were to rely entirely on national instruments of foreign policy.

CONSOLIDATION

To summarize, this period of foreign policy did not evince any significantly new postures or strategies. Malaysia's decision making elite remained fundamentally unaltered despite the inclusion of some "new blood" in the cabinet and considerable in-fighting within the ruling party which led to the expulsion of two deputy ministers.[14] However, there is no evidence that these domestic events had any effect on foreign policy. The fact that the Hussein-Rithaudeen team ignored innuendos that communists influenced Razak's foreign policy indicated that foreign policy remained routed on the course that the Razak period had set.

The most important foreign policy actions in the period were the signing of the Declaration of ASEAN Concord and the Treaty of Amity and Cooperation, representing the product for which Wisma Putra and other ASEAN officials had worked hard in the two preceding years or so. The amity treaty was clearly a follow-up of the K.L. Declaration, which was fast running out of steam. As such it was a necessary further step, as Malaysia's policymakers stressed, towards the neutralization goal. Promoting neutralization itself remained the most important foreign policy strategy in the security issue area, with perhaps the initial enthusiasm of the Razak period replaced by a more realist approach. The Kuantan Declaration with Indonesia provided this dimension of policy. However, the principle itself remained unfulfilled, and the larger policy of neutralization was hamstrung from an international law perspective, as well as in real terms. There were a number of major-power considerations and ramifications in terms of the new balance of power in the Southeast Asia region, as well as a host of intraregional imponderables, which we have discussed in the previous chapter.[15] The Hussein Onn government, one suspects, did not have the answers to many of these questions but if the proposal for neutralization was left purposely vague, it allowed for flexibility in the strategic sense and its eventual outcome or outcomes could incorporate whatever developments may occur in the international environment of Southeast Asia.

Towards the end of his tenure, the prime minister himself had already been weakened by political challenges from within the ruling UMNO party. His own health suffered a decline when in December 1980 he fell ill in Britain and returned in February for a heart bypass operation. He eventually retired from office in July 1981.

In Table 6.1, we provide a summary of Malaysia's most significant foreign policy actions and their relation to existing postures, objectives, and strategies for the Hussein period. Only the major actions and the most important postures, objectives, and strategies are listed.

TABLE 6.1
Foreign Policy Outputs 1976–77

Postures	Objectives	Strategies	Actions
Neutralism	• Maintaining political independence • Protecting territorial integrity	• Promoting a Zone of Peace, Freedom, and Neutrality in Southeast Asia • Promoting regional and national resilience	• Establishing diplomatic ties with Vietnam, Laos, and Kampuchea (1976) • Signing Declaration of ASEAN Concord Treaty of Amity can Cooperation (1976) • Launching with Thailand "Cahaya Bina" (1977) • Supporting UNCTAD, NIEO, and the Integrated Programme (1976)
Developing World Orientation	• Promoting economic development • Stabilizing commodity prices	• Promoting and participating in trade groupings and price stablization schemes	• Starting the following dialogues: • EEC-ASEAN (1972 onwards)
Economic Nationalism		• Pursuing regional and national self-reliance	• Japan-ASEAN (1978 onwards)
Regionalism	• Promoting cooperation and security	• Promoting goals and role of ASEAN	• US-ASEAN (1977 onwards) • Commitment to implement ASEAN regional industrialization Project (1976) • Reducing tariffs on 71 items of intra-ASEAN trade (1977)

Source: Author's own compilation.

NOTES

1. Furthermore, he had a weak political base. As Razak's brother-in-law, his ascension to deputy premier seemed to be less on the merit of party support, than on the personal prerogative of Razak.
2. Mahathir was reported by the *Far Eastern Economic Review* (29 June 1979) as saying: "If the illegal Vietnamese refugees continue to come in, we will shoot them on sight" (cited by Means 1991, p. 81).
3. By November 1980, 83,000 had been settled in countries of asylum, while 13,180 still remained in Malaysia (Means 1991, p. 76). Malaysia was open only to Muslim refugees and some Cambodian "Chams" settled in places such as Kelantan. The figure reported by the United Nations High Commission for Refugees (UNHCR) for the total number of boat refugees who had landed in Malaysia is 240,000 persons. Some 9,000 chose to return to Vietnam while the rest were repatriated to third countries. They were first housed on the island, Pulau Bidong, off the Terengganu coast, and subsequently moved in 1990 to the Sungai Besi camp in Selangor, near Kuala Lumpur. The last of the boat refugees were repatriated to third countries in 1996 (various sources, including from UNHRC webpage, <http://www.unhcr.org/> (accessed 25 September 2007).
4. *New Straits Times*, 1 March 1976.
5. The Laotian Foreign Minister Phoun Sipraseuth returned the visit in early 1978, making it the first official Laotian state visit to any ASEAN country.
6. See Amer, Saravanamuttu and Wallensteen (1996) for an account of ASEAN's role in the Cambodian conflict and peace process from the ASEAN perspective.
7. See Antolik (1990, p. 18ff.).
8. Retreived from *Foreign Affairs Malaysia* 8 (1975): 47.
9. Retreived from *Foreign Affairs Malaysia* 9 (1976): 23.
10. Retreived from *Foreign Affairs Malaysia* 8 (1975): 50–57.
11. The Lomé Convention was signed by the EEC and forty-five African, Caribbean, and Pacific countries in February 1975.
12. The only concrete results of the ASEAN-EEC dialogue was the GSP access for finished and semi-finished industrial goods accorded to the bulk of LDCs while the JSG succeeded only in launching various technical studies. See Malcolm Subhan, "ASEAN-EEC Relations", in *Southeast Asian Affairs* (1977, pp. 50–63) for a documentation of the outcome of this dialogue.
13. See Malaysia. Treasury. *Economy Report 1975–76.*
14. For an interesting if somewhat speculative account of the UMNO leadership manoeuverings and in-fighting, see Subky Latif, "UMNO: 30 Years After", in *Southeast Asian Affairs* (1977, pp. 160–72).
15. See also Rao and Ross-Larson (1977, pp. 162–70) for a succinct discussion of the neutralization proposal from this perspective.

7

CONFRONTING GLOBALIZATION WITH ICONOCLASM, 1981–96

ICONOCLASM

Datuk Sri Dr Mahathir Mohamad, Malaysia's fourth prime minister, rose to assume the reins of government on 17 July 1981 after the health-stricken Hussein Onn announced his retirement from political office earlier in May the same year. As Mahathir was already deputy prime minster under Hussein, there appeared to be no controversy over his taking over the leadership of the ruling UMNO and the premiership. Perhaps no other leader in Malaysia's history fits the bill of Third World iconoclast better than Mahathir Mohamed.[1] By the eleventh year of his office in 1992, Mahathir, who seemed to thrive on controversy, had virtually overhauled all aspects of Malaysia's domestic and foreign policy, including seeing the end to Malaysia's definitive New Economic Policy (NEP), ushered the country into the ranks of a second generation of Newly Industrializing Countries (NICs),[2] and emerged as *the* putative champion of Third World causes.

This chapter will focus on the years 1981–96, which may be seen as the period of Mahathir's political ascension, when he also confidently steered Malaysian foreign policy in a particular direction consonant with his own appraisal of the political and economic situation in the Malaysian state. However despite personal predilections, during these years, external policy could be said to be closely intertwined with the domestic policy. Such linkages are perhaps even more evident during Mahathir's tenure than in any other previous periods. In focusing on the iconoclasm of the Mahathir period, one is not by any means dismissing several other important elements in the political economy of foreign policy. First, however idiosyncratic a particular leader may appear to be, he is bound by the socio-economic connectivity with previous periods of foreign policy, that is, by the continuity of relationships, domestic and external, that he ignores at his own peril. Second, it is axiomatic that any leader's policies always tend to resonate with the elite perceptions of his particular regime, if not that of the whole political class. Third, and perhaps even more crucially, a particular leader's policies are bound to be constrained by societal and economic imperatives both internally and externally.[3] As such, the construction of new dimensions or notions in foreign policy will be subjected to these three sets of constraints even if high agential power may be attributed to a particular leader. My approach is somewhat in contrast to that of Dhillon (2008), who in writing a critical and comprehensive work on Mahathir's foreign policy, has been inclined to give great play to the idiosyncratic factor as the major driver behind foreign policy in the Mahathir era. Dhillon does not employ a constructivist perspective in foreign policy analysis, but rather a "comparative foreign policy approach" which he also attributes to my earlier work. According to Dhillon, two other major factors, "domestic" and "external" have also impinged on the policy outcomes beyond Mahathir's idiosyncrasies.[4] In particular, on the domestic front, the need for regime maintenance and the national imperative of development have determined how Mahathir had fashioned his foreign policy. Furthermore, globalization and regionalism had also greatly influenced Mahathir's foreign policy. My own conclusions do not greatly differ except for my devalorization of the idiosyncratic factor and my greater emphasis on Mahathir's iconoclasm, as opposed to his "idiosyncrasies".

Thus the chapter will attempt to account for Malaysian foreign policy in the Mahathir period in terms of the overall constraining elements. Besides paying close attention to the fact that the foreign policy outputs were closely tied with the usual goals of security and autonomy, we also note the fact that at that juncture of Malaysia's economic trajectory, these were intimately connected with the maintenance of a particular form of a developmental state, that is, an authoritarian, albeit largely democratic, political regime of the NIC variety greatly directed at the goals of state and nation building (Wurfel and Burton 1990, pp. 293–309). The restructuring of policy is especially important in the Mahathir period not only because of the unavoidable impact of globalization, but also because it impelled through the Mahathir leadership role, an aggressive pursuance of national goals. Thus, the iconoclasm of the Mahathir period needs to be cast in the context of an authoritarian capitalist political regime seeking its "neo-mercantilist" niche in the rapidly changing international division of labour of a post-Cold War regional and global political realignment. To be sure, the ideas, norms, and interests of a well established preceding foreign policy constructed in the Abdul Razak and Hussein Oon periods (of which, it must be remembered, Mahathir participated as a cabinet minster and deputy prime minister) remained as the "foundationalist" basis or point of departure for the new Mahathrian constructs in foreign relations. The manner the foreign policy narrative is undertaken in this chapter varies from previous chapters in that it adopts a more free-wheeling appreciation of foreign policy issue areas in terms of new policy postures and positions taken up by the Mahahtir government. Futhermore, in the Mahathir period, economic and political questions were invariably closely linked and it will be more difficult to conceive of clear-cut security and economic issue areas in this period. We will elaborate further on this as we elucidate the Mahathirian foreign policy postures, strategies and actions, which remain our basic descriptive labels for delineating foreign policy.

LOOKING EAST, 1981–85

From the outset it was clear that Mahathir was not about to leave untouched existing policies, both domestic and foreign. He tended to be more circumspect about matters of defence and security, which for the most part were left unaltered in the first phase of this period. However, he immediately turned his attention to questions of development and political economy, coming up with a radical new policy — the "Look East" policy — geared to propel Malaysia into becoming a Newly Industrializing Country (NIC). I have suggested that the "Look East" policy embodied the prime minister's proclivities in that it represented a two-pronged approach to lift Malaysia's economy on the road to rapid industrial growth, while at the same time, prod its predominantly Bumiputera population into becoming economic achievers (Saravanamuttu 1989, p. 24).

It also needs to be recalled that a series of incidents involving differences with Britain preceded the announcement of the "Look East" policy, such as the fees hike in U.K. universities and the rule changes made by the British Securities Council in the London Metal Exchange after Malaysia's "dawn raid" on British-owned Guthrie. These incidents provoked Mahathir to announce a "Buy British Last" policy (Stubbs 1990, p. 119) only some six months after he had assumed office. There have been suggestions that Mahathir's antipathy towards the British has a history which can be traced to his early writings in the *Sunday Times* under the pseudonym, "C.H.E. Det".[5] Thus, even from early days, the young Mahathir, who had his tertiary education in Singapore, had already shown antipathy towards "the West". As prime minister he showed an early disdain for the Commonwealth Heads of Government Meeting (CHOGM) by missing the Melbourne (1981) and New Delhi

(1983) meetings, but changed his mind when the heads met in Bahamas (1986), and by 1989 had decided to make peace with the Commonwealth by hosting its meeting in Kuala Lumpur. A scribe of Mahathir's policies, Chamil Wariya (1989, pp. 53–61), takes contention with the view that Mahathir was anti-British, arguing that "Buy British Last" was a rational retaliation against British policies which affected Malaysia adversely, such as the university fee increases. To give an idea of the importance of this, Chamil argues, one only needs to note that Malaysia had at its peak some 15,500 students studying in the United Kingdom. The annual fees for U.K. universities went up from £325 in 1975 to £940 in 1979. Moreover there was resistance to Malaysia's takeover of British companies, which besides Guthrie, included Sime Darby and Harrison and Crossfield, Dunlop and the like (Chamil 1989, p. 59; and Means 1991, pp. 91–92). The Malaysian action was enough to jolt the Thatcher government into dispatching Foreign Minster Lord Carrington and Defence Minister John Notts for a special visit to Malaysia in early February 1981. Mahathir obligingly dropped the policy just prior to his London visit in early 1983 although he had earlier hinted it would be a long-term policy. The declining value of the pound *vis-à-vis* the ringgit was possibly a sop for the change of heart.

What is beyond doubt, especially with hindsight, was that the "Look East" policy was certainly not a mere function of "Buy British Last", but rather that it was convenient then for Mahathir to ride on the wave of anti-British (and even anti-Commonwealth) sentiments to launch the "Look East" policy, a policy which had to ride roughshod over prejudices and memories against the Japanese, both within the country and regionally.[6] The policy was iconoclastic in a double sense. The Malay world view never resonated with "Eastern" work ethics or its aggressive economics. Nor did previous prime ministers ever see a Japan, South Korea, Taiwan, let alone, a Singapore, role model. But behind the "Look East" policy was the clear message that these late and newly industrializing success stories were the ones for Malaysia to emulate. Secondly, "Western" economic success was to be debunked as implicitly non-adaptive to new times and as exploitative, and even worse, still imperialistic and therefore not worthy of emulation.

Thus for most of the early 1980s, the Malaysian Government, through its formal and informal machinery, mounted a concerted campaign to publicize and propagate the "Look East" policy. The media lapped it up and the bureaucrats scrambled to discover and uncover all manner of ways to implement the prime minister's edict, and the Malaysian public was bombarded with a relentless barrage of propaganda about "the Japanese miracle" and the need to make the country into a "Malaysia Inc". Clearly it was politically less expedient to emulate Chinese-dominant Singapore, nor could Taiwan or Hong Kong serve as ideal models, and despite Mahathir's rhetoric about the new economic "dragons", Japan was seen the model *par excellence*.[7] Thus in a speech to the joint annual conference of the Malaysian-Japanese economic associations, MAJECA and JAMECA, in February 1982, the premier elucidated that the policy was an effort to emulate Japanese industrialization, work attitude, ethics, and skills, and also to seek the cooperation of the Japanese government and Japanese companies in various areas of technical training and industrial management directly (Saravanamuttu 1984, pp. 457–58).

Subsequently there appeared some elucidation and qualification of the earlier policy when, in his memorandum to senior government officials in June 1983, the prime minister said, "Looking East does not mean begging from the East or shifting the responsibility for developing Malaysia to them. Responsibility towards our country is our own and not that of others. Looking East also does not mean buying all goods from or granting all contracts to companies of the East, unless their offer is best" (Mahathir Mohamad 1989, p. 7). A negative turn in the policy came in August 1984. The prime minister delivered a speech in *absentia* to the inaugural Malaysia-Japan Colloquium, co-sponsored by Malaysia's Institute of Strategic and International Studies and Japan's Foreign Ministry, in which he took Japan to task for perpetuating a "colonial" relationship.

In March 1984 Dr Lin See Yan, deputy governor of Bank Negara (National Bank), in a speech to the MAJECA-JAMECA annual conference, detailed Malaysia's US$2.7 billion current account deficit in services (or invisibles) with Japan in tones calculated to signal that the "Look East" policy was no *carte blanche* for Japan to take economic excesses. Other irritations had also time and again emerged over Japan's adamance about protective trade barriers against Malaysian manufactures, the slow rate or lack of technology transfer, and the practice of transfer pricing by Japanese multinationals to avert taxation. However, the last straw was evidently Japan's blocking of the Malaysian Airline System's bid to operate a flight to the United States with Northwest Orient Airlines via Tokyo in 1984. Japan had refused to grant traffic rights for such a venture, and the holding of the Malaysia-Japan Colloquium in August that year provided the Malaysian premier with the ideal occasion to hammer home his point in calling for a "Second Opening" of Japan, lest the "black ships" of ASEAN beckoning at its door became impatient. Dr Mahathir subsequently met with his Japanese counterpart, Yasuhiro Nakasone, in November 1984 on the MAS flight issue and reportedly agreed on an arrangement involving Japan Airlines. But clearly this and other related irritations in Japan-Malaysia ties marked the nadir of four years of the implementation of the "Look East" policy. Indeed, the air rights issue, in retrospect, had provided the Malaysian Government with a convenient opportunity to jettison the less palatable aspects of the policy.[8]

THE GRAND VISION CIRCA 1990s[9]

By the early and mid-1990s, the prime minister had begun again to extol the virtues of the East and to lambast the West. The new Mahathirian vision was to turn Malaysia into a developed country by the year 2020. Accordingly, Malaysia was not interested in becoming or at least being labelled an "NIC". This was a "trick" of the West, said Dr Mahathir: "The rise of countries such as Japan and South Korea showed that the Asian countries can do just a well if not better than the Western nations. Japan has developed so well that it can now buy the whole of the United States." (*The Star*, 27 May 1991).

Thus it seemed that the Look East Policy was alive and well again, although this time it was tacked onto the larger goal of Malaysia's 2020 vision of becoming a "developed country". These ideas were enunciated in a policy speech on 28 February 1991, strategically pitched to the Malaysian Business Council, of which the prime minister was chairman. He suggested that by the year 2020, "Malaysia can be a united nation, with a confident Malaysian society, infused by strong moral and ethical values, living in a society that is democratic, liberal and tolerant, caring, economically just and equitable, progressive and prosperous, and in full possession of an economy that is competitive, dynamic, robust and resilient." (Mahathir 1991, p. 2). The speech spelt out nine challenges that would have to be met and ten economic objectives that had to be attained to achieve that goal.[10]

The "Wawasan 2020" (Vision 2020) policy was essentially Mahathir's answer to the post-NEP period of development in the country. It is believed that many portions of the speech were taken from the final report of the multi-ethnic National Economic Consultative Council (NECC), which was set up in 1988 to pave the way for the post-NEP period.[11] The main thrust of the policy was to inveigle the private sector to play the leading role in Malaysia's economic trajectory, with the government providing a steadying hand in line with the "Malaysian Inc." policy enunciated in the early 1980s. Among some of the more ambitious goals of Vision 2020, also known as the New Development Policy (NDP), was the doubling of gross domestic product every ten years between 1990 till 2020, arriving at a GDP of M$920 billion in real terms by that year. This could be achieved by an average GDP growth rate of 7 per cent over the thirty years anticipated for the materializing of the 2020 goal. Although this was extremely ambitious, it should be noted that Malaysia's growth topped 10 per cent in 1990 and remained positive until the financial crisis of 1997–98. Clearly, Vision 2020 was propounded when Malaysia was riding on a crest of economic confidence and real economic achievements. For example, by 1992, Malaysia boasted of having no unemployment problem, there being a labour shortage situation instead which had seen the influx of some 700,000 (legalized and semi-legalized) foreign workers that year.

Along with the Vision 2020 goal was a very definite strategy in external policy geared towards advancing ASEAN economic cooperation to its upper limits, in tandem with larger-than-ASEAN efforts of economic schemas such as the East Asia Economic Caucus (EAEC). It was Mahathir's overall disappointment with ASEAN's inability to move decisively in the economic sphere that prompted his EAEG (East Asia Economic Grouping), and subsequently, the EAEC idea. Mahathir made the policy speech about the EAEG idea to the Hong Kong Foreign Correspondents' Club on 14 October 1992. Touching on aspects of regional cooperation in the region, Mahathir alluded to ASEAN's inauspicious beginnings: "Economic development was not on the minds of the founding fathers of ASEAN," he averred. However, he noted that ASEAN, as a regional organization, had played a significant role in the growth of the member countries in ensuring regional stability and peace. Thus it was extended to the Indo-China states and Myanmar, which should rightly belong eventually to the grouping (*New Straits Times*, 15 October 1992).

But here ended ASEAN's role, that is, its function in enlarging a political concept to encompass all ten countries of Soutrheast Asia. Its economic agenda remained unfulfilled. Up until 1992, some twenty-five years after it had been formed, it had only succeeded in making inchoate steps towards setting up a free trade area, and following Mahathir's inexorable logic, ASEAN at its maximum strength could hardly encompass an area large enough to meet the challenge of either a unitary Europe (the European Union) or the North American Free Trade Area (NAFTA). Hence, the EAEG/EAEC was the logical outcome of an enlarged entity beyond ASEAN. Mahathir said that his idea was not new since South Korea had in 1970 proposed the Asian Common Market, while Japan's Ministry of International Trade and Industry suggested an "Asian Network" in 1988:

> The EAEG or EAEC should neither be a formal grouping like ASEAN nor should it be a trade bloc like NAFTA or the EC. As it is dedicated to world free trade, it cannot be protectionist and give its members preferential treatment in intra-regional trade. Its chief purpose is to provide a strong voice for East Asian countries in trade negotiations with the rest of world,

particularly the EC and NAFTA. It has been obvious for a long time that no one respects the voices of developing countries like Malaysia, or even of groups like ASEAN. But a regional forum with China, Japan together with the ASEAN six as members will have a much greater clout if they speak with one voice on common problems affecting them." (*New Straits Times*, 15 October 1992)

The EAEC idea was immediatly opposed by the U.S. which saw the grouping as a serious challenge to its preference for Asia Pacific regionalism. Thus, Secretary of State James Baker requested in a memorandum to Japan that it not be a party to the EAEC. This sparked a furore in Malaysian circles in November 1991, with Mahathir virtually accusing President Bush of reneging on a *quid pro quo* of Malaysian support for the American-sponsored Security Council resolution on the Gulf War.[12] Mahathir took his fight, appropriately enough, to the Hong Kong Foreign Correspondents' Club. In Hong Kong, Mahathir specifically chided the United States for its double standard on trade issues. The United States had already been instrumental in knocking back the EAEG idea when it was proposed by Mahathir in early 1991, and thanks to misgivings from ASEAN countries such as Indonesia and Singapore, the concept of the grouping was reduced to that of a "caucus" to mollify American fears that it was to be a trading bloc. On top of this, the United States insisted that any regional grouping in the Asia-Pacific area should have the United States as one of its members, hence preferring the earlier idea of the Asia Pacific Economic Council or Community (APEC). Mahathir argued that, "If being on the shores of a vast ocean qualifies one to be a member of a regional organisation, then the U.S. should also be a member of the EC [EU] which is made of countries of the Atlantic rim." Furthermore, he hinted more than once that there was an ethnocentric element in the U.S. attitude. Commenting on possible U.S. fears of Japanese domination in an EAEC grouping, he opined that China, Korea, and ASEAN would not allow such an eventuality.

It was therefore to be expected that Mahathir chose not to attend the 1993 APEC Summit in Seattle although Malaysia did send Minister of International Trade and Industry Rafidah Aziz. The Mahathir snub led the then Australian Premier Paul Keating to make the famous remark that the Malaysian premier was "recalcitrant". Mahathir, however, made an appearance in the 1994 APEC, held in Bogor, Indonesia, which proposed a Free Trade Area for APEC to achieve by 2020, but Malaysia continued to have reservations about the APEC enterprise.[13]

It could well be that with respect to East Asian and the Asia Pacific regionalism, hardnosed considerations linked to the prospect of a breakdown of the Uruguay Round and the need to create a counterweight to NAFTA were important elements behind Mahathir's postures and his preference for the EAEG/EAEC idea (Camroux 1994, p. 31). Additionally, there was always the strong element of Asian values in Mahathirian rhetoric and discourse, which no doubt influenced his projects, viz.

> In East Asia we are told that we may not call ourselves East Asians as Europeans call themselves Europeans and Americans call themselves Americans. We are told that we must call ourselves Pacific people and align with people who are partly Pacific, but more American, Atlantic and European. We may not have an identity that is not permitted, nor may we work together on the basis of that identity ... [T]he East Asian Economic Group or EAEG was proposed, not as a trade bloc, but as a forum for the nations of East Asia to confer with each other to reach agreement on a common stand for a common problem caused by the restricted trade practices of the rich. (Camroux, 1994, p 33)

It was evident that Indonesian and other ASEAN states were less ethusiatic about the EAEG idea than Malaysia, in part, because they were not consulted beforehand about it by Mahahtir. So, in late 1991 Indonesia proposed successfully that the EAEG be converted to East Asian Economic Caucus (EAEC). While accepting this, Malaysia made the further proposal that EAEC be sited within APEC, to which the ASEAN members agreed in 1993 (Milne and Mauzy 1999, p. 130). The EAEC continued to be an issue at the August 1995 Bandar Seri Begawan gathering of the ASEAN Regional Forum (ARF). Malaysian officials became rather irritated by the insistence of Japan and South Korea for an answer as to why Australia and New Zealand were not asked to be members of the caucus.[14] These issues were raised in light of Gareth Evans' suggestion that Australia, though not "Asian", could be said to be geographically situated in the "Eastern Hemisphere".

Without the member states wishing it, the East Asia issue had thereby begun to affect ASEAN policies, thanks to Dr Mahathir. Indeed, acceptance of the EAEC project by ASEAN, even nominally, meant it had to deal with all the tricky issues raised. However, Mahathir's perspective and his rather assertive positions on the issue may have affected ASEAN well into the future. The subsequent formation of ASEAN-Plus-Three, which excludes Australia and New Zealand, and the East Asian Summit, which includes the two countries, are perhaps testimony to this. Former Secretary General of ASEAN Rodolfo Severino writes that the ASEAN-Plus-Three proposal was first made in December 1990 by Mahathir at a dinner in honour of the Chinese Premier Li Peng, where Severino was present. In other words, according to Severino, the rather unclever idea of having EAEC as a caucus of APEC was abandoned for the idea of the ASEAN-Plus-Three.[15] An East Asia Study Group, formed by the ASEAN-Plus-Three, subsequently suggested the setting up of the East Asia Summit (EAS).[16]

SOUTHERN STANCE, ANTARCTICA, AND NAM

Characteristically, Mahathir hitched Malaysia's external economic orientation to that of the developing Southern countries. Although this was no departure from previous stances in Malaysian foreign policy, Mahathir took a much higher profile on North-South economic issues than other Malaysian leaders in the past had. In particular, he moved for the setting up of the South-South Commission in the Harare NAM summit of 1986. Mahathir had chaired the steering committee of the Second South-South Dialogue in Kuala Lumpur in 1985 which proposed the idea. The South-South Commission was to be set up with the cooperation of the South Foundation based in London. The Commission was headed by Julius Nyerere of Tanzania and Malaysia provided its secretary general in the person of retired foreign minister, Tan Sri Ghazali Shafie.

Not unconnected to his criticism of the North was Mahathir's Antarctica policy. In his 1982 maiden speech as Malaysia's head of government at the United Nations, he argued that Antarctica was the common heritage of mankind and as such should not be the preserve of a few countries and major powers via the 1959 and 1961 Antarctic Treaties. In the face of opposition from the Consultative Parties of the Treaty, Mahathir carried his battle into the 1984 and 1986 U.N. General Assemblies, but was not successful in his campaign.

Mahathir essentially maintained the overall thrust of Malaysia's non-aligned policy throughout his tenure of office, but with the movement in crisis — perhaps even losing its *raison d'être*, following on from the end of the Cold War by the 1990s — the Malaysian premier seized on the opportunity to refurbish a new role for NAM. Mahathir, although he diplomatically denied this, stole much of the thunder at the 1992 NAM conference in Jakarta. Not only was Malaysia instrumental in moving the resolution on the Bosnian crisis calling for the expulsion of the rump state of Yugoslavia from the United Nations, but Mahathir virtually became, as the *Far Eastern Economic Review* in a cover story put it, the "new voice for the Third World" or a "little Sukarno" as some of the Indonesian media opined, if sardonically.[17] Hype notwithstanding, the Malaysian government, perhaps mainly through its then Foreign Minister Abdullah Badawi, argued that NAM still had an important role to play in the so-called new world order, as a forum for the

Southern nations to air their grievances and views on issues ranging from the environment to political crises such as the Bosnia-Herzegovina imbroglio, and to questions of reforming the United Nations in keeping with the interests of Third World states.

Under Mahathir, Malaysia took a particularly strong Third World line on the environmental question ever since the surfacing of what it alleged were Western campaigns and the softwoods lobby against the logging of tropical rainforests. The *Far Eastern Economic Review*'s Michael Vatikiotis suggested that "Starting as far back as 1989, Mahathir took the view that developed countries were bent on blaming the earth's dismal state on the less developed South, while at the same time hindering the South's ability to protect the environment by failing to foster sustainable development." The *Review* writer said that Mahathir's stance won him recognition at the Rio de Janeiro June 1992 Earth Summit where Malaysia's position helped define the demands of the South:

> Simply put, the value of Mahathir's contribution was that by forcefully linking consideration of the environment to development, the North was prevented from shirking its responsibilities on such issues as carbon monoxide emissions because they could not shift the blame onto disappearing tropical forests. (*FEER*, 20 August 1992, p. 17)

MUSLIM POLITICS, PALESTINE, THE GULF WAR, AND BOSNIA

Most political analysts, including this one, would date the genesis of an overtly pro-Muslim World orientation in foreign policy to the Mahathir period.[18] In 1983 Mahathir declared that NAM and the Commonwealth were no longer as important as the Muslim world (Hussin Mutalib 1993, p. 32). However, as noted by Nair (1997), ASEAN remained in the innermost concentric circle of core relations, while relations with the Muslim world constituted the second circle. NAM and the South were probably in the third circle, while the Commonwealth was relegated to the fourth.[19] In the Mahathir perod, Palestine remained an enduring concern of foreign policy and the anti-Zionist posture of the government was constantly profiled at the United Nations. In each year after he made his maiden speech at this body, Mahathir did not fail to raise the Palestine question (Chamil 1989, p. 104). Malaysia's position has consistently been to derecognize the Israeli state so long as the Palestinian people are denied their homeland and a state.[20] Mahathir also took a particularly strident stance against the role of Western powers in propping up the Israeli state and not putting enough pressure on it to abide by U.N. resolutions 238 and 242, requiring the vacating of occupied Arab territories. However, in the latter years of Mahathir's tenure, Bosnia-Herzegovina took centre stage in Malaysian foreign policy because of Mahathir's own impassioned approach to the subject. The Bosnia issue dovetailed with Malaysia's increasing tendency to project itself as an aspirant middle power capable of contributing to international peacekeeping under the auspices of the United Nations. Mahathir was not averse to projecting such an image for Malaysia, particularly when a great deal of press was given to genocidal actions and other appalling events perpetrated by Serbians on Bosnian Muslims. By March 1995, Malaysia had some 2,555 officers and men serving in U.N. missions abroad, including 1,512 in Bosnia. Malaysia's involvement in the UNPROFOR (UN Protection Force) operation in Bosnia was as much motivated by politics targeted at an international Islamic audience and a Muslim population at home as it was at the same time one born of a genuine humanitarian concern with Western callousness and double standards in dealing with the Bosnia fiasco (Saravanamuttu 1994).[21] Mahathir believed that West clearly practised a double standard in Bosnia as it had done in other situations across the globe, such as in Rwanda and Cambodia, while at the same time lambasting the United Nations for dancing to the tune of the major powers (Milne and Mauzy 1991, p. 125). In one of his usually hard-hitting speeches on the Bosnia situation, he said:

> The Bosnian government desperately appealed for help from the vaunted defenders of the human rights of the world, but neither the European Union nor the United Nations Security Council took decisive action. Humanitarian aid was offered subject to permission being granted by the Serbian agressors. And, as can be expected, the Serbs were not quite cooperative... Bosnia-Herzegovina is the victim of the designs of certain people and powers who are quite happy to see the emergence of Slovenia and Croatia, but will do nothing for Bosnia, although Bosnia-Herzegovina has as much right as the other two to nationhood. (cited in Milne and Mauzy 1999, p. 136)

Issues relating to the Arab world and Islam had earlier come to a head for Malaysia during the Gulf War of 1991. Because it was then an alternate member of the U.N. Security Council, the event had become all the more significant for Malaysia. Added to this was the fact that its predominantly Muslim population was evidently emotionally stirred and palpably disturbed by the massive U.S. bombardment of Iraq, screened daily on Malaysian television, courtesy of CNN. It was therefore somewhat curious that Mahathir had earlier gone along with Resolution 678 of the Security Council, sanctioning full-scale military action against the Saddam Hussein regime. Given that at that time, Malaysian, especially Muslim, sentiment was decisively anti-U.S. and pro-Iraq, the government's support for Resolution 678 turned out to be something of a *faux pas*. An abstention on the vote was clearly the more logical course of action as it was perhaps later realized. It remains a puzzle why the Mahathir government had gone along with the U.S.-led action.

From the statement by the Malaysian Committee for the International War Crimes Commission on the Gulf War,[22] we can gather that then Foreign Minister Dato Abu Hassan Omar had argued that the "all necessary means" clause of Resolution 678 did not sanction the destruction of Iraq, only the recapture of Kuwait. In his address to the Security Council on 25 September 1990, the foreign minister stated what sounded like an admission of a mistake:

> "[W]e cannot but feel perturbed over the apparent headlong rush, moving from one resolution to another in a period of seven weeks. The question may be asked whether enough time is given for each resolution to take effect. Are we moving at this speed to make sanctions effective, or are we readying ourselves early for a situation where we will conclude that sanctions are not effective and other measures must therefore be taken? Malaysia will not accept the latter course being applied. We do not accept that war is inevitable or that we are escalating towards confrontation … Malaysia … is averse to the involvement of the armed forces of major powers in any region. That we had to be party to authorizing the use of forces of certain countries in respect of Resolution 665 (August 25) does not sit well with us." (*Statement 1991*, p. 3)

The committee rejected the "naive" hypothesis that the Malaysian Government was indeed unaware that the United States through the United Nations, would act on the level and scale that it did, notwithstanding the "all necessary means" mandate given in Resolution 678 and that it voted in good faith without undue pressure from any outside party. It instead concluded that the more plausible explanation was that the Malaysian Government was aware that the U.S./U.N. would act on the scale it did, but was pressured into voting for the resolution, in particular, by the United States.

After the Gulf War, the Mahathir government consistently argued against US domination of the "New World Order"[23] and its control of the U.N. Security Council, which, it argued, needed to be reformed to include more Third World states and Japan as permanent members. The United States earned more ire from Mahathir (as already noted above) after its attempt to dissuade Japan from becoming a party to the EAEC, which was perceived as part of an overall U.S. effort at hegemonic control of the world through propagating a unipolar international system under its rubric of a New World Order. The

Institute of Strategic and International Studies (ISIS), the acknowledged think tank of the government, in various communications and position papers, suggested that the establishment of a multipolar international system was the preferred scenario of the post-Cold War era. Despite being a strident critic of U.S. foreign policy, the Mahathir government continued to cooperate on defence matters with the United States through the Bilateral Training and Consultation (BITAC) agreement with the United States established in 1984, which allowed for military exercises, intelligence sharing, and logistics support. Wain writes that the U.S. Air Force and Navy made use of BITAC to establish air-to-air and air-to-ground training, and for the U.S. Army to get access to the jungle warfare training school at Pulada in Johore. The U.S. Navy also developed a small-ship repair facility in Lumut on the West Coast, and the U.S. Air Force later established a facility in Kuala Lumpur to repair C-130 Hercules transport aircraft.[24]

The foregoing discussion of new foreign policy positions straddling various issue areas demonstrates the constant interplay of domestic and external factors in influencing the Mahathir government's policies. The most characteristic aspect of foreign policy was its intense linkage with domestic or national goals. Thus the "Look East" policy and Vision 2020 were essentially postures and strategies linked to various national objectives as defined by Mahathir's government. This foreign policy positioning was used as the cutting edge in certain foreign relations and ventures. Such new foreign policy constructs were geared no doubt to national goals of development and clearly impelled the strong stances that Mahathir took on North-South issues, belying an exasperation with the attempts of Northern countries to block schemes he proposed such as the EAEG. The Mahathir government also saw the new approach to sustainable development of the North as damaging to Third World states such as Malaysia which had ample natural resources to exploit. This seems to be the rationale behind the strident views expressed in the Rio Earth Summit. However, Malaysia was not averse to cooperating with the North, including with the United States, even to the limits of adversely affecting societal sensibilities when such cooperation was thought to bear anticipated advantages. This factor characterized Malaysia's initial ambivalence over the Gulf War and its domestic *faux pas* as explicated above, which in some ways saw a correction in the strong stance taken on Bosnia.

Our next section deals with more regional, Southeast Asian, questions, and here again the concerns of nation and state tend to outweigh the goal of regional peace although a dovetailing of regional goals through ASEAN glossed over ideological differences with communist states.

INDO-CHINA STATES AND THE CAMBODIAN CONFLICT

ASEAN since its formation in 1967 has been a ready vehicle for Malaysian policymakers to propagate foreign policy pertaining particularly to regional security issues. The Mahathir government in this sense was the mere inheritor of such a foreign policy instrumentality, but it used this to great effect in the period ushering in the end of the Cold War and rapprochement between the ASEAN and Indo-Chinese states. Because highly significant developments occurred during this period, Mahathir did not fail to capitalize on them. When he assumed the reins of government, the Cambodian conflict loomed large as the most intractable of the regional security issues. In fact, that year, the ASEAN states had just won overwhelming support for a U.N.-sponsored International Conference on Kampuchea (ICK) which adopted a "Declaration on Kampuchea", reiterating the various ASEAN demands for a comprehensive political settlement of the Cambodian conflict through negotiations.

Malaysia was also particularly instrumental through then Foreign Minister Tan Sri Ghazali Shafie in setting up the Coalition Government of Democratic Kampuchea (CGDK), which held on to Cambodia's UN seat for most part of the 1982–90 period. The CGDK was formalized on 22 June 1982 in Kuala Lumpur, with Prince Sihanouk as president, Khieu Samphan as vice-president, and Son Sann as prime minister.

Malaysia was content thereon to let other ASEAN states take the lead on the Cambodian question in the ensuing period of diplomatic impasse between Indochina and ASEAN, which endured until 1987. In 1988, political developments in Thailand gave a fillip to breaking the impasse when the government of Chatichai Choonhavan started to pursue a new Indo-China policy, which was by degrees more friendly and flexible, and came to be known by its dictum of "turning battlefields of Indo-China into markets". This led to an immediate improvement of relations with Cambodia and Vietnam. This in turn led to Thailand's sponsorship of several dialogues and eventually saw the convening of the meeting of the newly formed Supreme National Council of Cambodia in June 1991 in Pattaya. However, even before the Thai initiatives, Indonesia, which also acted concurrently as co-chair of the Paris peace talks, had played a highly significant role in bringing together all parties to the Cambodian conflict in several rounds of the "Jakarta Informal Meetings" (JIM). The idea of such meetings was agreed on in July 1987 by Vietnam and Indonesia, with the blessings of Indo-China and ASEAN respectively. Malaysia had also earlier, at about the end of 1984, supported the idea of "proximity talks" with Indo-China.

Following on a "warm-up" meeting of Hun Sen, representing the State of Cambodia (the new name of the People's Republic of Kampuchea), with

Prince Sihanouk in Paris, Indonesia received the signal to hold the first JIM in July 1988. Besides the internal parties to the Cambodian conflict, JIM saw the participation of all the Indo-China and ASEAN states, thereby allowing for the first face-to-face meetings of all the regional parties in the conflict. Even though the first JIM failed to resolve outstanding issues, it nevertheless propelled a new dynamic in the peace process which led to other meetings among the various parties to the conflict, including the meeting between Sihanouk, Son Sann, and Hun Sen in Paris of November 1988; between Thailand and Vietnam in January 1989, and between Vietnam and China also in January 1989.

Since all ASEAN foreign policies were also *ipso facto* officially sanctioned by Malaysia, the above actions saw the full participation of Malaysia, although it should be stated that security and political questions did not appear to be an empahsis of the Mahathir government, especially after Ghazali Shafie retired as foreign minister. Malaysia's main initiative was to push gently for the eventual inclusion of the Indo-China states into ASEAN.

By the time of the ASEAN Summit of January 1992, Malaysia had already openly declared support for Vietnam's and Laos' intention to join the regional body. In the event, the Singapore Declaration reiterated support for the U.N. role in the Cambodian peace process and ASEAN's willingness to partake in international programmes for the reconstruction of Vietnam, Laos, and Cambodia, and in an obvious overture to Indo-China, it welcomed all Southeast Asian countries to accede to the ASEAN Treaty of Amity and Cooperation. As part of political and security cooperation, ASEAN commitment to ZOPFAN and the Southeast Asian Nuclear Weapon Free Zone (SEANWFZ) was re-emphasized. (*New Straits Times,* 31 January 1992). By the annual ASEAN Foreign Minister's meeting in Manila in July that year, both Laos and Vietnam had acceded to the Amity Treaty. The ASEAN Summit of July 1994 in Bangkok inaugurated the ASEAN Regional Forum (ARF) and the subsequent Ministerial Meeting in Brunei the following year saw Vietnam participating as a full-fledged ASEAN member, and the setting up of an Asia-Europe Meeting (ASEM) alongside the ARF. The SEANWFZ came to fruition in December 1995, when the ASEAN heads of government signed the draft treaty in Bangkok. With ASEAN developments coming fast and thick up till the mid-1990s, Malaysia may be said to have not only generally backed all these moves, but perhaps in some instances, even initiated some of them to fashion a more aggressive and frontal political role for the regional body.

Mahathir in his Hong Kong speech cited earlier had already called for an enlarged ten-nation grouping comprising the then ASEAN six to be joined by the three Indo-China states, plus Myanmar, a reiteration of an earlier call in speech in Kuala Lumpur to the First ASEAN Congress of the Strategic Studies Institutes of ASEAN countries (*New Straits Times*, 9 October 1992), and there was little doubt that this will soon become reality.

Thus, in the Mahathir period, ASEAN no doubt remained the primary instrumentality of Malaysia's regional diplomacy and its fallback for regional security. However, the idea of the EAEG/EAEC remained problematic and, as we have noted, was later replaced by the ASEAN-Plus-Three and the EAS. It is of some interest to note that the Singapore Summit of 1992 approved in principle the EAEC idea which Malaysia was keen to sell to its ASEAN partners, despite the flak that some members were unhappy over Mahathir's announcement of the idea before consulting other ASEAN member states. The Singapore Summit also endorsed and initiated the first steps of an ASEAN Free Trade Area (AFTA) called the Common Effective Preferential Tariff (CEPT) scheme, with Malaysia immediately offering some 4,000 items to be traded under this system which took effect on 1 January 1993. Import duties would range from 0 to 5 per cent and AFTA was initially due to come into full maturation by the year 2008, but later the timetable was advanced to the year 2003.[25]

POLITICAL ECONOMY AND FOREIGN POLICY, 1981–96

Foreign policy under Mahathir's tenure epitomized the linkage of politics and economics, which is taken to mean both the linkage of the national unit with the external world, as well as the linkage between domestic and external policy. Malaysia's foreign policy in this first Mahathir period can be appreciated in terms of its economic ambitions to be imaginatively exploiting the new international division of labour, and in terms of domestic developments and forces garnered by the irrepressible Mahathir to propagate and, to a great extent, realize his vision of turning Malaysia into a high-growth, rapidly industrializing, developmental state. This trajectory of development was aggressively orchestrated by Mahathir and foreign policy was creatively geared to serve national interests as defined by his government. The domestic instrumentality for bringing about this state of affairs was an authoritarian state structure articulating within a capitalist framework.[26] The imaginative constructions of new foreign policy positions and strategies did not alter fundamental policies that were laid down in the Abdul Razak period. Rather they added new elements of iconoclasm and developmental assertiveness. Mahathir's era also epitomizes — more than any other period — the deliberate use of foreign policy for the pursuance of national goals and national needs as defined by the policymakers of the day.[27]

Like foreign policy in the previous periods, the basis of Malaysian foreign policy during the Mahathir tenure can be explained by reference to four generic sources of policy: historical, external, internal, and idiosyncratic (or elite) factors as depicted in Figure 7.1. It also may be useful to conceive of this first period of foreign policy under Mahathir as traversing two major phases; 1981–87 and 1987–96. The reason for selecting 1987 as the end of the first phase is that Mahathir overcame intense internal politicking within UMNO that year and it was also the year when the infamous "Operation Lalang" saw the detention without trial of some 106 to 107 politicians, activists, and intellectuals. There was considerable international protest over the arrests, especially from NGO circles, and many of the social activists were designated by Amnesty International as "prisoners of conscience".

Core foreign policy objectives of political independence and territorial integrity remained stable in the first Mahathir period, but middle-range possession goals of enhancing the nation state were evident in the quest for NIC status, while long-range objectives were now linked to Malaysia's aspiration to become a developed country by the year 2020. This explains the various high-profile postures and new strategies of economic development such as the "Look East" policy and the EAEC. The intervening variable would comprise a combination of Mahathir's proclivities (the idiosyncratic factor) and the NIC concept of capitalist modernization, which had become the touchstone of the Mahathir period. This ideology differs from that of the NEP period when a state-capitalism approach was promoted in contrast to the Mahathirian period when the new watchword was "Malaysia Inc". It is undeniable that most of Mahathir's cabinet colleagues, the upper echelons of the newly furbished UMNO, share this ideological orientation. The local bourgeoisie, Bumiputera and non-Bumiputera, were clearly not opposed to the economic thrust of the Mahathir policies. The UMNO Team A-Team B struggle in the late 1980s perhaps saw Mahathir's vision triumph over that of the bureaucratic and royalist wings of the party, led by Tengku Razaleigh, who then went on to form the splinter Semangat 46 political party.[28] Khoo (1992) propounds the idea of Mahathir as the harbinger of a grand modernization vision and programme, perhaps somewhat at variance with more traditional views in UMNO circles, more or less backed by a bureaucratic class, which wanted to see a continuance of the old NEP. As suggested above, the programmes envisaged by the NDP's Vision 2020 plan seem to confirm such an interpretation. Despite Khoo's notion of an implied resistance to this by the bureaucratic class, one need not necessarily accept the view that the whole bureaucracy *en masse* was against the new vision. Often bureaucrats are quick to spot the changes and move with the times or with the predilections of a new leader. Indeed, in the NDP period, the government began openly to promote English and downplay Malay as the medium for the acquisition of new knowledge and skills necessary for Malaysia's 2020 vision. A controversy boiled over, for example, between Mahathir and the leading Malay daily, *Utusan Malaysia*, over this issue, but it was a forgone conclusion as to whose views would prevail.[29] Gordon Means (1991) also talks about Mahathir's "new political idiom" of politics, but relates it more to domestic issues such as the declining role of the royalty (Means 1991, pp. 110ff). Although Means' analysis predates the Vision 2020 policy, he had, by and large, captured the Mahathirian shift in spirit. The general thrust of all the above analyses supports my notion that whatever one's assessment of Mahathir, he was the iconoclast *par excellence*.[30] Generally considered to be the "brains" behind the NEP, through the ideas expressed in his controversial *The Malay Dilemma*, Mahathir became the very person who would hasten the NEP's formal demise. Foreign policy mirrored Mahathir's domestic politics. Although a little more circumspect about foreign policy than domestic matters, he had already early on acquired accolades (if disputed) for his steadfast stances against the hegemony of the West, and was virtually the main spokesman for the Third World on issues of the day, such as environment degradation and sustainable development. However, the external agency of even a Mahathir was, needless to say, constrained by a global order that constantly frustrated his ambitions.

Nesadurai has written of the primacy of economics and Islam in Mahathir's foreign policy (Nesadurai 2004, pp. 7–9). According to her, Mahathir also used the Asian values discourse as a counter-hegemonic trope to reject both Westernism in the larger sense and neo-liberalism in the global order, viz. "The "Asian Values" counter-discourse, thus, sought to ideologically de-legitmize American or Western models and practices of human rights and liberal democracy, while it also helped to legitimize the interventionist approach to economic development based on communitarian end-goals rather than the maiximisation of individual self-interest" (Nesadurai 2004, p. 12).

We will also see in the next chapter how Mahathir's counter-hegemonic discourse became particularly prominent in the 1997–98 financial crisis, which Nesadurai also analyses (pp. 12ff). However, I would be loath to suggest that the Mahathir counter-hegemonic discourse was based on any radical thorough-going anti-capitalist or even anti-imperialist politics. Mahathir was able to employ astutely a capitalist developmental approach (with increasing neo-liberal attributes) in the domestic realm even as he railed against the injustices of the neo-liberal international order. Below is an attempt to depict graphically in a constructivist vein the character of foreign policy formulation in the Mahathir period, particularly in terms of its political economy linkages.

TABLE 7.1
Foreign Policy Outputs 1981–96

Postures	Objectives	Strategies	Actions
Non-aligment South-South, Islamist Orientations	• Maintaining political independence, territorial integrity	• Promoting ZOPFAN • Promoting regional security cooperation • Championing NAM	• Initiating/signing the SEA Nuclear Weapons Free Zone • Occupying Spratly island (T. Layang Layang) • Promoting and supporting CGDK through ASEAN • Support Cambodian peace move
Anti-Imperialist Champion of the Third World Neo-mercantilist Orientations	• Enhancing economy and status towards becoming developed country	• Iconoclasm • Promoting and participating in South-South schemes	• Sending peacekeeping forces to Cambodia (UNTAC), Bosnia (UNPROFOR), and Somalia (UNISOM) • Supporting Bosnia and expulsion of Yugloslavia from U.N. • Anti-U.S. statements, Gulf War decisions 1991
Internationalist & Regionalist (ASEAN) and East Asian Orientations	• Enhancing national status and global presence • Promoting Asian regional cooperation and security • Increased cooperation with Japan and NIEs	• "Buy British Last" • "Look East" Policy • Promoting goals and role of ASEAN • Promote Japan's regional/global role	• Forex trading • Tin market foray • Approval of Japanese PKO bill and peacekeeping in Cambodia • MAS flights economic agreements, etc. with Indo-China

Source: Author's own compilation.

FIGURE 7.1

Malaysian Foreign Policy under Mahathir Mohamad, 1981–2003

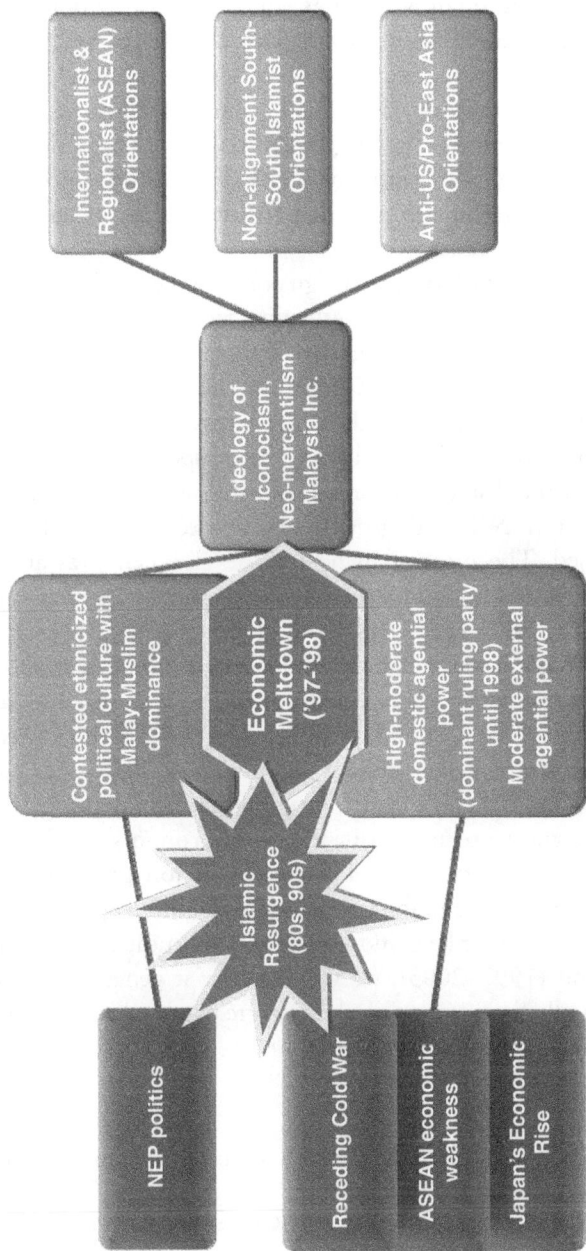

Source: Author's own compilation.

CONCLUSION

Underneath the facade of Mahathir's iconoclasm was a political astuteness which was ably geared to propel regime change, as well as maintain a form of authoritarian regime which best served essentially national goals of modernization towards "NIChood". The Mahathir government was ruthless in implementing this objective, brooking no opposition in its path, and was ready to go the gamut of social controls on objectors to such a plan, although latterly, also prepared to use the carrot to lure would-be oppositionists to its cause.

One may say that Malaysian foreign policy in the first Mahathir period saw the iconoclastic prime minister overhauling significant old domestic policies and charting new, bold and aggressive foreign economic policies geared to launching Malaysia first into "NICdom" and the anticipated onward trajectory to developed country status by the suggested year, 2020. His foreign policy yielded much domestic dividend from the perspective of his pro-modernist and national-capitalist vision for the country, and turned Malaysia into a second-generation NIC with growth rates and economic performance never before attained. The price of such rapid development was an increasingly authoritarian state structure which saw its worst excesses in the arbitrary mass arrests of 1987. The event occurred after two bad years in which the country suffered a negative growth of 1 per cent and 0 growth respectively. Subsequent inordinately high growth rates, plus a virtual full employment situation, allowed for a confident pursuance of Mahathir's new vision for the country. However, the country's attainment of NIC status paradoxically locked it even more firmly into the new international division of labour, and any major downturn or upturn in the world economy was bound to affect the Malaysian state very swiftly and thereby its foreign policy as well. This political economy factor in foreign policy, with both its positive and negative ramifications, has never been more evident than in the first Mahathir period. In next period (1997–2003), we will see how it generated an impact that would eventually force the political departure of arguably the most dominant figure of Malaysian politics to date.

NOTES

1. See Saravanamuttu (1996*a*). Substantial factual portions of this chapter are drawn from this earlier article of mine.
2. If we take it that the acknowledged NICs are the four "tigers" of Asia, namely, Hong Kong, Taiwan, South Korea and Singapore, I would argue that by the World Bank's reckoning (World Bank 1993), Malaysia, Thailand and possibly Indonesia rank as "second generation" NICs.

3. Cf. Milne and Mauzy (1999, p. 123) who make a similar point, viz. "It takes time for the unwieldy ship of state to make a big change of course."
4. See his conclusions (Dhillon 2008, p. 267).
5. See Khoo's (1995, pp. 81–88) studied interpretation of the young Mahathir's essays.
6. The policy was announced, after all, no more than seven years after the the infamous "Maluri" anti-Japanese riots in Jakarta during Premier Fukuda's visit, and student demonstrations against the Japanese in Bangkok at about the same time. The incidents jolted Japan into extending a US$2 billion aid programme to mollify the frayed emotions of its ASEAN partners under the so-called Fukuda Doctrine of 1976.
7. However, the policy emulation was extended to South Korea, sealed through scholarships and exchanges just as with Japan, which proffered "Mombushu" scholarships to Malaysians. One could well surmise why two other Chinese-populated NICs, Taiwan, with no diplomatic ties with Malaysia, and Hong Kong, not an independent state, were not accorded the same privilege as South Korea.
8. See Saravanamuttu, 1992*a*, for a discussion of both the positive and negative consequences of "Looking East".
9. Cf. Khoo, 1992, for an interpretation of Mahathir's grand vision, mainly from the perspective of internal politics.
10. The nine challenges were: national integration and the development of a "Bangsa Malaysia" (Malaysian Race), creating a psychologically liberated and secure Malaysian society, developing a mature democratic society based on a communitarian democracy, establishing a moral and ethical society, establishing a matured liberal and tolerant society, establishing a scientific and progressive society, establishing a caring society and caring culture, ensuring an economically just society, and, establishing a prosperous society that is dynamic, robust and resilient. These challenges were to be met by an economy that is diversified and balanced, quick to adapt to changing patterns of supply and demand and competition, technologically proficient, strong and cohesive, and driven by brain-power, with high, escalating productivity, an economy which was entrepreneurial and self-reliant, sustained by exemplary work ethics, characterized by low inflation, and subjected to the full discipline and rigour of market forces (Mahathir 1991, pp. 2–4 and 8–9).
11. I gathered this from private communications with NECC members whom I know. Another known fact is the tract, *The Way Forward* (1991), which embodied these NECC recommendations, was chiefly prepared by the Institute of Strategic and International Studies, then headed by Nordin Sopiee; the institute no doubt took liberties at embellishing its text.
12. There was a strong rumour that Mahathir at the height of the Gulf crisis had received a phone call from Bush when he was in Tokyo for support of resolution 678, which sanctioned military action against Iraq. Mahathir divulged this later in anger over the EAEC issue, See *The Star*, 8 November 1991.

13. See Camroux (1994, pp. 30–36), Saravanamuttu (1996*b*, pp. 116–19) and Higgott and Stubbs (1995) for three expositions on why Mahathir remained adamant in his views about APEC.

14. The Japanese Foreign Minister, Yohei Komo, in raising his queries implied that Japan would not participate in EAEC, if it were to drive a wedge in the APEC formation, while South Korean Foreign Minister Gong Ro-Myong similarly wanted a consensus from APEC members on EAEC if his country were to be part of it. See *New Straits Times*, 4 August 1995.

15. See Severino (2006, pp. 265–66).

16. See Severino (2006, pp. 269–74) for a discussion of this and the steps involved in the establishment of the EAS.

17. See *FEER*, 20 August 1992.

18. Cf. Nair (1997, p. 80ff.) and Hussin (1993, pp. 32–33).

19. According to Nair (1997, p. 80), Mahathir, on assumption of the premiership in 1981, came up with a formal ranking of foreign relations as follows: 1. ASEAN, 2. Islamic countries, 3. the nonaliged community, 4. the Commonwealth. A senior official Nair spoke with rated Isalmic counties as a "very distant" second priority (Nair 1997, p. 90). Surely such a rigid rendering of priorities could hardly be maintained for long and the absence of the United States or Europe is rather conspicuous.

20. Malaysia has insisted on a two-state solution to the Palestinian-Israeli impasse and a comprehensive peace agreement acceptable to the Palestinians, with the provision for a full-fledged Palestinian state, with Arab East Jerusalem as its capital (Wisma Putra webpage <http://www.kln.gov.my> (accessed 16 October 2008). See also speeches by Foreign Minister Syed Hamid Albar, *Multilateral Issues, 2005–2007* (2007).

21. A testimony to the humanitarian aspect of the policy was the willingness of Malaysia to accept Bosnian refugees as residents in Malaysia. Many campaigns and fund-rasing events were also held. Of course, it could hardly be denied that the Muslim or "Islamic" factor was an important driver of the policy.

22. This was a five-page statement (1991) prepared by Malaysian civil society organizations which were against the war in Iraq (hereafter cited as Statement 1991).

23. This, of course, was the well known expression used by the George Bush (Senior) administration.

24. See Wain (2009, Chapter 10). Mak reveals the extent of U.S.-Malaysia collaboration as told by then Defence Minister Najib Razak in May 2002 in a lecure entitled "U.S.-Malaysia Defence Cooperation: A Solid Success Story" at a Heritage Foundation Centre for Strategic and International Studies event. Najib said there had been more than seventy-five U.S. military ships visiting in two and a half years, the U.S. Air Force conducts mock battles with the Royal Malaysian Air Force, the U.S. Navy SEALS has training in Malaysia twice a year, and 1,500 Malaysian personnel have benefited from IMET (Mak [2004], pp. 147–48).

25. See *The Star,* 29 January 1992 and *Asiaweek,* 7 February 1992, pp. 23–25. Clearly, ASEAN's AFTA ambitions remain stalled up to the time of writing (2009).
26. An intrepretation of the character of the Malaysian authoritarian state as it is related to the push for rapid industrialization is found in Saravanamuttu (1987). I have characterized the Malaysian state as a variant of O'Donnell's Bureaucratic-Authoritarian state.
27. See Weinstein (1972) and my earlier work, Saravanamuttu (1983), pp. 6–7, for an explication of this idea.
28. An interpretation of this split is given by Khoo (1992) and Shamsul (1988). See also Chamil (1988), for a portrayal of the conflict from the perspective of Mahathir supporters.
29. See Mahathir's letter to *Utusan Malaysia,* 19 September 1992. Subsequent to the publication of Mahathir's letter, there was a major shake-up of the top brass of the paper in which Mahathir's detractors were removed.
30. An interesting interpretation of "Mahathirism" is given by Khoo's (1995) in-depth study of Mahathir's paradoxical intellectualism. Khoo sees in Mahathir's thinking, a shift in the definition of "the enemy" away from the Chinese domestically to "the West" externally. See his Chapter 3 (especially pp. 54–81) which deals in large part with Mahathir's foreign policy.

8

CRISIS, RECOVERY, AND DENOUEMENT OF AN ERA, 1997–2003

PHASES OF MAHATHIR'S TENURE

As Mahathir Mohamad approached the sixteenth year of his premiership, he was looking rather comfortable politically. He had overcome the internal factionalism of UMNO which exploded into the open conflict of Team A versus Team B, and by dint of authoritarian power, had contained other dissident and oppositional voices through the 1987 political detentions, while seeing through two general elections in 1990 and 1995. Indeed in the second election, he had led the Barisan Nasional (BN) to a famous electoral victory which saw the coalition garnering an unprecedented 65.1 per cent of the popular votes.[1] Indeed, as one writer puts it, regime maintenance through "personalized dominance" in politics was at its zenith (Hwang 2003).

Although for the purposes of analysing foreign policy I have divided Mahathir's tenure into two major periods, analysts such as Ho Khai Leong (2001) have found four distinct phases in Mahathir's term, namely: 1981–84 — an early reformist phase of purportedly instituting a "Clean, Efficient and Trustworthy" government; 1985–89 — when the Mahathir administration was buffeted with charges of corruption and an economic recession, which also saw the emergence of intra-UMNO acrimonious politics and outright political repression; 1990–96 — a confident phase when the Vision 2020 and NDP were propounded, and when Islamization was implemented *a fortiori;*[2] 1997–2003 — a period of economic and political uncertainties marked by the financial crisis and meltdown, the Anwar Ibrahim embroilment, the concomitant *Reformasi* movement, and Mahathir's political decline.[3] Thus, as suggested by an astute analyst of Mahathir's politics, the four periods could be dubbed as follows:

- Early Mahathirism, 1981–84
- Mid-Mahathirism, 1985–89
- Late Mahathirism, 1990–96
- Crisis Mahathirism, 1997–2003[4]

Clearly, foreign policy construction would have closely mirrored these domestic phases of the Mahathirian tenure as pointed out, for example, by Joseph Liow.[5] It would be germane for me to briefly revisit the broad thrusts of foreign policy in the first three phases before delving into the final phase, which will be the main burden of this chapter.

As we know, in the first phase of Mahathirian reformism, the "Look East" policy was proffered as the distinctive foreign policy strategy that would help Malaysia and Malaysians through a Japanese-styled work ethnic to institute what in contemporary parlance would be "good governance". The policy was vigorously pursued on the domestic plane by such measures as "quality control circles' in companies and government departments. On the economic front, the Japanese-styled *sogoshosha* (or general trading company) became the model for government-link companies (Saravanamuttu 1991, p. 81). There was also the introduction of the "Malaysia Inc." notion in tandem with the government privatization policy and the creation of the Heavy Industries Corporation of Malaysia (HICOM) in 1983, and the elaborate and expensive collaboration with Japan in the Perwaja Steel enterprise, which ultimately failed. The deliberate attempts to link domestic and external economic policies were clearly evident in this phase of Mahathir's tenure.

In the second phase, the domestic economic downturn and problems may be said to have sparked some "tail-wag-dog" manoeuvres. Foreign policy was enlisted for deflecting domestic issues. One could detect that Mahathir was particularly strident in this phase in championing the South-South and also Muslim causes. An example of such Third World posturing was the Mahathir initiative in creating of the Group of 15 among LDCs in 1988 (Camroux 1994, p. 22).

However, a more strident Islamic stance did not come until the third phase, during which occurred the Bosnia-Herzegovina imbroglio and when, it must be said, Mahathir's position on the 1991 Gulf War paradoxically became a problem for his government. This phase was also marked by greater engagement with the OIC and the creation the Institute of Islamic Understanding (IKIM), directly under the patronage of the prime minister in 1992.[6] The role of IKIM was to propagate a state defined Islam to meet challenges of the internal Islamic resurgence and to establish a dialogue with non-Muslims inside and outside Malaysia (Milne and Mauzy 1999, p. 86).

This leads us to the final phase and period of the Mahathir tenure, to which we will now turn our attention. We will give the main focus to the events related to the financial crisis of 1997–98 and its external and internal impact. In this sense, this chapter will not follow the previous chapters by way of depicting foreign policy outputs of the years concerned. Rather, this chapter will adopt an international political economy approach to examine both the domestic and external ramifications of the financial crisis for Malaysia. The second part of the chapter deals with matters which are also largely domestic, revolving around the *Reformasi* Movement, sparked by the financial meltdown and Anwar Ibrahim's incarceration after a sensational, politicized trial. The external implications of these events will be teased out. Finally, the chapter ends with the suggestion that a political denouement of the period effectively meant Mahathir's departure from the political stage. In many senses, the normalization of foreign policy could only occur after the various aspects of this economic and political crisis were resolved. Of course, in matters of security and other core foreign policy postures and objectives, such as relations with ASEAN, major powers and the Islamic World, policies remained stable and largely unchanged throughout the crisis.

THE FINANCIAL CRISIS AND MELTDOWN[7]

A brief note on the state of the global financial order may be useful before we examine the actual crisis and its impact on Southeast Asia and Malaysia. It is generally recognized that the Bretton Woods arrangements were overtaken by events by the 1970s, wherein among other things, the fixed exchange rates system based on gold convertibility was replaced by flexible exchange rates. Since then, the world's financial system has been marked by only intermittent attempts to stabilize exchange rates — and then only among the important currencies such as the U.S. dollar, the German mark, and the Japanese yen for example, the Bonn summit of 1978, the Plaza Agreement of 1985, and the Louvre Accord of 1987 (Pauly 1997, p. 27). The somewhat freewheeling situation in the financial sector was not unrelated to the ascendancy of neoliberalism, since states, which lacked political will or authority, could hardly institute systematic measures to check the market players, who by the 1990s, had grown by proportions that were truly phenomenal. This is not to say that private market players did not try to institute international regimes for the control of financial subsectors such as international banking and the securities markets (Coleman and Porter 1994). However, such regimes were, by and large, weak and poorly supervised. These broad economic and financial developments of globalization in 1990s have provided the context, if not the impetus, for the spectacular events of 1997 and 1998 which have come to be called East Asia's financial "crisis", "turmoil", and "meltdown". An even more far-reaching global economic meltdown was sparked in 2008, a matter beyond the scope of this book. Suffice it to say that the 1997–98 crisis was practically a prelude to that event ten years later.

Many explanations to the East Asian economic turmoil now fill copious pages of writings in books and articles.[8] The crisis essentially began after an extraordinary spate of developments sparked by the devaluation of the Thai baht in June 1997. With hindsight, most analysts agree that a major reason for the financial crisis and meltdown was that Southeast Asian countries had been running large current account deficits for several years, with effects on local financial markets even prior to the 1997 situation.[9] Indeed, in the second half of 1996, high interest rates in Thailand caused a stock market slump, but the central bank moved in to stabilize the baht by spending some of its $40 billion foreign reserve. In addition to this, export growth had also ground to a halt by the end of 1996.

In retrospect, the problem of large current account deficits and the concomitant of overheated economies can be traced to the global developments in the financial sector arising out of the 1985 Plaza Accord. Taking Thailand as the template, the accord, which revalued the yen upwards *vis-à-vis* the dollar, had the effect of making Thailand (and much of Southeast Asia) increasingly indebted in yen-denominated loans. This proportion reached 52 per cent in Thailand's case and brought about massive influxes of Japanese capital and an equally large outflow of exports. The Plaza Accord also made credit in U.S. dollars cheap for Thailand, allowing for a decade-long boom of the Thai corporate sector. However, as the dollar value rose against the yen in 1995 and 1996,[10] in tandem with a drop in exports as a result of the Japanese slowdown, Thailand's troubles began to multiply.

Some months before the actual meltdown, analysts such as David Hale (1997), however, did not think that the Mexican scenario which the *Economist* had begun to foist on Southeast Asia was valid. He argued that ineffective exchange rate and banking policies could be corrected, especially in the Thai case, to avert a Mexican-style crisis.[11] While one could say that such policies failed to be implemented by the Thai government prior to the July 1997 crash, it would be counterfactual to suggest that had such policies been put into place, the crisis could have been averted. Certainly even the stronger economies such as Malaysia and Singapore, with their tighter monetary policies, were by no means insulated from the 'contagion' that swept across the region. Virtually all of East Asia suffered from the financial meltdown with South Korea taking the worst beating in the second phase, after Thailand.

Jomo (1998) argues that the root of the crisis was economic vulnerability. The major reasons for this vulnerability were both internal and external, anchored on the twin problems of a quasi-peg of Southeast Asian currencies to the dollar, and the unprecedented level of financial liberalization in the region spawning cheap liquidity, which became unaffordable when events turned sour for the "tiger" economies. However, explanations based on the macroeconomic and microeconomic vulnerabilities of the Southeast Asian economies only provide part of the picture. The fact of the matter was that global financial markets and the financial sectors in most economies had become effectively decoupled from their real economies (Saravanamuttu 1998, pp. 122–23).

Early in the crisis, Mahathir charged that Asian currencies had suffered at the hands of "rogue speculators", blaming George Soros, the Hungarian-born American financier-international fund manager-cum-philantrophist, for launching an assault on the ASEAN economies because of ASEAN's decision to admit Myanmar (Burma) into the regional association. Soros denied this and countered that he had been promoting the idea that the global economy was in deep crisis and needed fundamental reform (Soros 1998). Soros and Mahathir had a war of words in Hong Kong during the World Bank-IMF meetings in September, in which the former said the prime minister was a "menace to his own country". Mahathir, meanwhile, went to different international forums to suggest his ideas for reforming the international financial system.[12] On 1 September 1998, the premier made the unprecedented move of instituting capital controls for the country and the non-tradability (or convertibility) of the Malaysian ringgit. The next day, 2 September 1998, Mahathir sacked Anwar Ibrahim, his finance minister.

The differences between Anwar and Mahathir were apparent since the World Bank-IMF annual meetings in Hong Kong of September 1997. By December 1997, Anwar had introduced austerity measures aimed at curbing support for companies favoured by Mahathir. Rather conspicuously, he had frozen the Bakun Dam project. However, Jomo has argued that even though Anwar approved tighter fiscal and monetary measures in late 1997 in line with IMF recommendations, by June 1998, he had increased public spending, especially to provide for credit and investment in food and agriculture, and also sought to increase liquidity and banking margins.[13] When the National Economic Action Council was formed on 7 January 1998, Mahathir had put former Finance Minister Daim Zainuddin, in charge of it as executive director. By 25 August, Daim had assumed the position of special functions minister, in charge of the economy, a move seen as the writing on the wall for Anwar Ibrahim.

DEBUNKING THE IMF

Just prior to the crisis, the basic vulnerability of the Malaysian economy to the forces of financial globalization was clearly in evidence, despite the usual strong indicators of economic health. Several macroeconomic indicators of such vulnerability emerged by the mid-1990s:

*   The savings-investment gap was at 5 per cent in 1997, fuelling a current account deficit in the order of RM12 billion since 1994 and remained high throughout the 1990s. This gap was bridged by foreign direct investment traditionally, but increasingly by short-term capital inflows.
*   The sourcing of short-term investment flows through the Kuala Lumpur Stock Exchange (KLSE) had reached feverish levels by the early 1990s owing to the establishment of the Securities Commission, and the passing of legislation allowing for easy credit. This led to the collapse of the market in early 1994, but a rebound by early 1997 wherein market capitalization exceeded by five times the annual national income.
*   An explosion of private sector debt, commercial bank liabilities increasing from RM10.3 billion at the end of 1995 to RM25.2 billion in June 1997, while their net external reserves position declined from negative RM5.3 billion to negative RM17.1 billion over the same period.

                                                        (Jomo 1998, pp. 181–82)

As reported in the *Mid-Term Review of the Seventh Plan*, the financial crisis impacted heavily on the Malaysian economy. The ringgit depreciated from RM2.52 *vis-à-vis* the USD on 1 July 1997 to RM3.53 by the end of the same month, before reaching an all-time low of RM4.88 in early January 1998. It was subsequently fixed at RM3.80 on 2 September 1998, along with the introduction of exchange control. The KLSE Composite Index fell by 73 per cent and market capitalization decreased by 74 per cent between July 1997 and September 1998. In the banking sector, NPLs (non-performing loans) rose to 11.4 per cent by August 1998. For the year 1998, real output of the economy contracted by 6.7 per cent, the inflation rate rose 5.3 per cent, and the rate of unemployment to 3.9 per cent. The federal government account registered a deficit for the first time since 1993, and external debt.

The Malaysian government's initial response to the crisis — and especially Mahathir's responses — was one of a series of unorthodox interventions. Several direct steps were then taken to insulate the domestic interest rate from capital mobility. The offshore, over-the-counter CLOB (Central Limit Order Book) in Singapore was stopped to prevent illegal short selling of Malaysian shares. There was also the step of banning the short selling of

100 blue-chip stocks and the plan to use funds of the Employees' Provident Fund to shore up share prices. This was followed up, most importantly, by the announcement of capital controls on 1 September as indicated earlier. In such a move, Mahathir supposedly followed a proposal by MIT Professor Paul Krugman who had argued in an article in *Fortune* magazine that such capital controls could give crisis-ridden Asian economies breathing space in which to resume growth.

The controls remained in place for almost eight years and were lifted only in July 2005 when the ringgit peg was removed. Mahathir and the government claimed that they made the difference in Malaysia's economic recovery when compared with the other crisis-stricken East Asian economies. In retrospect, it is true that by doing so, and in tandem with various other fiscal and monetary measures, Malaysia was able to avoid an IMF rescue package. By the middle of 1999, the Malaysian authorities were already trumpeting that the recovery was more than evident, with the stock market showing signs of new life, indicated by the KLSE-CI breaching 800 points by August after a low of about 260 points at the nadir of the crisis. By August, regular monthly surpluses in the current account had also boosted Malaysia's international reserves to US$31 billion, good for seven months of imports. Although 1998 saw a decline in GDP of negative 6.7 per cent, the government towards the end of 1999 forecasted a 5 per cent growth.[14]

Throughout the handling of the crisis, the Malaysian government and the central bank, Bank Negara, avoided any borrowing from the IMF. Instead funds were sourced from Japan, ADB, and the World Bank, and through the issue of international bonds. In July 1999, Bank Negara issued US$1 billion bond in New York, which although oversubscribed, was issued at a rate 330 basis points above that of U.S. Treasury bonds.[15] A second bond issue of US$659 million was conducted in August 1999 by the national oil corporation, Petronas. This was short of the original one billion target because market conditions were unfavourable. The bonds were issued at 320 basis points above U.S. Treasury bonds (*New Straits Times*, 6 August 1999).

Other measures included the setting up of an Asset Management Corporation (Danaharta) in March 1998 to undertake restructuring and recapitalization of the banking system. A "special purpose vehicle", Danamodal, was also set up to mop up NPLs and generally to source funding for recapitalization of companies and to improve liquidity. Bank Negara, which supervised both bodies, moved to restructure the banking sector and to cushion debt-ridden companies by keeping interest rates low and by injecting liquidity through measures such as the bond issues.

In a radical banking move, the central bank in early August 1999 announced that Malaysian banks would be merged into six major groups. The first step was for Malayan Banking, the country's largest state-backed bank, to take over eight financial institutions. Public Bank, a Chinese flagship, was to merge with other Chinese-owned financial holdings, while Bank of Commerce was to merge with Bank Bumiputera, the Malay flagship which had become insolvent. Multipurpose Bank was to merge with RHB Bank, thought to be the second largest bank, together with some others, and Southern Bank, was expected to take over some other banks, including Penang Chinese-based Ban Hin Lee Bank.[16] However, by the next month, it became clear that the plan was too ambitious and could not be pulled off without encountering problems. By October, Bank Negara was forced to announce that the banks were free to choose their own partners for merger, following Prime Minister Mahathir's own statements to the same effect.[17]

CRISIS AND POLITICAL LEGITIMACY

In this section we will undertake a general analysis of the crisis and its impact linking capital, ethnicity, and political legitimacy as the key elements in a political economy analysis of the financial crisis.

In this book, I have persistently argued that Malaysia's plural society frames and constrains the character of politics, economy, and foreign relations. By the 1990s, Malaysian society had become much more middle class and with a large proportion of *Bumiputeras* in the working class. The NEP, which was aimed at restructuring society and eradicating poverty, had been highly successful in the second objective and to some extent, in the first as well. The globalization and liberalization phase of Malaysia's political economy since the 1980s coincided with the ascendancy of Mahathir as prime minister. While confronting globalization in his inimical way, as we have pointed out in the previous chapter, Mahathir was clearly still subject to its overwhelming force. In a volume devoted to Mahathir's correspondence with world leaders, Abdullah Ahmad (2008, p. 78) writes that Mahathir was not against globalization, but wanted some form of accommodation from the West. The financial crisis and meltdown of 1997/98 was clear evidence of how globalization had adversely affected Malaysia, but Mahathir was apparently able to find broad common ground with French President Jacques Chirac who wrote that he shared Mahathir's view that "global governance has to be improved if the challenges of globalization are to be successfully met" (Abdullah Ahmad 2008, p. 99). In the manner in which he addressed the crisis, Mahathir clearly did again take up the cudgels against the economic "demons" of globalization. An important question in this analysis is how Mahathir was able to ride through this crisis and its consequences and to maintain both the legitimacy of the political regime and the economic goals he had set for Malaysia. A broader question relates to whether a bending of the political rules of the game became imperative for Mahathir in order to maintain a dubious legitimacy in the face of a political challenge from his political opponents, most importantly, from Anwar Ibrahim and the political opposition, and also from an increasingly vociferous and critical civil society.

Without doubt, the NIC pattern of economic growth continued to be the mainstay of the Malaysian economy as evidenced by developments well into the 2000s. The role for foreign capital continued to be important despite the incessant rhetoric of the prime minister on foreign domination and recolonization of the Malaysian economy. The fact remains that whether it is in trade or in export-led industrialization, Malaysia has depended and continues to depend on foreign demand, foreign capital, and foreign technology. The joint venture form of foreign involvement in the Malaysian manufacturing sector remains the preferred and most effective strategy of garnering both foreign capital and technology. In the 1990s, Japan remained the foremost foreign, direct investment contributor. However, in the late 1990s the United States substantially overtook Japan in FDI, and interestingly, first-tier NICs, especially Korea, Taiwan, and Singapore, had become increasingly important as foreign investors. If benefits from industrialization were the basis for a large part of Malaysia's political legitimacy, it was unlikely that there would have been any major change to the model of foreign-propelled industrialization even in the Mahathir era.

There is another level of activity in which foreign capital had become increasingly important. This is in the area of financial flows and portfolio investment. It is apparent that the KLSE had become a major source of capital for many Malaysian companies seeking capitalization. Foreign participation in the Malaysian stock market is not only important for the actual capital brought in, but is also highly desired as a boost to the local bourse's long-term credibility and performance. In the era of neoliberal financial liberalization, the lack of a high performing bourse is in itself an indicator of poor economic fundamentals. The Malaysian bourse saw a turnover of some RM408.55 billion in 1998. Total equity held was some RM117.06 billion with foreigners holding some RM23.35 billion or almost 20 per cent. Again, given the neoliberal dictates of global capitalism, foreign portfolio capital, therefore, became a crucial element for regime legitimacy in Malaysia, notwithstanding the rhetorical pronouncements of the prime minister to the contrary. Needless to say, legitimacy took a precipitous slide when the financial crisis struck in 1997/98. The KLSE, which plunged some 80 per cent, collapsed to only a quarter of its pre-crisis value at the height of the turmoil.

The NDP and Vision 2020 policies with their emphasis on growth already had an impact on the Malaysian share of corporate assets as reported in the *Mid-Term Review of the Seventh Plan*. The *Bumiputera* share fell slightly from 18.6 per cent in 1995 to 17.7 per cent in 1998. The Chinese share of 40.9 per cent in 1995 dropped slightly to 38.5 per cent by 1998. By contrast, foreigners in 1998 held 31.8 per cent of the corporate sector, which was 4.1 per cent more than in 1995. The growth strategies seem to have had an effect on Malaysian holdings in the corporate sector and it was evident that the middle class continued to expand along with the NDP.

In 1997, *Bumiputera* professionals roughly kept pace with Chinese and Indian professionals (32 per cent, 52.1 per cent, 13.1 per cent respectively of the total), but the professional and technical categories had some 63.1 per cent *Bumiputeras* in 1998. Other categories such as clerical and administrative workers also show a high percentage of *Bumiputeras*. Admittedly *Bumiputeras* predominate as agricultural workers (61 per cent), but so do they as production workers (43.6 per cent). A large *Bumiputera* middle class, along with that of other ethnic groups, increasingly impacted on Malaysian civil society. This factor had highly significant implications for political legitimacy. Certainly, it became self-evident that the political base of the ruling coalition would shift from its rural and non-urban sectors to more urban locales, given that middle class Malaysians would tend to be found in urban settings. More importantly, for the United Malay National Organization (UMNO), *primus inter pares* in the ruling coalition, such a change could mean the erosion of its traditional source of support which had been in rural constituencies.

Works on Malaysian capitalism by Gomez (1999), Gomez and Jomo (1997), and Searle (1999) give interesting insights on how the NEP and, to some extent, the NDP, affected capitalist development at the micro level of political economy. These findings throw new light on how cronyism, defined broadly as the phenomenon of favoring particular individuals in business dealings and contracts, affected political legitimacy. While the macro picture of corporate ownership of the economy provides fairly credible evidence for the achievements of the NEP, and by the end of the 1990s, also the NDP, there were many disturbing signs that the distribution of the economic cake had been somewhat skewed. Furthermore, these analysts have suggested that the NEP created "rentier" or rent-seeking capitalists especially among the *Bumiputeras* (Gomez and Jomo 1997, p. 179).

The authors suggest that the *Bumiputera* holdings in the corporate sector shown in official statistics probably underestimate the share, as well as the strategic holdings, of particularly influential *Bumiputeras*. Another interesting point made is that although Chinese businessmen have been able to hold their own to maintain their grip on the economy, the Mahathir era also spawned crony Chinese capitalists who were closely associated with, and cultivated close connections with leading politicians. Speculation was rife that many of these not-so-independent Chinese and other non-Malay businessmen also operated as proxies for certain UMNO leaders, particularly Daim Zainuddin (Gomez and Jomo 1997, p. 181).

Gomez gives more evidence of such connections and associations in his book on Chinese business in Malaysia (1999), but we can only touch briefly on some of the material here. The author examines how Chinese capital has withstood, or indeed, has taken advantage of the era of the NEP and NDP. It is evident from his eight case studies of prominent Chinese businessmen that although there has always been pressure to ensure *Bumiputera* participation in their enterprises, these businessmen have been able to maintain personal or family control. By deftly including prominent Malay directors in their respective companies and operations, there has been little necessity to relinquish full control to the state or to *Bumiputeras*. Such had been the *modus operandi* of Chinese corporate giants such as Robert Kuok (Perlis Plantations Bhd), Lim Goh Tong (Genting Bhd), and Loh Boon Siew (Oriental Holdings Bhd), the older set of the more etablished rich, and newer players such as William Cheng (Amsteel Corp. Bhd), Khoo Khay Peng (Mui Bhd), Vincent Tan Chee Yioun (Berjaya Group, Bhd), as well as a newer crop of Chinese capitalists such as Francis Yeoh (YTL Corp. Bhd) and Ting Pek Khiing (Ekran Bhd). Various names in last two groups of individuals had been known for their close association with the prime minister.

Searle's (1999) study of the NEP period takes on the issue of rentier capitalism head-on and concludes that, "there has been a blurring of categories of state, party and private in the development of Malay capitalism, so from that amalgam have emerged both rent-seekers and entrepreneurs and many groups between the two" (Searle 1999, p. 246). His measured conclusion about the character of Malaysian capitalism suggests that the political legitimacy of the Mahathir regime may have remained largely intact at least up till the eve of the political turmoil in UMNO, before Anwar Ibrahim's sacking. These new domestic considerations will need to be weighed along with the impact of globalization, via the financial crisis, which is addressed in the section below.

POLITICAL BAILOUTS AND RECOVERY

If there is one main lesson to be drawn from the 1997/98 financial crisis and meltdown, it is that nation states especially of the NIC variety, are prone and vulnerable to the vicissitudes of the international economic order. The latitude for action for individual states has become extremely narrow. Such was the case for Thailand and Indonesia, which had Hobson's choice in accepting IMF rescue packages. Malaysia apparently had much more room for manoeuvre as indicated by its response to the crisis. Jomo has argued that Mahathir's recovery package "was probably too late, flawed, biased (towards those interests he favoured) and arguably, unnecessary" (Jomo 2004, p. 258).[18] He argues that the introduction of capital controls fourteen months after the beginning of crisis was probably unnecessary. However, he allows that the package's counter-cyclical measures and capital flow management approach, as opposed to the IMF's pro-cyclical and account convertibility preferences, was the correct response. Jomo's critique centres on the "moral hazard" issue where privatized assets were recapitalized with apparently no penalties: "Thus, cronies are cynically said to have been doubly 'blessed' — first, when chosen to benefit from privatization and, then, by being allowed to 'walk away' virtually unscathed — at public expense" (Jomo 2004, p. 258). Among one of the more controversial measures was the closing of the offshore over-the-counter CLOB (Central Limit Order Book) catering mostly to Singapore investors and the banning of short-selling of 100 blue-chip stocks just prior to capital controls on 1 September.

Moreover, one could well argue that the recovery would not have been as smooth were it not for the easy availability to the government of "cash cows" such as the national oil corporation, Petronas, the Employee's Provident Fund (EPF), and the Muslim Pilgrims' Fund (*Tabung Haji*). Had it not been for this factor, the political legitimacy of the Mahathir regime may have been seriously or even mortally stricken by the impact of the crisis. We will give focus to the role of Petronas in bailing Malaysia out of the crisis, as revealed in media disclosures.

According to the *Far Eastern Economic Review,* for the year that ended in March 1999, Petronas paid more than RM6 billion in federal taxes, plus RM4.1 billion in dividends, which represented a sixth of the total expected government revenue for 1999.[19] It also repatriated some RM250 million monthly to local banks. Petronas posted net profits attributable to shareholders of RM6.8 billion in fiscal year 1998, down 32 per cent due to falling oil prices. In the upshot of the financial crisis, Petronas' most controversial acquisition was a RM1.8-billion controlling stake in the Malaysian International Shipping Corp (MISC), the country's largest shipper. However, this move was merely a precursor to MISC's buy up of Konsortium Perkapalan, the ailing shipping firm of Mirzan Mahathir, the prime minister's eldest son. MISC paid Konsortium RM836 million in cash and also inherited RM1.2 billion Ringgit of its debt. At the same time, Petronas raised its stake in MISC to 62 per cent to allow it to undertake the Konsortium acquisition. Needless to say, the deal raised more than a few eyebrows. At that time Anwar Ibrahim filed a report with the police charging nepotism and calling for a full investigation. Another "non-core" acquisition of Petronas occurred in early August 1999. The oil company bought a 27.2 per cent stake in national carmaker Perusahaan Otomobil Nasional Bhd (Proton), at a cost of RM1billion (*New Straits Times*, 7 August 1999). Proton was already known to have been burdened by heavy debts although its distribution and sales arm, Edaran Otomobil Nasional (EON), was reaping profits. Other rescues by Petronas in the past included the following:

- September 1984: RM 2.3 billion into state-owned Bank Bumiputera after it had to take heavy provisions for bad loans to Hong Kong's property sector.
- July 1985:Buys Pratt & Whitney-powered Boeing for lease to MAS so that the airline could get out of a contract with Rolls-Royce.
- March 1988: Pays a state agency nearly twice the market value of Dayabumi, a 36-storey building that served as its headquarters until it moved to the Twin Towers.
- October 1989: Bails out Bank Bumiputera with RM982 million after the bank was battered by falling property prices.

Apart from bailouts, Petronas was in the forefront of acquisitions and projects of particular interest to the prime minister. It bankrolled the US$800 million (RM4 billion) Petronas Twin Towers, the tallest buildings in the world, which it then occupied. Even more awesome was its financial backing of the new RM22 billion hi-tech administrative centre of the government known as Putrajaya, situated twenty-five kilometres from Kuala Lumpur. Putrajaya houses the prime minister's magnificent office and his palatial residence. Petronas was the major shareholder in a fund known as National Heritage Fund, set up for Putrajaya's construction.

From the foregoing expose of the 1998 activities of the national oil corporation, it can be surmised that the Mahathir government was heavily dependent on it for not only favourite projects, but also to mend fissures in the economy caused by the financial crisis and meltdown. From a critical perspective, the prevalence of such activities confirmed for many the prevalence of crony capitalism and rentier capitalism during the Mahathir regime. When charged with this, Mahathir facetiously remarked that all *Bumiputeras* and all businessmen were his cronies (*The Star*, 4 August 1999). This said, Mahathir had nonetheless successfully engineered an economic recovery visible to the man on the street.

THE *REFORMASI* MOVEMENT

It can be said that the political legitimacy of the Mahathir government eventually found its nemesis in the emergence of a strong Malaysian civil society. Weiss (2004) calls this Mahathir's unintended legacy. In the aftermath of the financial and economic crisis at the end of 1997, an unparalleled spate of events spilled over into the political arena at a remarkable and frenetic pace. These developments led to the sacking of Anwar Ibrahim as deputy president, and as deputy prime minister, and finance minister. Even more bizarre was Anwar's so-called corruption trial of seventy-seven days. It concluded with the sentencing of Anwar's to a six-year prison term on 14 April 1998. A new political party had already been formed on 4 April, helmed by Wan Azizah Ismail, Anwar's wife. The Parti Keadilan Nasional (later Parti Keadilan Rakyat, PKR) became the political vehicle for the forces of the *Reformasi* to direct their energies to electoral politics and political change, including seeking justice for Anwar as well as for other victims of the post-crisis political repression.

It became clear that Malaysia was in the grips of yet another bout of political turmoil, which raised new questions about the legitimacy of the UMNO-led political regime. Without doubt, the *Reformasi* related events, wittingly or otherwise, impelled new awakenings of political consciousness in Malaysian civil society. The actual outburst of peaceful street demonstrations had a sustaining power few would have predicted. Furthermore, more Malaysians were seemingly choosing to ignore the official and government-backed media and turning to information from alternative news purveyors. The circulation of the Parti Islam Se Malaysia (PAS) weekly newspaper *Harakah*, swelled to more than 380,000 readers before it was forced by the Home Ministry to become a bi-monthly paper. Indeed, certain strata of the knowing public created and began to propagate a host of alternative news sources on the internet, thereby supplementing or allowing Malaysians to ignore the existing, government-dominated media.

For the estimated 900,000 Malaysian internet users of that period,[20] they could log on to numerous *Reformasi* internet sites which had mushroomed, and the number of hits on the most popular ones was nothing short of remarkable. For example, *Laman Reformasi* (Reformasi Website) reported well over 20 million hits from October 1998 till the end of 1999. At the height of the Anwar affair there were at least some 30 *Reformasi*-related sites in cyberspace. There were also a number of ongoing list serves and websites — *freemalaysia, sangkancil, adilnet, saksi* — which regularly carried spirited, alternative reports and commentaries on the unfolding events. An internet newspaper, *malaysiakini*, was launched.[21]

The *Reformasi* movement has brought onto the political centre stage a new political culture of peaceful, political protest and dissent. Ironically, the reflexive intolerance of the Mahathir government to the *Reformasi* movement served only to enhance the imperative for political reform. The new political party, PKN, which was multiracial in approach and membership, and the other main opposition parties — PAS, DAP and PRM — were propelled by the political events to band together to form an Alternative Front against the BN government. Although the November 1999 elections returned the Barisan Nasional to power, the BA, through PAS, captured both the Kelantan and Terengganu state governments. Both PKN and DAP fared poorer than PAS, but obtained ten and five parliamentary seats respectively, and together with the twenty-seven PAS seats, constituted the strongest opposition in Parliament in the peninsula since 1969.[22]

The above depiction of events and developments shows an interesting new trend in Malaysian politics, namely, the increasing involvement of Malays in issues relating to justice and human rights that were premised on universal political discourse. The formation of Barisan Alternative also suggests that political practices were shifting in the direction of multi-ethnic coalitions, which put the accent on non-ethnic, rather than ethnically slanted political discourses.[23]

The broad argument advanced here is that the political economy factors, which provided the basis for the performance legitimacy of the Mahathir government, were contraindicated by developments within civil society, described above. Genuine political legitimacy remains problematic for a political regime, which not only continually failed to redress fundamental economic problems, but proved to be one which also persistently ignored the demands, interests, and concerns of civil society.

POLITICAL FALLOUT IN FOREIGN RELATIONS

Perhaps it could be said that the major fallout of the financial crisis was its dampening effect on the more grandiose foreign policy constructions of the Mahathir era. While most core interests and orientations remained unaltered, the "Look East" policy clearly took a beating. As one analyst put it, the Japanese model was greatly discredited when the Japanese bubble burst in the 1990s, but worse was to come with the financial crisis (Lee 2004, p. 323). Admittedly there was no direct link of the crisis with Japan, which actually tried to rescue, if belatedly, its Asian neighbours with various financial initiatives, including the proposal for an Asian Monetary Fund. However, there was the presumption that countries such as Malaysia, Thailand, or Indonesia had deliberately copied the Japanese model and failed. Although there was no official debunking of the "Look East" policy, at the end of the two decades of its dubious implementation, many of its distinctive features such as the *sogososha* or, Japanese-styled in-house unions, and collaborative ventures such as Mitsubishi's involvement in the national car project, has all but evaporated. Clearly, too, Mahathir's vision of an East Asian resurgence and East Asian regionalism suffered a major blow and the idea of the EAEC was fast becoming a dead letter, although as we had indicated earlier, it was latterly reincarnated under the ASEAN-Plus-Three rubric. Towards the very end of his tenure, in August 2003, Mahathir was able to deliver a speech on "Building the East Asian Community: The Way Forward" at the First East Asia Congress at the Putra World Trade Centre in Kuala Lumpur.

At the height of the *Reformasi* Movement there were various events that had direct foreign policy fallout for the Mahathir government. U.S. Vice-President Al Gore who attended the APEC meeting in Kuala Lumpur in November 1998, created a stir when he made a speech saluting the "brave people of Malaysia", that is, those of the *Reformasi* movement, more than hinting the United States was displeased with the government's treatment of political dissent and Anwar's incarceration.[24] Gore, who made the speech at a dinner hosted by the Malaysian Government left after his speech, which prompted a spirited response from Noordin Sopiee, director of the Malaysian think tank, Institute of Strategic and International Studies. Nordin, in a full-page ad in the mainstream *New Straits Times*, criticized the American vice president for being "kurang ajar" (ill-mannered), besides rebutting him on other points.[25] Mahathir himself obviously took umbrage and wrote much later in 2007 that Gore had "intended to offend and to incite and encourage my opponents ... to overthrow my government".[26] Mahathir's own visits to the United States and United Kingdom took on a different sort of tone after a Free Anwar Campaign (FAC) was launched in August 2000, with chapters abroad. The FAC arranged for protests and demonstrations during the Mahathir visits and secured the support of the Islamic Society of North America ((ISNA) to withdraw an invitation to him as a keynote speaker for a conference (Funston 2001, p. 205). Trade Minister Rafidah Aziz was similarly embarrassed by the FAC, which had inserted materials into handouts during a trade mission to attract potential visitors from the United States. By the end of 2000, Mahathir had even accused unnamed Muslim countries of helping the opposition to bring down his government (Funston, p. 205).[27]

The Anwar factor affected Malaysia's relations with many countries, not just the United States. Canada, Australia, New Zealand, and the European Union raised questions about due process in the Anwar trial. Lee Kuan Yew of Singapore remarked that it was "an unmitigated disaster", U.N. Secretary General Kofi Anan met with KeADILan leader Wan Azizah, and Malaysian senior lawyer Param Cumaraswamy was appointed as U.N. Special Rapporteur on the Independence of Judges and Lawyers. All of these events clearly indicated a global unease about, if not outright condemnation of the manner the Anwar trial had been conducted, capped by his being sentenced to nine years of imprisonment in August 2000.[28]

Other fallout of Mahathir's high-profile pro-Muslim policies came as a result of the 11 September 2001 bombing of the New York World Trade Center. Although this provided the opportunity for Muslim states such as Malaysia to toe the line of the U.S. policy of counterterrorism or global war against terrorism, it may have turned out to be a double-edged sword. Initially, the Malaysian government was able to put Islamic opponent PAS on the defensive, but the definition of "terrorism" remained problematic. In a conference organized by Kuala Lumpur under the auspices of the OIC in 2002, there was no agreement on what the term meant and even the issue of "suicide bombing" found no consensus.[29] As one writer put it, in its relations with the United States, Malaysia was "both courted and implicated" in its war against terrorism (Maznah 2002, p. 161). Some of those detained under Malaysia's Internal Security Act (ISA) were alleged by the U.S. authorities to have had links to the actual planners of the September 11 attacks and the United States also issued travel warnings blacklisting Malaysia as one of the places for tourists to avoid.[30] The Mahathir government's Muslim politics has clearly created contradictions and dilemmas for its foreign policy as noted by Maznah Mohamad:

> While 11 September may be may have breathed a new lease of life into a once beleaguered government under threat from the Islamic opposition, it has also brought forth new dilemmas. The government does not want to acknowledge foreign intelligence presence in weeding out terrorist cells in the country, but it wants to use this opportunity presented by the anti-terror law to discredit the Islamic opposition. However, the latter gives credence to foreign allegations that Malaysia may not be a safe haven for foreign investors nor a desirable destination for tourists. (Maznah 2002, p. 162)

Towards the end of the Mahathir era, it could well be argued that that counterterrorism policies had taken their own "institutionalized course (Welsh 2004, p. 143). The August 2003 capture of Hambali, the Jemaah Islamiyah (JI) leader married to a Malaysian, was touted as a success.[31] The government estimated that there were 465 JI members in Malaysia, sixty-nine of whom were still held in the Kamunting detention camp. It had introduced counterterrorism laws, and money-laundering related measures, naval patrols, and the like (Welsh 2004, p. 143). The use of the ISA, however, has drawn criticism domestically and so too has the government's cooperation with the United States, all of which, many would argue, seem rather at odds with the Mahathirian counterhegemonic rhetoric of the past.

POLITICAL DENOUEMENT

Without doubt, the decline of Mahathir's political leadership and credibility came as a concomitant of the Anwar Ibrahim saga. Although Mahathir was able to lead the UMNO and BN through another electoral victory in a snap election called in November 1999, the emergence of the Barisan Alternative and a plethora of civil society organizations around the *Reformasi* banner, and the multi-ethnic campaigns directly and indirectly calling for Mahathir to leave the political stage, clearly left a mortal scar on his regime. As Hwang puts it:

> [T]he Anwar episode and its social, cultural, and political consequences disclosed a possible erosion of the politics of racialism. What distinguished Malaysian politics after Anwar's dismissal from the previous UMNO crisis of 1987 is the emergence of multi-ethnic awareness in Malaysian civil society, especially among the young Malaysian middle class. (Hwang 2003, p. 331)

Moreover, analysts had shown that Mahathir actually lost the Malay vote in 1999. Writers have shown through an analysis of the Malay vote that UMNO's slippage was evident in every Malay-majority area, with popular margins greatly reduced compared with the previous election of 1995. Moreover, not only did UMNO lose the state contests in Kelantan and Terengganu, it virtually lost the contest in Kedah as well, polling a precarious 49.9 per cent of the popular vote (Maznah 2003, p. 74). Moreover, it has also been argued that there was an "unravelling" of the Malay consensus as a result of the Anwar episode. In September 2000, Mahathir experienced his first international snub when the Islamic Society of North America (ISNA) withdrew its invitation to him to be the keynote speaker at one of its meetings (Maznah 2001, p. 219). On the domestic front, another electoral blow came in the Lunas by-election of 29 November 2000. Although this was a mixed constituency in Mahathir's home state, Kedah, it was a KeADILan candidate who defeated the BN man by 530 votes, showing that the Mahathir regime had still not recovered one year later from the poor showing of the last election (Maznah 2001, p. 220). The fact that alternative Malay-based parties had become effective voices against UMNO evidently dented Mahathir's mantle of leadership and dealt a lethal blow to his legitimacy as putative leader of the community. Some relief came to Mahathir only in 2001 when it became evident that the DAP was in an unhappy marriage with the PAS in the Alternative Front. DAP left the front in September because of the Islamic state issue.

Mahathir's post-financial crisis woes were not over even though he had apparently steered Malaysia to economic recovery. Politically-charged bailouts of Malay businessmen such as Mirzan Mahathir (discussed above) and, conspicuously, of Tajuddin Ramli through the governmental buy-back of Malaysian Airlines, which Tajuddin headed, further eroded Mahathir's credibility.[32] So too did the bailout of alleged erstwhile UMNO proxy (and Daim protégé), Halim Saad's Timedotcom, by the use of state pension funds (Salazar 2004, p. 288). In fact, Halim's loss-laden flagship, the Renong conglomerate, had debts which totalled RM13 billion, and was subjected to a restructuring which saw the removal of its chairman. By June 2001, Daim Zainuddin had resigned from the government, indicating that there was a rift within the UMNO elite over the problem of dealing with fallen Malay corporate figures. A Mahathir in denial argued that the collapse of Malay corporate empires did not reflect the failure of Malay businessmen in general. As Salazar (2004, p. 291) suggests, it appeared that renationalization and corporate restructuring of highly leveraged conglomerates was fuelled by political factionalism, in particular, disagreement between Mahathir and Daim, rather than by economic logic. Mahathir in the 55th UMNO General Assembly in June went on an attack against money politics and corruption, at the same time lambasting the Malays yet again for their complacent attitudes (Nathan 2002, p. 170). Perhaps it was in the backdrop of all his travails that Mahathir was impelled to declare in September 2001 that Malaysian was already an "Islamic State". Such a declaration at the same time was an acknowledgement by Mahathir that his strongest and most persistent critics were the Islamists of PAS. Here then was a last-ditch effort to reinvigorate the Malay agenda for UMNO and simultaneously attempt to undercut the growing clout of PAS.

At the 2002 UMNO General Assembly, Mahathir made his announcement of his intention to resign on 22 June. It may have been unexpected and baffling at that point of time, but in retrospect, it was hardly possibly for Mahathir to hang on, given a legitimacy that had been eroded threadbare by events harking back to the Anwar imbroglio. In his last UMNO Assembly speech in June 2003, Mahathir reverted to a racialist discourse on the moral decay of the West as the cause of its domestic problems, from theft to incest, but his last hurrah came in the OIC meeting of mid-October where he spoke on fairer treatment for the Palestinians and the disconnect between Islam and terrorism. However, these moderate tones were apparently "drown[ed] out by twenty-eight controversial words about Jews in which he claimed they ruled the world".[33] Mahathir seemed true to iconoclasm till the end of his tenure, but his final acts lacked the credibility, let alone the sting, of the Mahathir of lore.

CONCLUSION

In this chapter we have dealt mostly with Mahathir's attempt to grapple with the onset and impact of the economic crisis of 1997–98, which itself sparked a political crisis that in turn saw his sacking of deputy premier and finance minister, Anwar Ibrahim. In the ensuing five years or so when Mahathir continued to helm the government, the defiant leader led Malaysia to an economic recovery with unorthodox economic policies. Mahathir may have been vindicated in an overall sense for his bold actions, as even former World Bank chief economist and Nobel laureate Joseph Stiglitz had begun to criticize the IMF.[34] However, the Malaysian premier was ultimately unable to hang on to political power. The political fallout of the episode eroded Mahathir's credibility and legitimacy to a point where he may himself have realized that he had become a liability to his own political party, UMNO.

Mahathirian "constructivism" in foreign-cum-domestic policy, which had flourished in the first period of his tenure, became decidedly hamstrung in the second stage of his tenure. And, had it not been for the availability of copious economic resources, such as from the national oil corporation, the latitude for his introduction of counter-IMF policies may have failed. In any case, the political fallout of such policies domestically and externally exerted an irrepressible pressure on his government, and damage control, rather than innovation, became the order of the day. Even the post-9/11 political environment was no sop for the damage already done by the political ramifications of the Anwar saga. As Hilly puts it, Mahathir was faced with three "crises of hegemony", economic, political, and ideological. In the first instance, despite a recovery from the financial crisis, the rupture with foreign capital remained unresolved; in the second, UMNO's decline in the face of PAS resurgence was a legacy which Mahathir could hardy live down, and finally, the excesses committed in the Anwar episode undermined any measure of moral authority of "late Mahathirism".[35] It is true and ironic that the political denouement of the Mahathir era, both in terms its domestic and external dimensions, inexorably called for the departure of its very progenitor from the political stage.

NOTES

1. The BN had increased its popular vote from the 53.4 per cent won in the 1990 election. In terms of seats, it captured a total 162 parliamentary seats, or 84.4 per cent of the total, and 338 state seats, 85.8 per cent of the total (Hwang 2003, p. 230).

2. Much has been written about Islamization in Malaysia. See, *inter alia*, Martinez (2003), Jomo and Shabery (1992), Mauzy and Milne (1983), and Nair's study of Islam in foreign policy (1997). Dhillon (2007) prefers to see Mahathir's polices as a case of "Islamic posturing". I have myself written that the following phases of Islamization may be discerned: Islamic resurgence in the late 1970s, Islamization policies from the 1980s and contestation over Islamization from the 1990s (Saravanamuttu 2004*b*, pp. 105–06). I would argue that it is in the third phase that the Mahathir government implemented state-defined Islamic polices. See endnote 5.

3. Since Ho's periodization ends at about the point of publication (2001), I've added the other two years. Jomo's periodization (2004) is more or less similar, collapsing periods two and three into one, viz. early years — 1981–85; boom and bust — 1986–97; unorthodox economic interventions — 1998–2003.

4. See Hilly's study (2001, pp. 254–56), which specifies four periods almost identical to that adopted here, except for the variation of years, viz. Early Mahathirism (1981-85), Mid-Mahathirism (1985–90), Late Mahathirism (1991–96), and Crisis Mahathirism (1997–2000).

5. See Liow's (2001) comprehensive essay on the Mahathir's foreign policy. Liow, however, identifies only three phases, the final phase starting in 1990.

6. Earlier, in 1983, the government had launched the International Islamic University of Malaysia (IIUM), or University Islam Antarabangsa Malaysia (UIAM) in Malay, with an initial grant of RM500million. (Means 1991, p. 101). The UIAM was co-sponsored by the OIC and has an international faculty and students. It could well be said that the Mahathir's government's Islamic thrust began much earlier, especially after the ABIM leader Anwar Ibrahim was brought into the Cabinet in 1981. Anwar was later made the second president of IIUM in 1988, after the demise of Tun Hussein, the first president.

7. Substantial factual portions of this section are drawn from Saravanamuttu (1998).

8. Among the earlier, more competent and better accounts are Jomo (1998), Rosenberger (1997) and Krugman (1997, 1998). The edited book by Arndt and Hill (1999) and the collection by Kwan, Vandenbrink and Chia (1998) give technical analysis of the crisis. My own effort, Saravanamuttu (1998), takes a political economy approach. See also later works such as Haggard (2000) and Yu and Xu (2001).

9. Rosenberger (1997, p. 226) points out that unlike the Mexican consumption-driven current account deficit in 1995, the Southeast Asian current account deficits were investment-driven. That is, they represented capital borrowed for a plethora of development projects, of which property development and infrastructure development featured prominently.

10. In these two years, through mutual agreement, the U.S. dollar rose 40 per cent *vis-à-vis* the yen. Meanwhile, the Southeast Asian currencies remained largely pegged to the US dollar at the old values. Additionally, in January 1994, China devalued the yuan by 50 per cent against the U.S. dollar. The export price capacity of China clearly affected the Southeast Asian economies in 1996 (Rosenberger 1997, p. 225).

11. There was the 1995 monetary agreement, orchestrated by Thailand, to avert financial crisis, which was signed by the central banks of Hong Kong, Australia, Thailand, Malaysia, and Indonesia. However, when it came to the test, it appears that this scheme failed to live up to expectations.

12. For example, during the G-15 meeting in Jamaica, it was reported that his ideas were well received by leaders of the developing world. It was also reported that the French Premier Jacques Chirac, whom Mahathir visited immediately after the G-15 meeting, was sympathetic to ideas of reforming the international financial architecture (*New Straits Times*, 15 February 1999).

13. Jomo (2001) states further: "With an estimated 25–30 billion Malaysian Ringgit in Singapore, the Malaysian monetary authorities could not expect to altogether prevent interest rates from rising with the much higher interest rates available in the island republic. This was a situation which Anwar was acutely aware of. Jomo adds: "[W]hile Anwar was undoubtedly more inclined to cater to 'market sentiments', his post-September 1998 demonisation by Mahathirists as an IMF stooge and agent of the West is certainly not supported by his economic policy record" (pp. xxiv–v).

14. This was the projection of the 1999/2000 Economic Report that was tabled in October. See *The Star*, 30 October 1999. In fact, the GDP decline was 7.4 per cent in 1998, and the 1999 growth rate was later revised upwards anyway from 5.4 to 5.8 per cent. According to a WTO report, the economy rebounded with GDP growing by 6.1 per cent in 1999, and by 8.3 per cent in 2000, so that at the end of 2000, real output in value terms exceeded the pre-crisis level. However, per capita income was US$3,531 in 2000, around 20 per cent lower than the pre-crisis level.

15. However, critics have pointed out that this rate showed a low confidence in the

Malaysian economy since Korea and Thailand have been able to issue bonds at a lower rate (Pillay 1999, p. 4).

16. See *New Straits Times, The Star*, 7 August 1999, *FEER*, 9 September, 1999. Thomas Fuller, writing for the *International Herald Tribune*, 7–8 August 1999, suggested that the move was one of East Asia's most radical and ambitious bank restructuring effort wherein some twenty-one commercial banks, twenty-five financial institutions and twelve merchant banks were being downsized into six major banks. A political reading of the move suggests that ethnic and crony considerations were also at stake besides the purported objective of strengthening the banking sector. There was allegedly an indirect admission that an ally of Finance Minister Daim Zainuddin's would take over Chinese-based Multipurpose Bank, which only ranked a lowly tenth, which will then merge with or take over RHB Bank, ranked second and supposedly favoured in the past by the deposed Anwar Ibrahim.

17. In the new Bank Negara directives, greater responsibility was to be passed on to the shareholders of the banking institutions to carry out the merger process. Certain banks, notably, RHB Bank and Arab Malaysia Bank, had indicated their interest to become anchor banks with the likelihood that the final count would go beyond six anchor banks by the time the exercise ended in January 2000. (*The Star*, 9 December 1999). As it turned out, by 2000, there emerged ten banks, namely (in order of asset ranking), Malayan Banking, Bumiputera-Commerce Bank, RHB Bank, Public Bank, Hong Leong Bank, HSBC Bank, Southern Bank, OCBC Bank, Standard Chartered Bank, and Citibank. Later, Commerce International Merchant Bankers (CIMB), said to be the Southeast Asian region's largest investment bank, acquired Bumiputra-Commerce Bank in June 2005, and Southern Bank in March 2006. *The Edge* business weekly (December 2005, accessed online 10 October 2007), reported that a whopping RM23 billion was the cost of the whole bank restructuring exercise, with the government footing as much as RM12.5 billion of the total bill.

18. Ariff and Yap (2001, p. 240), on the other hand, argue that capital control measure brought about the stability that enabled recovery and reforms to the financial sector to be implemented swiftly.

19. See S. Jayasankaran's exposé on Petronas in *Far Eastern Economic Review*, 12 August 1999.

20. Internet usage in Malaysia has increased manifold since then; from 3.7 million in 2000 to 14.9 million in 2008, *Internet World Stats*, <http://www.internetworldstats.com/asia/m.htm> (accessed 21 October 2008).

21. *Malaysiakini* has remained an alternative media force to be reckoned with up till the time of writing (2009). It is ironic that Mahathir in 2005/6 regularly used *Malaysiakini* to air his criticisms and differences with the Abdullah government and even started his own blog, *"Che Det"*.

22. See Loh and Saravanamuttu (2003) for a study of the 1999 general election.

23. I have written concertedly about the middle class factor in engendering multi-ethnic Malaysian politics. See Saravanamuttu (1992, 2001, 2005).

24. His exact words were "We continue to hear calls for democracy, calls for 'Reformasi.' We hear them today — right here, right now — among the brave people of Malaysia", as cited by David DeRosa of Bloomberg (28 November 1998).

25. In a subsequent letter entitled "We won't stand for 'kurang ajar' idiots" in *New Straits Times*, 21 November 1998, Noordin wrote: "I sat through the entire proceedings and I must confess that I was stung by his final comments. When Mr Gore finished, I started to clap and it took me a full five seconds before I stopped. I suppose a lifetime of training and conditioning got in the way of what I should have done. I was so upset that the first thing the next day, I called up the *New Straits Times* and asked them whether I could take a one-page advertisement to express my views. I asked them how much it would cost. The paper came back two hours later to say that a page could indeed be found and that the lowest, absolutely lowest cost (special to me because I had once worked with the newspaper) would be RM14,500. I took a deep breath and proceeded to write the text."

26. See his prologue in the book by Abdullah Ahmad (2008, p. 13).

27. It has transpired more recently that Mahathir's efforts at damage control over the Anwar issue in the United States even involved the hiring of the dubious American lobbyist, Jack Abramoff. The Malaysian government allegedly paid $1.2 million to Abramoff to arrange a meeting of Mahathir with Bush in 2002. Abramoff has since been sentenced to jail for fraud, tax evasion and conspiracy <http://www.washingtonpost.com/wp-dyn/content/linkset/2005/06/22/LI2005062200936.html> (accessed 23 January 2009).

28. Anwar was found guilty of "unnatural sex acts". The nine years was in addition to the six years he was handed down in 1999 for political "corruption" (or abuse of power). See Maznah (2001, p. 217) and Martinez (2001, p. 195).

29. Malaysia has since set up the ASEAN Centre for Counter Terrorism. See Chapter 2.

30. Yazid Sufaat, one of about seventy suspected Islamic militants detained by the Malaysian Government, was interviewed by FBI officers in November 2002 for alleged links to the hijackers of the American Airlines jet that crashed into the Pentagon (Maznah 2002, pp. n29, 166).

31. Two other JI leaders, Noordin Mat Top and Azhari Hussein a.k.a Amran Mansour, were Malaysians. The latter used to be lecturer at the Technological University of Malaysia. An Iranian paper has called them the "Asian Al-Zarqawi's" together with Indonesian Ridzuan Isamuddin a.k.a. Hambali captured in 2003 by Thailand. Nordin is known as the "Moneyman" while Azhari was dubbed the "Demolition Man", both being implicated in the Bali bombing of 27 October 2002 in which 202 persons died, and the Jakarta Marriott Hotel blast of 2003. (*Iran Daily*, 27 October 2005). Noordin was tracked down and killed in Solo

on 17 September 2009, while Azhari was hunted down and killed by Indonesian authorities in an incident near Jakarta on 9 November 2005 (*New York Times*, 10 November 2005, *Malaysain Insider*, 20 November 2009).

32. The details of the MAS bailout are worth recalling. Parcelled out in boom times in 1994 to private ownership, it was repossessed by the government in early 2001 with a debt of RM2.7 billion, but with executive chairman Tajuddin Ramli disposing his 29 per cent stake to the government at a premium share price of RM8. The market price of MAS shares at the time was RM3.68. In a restructuring in early 2002, it was revealed that the MAS debt had ballooned to RM9.2 billion. The Malaysian police commercial crime division then went on to investigate Tajuddin Ramli for alleged irregularities centring around cargo operations involving a Germany-based handler controlled by the erstwhile chairman. (See *Asian Wall Street Journal*, 20 February 2002). In May 2006, Tajuddin was sued by Pengurusan Danaharta Nasional Bhd and two subsidiaries for RM589 million of in relation to a RM1.792 billion loan which enabled him to buy a controlling interest in the airline in 1994. (See *The Sun*, 22 May 2006.) In various news reports, Tajuddin has claimed that he did what he was told by Mahathir and Daim. At the time of writing (2009), the case apparently remained in the courts.

33. See Welsh (2003, pp. 140–41).

34. This was done on various international appearances after his retirement from the World Bank after 2000. His critique of the IMF is found in his best-selling book, *Globalization and Its Discontents* (2002).

35. See Hilly (2002, pp. 257–60).

9

EMBEDDING ISLAM, EMBRACING GLOBALIZATION, 2004–08

THE ABDULLAH TRANSITION

Abdullah Badawi assumed the reins of government on 31 October 2003 after his predecessor Mahathir Mohamad had been at the helm for the previous twenty-two years. Abdullah was Mahathir's choice to succeed him. It was therefore quite surprising that he was soon rolling back a number of Mahathir's policies and decisions, in particular, megaprojects. At the same time, the new premier also initiated an anti-corruption drive and various efforts at reform within the government structure and machinery.

Even within a month of becoming the prime minister, Abdullah Badawi (or "Pak Lah" as he had come to be known) started to "tinker with" Mahathirist policies and decisions as one journalist put it (Netto 2004). Most prominently, he put up front the new anti-corruption thrust of his government and also promised to correct the low efficiency and ineptness of various branches of government service. He made it clear that he would put a hold on megaprojects, most prominently of which was the action to scuttle immediately a RM14.5-billion double-track railway line awarded to Gamuda and the Malaysian Mining Corporation (MMC). This was carried out despite the fact that Mahathir had given the project the green light just before his retirement. The awarding of the contract to private contractors Gamuda-MMC was complicated by the government's letter of intent stating that it would involve the Governments of India and China in the project. The project was particularly controversial because it involved business tycoon Mokhtar Al-Bhukary whose growing business empire had become the subject of much speculation that he had strong political patrons.

On the ideational dimension and in diplomacy, Abdullah introduced palpably a much softer style of dealing with the outside world, and through a softer version of a modernist and moderate Islam known by the term his government had coined, "*Islam Hadhari*" or "civilizational Islam". This concept of Islam was the hallmark of his orientation towards the Western world and especially in the face of the American-led "global war against terrorism". It must have been calculated by Abdullah's advisors that Malaysia as leader of the Organization of The Islamic Conference (OIC) and the Non-aligned Movement (NAM), should project such an image in order to optimize not just the objectives of these umbrella organizations, but also its own national interests. The ten purported principles of *Islam Hadhari*, which have been the mantra in numerous speeches by Abdullah and his spokespersons were: faith and piety in the Almighty; a just and trustworthy government; a free and independent people; the vigorous pursuit and mastery of knowledge; balanced and comprehensive economic development; a good quality of life for the people; protection of the rights of minority groups and women; cultural and moral integrity; safeguarding natural resources and the environment; and, strong defence capabilities.[1]

The *Islam Hadhari* concept was also used to optimum effect in the campaign of the general election of March 2004 to upstage the Islamic party, PAS. Thus a substantial political development for the Abdullah government came in the form of the landslide electoral victory of the BN under his leadership, whereby the ruling coalition not only captured 90 per cent of the parliamentary seats, but also dealt a serious blow to PAS, as well as to Parti KeADILan Nasional (PKN). PAS failed to retain control of Tereggannu and nearly lost its base in Kelantan as well. PKN, despite an effective merger with the Parti Rakyat Malaysia (PRM), was only barely able to hold on to the seat held by its president, Wan Azizah Ismail, the wife of the jailed Anwar Ibrahim. In short, the BN's electoral victory dealt a double blow to both political Islam of the PAS variety, and the *Reformasi* movement. However, one hastens to add that this did not automatically mean that either political Islam or *Reformasi* were spent forces. Rather, with Mahathir leaving the political stage, Abdullah was able to capitalize on the event, and along with the DAP's departure from Barisan Alternative, Pak Lah was able to co-opt astutely some of the ideas *Reformasi* into the government's programmes and take most of the wind out of the opposition's sails.

Flushed with his electoral victory, Pak Lah perhaps felt more confident in pushing forward with his own plans. Most controversially, on 11 April 2006, Abdullah cancelled the "crooked (or scenic) half-bridge" project of Mahathir, which was to build a link on the Malaysian side over the Singapore-Malaysia causeway. This bridge would allow for ships to pass under it and access the South China Sea without passing though Singapore. Related to an implied criticism of megaprojects was the initiation of the much-publicized CBT RM76.4 million trial of Eric Chia, the erstwhile chief executive officer of Perwaja Steel Sdn. Bhd. Chia had been appointed by Mahathir to head the troubled steel company.[2] Although it must be said the Anti-Corruption Agency (ACA) had begun its investigations much earlier on Perwaja Steel, the new prime minister had promised that some eighteen or so high-profile ACA cases will be pursued during his tenure. The Abdullah government also set up a Royal Commission to investigate reforming the police. Headed by former Chief Justice Mohamed Dzaiddin Abdullah, the commission already produced a preliminary report in August 2004, which found that corrupt practices involve officers and personnel "at all levels" (*New Straits Times*, 10 August 2004). However, after the final report was completed in May 2005, few of the 24 recommendations of the commission have been implemented, including the most important one of setting up an Independent Police Complaints and Misconduct Commission (IPCMC).[3]

Thus it seems clear that while the general change over the first two years of Pak Lah's ascension to power boosted his image and reputation, the subsequent slide in the lack of implementation of some stated polices, such as his anti-corruption plan, the mounting concerns of non-Malay constituencies over polices related to questions of Islam, the international publicity of a murder trial implicating persons in high places, and other negative events, had dogged an increasingly defensive Pak Lah government. By April 2006, Mahathir had also begun to fire a salvo of attacks on Abdullah's policies. Indeed, by the middle of 2007, there were rumblings that an early election could be held to stem the mounting criticism and dissatisfaction with Pak Lah's leadership or the lack if it.

Furthermore, under Pak Lah, much was also in evidence that old-style ethnically divisive (even racist) UMNO politics had come to stay. Mahathir himself bitterly complained of his failure to be elected to be a delegate in his old constituency to attend the UMNO General Assembly in November 2006. He openly accused Pak Lah's supporters of bribing the divisional delegates. In the run-up to the UMNO General Assembly, Abdullah nominated as his deputy, Najib Abdul Razak, after months of speculation, and the pair secured virtually all the nominations of the party divisions. Abdullah lost one nomination to the lame challenge of Tengku Razaleigh Hamzah, who managed to receive a sole vote from his own division. During the Assembly proceedings, UMNO Youth leader Hishamuddin Hussein Onn spectacularly whipped out a Malay *keris* during the UMNO General Assembly to berate his audience again about the virtue of *ketuanan Melayu* (Malay supremacy). More was to come by way of incendiary racist statements made against the Chinese by other delegates, all of which was telecast live for the first time for all Malaysians to witness.

On 31 March of 2006, Pak Lah had unveiled the Ninth Malaysia Plan which would see an expenditure in access of RM200 billion from 2007–12. The plan itself drew flak from independent research findings of the Centre for Public Policy (CPP) of the Asian Strategy and Leadership Institute (ASLI). The CPP claimed that the NEP target of 30 per cent of ownership of the economy had been surpassed, leading to a series of public debates, which ultimately led to the resignation of CPP director Dr Lim Teck Ghee (Ooi 2007, pp. 187–88).

Even more controversial have been the contestations and court decisions regarding conversions into Islam and out of Islam (apostasy) that have led to acrimonious public debates and even street demonstrations.[4] Matters came to a head when, in January 2006, all of Pak Lah's ten non-Muslim cabinet ministers signed a memorandum requesting that Article 121 (1A), which gives jurisdiction of Islamic matters to Shariah courts, be reviewed. Pak Lah managed to prevail on his ministers to withdraw their memorandum (Ooi 2007, p. 185). The prime minister also deemed it fit to step in to halt the "Article 11" forums, organized by a coalition of NGOs, to discuss the federal Constitution and protection under the law on questions of religion. On two occasions when Article 11 forums were held, one in Penang and the other in Johor Baru, Muslims held demonstrations to protest the group's alleged "hidden agenda" to revive the moribund Inter Faith Council, which incidentally was scuttled by the government. In Penang, protesters heckled the panelists, which included speakers such as Shad Saleem Faruqi, professor of constitutional law at UiTM; Imtiaz Malik, president of the human rights body HAKAM; and Zaid Ibrahim, Kota Bharu Member of Parliament. The police who appeared on the scene forced the forum to end early, without all the scheduled speakers having their say. The forum in Johor was similarly ended early, but all speakers were able to deliver their talks.

On the heels of the Article 11 forums was a reported gathering of 10,000 Muslims at the Masjid Wilayah on 24 July 2006. Among the personalities who spoke at the forum titled "The Syariah and Current Issues" were former Bar Council presidents Sulaiman Abdullah and Zainur Zakaria, Perak *mufti* Harussani Zakaria, constitutional expert Abdul Aziz Bari, and Muslim Youth Movement of Malaysia (ABIM) president Yusri Mohamad. Other speakers were Syariah lawyer Kamar Ainiah Kamaruzaman, former Penang *mufti* Sheikh

Azmi Ahmad, and forum chairperson Azmi Abdul Hamid, who headed the Malay-advocacy group Teras. The speakers called on the government to strengthen the country's Islamic institutions and not weaken them.[5]

More issues and controversies peppered the Abdullah administration as he moved into the fourth and fifth years of his stewardship of Malaysia. The "Bersih" coalition of political parties and NGOs calling for clean elections on 10 November reportedly saw 40,000 people taking to the streets, and the HINDRAF rally of some 30,000 Indians came close on its heels on 25 November 2007. Abdullah took the heavy-handed action of detaining five HINDRAF leaders under the draconian Internal Security Act (ISA), which he did not appear to relish. Some of these developments were truly remarkable in exposing the mendacity, incompetence, and corruption of the government, its leaders, political cronies, and institutions in years past. Abdullah himself became embroiled in charges of nepotism. Amongst the more damning revelations were those related to the judiciary, albeit acts of the past during the Mahathir era. The sensational V.K. Lingam video recording impelled Abdullah himself to call for a Royal Commission to ascertain the extent of judge-fixing and case-fixing by the eponymous lawyer named in the scandal. The hearings revealed the alleged writing of judgments by the same defence lawyer for the presiding judge.

More than ever before, as the prime minister himself pointed out, the government needed a fresh mandate. There could even have been a more mundane factor that caused the early calling of a general election, namely the new blood or generational shift factor. Many untested, younger UMNO and Barisan National politicians were anxiously waiting in the wings to rise in the hierarchy and to seek their baptism of fire. Among them was Abdullah's son-in-law, the fast rising Khairy Jamaluddin, as well as the son of the receding Gerakan Party leader, Lim Si Pin. The Malaysian Chinese Association's (MCA) also needed to jettison some so-called "Team A" members although one of them, former Health Minister Chua Soi Lek conveniently disqualified himself after a widely distributed sex video led to his resignation. Then, in the tiny northern state of Perlis, two UMNO ministers were evidently on the chopping block. There were also political trimming exercises to be undertaken within the Malaysian Indian Congress (MIC) in its desperate attempt to retain the Indian vote. A whole year ahead of the mandatory five years, Abdullah announced that he would call for a general election. The date was set for 8 March 2008. Much of the reasoning revolved around two factors; the economy and Anwar Ibrahim. The economic situation seemed destined to deteriorate, with the American economy likely to go into recession with its knock-on effects on Malaysia. Anwar Ibrahim, former deputy premier, now *de facto* leader of the opposition People's Justice Party (PKR)[6] would have been eligible to contest by mid-April, five years after his release from jail, on charges for which he was cleared in 2004. It was entirely credible that the Abdullah Badawi government would have agonized that an elected Anwar as a Member of Parliament meant trouble.

In the event, the 2008 general election turned out to be a political disaster for Abdullah. The National Front (Barisan Nasional, BN) government arguably suffered its worst defeat in history with a loss of its two-thirds majority of seats.[7] The BN government also just about lost the popular vote in Peninsular Malaysia, including the loss of four state governments while one continued to be in opposition hands. Chinese and Indian voters clearly preferred the opposition parties while Malays still had a preference, but a reduced one, for the BN parties. The most significant swing came from Indians, who evidently abandoned the ethnically constituted Malaysian Indian Congress (MIC). The Chinese voters also swung palpably in the direction of ostensibly non-Chinese parties, giving to the Malaysian Chinese Association (MCA) its poorest showing since 1969. Under constant pressure from his own party, UMNO, to step down, Abdullah later announced on 8 Ocotber 2008 that he would relinquish the UMNO presidency, and, by implication, leadership of the government. To assuage the embattled prime minister, the UMNO Supreme Council announced the postponement of party elections of December 2008 till March 2009.

It is against the backdrop of these domestic developments that we will now assess the foreign policy orientations, initiatives, and actions of the Abdullah Badawi government.

EMBEDDING ISLAM *HADHARI*

A constructivist approach to Abdullah Badawi's government's formulation of foreign policy could well locate Islam as its strongest social-cultural "structure", constraining or enabling agential power of the Malaysian state under his tenure. The Pak Lah government itself proffered its own ideational construct of *Islam Hadhari* (or "civilizational Islam") as the basis for decision making on a number of policy terrains, inclusive of foreign policy. It may be germane at this point to further explicate the broad contours of this notion of Islam as propounded by the Abdullah government. Before this, it may be important to point out that Abdullah's predilection for an Islamic perspective not only comes from a background of Islamic studies at the University of Malaya, but even more so, a strong Arab pedigree of religious personages. His grandfather Abdullah Fahim was the first official *mufti* (scholar and proponent of Islamic law) of Penang.[8]

The first comprehensive statement on the concept of Islam *Hadhari* by the prime minister himself was made before the 55th UMNO General Assembly in September 2004. Cutting through the fog of rhetoric and Islamic injunctions that embellished the speech, one finds the unmistakable exhortation to Malays and the *Ummah* to revive the "civilization" aspects of Islam for moderation, competitiveness, progress, quality, pursuit of knowledge, open-mindedness to science and technology, and modernity in general. There is also the important emphasis on moral integrity.[9] In the same speech, Abdullah reiterated Malaysia's support of the stock principles of international relations to which Malaysia adhered, viz.:

*   respect for international laws and institutions
*   respect for sovereignty and territorial integrity
*   settlement of disputes through negotiation
*   refraining from the use of force unless sanctioned by the United Nations, and
*   equitable distribution for the benefit of mankind (Abdullah Badawi 2006, p. 10).

The prime minister also said the following to his Malay audience:

> We must reject violence that targets innocent civilians. Similarly, violence that is caused by any party, whether by nations or by militant groups, cannot be accepted nor tolerated. The term, *'jihad'* should not be misused and should not be misinterpreted to justify terrorism. Such actions only serve to tarnish the teachings of Islam. Islam does not permit such violence. (Abdullah Badawi, p. 12)

The second important exposition of the idea came a week later in an address to the Oxford Centre for Islamic Studies entitled, "Islam, Malaysia and the Wider World". Underlining Malaysia's leadership role in the OIC, Abdullah stressed the urgency of resolving conflicts among Muslim countries and proposed the setting up of a centre of conflict resolution in Malaysia. He also offered Malaysia as the focal point for a "more open and diverse Islamic discourse", viz.

> Our universities will work together with institutions around the world, such as the Oxford Centre for Islamic Studies, to promote dialogue within the Muslim world. As much as it is necessary for Muslims to find common ground with people of other faiths, we must also open up the discourse within the *ummah*. Malaysia will invite Muslim scholars from all over the world to initiate the process of intellectual reform and renewal. (Abdullah Badawi, p. 49)

Abdullah has also tried to tweak Islam *Hadhari* for the multicultural context of Malaysian society. In a speech to the Asia Society of Australia in Sydney in April 2005, he argued that the ten principles of the concept "are acceptable to our non-Muslim population". Mentioning that some 100,000 Malaysians have graduated from Australian universities, he said that Islam *Hadhari* puts a high premium on education and the acquisition of knowledge. Human capital development was also the key to poverty eradication. Stressing that the concept was consistent with democracy and a multireligious and multiracial country such as Malaysia, the premier averred that Australia could play a part in promoting a critical dialogue between the non-Muslim and Muslim world, and offered Malaysia as "the focal point for promoting more open and diverse Islamic discourse". (Abdullah Badawi, p. 127)

The quote below from the speech at Islamabad, on the occasion of the conferment of an honorary doctorate of laws to the Malaysian premier by the International Islamic University, sums up well the Abdullah government's approach to embedding Islam *Hadhari* in Malaysian society:

> Malaysia has…embarked upon 'Islam Hadhari' as an approach adopted in the conduct of our everyday lives. Islam Hadhari is not a new religion. Islam Hadhari is not a new *mazhab*. Islam Hadhari is merely an approach to foster a progressive Islamic civilization, built upon the noble values and realities of Islam. It places substance over form. It is both practical and pragmatic. It emphasizes development, consistent with the tenets of Islam, which focuses on enhancing the quality of life of every citizen, regardless of his or her religion. This approach is also inspired by our firm belief that the tide of radicalism and extremism may be halted and replaced with good governance, healthy democratic practices, and empowerment of it citizens through proper education along with an equal share of the benefits of economic growth. (Abdullah Badawi, p. 73)

ENGAGING ISLAM GLOBALLY

The Abdullah government fortuitously took over the mantle of the 57-country OIC, after Malaysia hosted its 10th Summit Conference at Putrajaya in October 2003.[10] This gave the prime minister ample opportunity on several occasions early in his tenure to profile Malaysia as a moderate "Muslim state".[11] We have already mentioned the event at Oxford University. Abdullah also spoke at some length on "Islam, International Peace and Security" at the Bertelsmann Foundation in Berlin in May 2005. Profiling Malaysia's role as OIC chair, the premier called for "inter-civilization dialogues" at both the official and the second track levels, arguing that in the quest for global development and prosperity, the West could not ignore the 1.4 billion Muslims represented by the OIC members who also produced 70 per cent of the world's energy requirements. He called for five fundamental shifts to the approach to peace and security: from a security order based on amorality to one based on moral purpose; from state security to people security as the central object; from the pursuit of narrow national interest to enlightened national interest; from conflictual security to cooperative security; from a focus on narrow military security to a focus on wider, comprehensive security. Explaining the second shift, he said: "The welfare of the people must lie at the heart of all our struggles, not least the struggle for security." (Abdullah Badawi, p. 159)

One of Abdullah's first foreign undertakings was an official visit to the United States in July 2004 (see below). Following the prime minister's meeting with Bush, there were suggestions that Malaysia was initiating a move to send an OIC peacekeeping force to Iraq. The idea was publicized by Foreign Minister Syed Hamid Syed Albar (*Utusan Malaysia*, 1 August 2004), but up to date, no such move has materialized. In the event, Malaysia on its own did send a medical team to Iraq. Abdullah revealed that he conveyed to the American president his views about Muslim-Western relations, viz.

> [I] did also convey to president Bush my belief that now, more than ever, we need to find the moderate center[,] we must not be driven by extremist impulses or extremist elements on both sides of the spectrum[,] the world can ill afford to continue down its present trajectory[,] we need to bridge the great divide that has been created between the Muslim world and the west[,] our efforts to bridge this divide must go beyond elite diplomacy western governments, and in particular the government of the United States, must continue to convince the peoples of the Muslim world that this is not a war against Islam and that the legitimate grievances of the Muslim world are taken seriously and acted upon.[12]

BROKERING THE MINDANAO PEACE TALKS

In keeping with its Islamic credentials and involvement in OIC, the Abdullah government continued its role as third-party facilitator in the Southern Philippines conflict. Malaysia's active involvement in the Southern Philippines peace process began in the late 1990s during Mahathir's tenure. Malaysia's encounter with the Philippine over the Sabah claim may well be a factor that predisposed it towards brokering the peace talks in Southern Philippines. The peace talks were initiated by Kuala Lumpur in 1997 soon after the Philippine implementation of the Autonomous Region of Muslim Mindanao (ARMM) collapsed under the leadership and governorship of Nur Musuari of the Moro

National Liberation Front (MNLF). Nur Musuari lost control of the MNLF and was later detained by the Philippine government on various charges.[13] While the Mindanao problem is complicated by the emergence of the militant terrorist group, Abu Sayyaf, most observers would recognize that the struggle of the Muslim South has since fallen mostly on the shoulders of the MILF (Moro Islamic Liberation Front) which has replaced the MNLF as the main representive voice of the Muslims.

From 2003, there was a level of cooperation between Malaysia and the United States (more specifically, the State Department) which participated indirectly in the peace process through the United States Institute of Peace (USIP). While the United States encouraged or gave support to the Malaysian government's role as a third-party facilitator, this was not reciprocated by the Malaysia Government which did not allow for a USIP presence, even as observers, at the negotiation table of the exploratory talks between the GRP and MILF. It may well be that the MILF also resisted USIP formal presence at the table.[14] However, this did not prevent USIP from working with the GRP and MILF and other related parties, including civil groups, to arrive at a consensus and broad agreement on substantial points such as the nature and coverage of the ancestral domain.

By September 2006, the talks were stalled at the stage of determining the ancestral domain of the Bangsamoro people.[15] Towards the end of 2007, this complex and difficult issue remained deadlocked. Malaysia had maintained a monitoring team of fifty-one officers from the Malaysian Defence Forces, the Royal Malaysian Police, and from the Prime Minister's Department. There were also ten military officers from Brunei Darussalam and five from Libya.[16] On 16 April 2008, Malaysia announced that it would pull out its monitoring team in stages beginning on 10 May. While announcing this, then Malaysian Foreign Minister Rais Yatim said that his country was willing to continue playing a role in the peace process and was quoted as saying: "Though Malaysia is no longer willing to participate in the International Monitoring Team, in the context of ASEAN brotherhood, Malaysia is ready to cooperate with the Philippines and study the form of assistance that could be channeled." (*Bernama*, 8 May 2008)

With its team reduced to twelve later that year, Malaysia opted to pull out all its monitors by 30 November. However, there have been offers to participate coming from Australia and even Sweden. The OIC, which oversees the IMT (International Monitoring Team), later allowed for the participation of Japan and Canada in the IMT.[17] Clearly, many more players, state and non-state, may be entering the new stage of the peace process. After President Arroyo's visit to the United States and meeting with President Obama in July 2009, and the government's suspension of military operations in the south, there are now suggestions that a combination of state and non-state actors may be able to take up the cudgels for a new peace process.

ENGAGING THE WEST AND THE UNITED STATES

The new prime minister's meetings with President George Bush, President Jacques Chirac and Prime Minister Tony Blair all in the space of one week from 19–23 July marked an important foreign policy initiative and one which put a stamp of his personal style, if not an actual change in substantive policy. His speech to the U.S.-ASEAN Business Council on 19 July is perhaps indicative of the broad style of Abdullah, while in substance, he maintained previous policy positions on the issues of Palestine, Iraq and global terrorism, and Malaysia's economic priorities. Excerpts of that speech which is in the reported tense, do convey seemingly candid positions and views of an Abdullah *sans* rhetoric, and I reproduced some sections below with brief commentaries.

Abdullah showed considerable firmness and no substantial change on Iraq and Palestine compared with the gist of policy in these areas in the Mahathir era:[18] Excerpts of Abdullah's speech in the United States are reproduced below:

> In my meeting with President Bush earlier today, I reiterated some of my concerns about Iraq, Palestine and the direction in which the war against terrorism was taking[,] the Muslim world still needs some demonstration of good faith from the United States in addressing the root causes of terrorism, in particular the unresolved question of Palestine[;] the transfer of sovereignty to the Iraqis was merely a first step in returning to multilateralism, and the U.N. should be fully engaged when it stands in defence of the sovereignty and territorial integrity of member states.

As was his wont, he touted the success of Malaysian multiculturalism and the fact that being a "Muslim country" did not prevent Malaysia from being cognizant of its diverse cultural heritage nor its need for technological advancement:

> Our election victory [2004] showcased Malaysia as a multiracial and multireligious nation that protects freedom of worship and celebrates our diverse cultural heritage[;] we have also demonstrated that a Muslim country can be modern, democratic, tolerant and economically competitive[,] Islam does not teach us to turn our backs against the rest of the world[,] neither does it enjoin us to preach hatred and commit violence[,] conversely, it makes it an obligation for all Muslims to fulfill their potential, not only for the hereafter, but also in this world[,] this means technological advancement,

scientific innovation, academic excellence, economic development, entrepreneurship and trade.

Reiterating Malaysia's commitment to democracy, he averred that "we believe that with good governance, a healthy democracy, the empowerment of our citizens through education and economic growth with equity, we can withstand the tide of radicalism and it is a prescription which I hope others in the Muslim world can apply so that we are able to rollback extremists and terrorists, not just in Southeast Asia, but also throughout the world."

He stressed the importance of US-Malaysia relations with respect to trade, alluding to the impending FTA to be signed with the United States:[19]

> The United States and Malaysia have a profound and deep relationship[;] beneath the occasional political rhetoric, there are strongly positive numbers[,] Malaysia is the United States' 10th largest trading partner and for Malaysia the U.S. is not only our largest trading partner[,] but an important source of investments[;] your companies have invested almost 12 billion dollars in the last two decades in our economy[;] in order to strengthen this economic relationship, we recently concluded the signing of a trade and investment framework agreement which represents the first step towards a free trade agreement.

As he was speaking to businessmen, he then made the expected pitch for U.S. foreign investment in Malaysia:

> We are encouraging more U.S. companies to set up their regional distribution centers, operational headquarters and international procurement centers in Malaysia business process outsourcing is a burgeoning sector in Malaysia[;] where we offer the competitive advantage of a highly-trained, English-speaking workforce and world-class ICT infrastructure[;] I would also encourage U.S. companies to set up research laboratories and centers in Malaysia, especially in the field of biotechnology[;] it is important that Malaysia moves up the value chain and in order to do this, we need real technology transfer[;] Malaysia has the potential to be more than just an assembly line for the developed world, and I hope new investments will be reflective of the higher value-added capacity of our economy today.

The final quote deals with special areas of cooperation which the Abdullah government particularly wished to promote, including with respect to the issue of counterterrorism:

> Our close cooperation also extends into other areas, notably education, defense and in counter-terrorism initiatives[;] ever since the tragic events of September 11, 2001, Malaysia has extended our full cooperation in ensuring that the international network of terror is crippled and eventually

eliminated[;] our governments are in an advanced stage of negotiating a mutual legal assistance treaty which will facilitate further cooperation in legal, law enforcement and security matters[;] US commitment in the Southeast Asia regional center for counter-terrorism, located in Kuala Lumpur, has also been most encouraging.

RATCHETING UP BILATERAL RELATIONS

The Abdullah government also paid new attention to other bilateral relations where there have been issues or problems, or which have become increasingly important to Malaysia. Thus there were early prominent shifts made by Abdullah with respect to relations with Singapore, Australia, and China.

Let us briefly take a look at Malaysia-Singapore relations first. In an extended section later in this chapter we will examine these relations in even greater detail, especially with respect to developments in 2007.[20] Almost immediately after Abdullah took over the reins of government, there had been a palpable warming up of relations south of the border. Among other things, Singapore's investment arm Temasek Holding had acquired a 5 per cent interest in Telekom Malaysia, something unthinkable in the Mahathir period. In May Malaysian Trade Minister Rafidah Aziz made a further overture to Singapore in announcing the setting up of a RM10-million business development fund. This was announced at a dialogue with a seventy-member Malaysian-Singapore business council, led by counterpart George Yeo. For the record, Singapore companies invested RM8.1 billion between 1998–2003 in Malaysia, while Malaysian firms put RM13.8 billion into Singapore between 1996–2003 (*Malysiakini.com*, 24 May 2004). By December 2004, talks on unresolved bilateral issues were held between Abdullah and Senior Minster Goh Chok Tong, with both seemingly upbeat about future relations despite the absence of any formal agreement. Goh intimated that "where issues can be resolved by the foreign ministers, they can resolve them, where they think they cannot resolve them, they should not try to resolve them". Leave that to Abdullah and him to be the final arbiters, he had added. (*Bernama*, 13 December 2004)

Bilateral relations with Australia were also given a fillip in the wake of Abdullah's ascendancy as prime minister. By early July, Australia and Malaysia announced that talks on a free trade pact would be underway. This represented a dramatic shift in relations, given Mahathir's most recent tiff with Australia over its role as "deputy sheriff" of the United States in the region. Interestingly, over the controversial issue of the possible involvement of U.S. marines patrolling the Malacca Strait, Australian foreign minister Alexander

Downer offered support to Malaysia's position and said that security was the responsibility of littoral states (*Malaysiskini.com*, 4 June 2004).

Finally, an interesting geostrategic move by the new prime minister was his June 2004 visit to China, ahead of visits to the United States and Japan. Over the years, Malaysia has become ASEAN's largest trading partner with China, with a massive US$20 billion in two-way trade in 2003 (*People's Daily Online*, 1 June 2004). Abdullah's visit also commemorated the 30th anniversary of diplomatic ties with China, important as a statement itself, given Malaysia's large Chinese population and the fact that it was the first ASEAN country to recognize the People's Republic of China in 1974. However, relations with China took a rude knock in November and December 2005 in what has come to be known as "the nude ear squat incident".[21] The incident began when DAP Member of Parliament Teresa Kok alleged that the police had sexually outraged a woman who was a Chinese national, also making her do ear squats. Other reports of similar abuses then started to surface. An anonymous whistle-blower then produced a video depicting a female police officer ordering a female detainee (later identified as a Malay woman) to perform ear squats in the nude. A public inquiry was instituted with regard to the video incident and clearly the suggestion that Chinese nationals were given the short shrift by Malaysian authorities created enough flak to send Home Minister Azmi Khalid to Beijing on 5 December to mend fences with China. Azmi explained that his visit was meant to explain several matters related to the perception of the public and government there regarding immigration enforcement issues and other enforcement on Chinese tourists in Malaysia. Earlier, on 29 November, Deputy Internal Security Minister Noh Omar had made the unfortunate remark that if foreigners thought that Malaysian police were brutal, they should go back to their own countries and not stay in Malaysia.[22]

"NORMALIZING" RELATIONS WITH SINGAPORE

With respect to relations with Singapore, one of the major decisions of the Abdullah government was to cancel a project of the Mahathir government to build a bridge to Singapore to replace the current causeway from Johor Baru. When the project stalled in the Mahathir period because the terms of agreement could not be concluded with the Singapore Government,[23] the Mahathir government had decided to go it alone by building on the Malaysian side, a half-bridge, also known by its more colourful appellations as "scenic bridge" or "crooked bridge". The project was lying fallow when Abdullah took over the reins of government although the motions were started to build the Customs, Immigration, and Quarantine (CIQ) Complex on the Malaysian side.[24] On 12 April 2005, the Abdullah government decided to scuttle the building of the half-bridge. This led to a barrage of criticisms from Mahathir and his supporters. On 14 July, Abdullah made a lengthy press statement explaining why the half-bridge had to be stopped, releasing in the statement the content of several declassified documents purportedly dealing with the matter, including letters from Senior Minister Goh Chok Tong. According to this document, the main argument for not proceeding with the half-bridge was as follows:

> Comprehensive advice by the Attorney General's Chambers showed that Malaysia should not proceed to build a bridge unilaterally without complying with our legal obligations. In particular, Malaysia had obligations under the Johor-Singapore water agreements 1961 and 1962, the Wayleave Agreements and the Separation Agreement 1965. The main obstacle was that the construction of the crooked bridge will involve the demolition of the Malaysian side of the Johor Causeway. The said demolition would directly affect the water pipeline located inside the Johor Causeway and water pipelines straddling the Johor Causeway in which the ownership thereof vests with the Public Utilities Board of Singapore. The Attorney General's Chambers also stated that under the 1961 and 1962 Johor-Singapore Water Agreements, "Malaysia is required to obtain approval of PUB in relation to the alteration of water pipelines as a result of the construction of a full straight bridge or a scenic half bridge."[25]

Early in Abdullah's tenure as prime minister, in October 2004, Singapore Premier Lee Hsien Loong made an official visit to Malaysia and by December of the same year, Abdullah had met with Senior Minister Goh Chok Tong to discuss outstanding bilateral issues. The controversy over the half-bridge broke out in September 2005 after Abdullah had evidently been convinced by his Singapore counterparts not to go ahead with the project.

The new stage of relations came in mid-May 2007 when the Malaysian and Singapore premiers, Abdullah Badawi and Lee Hsien Loong, and their cabinet-level entourages met on Pulau Langkawi and sealed an important bilateral agreement. The centrepiece of the diplomatic effort was no doubt the agreement to set up a Joint Ministerial Committee with oversight over economic cooperation in the Iskandar Development Region (IDR) in the state of Johor. Both sides agreed to the introduction of "smart cards" to facilitate the two-way traffic of Malaysians and Singaporeans to the IDR. Both governments also issued a categorical statement that they would accept the ruling of the International Court of Justice on the Pulau Batu Putih/Pedra Branca dispute by November 2007. Without doubt this event represents the high watermark in some two decades of bumpy and, oftentimes, acrimonious Singapore-Malaysia relations. It is particularly interesting that globalization and economic diplomacy had seemingly led the way to a significant turn in Malaysian-Singapore relations of recent years.

According to the Malaysian prime minister, more could be in the offing after his new warming up of relations. Even prior to the diplomatic retreat, there was already talk of a new fast train link between Kuala Lumpur and Singapore undertaken by the YTL Corporation and the building of "several bridges" linking Singapore and Malaysia (much like in New York and Manhattan) to supplement the overcrowded causeway and the underutilized Second Link. Earlier on, Abdullah had remarked that the project could develop into a relationship much like Hong Kong's with Shenzhen. It could well be that IDR could become a prime and actual example of how economic diplomacy may have paved the way for more sustainable economic relations between Malaysia and Singapore in years to come. One hastens to add, however, that UMNO politics has spooked such mutually exclusive projects time and again. This is also not helped by the periodic insensitive remarks of some Singapore leaders.

The IDR, renamed "Iskandar Malaysia", spans an area of 2,217 sq. km., which is about thrice Singapore's size. Initially it was reported that US$105 billion was to be expended in the IDR, although there appeared to be little information about the actual phases of investment over the period of the Ninth Malaysia Plan. The Malaysian committee that would have oversight over the IDR was to be chaired by the Malaysian premier himself and one of its members was to be the veteran UMNO politician of the Johor, Tan Sri Musa Hitam. To provide clout to the project, the main stakeholder of the IDR will be the government's sovereign fund, Khazanah Holdings, while the primary developer would be UEM Land, a subsidiary of United Engineers Malaysia, known for its huge infrastructure projects.

In a seminar in Singapore on 23 May 2007, the managing director of UEM Land, Wan Abdullah Wan Ibrahim, was upbeat about the prospect of private sector investment from across the border. He said that by the year's end, some S$38.5 million would be purchased by Singaporeans in industrial lots in the IDR. The Nusajaya area, the first to be developed, will see the establishment of an industrial park, a waterfront precinct, theme parks, an educational city, a medical park, and residential areas. Plans were in place for a medical faculty to be run by Newcastle University and a private institution run by iCarnegie of Carnegie Mellon University. On 28 August, at a seminar on business opportunities in Singapore, Minister for International Trade and Industry Rafidah Aziz put her weight behind both the IDR and the "Northern

Corridor Economic Region" as the most attractive investment destinations for Singaporeans. She also said that under Malaysia's Third Industrial Master Plan, over the next fifteen years, $300 billion in foreign investments was targeted. (*Business Times*, 29 August 2007).[26] On the eve of Malaysia's 50th anniversary celebrations in August 2007, the government appropriately announced that a group of Middle Eastern investors had agreed to invest RM4.1 billion (US$1.2 billion) in the IDR. According to news reports, Abu Dhabi state investment agency Mubadala Development Co., Kuwait Finance House, and Dubai-based property developer Saraya Holdings Ltd., agreed to develop a total 2,230 acres (902 hectares) in the IDR. Projects include a golf village, an amusement bay, a residential district, a medical centre, and a financial hub for Islamic banking services. (*AP*, 29 August 2007). A further important development by 2009 was the idea of the Singapore-Johor Bahru Ring Road spanning the Ayer Rajah, Pan Island, and Kranji highways on the Singapore side, and Tuas-Second Link and Skudai highways on the Malaysian side. The two connecting points were the Causeway and the second link bridge.[27]

The overseeing structure for Iskandar Malaysia is the Iskandar Regional Development Authority co-chaired by the prime minister and chief minister of Johor. It could prove to be the lynchpin for the beginnings of the economic integration of this region of Johor with the industrial and financial hub of Singapore, ushering a bilateral economic zone as against the moribund ASEAN "growth triangles" which have not made much progress. The ultimate goal for the IM-Singapore economic zone could be a customs union, where tariff and non-tariff barriers are harmonized, or even a common market in which one could see the free flow of the factors of production, in particular, capital and labour. The first Joint Ministerial Committee (JMC) meeting on the IDR was held on 23 July 2007. It was jointly chaired by Malaysia's Effendi Norwawi, minister in the Prime Minister's Department, and Singapore's Mah Bow Tan, minister for national development, and also included as members the Chief Minister of Johor Abdul Ghani Othman and Raymond Lim, minister for transport, Singapore. The JMC formed four workgroups to look into facilitating immigration clearance, enhancing transportation links, tourism cooperation, and environmental collaboration.[28]

REFURBISHING REGIONALISM

Abdullah has largely maintained the thrust of foreign policy *vis-à-vis* ASEAN and East Asian relations. ASEAN remains the anchor of Malaysia's overall orientation towards the rest of the world, but the new prime minister continued to push for greater East Asian regional integration via the ASEAN Plus Three grouping. In his speech to the Second East Asia Congress in Kuala Lumpur on 21 June, Abdullah called for the establishment of an East Asian Community based on 'six cardinal imperatives", namely, egalitarian and democratic; omni-directional and embracing, turning its back on no one; caring and mutually beneficial; committed to global empowerment; devoted to economic prosperity, and, obsessive about regional peace and friendship.

Even before Malaysia assumed the chair of ASEAN in 2005, Abdullah had perceptibly pushed for a much higher level of collaboration within ASEAN. Among other things, the new prime minister called for the regional body to explore the possibilities of a common time zone, common travel document, and common currency. In the National Colloquium on ASEAN held in Kuala Lumpur on 8 August 2004, Abdullah also stressed that Malaysia would try to work towards the following objectives:

- Prepare the groundwork or building blocks for the nucleus of the ASEAN Community idea
- Strengthen ASEAN external relations, especially with respect to the ASEAN Plus Three relationship
- Work towards the ASEAN Charter which would confer upon it an "international legal personality" (*The Star*, 8 August 2004).

In 2005, among some of the matters Abdullah took up in ASEAN's name was to seek the Asian-Europe Meeting to accept the ASEAN Secretariat as part of its formal structure because it was already the secretariat for the ASEAN Plus Three process. In the run-up to Malaysia's hosting of the ASEAN and East Asian Summits in December 2005, in an interview on the official television channel (*RTM1*), he said : "For ASEAN to become a truly strong cohesion, it must involve people at all levels. We need to engage the views from all strata of society ... from civil societies, because ASEAN belongs to them, so that they are more concerned about the grouping in the future." (*Bernama*, 11 December 2005). On 8 August 2006 (ASEAN Day), Abdullah delivered the 2006 ASEAN Lecture. In his speech, he placed considerable emphasis on the importance of the ASEAN Charter as the instrument to carry the regional body forward. Arguing that while the cardinal principle of ASEAN has been "non-interference", the concept required refinement and the regional body needed to upgrade itself:

> I believe the new ASEAN Charter which is yet to be written is the right instrument to update the enduring principle of the TAC (Treaty of Amity and Cooperation)...The concept and principle contained in the treaty may indeed require refining or updating in order to be relevant and responsive to the changing needs of member countries. (*Bernama,* 8 August 2006)

In October of the same year, Abdullah attended the ASEAN-China Commemorative Summit in Nanning, marking fifteen years of dialogue relations, where he spoke positively about China's endorsement of the Southeast Asian Nuclear Weapons-Free Zone, and also urged China to adhere to the Declaration on the Conduct of Parties in the South China Sea signed by ASEAN and China in 2002.

EMBRACING GLOBALIZATION

If one took the conventional meaning of globalization as the increasing objective spread of the neoliberal economy on a global scale, then the external policy of all governments of this era, large or small, could hardly be insulated from it. Given its strong external orientation, the Malaysian economy has since its early days been more subject to the vicissitudes of the global economy than most. In the previous chapter, we have argued that Mahathir's polices attempted to confront globalization in various ways, but at the end of the day succumbed to its overwhelming impact. In Abdullah Badawi's tenure, there was an evident shift away from confrontational postures and policies towards the forces of globalization.

What is undeniable is that even in the Mahathir period, Malaysia had begun to engage actively with globalization via the World Trade Organization (WTO) by becoming a founding member since 1995. Malaysia, however, maintains a Third World position on most matters, such as with respect to the "Singapore Issues".[29] In 2007 it chaired the WTO General Council. The Ministry of Trade and Industry (MITI) actively pursues a trade liberalization policy and signed in 2006 a Free Trade Agreement with Japan and one with Pakistan, and is actively negotiating FTAs with the United States, Australia, New Zealand. The fact that Malaysian external trade has grown immensely[30] had been MITI's rationale for trade liberalization, Malaysia's trade policy, as outlined by MITI, is summarized as follows:

- Malaysia's trade policy is to pursue trade liberalization through the rule-based multilateral trading system under the World Trade Organization (WTO). To complement this, Malaysia has also chosen to pursue regional and bilateral trading arrangements.
- The WTO allows for free trade agreements (FTAs) provided that tariffs are eliminated substantially on all trade. One of the important principles is that all parties to the agreement must eliminate duties according to mutually agreed rules and timeframes. Furthermore, it must not be more trade restrictive to non-members of the FTA concerned.

- FTAs have traditionally been confined to trade in goods. However, after the establishment of the WTO, trade in services has been included in many FTAs. FTAs provide the means to achieve quicker and higher levels of liberalization that would create effective market access.
- Recent trends indicate that countries prefer Closer Economic Partnership (CEP) agreements that are more comprehensive in scope and coverage. Consequently, CEP agreements cover not only liberalization of the goods and services sector, but also include investment, trade facilitation, and economic and technical cooperation.
- FTAs essentially grant preferential treatment to participants of the FTA. In order to ensure that only members of the FTA enjoy tariff preferences, specific rules and disciplines are incorporated in such agreements. One such discipline is Rules of Origin (ROO). ROO stipulate the conditions under which only products originating from parties to the FTAs benefit from preferential market access.[31]

WTO Secretary General Pascal Lamy delivered a speech in Kuala Lumpur on 17 August 2007 at the invitation of long-serving MITI Minister Rafidah Aziz. The Secretary General heaped praised on Malaysia's open trading policy and argued that trade contributed to Malaysia's "take-off" and helped it overcome the financial meltdown of 1997–98.[32]

It is interesting to note that the Malaysia-U.S. FTA had stalled largely on the objections on the U.S. side over Malaysia's discriminatory ethnic policies and the issue of government procurements.[33] The first round of talks were held from 12–16 June 2006 in Penang at a local beach hotel. Various sections of civil society mounted a demonstration against the FTA. Among the groups heading the protest was the Third World Network (TWN), based in Penang, and known for its anti-globalization posture. The TWN, along with the Consumer Association of Penang and Friends of the Earth, set up a webpage providing readers with information on the impending FTA and its implications for Malaysia, particularly for agricultural producers and labour.[34] MITI on its part has posted a statement in answer to the U.S. congressman, the late Tom Lantos, who called on the United States to suspend the FTA negotiations with Malaysia. MITI's response is worth noting, viz.:

> The call by Tom Lantos to suspend the free trade agreement negotiations because of a business deal by a Malaysian company with the National Iranian Oil company does not augur well for the negotiations . No country can determine how companies in another country should conduct business. (Accessed from MITI portal, 21 August 2007)

It was evident that several sticking points had bogged down the negotiations. According to one report, besides the issue of ethnic preferential policies, intellectual property, environmental and labour matters appear to remain outstanding. The reference to a company dealing with Iran above was apparently a reference to a deal between Malaysian private corporation SKS and state-owned National Iranian Oil Company.[35] It may be argued by detractors that Malaysia's FTA policy runs counter to its overall stance on South-South issues, to which Abdullah's continued to pay lip service to in such forums as the Group of 77 (Plus China). The prime minister attended the group's summit at Doha in June 2005, speaking out on the need for a self-empowered "independent developing world" (*Bernama,* 16 June 2005).

MAJOR SCANDALS AND IMPLICATIONS FOR FOREIGN POLICY

As Abdullah entered the third and fourth years of his tenure, an increasing number of disruptive domestic issues and political scandals begun to surface and plague his government. Many of these scandals had negative implications for the foreign policy of the Malaysian Government. In this section, we will focus on four major scandals of the Abdullah period, namely, the SCOMI centrifuges trans-shipment and other military component transshipments, the oil-for-food issue, the Altantuya murder, and the Port Klang bailout.

Nuclear Parts Trans-shipment

An issue which emerged early in his tenure in February 2004 involved the sale of nuclear centrifuge parts to Iran, sourced from the Malaysian company SCOMI Precision Engineering, or SCOPE.[36] SCOPE was a subsidiary of the SCOMI Group, an oil-and-gas firm whose biggest stakeholder was Kaspadu, an investment company owned by the Malaysian prime minister's son, Kamaluddin Abdullah. The key figure in the alleged sale was a shady Sri Lankan businessman, Bhukary Syed Abu Tahir, who in a confession revealed that he helped Pakistan's Abdul Qadeer Khan (father of Pakistan's nuclear programme) leak or sell nuclear technology to Libya, North Korea, and Iran. According to media reports, SCOPE produced more than 25,000 individual parts for a Dubai-based company owned by Gulf Technical Industries, under a contract negotiated by Tahir, and shipped by a German freighter between December 2002 and August 2003. The parts, in boxes marked with SCOPE's name, were seized in the Mediterranean by German and Italian authorities in October 2003, while en route from Dubai to Libya. U.S. President George

Bush in a speech to Congress revealed details of the case, obviously gathered from CIA sources. The Malaysian police, which was contacted by the U.S. government over the matter, subsequently arrested Tahir on 28 May 2004 under the Internal Security Act. Tahir was released sometime in 2008.[37] In a labyrinthine connection with the case, in August 2006, five Japanese executives of the Mitutoyo company were arrested by the Tokyo Metropolitan Police for allegedly exporting advanced measuring devices without government permission in late 2001 to an unspecified recipient in Malaysia, which was allegedly thought to have been SCOPE. The Japanese police were reportedly trying to determine whether Mitutoyo's devices were used by SCOPE to manufacture centrifuge parts that were sold to Libya to enrich uranium for its nuclear weapons programme, which was discontinued.[38]

Clearly the SCOMI-SCOPE affair had grave implications for Malaysian foreign policy and particularly for relations with the United States even though the actions taken were those of a private company. The fact that the company was linked to the prime minister's son adds a further complication to the case. In fact, in January 2009, the U.S. government imposed sanctions on a number of individuals connected to "rogue" scientist A.Q. Khan. Among them were Shah Hakim Shahzanim Zain, chief executive officer (CEO) and major shareholder of the Scomi Group. The sanctions, which the U.S. State Department said came after a multiyear U.S. government review, mean that the individuals designated by the censure order are banned, among other things, from doing business with the American government.[39] The Malaysian police investigation that was carried out on the affair put the blame on Tahir, suggesting that he had deceived SCOMI into believing that the parts were being made for the oil and gas industry in Dubai and that foreigners from Germany, Turkey, Switzerland, and Britain were allegedly involved as middlemen to help procure the nuclear parts from A.Q. Khan. (Sodhy 2007, p. 39). The Foreign Ministry also sent a protest to the U.S. Embassy to say that Malaysia had been unfairly targeted and lumped together with countries such as Iran, North Korea, and Libya. In the event, the matter was settled by the intervention of the International Atomic Energy Agency (IAEA) which asked Malaysia to submit a report on the affair to which the latter agreed. The government directed the Institute for Nuclear Technology Research and the Atomic Energy Licensing Board to say that Malaysia would submit a report in line with the multilateral approach to nuclear proliferation and weapons of mass destruction (Sodhy 2007, p. 40).

In the circumstances, the Malaysian Government took the "politically correct" decision to arrest Tahir but, on the other hand, took no action against SCOPE. It deflected U.S. criticism with its multilateral approach tactic. From another perspective, it could well have been that parties involved were not unaware of the implications of the sales and may have assumed it was consistent with Malaysia's national interest to trade or sell even sensitive nuclear equipment to whichever country it chose. However, if that were the argument, the arrest of Tahir under the ISA would then remain a puzzle, or perhaps could be seen as an *ex post facto* decision.

Evidence subsequently surfaced that the nuclear and military component sales issue extended beyond the SCOMI group. According to a report in *Asia Times Online*,[40] in April 2007 the United States, under its Syria and Iran Non-proliferation Act, imposed sanctions on fourteen companies, individuals, and government agencies accused of dealing in advanced weapon technology with Iran or Syria. Two of the companies were listed as Challenger Corporation (Malaysia) and Target Airfreight (Malaysia).[41] Furthermore, in July, U.S. authorities arrested and charged a 59-year old Pakistani national, Jilani Humayun, for shipping F-5 and F-14 fighter jet components to Malaysia, from where they were alledgedly re-exported to Iran. Interestingly, a Singapore connection has also been named in military trans-shipments through Malaysia. A federal jury in Eastern District of New York in May 2006 convicted Singaporean businessman Ernest Koh Chong Tek of smuggling U.S. aircraft parts via Malaysia for trans-shipment to Iran.[42] Needless to say, the trans-shipments of U.S. contraband military components through Malaysia by various individuals and companies raises many issues of U.S.-Malaysia relations which appear to be unresolved from a foreign policy perspective. A simple question to be raised is what indeed is the Malaysian policy on such matters? If it accepts the U.S. policy as given, there should logically be a clear policy position and measures taken to check such activities. Another related issue is whether Malaysian companies and inviduals involved in such trans-shipments should be blacklisted, penalized, or even charged for such conduct by the Malaysian government.

OIL-FOR-FOOD SCANDAL

When the oil-for-food scandal made the headlines in the middle of 2006, then U.N. Secretary General Kofi Annan was embarrassed by the allegation that his son had been obliquely implicated for his part in a company that had benefited from the programme. In Malaysia, a similar situation apparently confronted Prime Minister Abdullah Badawi when allegations surfaced that either he or his family members may have benefited from illicit Oil-for-Food contracts to Iraq. Unlike Kofi Annan, to date Abdullah has not given a full public statement about the matter. According to *Asia Times Online*,[43] an "Abdullah Badawi" is listed as a recipient of the Oil-for-Food scam. The Malaysian prime minister has admitted to helping Malaysian businessmen take part in the Oil-for-Food programme, but has said at the time the accusations surfaced that he was not personally involved.

Malaysia Today's coordinator Raja Petra Kamarudin has made a number of highly damaging allegations,[44] about Malaysian companies and individuals involved in the scandal, based on two independent inquiries: [45]

- Tradeyear Sdn. Bhd., which entered into two contracts, is beneficiary to 5,600,000 barrels of Iraqi oil under the name of Abdullah Badawi.
- Mastek Sdn Bhd, which entered into four contracts, is beneficiary to 45,000,000 barrels of Iraqi oil under the name of Faek Ahmad Shareef. Mastek Sdn. Bhd. is owned by Obata-Ambak Holdings Sdn. Bhd. and Noor Asiah binti Mahmood (Prime Minister Abdullah Ahmad Badawi's sister-in-law). Obata-Ambak Holdings Sdn. Bhd. is in turn owned by Noor Asiah binti Mahmood, plus three others of the same surname and living at the same address as Noor Asiah.

It is unprecedented that a Malaysian prime minister has been linked directly to an international scandal of the scale of the Oil-for-Food proportions. It remains a puzzle that the Abdullah government has not formally responded to these accusations and to revelations found in the independent inquires which are now publicly available documents.

ALTANTUYA MURDER [46]

Another issue that has hit the international headlines concerned the bizarre murder of a twenty-eight-year-old Mongolian woman, Altantuya Shaaribuu, whose skeletal remains were found on a hilltop in Puncak Alam in Shah Alam on 6 November 2006. The murder itself would not have been brought to light had it not been for the Mongolian honorary consul in Kuala Lumpur, Syed Abdul Rahman Alhabshi, making a missing person's report and his persistent attempts to press the police about the matter. It was subsequently revealed by the police that Altantuya's body was blown up by military-grade C4 explosives and that she had also been shot. A chief inspector and a corporal of the police's Special Action Squad were charged with Altantuya's murder at the Shah Alam magistrate's court on 15 November. More sensationally, political analyst Abdul Razak Abdullah Baginda, director of the Malaysian Strategic Research Centre (MSRC) was charged the next day with abetting the crime. The bare facts of the case are that Chief Inspector Azilah Hadri,

31, and Corporal Sirul Azhar Umar, 36, were charged with killing Altantuya between 10 p.m. on 19 October and 1 a.m. on 20 October 2005, while Abdul Razak Baginda, 47, was charged with abetting them. In plain language, Abdul Razak Baginda was alleged to have persuaded the pair to commit the murder. Altantuya, by Abdul Razak's own admission in an affidavit, was his lover, and had allegedly come Kuala Lumpur to blackmail him, asking for some RM500,000, according to one testimony. All three faced the death penalty if convicted, but Abdul Razak was acquitted on 31 October 2008 after the judge found no *prima facie* evidence to prosecute him. Interestingly, the MSRC was a think tank closely associated with Deputy Prime Minister and Defence Minister Najib Abdul Razak. Altantuya was alleged to have been the interpreter in the Malaysian Government's purchase of eighteen Russian Sukhoi-30 jets and three French submarines contracted by the Malaysian Defence Ministry in 2003 and 2002 respectively. The Russian-educated Altantuya was fluent in Chinese, Russian, French, and English. The trial, which began on 16 June 2007, was concluded on 9 April 2009 with the conviction of the two policemen. Among the interesting developments, related events, and facts of the murder are the following:

- The trial was originally scheduled for March 2008, but later brought forward to June 2007.
- Controversial changes have been made with respect to the presiding judge, prosecution, and defence teams.[47]
- A cousin of Altantuya, Uuriintuya Gal Ochir, testified that her arrival with her murdered cousin and a friend in October 2006 was not found on immigration records.
- Uuriintuya claimed to have seen a picture of Defence Minister Najib Abdul Razak together with Abdul Razak Baginda and her cousin Altantuya.
- The evidence of Sirul Azhar Umar was found to be inadmissible by High Court judge, Justice Mohd Zaki Mohd Yasin.
- A third member of the Special Action Squad, who was allegedly at the scene of the murder, but not charged, was alleged to be the aide-de-camp to Rosmah Mansor, wife of the deputy prime minister.
- The father of Altantuya, Shaaribuu Setev, has filed a RM100 million legal suit of negligence against the Malaysian Government for the murder of his daughter.

Whatever the outcome of the trial, the fact that it has received front-page publicity for weeks and months would no doubt put the Abdullah government in an unenviable situation not just *vis-à-vis* a domestic audience, but also an international one. The most obvious link to foreign policy concerns Malaysian-Mongolian relations. Already, early in the proceedings, the Mongolian Government had asked Wisma Putra for an update and explanation of the murder (*Bernama*, 11 November 2006). The alleged link of the murder to the defence minister (who was also deputy prime minister) could not but be a major source of discomfort for the Abdullah government. Furthermore, the fact that the murdered woman may have been involved in dealings concerning Malaysian defence contracts with the Russian and French Governments raised the whole question of disclosures about defence issues and polices of the government. It is not uncommon in other political climes for implicated ministers to step down when a hint of scandal affects a ministry.[48] A further, if yet unproven issue, was that kickbacks were allegedly received by various parties for the defence contracts and that the murder was connected to this dimension of the affair.[49] This latter, if it surfaced at some point during court proceedings, would have embarrassed the Abdullah government and possibly even its foreign associates. Allegations of large commissions received by Razak Baginda for the defence deals have already been circulated by opposition leaders and detractors of the government in numerous postings in the highly accessible and open terrain of cyberspace.

THE PORT KLANG FREE ZONE BAILOUT[50]

The story of the Port Klang Free Zone (PKFZ) begins in the Mahathir period in 1999 when the company Kuala Dimensi Sdn. Bhd. bought 405 hectares of land in Pulau Indah for RM95 million from a fishermen's cooperative, Pulau Lumut Development Cooperative Bhd. Abdul Rahman Palil, the cooperative's chairman, was a Selangor executive councillor as well as Kapar divisional head of UMNO. The Port Klang Authority (PKA) subsequently bought the land in 2002 for RM1.08 billion or roughly ten times the original price. Kuala Dimensi, headed by chairman Azim Zabidi, who was also UMNO treasurer, was appointed the turnkey contractor to develop 514 warehouses, 2,000 parking bays, four office buildings, an exhibition centre, and a four-star hotel. The company reported more than RM3.3 billion in cost overruns in 2003. The legal firm responsible for drawing up the contract between PKA and Kuala Dimensi was headed by Abdul Rashid Asari, Kapar's UMNO vice-chief while Kapar UMNO youth chief, Faizal Abdullah, was deputy CEO of the property developer and investment firm for the sale and devlopment of PKFZ. Furthermore, Faizal's father-in-law, Onn Ismail, was the Kapar UMNO's chairperson and former chairperson of the fishermen's cooperative which originally sold the land. Total costs for the project stood at RM4.63 billion, plus a further RM1.08 billion for the land. The Jebel Ali Free Zone (Jafza), which was appointed operator of PKFZ and awarded a fifteen-year contract pulled out of the management deal citing red-tape and inefficiency on the part of its partner as the cause (*Business Times*, 17 August 2007). The PKFZ had up till mid-2007 attracted RM468 million worth of investments.

The Abdullah government on 23 August 2007 agreed to a bailout for the PKA with a soft loan after meetings between the transport minister, Chan Kong Choy and the prime minister. A Transport Ministry spokesman said:

> Port Klang is our main port and we have much [sic] big plans for it. We cannot continue to let debt problems persist as it holds back all the plans to enhance this venture…with the high overall cost of the PKFZ in mind, the government has agreed to give the soft loan and details are being worked out on the repayment scheme. It will be a scheme that will help them to get back on their feet again. (*Malaysiakini*, 24 August 2007)

At the peak of the controversy and amidst a possible public inquiry over the PKFZ fiasco called by Shahrir Samad, chairperson of the government's Public Accounts Committee, a director of the project's turnkey contractor, Kuala Dimensi Sdn. Bhd., warned of legal action against *Malaysiakini*. Tiong King Sing lambasted *Malaysiakini's* irresponsibility in writing reports that he said were inaccurate and jeopardized plans to develop the country. Tiong, who is also Bintulu MP, is youth chief of the Sarawak Progressive Democratic Party, a member of the ruling Barisan Nasional coalition (*Malaysiakini*, 25 August 2007).

The implications of the PKFZ fiasco are already apparent, if not palpable. The withdrawal of Dubai-based Jazra as managers did not augur well for Malaysian foreign partnerships with Middle Eastern countries or other parts of the world for that matter. Jafza managing director for international operations, Chuck Heath, was quoted as saying that "Jafza does not see this as the failure of PKA or any individual, but rather the Malaysian political and business environment that does not support quick change and innovative plans" (*Business Times*, 17 August, 2007). A more serious implication is that business cronyism, based on political party links, appears to afflict government projects in a highly negative way, leading to grave questions about governance and transparency in the Malaysian economic environment.

SOURCES OF FOREIGN POLICY IN THE ABDULLAH PERIOD

In a previous chapter, we referred to the "iconoclasm" of Mahathir Mohamad as his penchant for "the debunking of established beliefs and ideas about politics". We suggested further that in Mahathir's foreign policy, this led to "[A] genuine critique of existing inequitable relations between rich and poor countries, a disdain for 'Western' democracy, and persistent attempts to promote a modernist Islamic perspective in foreign policy". (Saravanamuttu 2004, p. 307)

The question that arises is to what extent Abdullah would follow such a style or even modify the iconoclastic substance of Mahathir's policies, especially in Malaysia's relations with certain countries. My reading is that while there was a palpable change in style, not much by way of the substance of policies changed, except perhaps in bilateral policies with some countries, notably Singapore, Australia, and the United States. We have already discussed the shift in domestic policy where a change in political climate allowed Abdullah to effect some real changes of policy domestically. However in foreign relations much of the substantive aspects of policy have firmly been laid down in Mahathir's time. One should also not forget that Abdullah had for nine years (1991–99) been a foreign minister himself in the Mahathir cabinet. This notwithstanding, since assuming leadership, Abdullah did introduce a much softer style of dealing with the outside world and, most importantly, a version of a modernist and moderate Islam, "Islam *Hadhari*" or "civilizational Islam". Cynics may argue that the concept was vacuous but nonetheless this concept of Islam was deployed as the hallmark of Malaysia's orientation towards the Western world, especially in the face of the American-led "global war against terrorism". It must have been calculated by Abdullah's advisors that Malaysia, as leader of the OIC and NAM, should project such an image in order to optimize not just the objectives of these umbrella organizations, but also Malaysia's own national interests. I would also add that Abdullah's moderate approach to foreign policy dovetailed well with the middlepowermanship posture and strategy of Malaysia, which we will discuss further in the conclusion of this book. Suffice it to say that the softer and non-abrasive style of Abdullah helped greatly to mend bilateral relations with some countries, which had no end of persistent problems and irritations with Malaysia under the Mahathir regime.

This chapter argues that there has been a shift in domestic and foreign policy since the political retirement of Mahathir Mohamad. New Premier Abdullah Badawi was responsible for ushering in this shift. This occurred despite the fact that much of substance and broad directions of policy remained largely unaltered or intact. Put differently, the dominant sectors of society, the ruling political party or parties, the most significant social strata (such as the capitalist class and middle class, and the working population, for example) were the agents or actors which continue to bestow agential power to the regime and also act as the ultimate checks and parameters for what could or could not be executed as domestic or foreign policy. Even in a strong and authoritarian state such as Malaysia, the above forces of society can and will often influence significant change. Leaders act and initiate changes according to such influences. I contend that only in exceptional circumstances will leaders initiate changes that go against the grain of society. Abdullah Badawi found to his chagrin that when he failed to implement with any level of satisfaction his proposed policies of reform after the overwhelming mandate given to him in 2004, his legitimacy was mortally eroded. The unmistakable signal came in the devastating results of the 8 March 2008 general election.

Abdullah was also the "victim" as it were of other larger political changes. It was clear that two major factors changed in the Malaysian political scene during his time. First, there was the political climate post-Mahathir, represented by the continued strength of *Reformasi* which was an anti-Mahathir movement sparked by the Anwar incarceration. Anwar's release from prison could not but add agential power to the *Reformasi* forces. This in turn put a greater impetus on an already strong Islamic resurgence, which was capitalized again by PAS.

Second, Islam *Hadhari* became the new elite ideology of the Abdullah government, but it eventually proved weak as a construct. In particular Abdullah failed to contain interfaith fractures despite his "moderate" Islam. It was clearly an opportune ideological construct propounded at a "ripe" moment of Malaysian political history. It certainly helped to legitimize and enhance the reputation of the Abdullah government, especially for his first three years in office, but it should be noted that the Mahathir era had already laid the groundwork with a wave of Islamization. Again, Abdullah's change was more in style than substance. Towards the latter half of 2006 and 2007, Abdullah's brand of Islamization began to generate its own negative reflexivity, especially within the domestic realm in terms of ethnic relations. This in turn had impacted on Abdullah's legitimacy and leadership of a multicultural coalition of political forces, straining to outer limits the parameters of consociational politics. Overplaying the discursive elements of an "Islamic State" also produced negative reflexivity in foreign relations, especially *vis-à-vis* non-Muslim countries and partnerships. Ethnic relations reached an all-time low for the prime minister with the HINDRAF street protests of November 2007. The disastrous outing at the hustings of March 2008 proved this as I have explained earlier on. In a constructivist rendering of the Abdullah period, one could say that the agential power of his regime was reduced to "weak" or "moderate", especially when it failed egregiously to manage ethnic relations and interfaith issues. Eventually this would impact on foreign policy capacity and capability. Figure 9.1 attempts such an interpretation in diagrammatic format.

In conclusion, the new premier Abdullah Badawi was clearly both the receptacle of political changes, and an agent of change in the new political climate created by the departure of Mahathir Mohamad from the political stage. Abdullah's softer and less abrasive style has definitely led to some significant shifts in foreign policy, in particular, in his projection of Malaysia as a "moderate" Muslim state, willing and able to participate actively in global politics. This shift has brought about a more collaborative relationship with major powers and also several bilateral relationships which have been problematic in the past.

FIGURE 9.1
Malaysian Foreign Policy under Abdullah Badawi

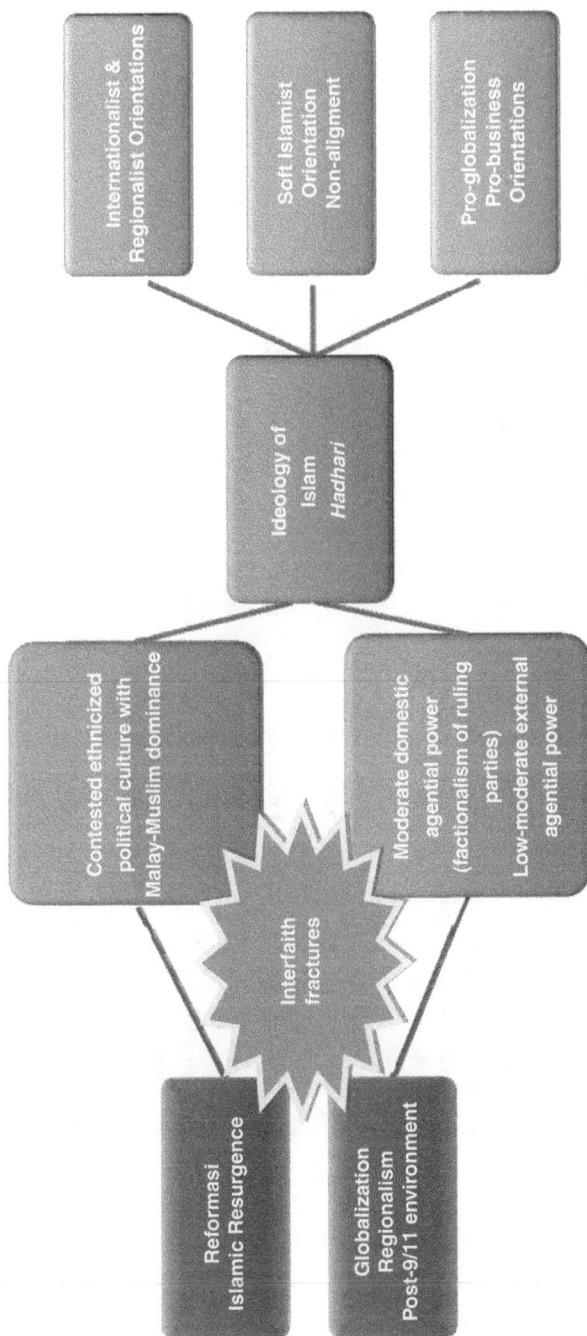

Source: Author's own illustration.

TABLE 9.1
Foreign Policy Output in the Abdullah Badawi Period

Policy Terrains → & Policy Outputs →	Special Relations (including bilateral)	Regionalism	Globalization	Global Security & Terrorism
	(US, "West", OIC, Commonwealth, Singapore, Indonesia, Thailand, Japan, China, Australia)	(ASEAN, East Asia, APEC)	(FTAs, WTO, G77, APEC, South-South)	
Objectives	Political Independence Sovereignty	Political Independence Sovereignty	Political Independence Sovereignty	Political Independence Sovereignty
	Territorial Integrity	Enhancing role of ASEAN as regional actor	Enhancing role as developmental state	Enhancing role as Muslim/Islamic state
Strategies	Enhancing role as developmental state	Promoting ASEAN, East Asian & Asia Pacific "open" regionalism	Engaging Globalization	Promoting Islamic perspectives, civilizational dialogue
	Championing Muslim causes	Championing Muslim causes	Promoting Islamic Finance	
			Promoting Islamic Finance	

continued on next page

TABLE 9.1 — *cont'd*

Actions			
Meeting Bush, Chirac, Blair (2004)	Chairing and attending ASEAN-related meetings	Engaging in WTO activities, negotiations	Chairing OIC and NAM
Signing Trade & Investment Framework Agreement (TIFA) with U.S. (2004)	Hosting first East Asian Summit (2006)	Participating in Doha Development Agenda negotiations (ongoing)	Attending Arab Summit 2007
China Visit on 30th Anniversary of diplomatic relations (2004)	Facilitating AFTA	Signing FTA with Japan (2006)	Statements and actions on Palestine, Iraq
	Supporting ASEAN Charter		Intensifying relations and visits to Muslim, Middle Eastern states
Indonesian Visits and agreements (2006, 2007)	Participation in APEC	Negotiating FTAs (since 2005/06) with US, Australia, New Zealand & Pakistan	
Thai visits (2004, 2006, 2007)	Chairing WTO General Council (2006)		
Australian visits (2004, 2006)	Inviting WTO Sec Gen Pascal Lamy to deliver lecture in KL (2007)	Meeting US-ASEAN Business Council (2004)	
Meeting with Singapore leaders (SM Goh, PM Lee, 2004, 2006, 2007) Summit (2006)		Attending G77 Summit + China	
Setting up Joint Ministerial Committee on Iskandar Development Region		Three-nation African tour in 2007	
Maintaining South China Sea presence			

Source: Author's own compilation.

Appendix 9.1

Selected Actions of Abdullah Ahmad Badawi, 2004–07

Year 2004

22 May	Interview with *CNBC*
28 May	Speech in Beijing, China
1 June	Keynote Address at Asia Pacific Roundtable, KL
21 June	Keynote Address at Second East Asia Congress, KL
2 July	Official Visit to Saudi Arabia
23 August	Speech on "Look East" policy in Seoul
26 August	Launch of Invest Malaysia
15 September	Meeting with Sultan of Brunei at Putrajaya
26–27 September	At the 59th U.N. General Assembly
5 October	Official Visit of PM Lee Hsien Loong of Singapore
11 October	Official Visit to Ireland
13 October	Working Visit to Thailand
11 November	Condolence on Yasser Arafat's passing
20–21 November	Attends APEC Summit at Santiago
25 November	Conferred Cuba's highest state award, Havana
28–30 December	Attends 10th ASEAN Summit at Vientiane
13 December	Meeting with Singapore's Senior Minister Goh Chok Tong, KL
15 December	Attends Arab Strategic Forum, Dubai
19–22 December	Official visit to India Conferred Honorary Doctorate

Year 2005

5 January	Attends Conference on Tsunami relief
23–24 January	Attends Biodiversity Conference, Paris
29 January	Launches Islam Hadhari portal
14 February	Malaysia and Indonesia agree to overcome problem of "illegals" in joint statement in Jakarta
15–18 February	Four-day Official Visit to Pakistan
18–20 February	Three-day Working Visit to Jeddah
1 March	Bilateral talks with SM Goh Chok Tong
14 March	Statement that Malaysia will not stake claim on Indonesian territory
31 March–2 April	Three-day Official Visit to New Zealand
6–8 April	Three-day Official Visit to Australia Malaysia and Australia pledge to enhance ties

21–22 April	Attends Asia-Africa Summit
	Pledges development assistance to Africa
3, 8 May	Hits out at those distorting Islam *Hadhari*
	Says Malaysia not turning into extreme state
13 May	Malaysia and Iran set up Joint Trade Committee
20 May	Has audience with Queen Beatrice of the Netherlands
25 May	Tells Japanese MPs Asian economic integration achievable
14–16 June	Attends G77 Summit Plus China in Doha
	Bilateral meetings with G77 leaders
	Speaks on "independent developing world"
23 June	Malaysia proposes OIC Infrastructure Fund and Wakaf Fund
8 July	Condemns London bombings
21 July	Says Malaysia does not want to just warm its seat as OIC, NAM chairs
25–27 July	Three-day visit to South Africa
11 September	Attends World Leaders Summit in Abu Dhabi
14 September	Announces Malaysia as "launchpad" for investment in Islamic countries
20 September	Chairs Biotech Roundtable in San Francisco
20 October	Passing of wife Endon Mahmood , receive condolences
10 November	Condemns Amman bombings
14 November	Red carpet welcome for Bosnian PM Adnan Terzic
18–19 November	Attends APEC Summit in Busan, S. Korea
	ASEAN leaders hold talks with Bush
26–27 November	Attends Commonwealth Heads of Governments Meeting (CHOGM) in Hong Kong
9 December	Endorses Mecca Declaration of 3rd Extraordinary Summit of OIC
12–14 December	ASEAN and ASEAN+3 meetings in KL Kuala Lumpur Declaration at first East Asia Summit
13 December	Japan and Malaysia sign economic partnership pact

Year 2006

13 January	Talks on greater cooperation in annual consultation with Indonesia's Susilo Bambang Yudhoyono in Padang
15 January	Says style is different from Mahathir in the column "Global Viewpoint" in the Bangkok Post
10 February	Calls on West and Muslims to multiply bridge builders
15 February	Announces Ninth Malaysia Plan
21 February	Visits Western Australia, meets Malaysian students
12 April	Malaysia stops construction of "Scenic Bridge" to Singapore

13 May	Attends D-8 Muslim countries meeting in Bali and suggests group spearhead Islamic financing
12 June	Putrajaya and Kazakhstan's capital Astana made twin cities
14 July	Press statement on declassified documents pertaining to Scenic/Crooked Bridge
25 July	Calls for ASEAN to stake its relevance
30 July	Speech on South Johor Development as growth catalyst
8 August	Delivers 2006 ASEAN Lecture in KL, says ASEAN Charter is the instrument to "update" non-interference policy
14 August	Reiterates decision to cancel crooked bridge
18 August	Launches Third Malaysian Industrial Master Plan 2006–20
7 September	Malaysia urges Israel to recognize Palestinian "unity government" at G-15 and NAM Summit in Havana
10 September	Attends ASEM at Helsinki, calls for ASEAN Secretariat to be included into ASEM
19 September	Attends U.N. General Assembly
5 October	Calls for North Korea to return to six-party talks
18 October	Ready for talks on Muslim South with new Thai PM Sarayud
29–30 October	Attends ASEAN-China Commemorative Summit in Nanning, lauds China's joining ASEAN's nuclear weapons-free treaty
19 November	Attends APEC Summit in Hanoi
4 December	Officiates conference on "Asian Community Building: Strategic Issues, Critical Imperatives", organized by the Institute of Strategic and International Studies (ISIS) in KL.

Year 2007

21 January	Arrives in London for interviews, LSE visit
23 January	Reiterates policy of Palestinian state with East Jerusalem as its capital at World Economic Forum in Davos
11 February	Arrives for three-day visit to Phuket for talks with Thai counterpart Sarayud
22 February	Receives Indonesia's highest award
26 February	Official maiden visit to Syria
1–2 March	Three-day official visit to Yemen
16 March	Opens three-day Islam Hadhari programme at "Hadhari Village" in Kepala Batas
28 March	Speaks at the 19th Arab Summit in Riyadh
2 April	Gives interview to Asian media group at 13th Nikkei International Conference
15–17 April	Three-day Official visit to Sudan
17 April	Arrives in Nairobi, First Malaysian PM to visit Kenya

20–22 April	Three-day official visit to Namibia
15–16 May	Two-day talks in Langkawi with PM Lee Hsien Loong. Decision to set up Joint Ministerial Committee on the Iskandar Development Region (IDR).
22 May	Invites Japan to participate in IDR in visit to Tsukuba Space Centre
18–20 June	Three-Day official visit to Russia
21–22 June	Two-day official visit to Bosnia
24 June	Malaysia to sign agreements on cooperation in trade and agriculture with Italy
27 June	The PM has made eighty official and working visits overseas since 2004, the Dewan Rakyat was told by Foreign Minister Datuk Seri Syed Hamid Albar. The visits had contributed to Malaysia's achievement as the world's 19th largest trading nation.
16 July	Speech to 18th Session of the World Islamic Call Council in KL, stressing importance of education
5–6 August	Attends three-day Langkawi International dialogue. The Dialogue, first held in 1995, has drawn about 500 participants from forty nations, mostly southern and eastern African countries, including ten heads of state and government.

Notes

1. An early and detailed version of the concept was delivered by minister without portfolio Dr Abdullah Mat Zin at a talk at Universiti Sains Malaysia on 30 July 2004, at which I was present. A major tenet of the concept as propounded by this minister was that Malaysia was to be a role model for an Islamic state. See further Abdullah's own explication of the concept which will be discussed later (Abdullah Badawi, 2006).

2. Eric Chia, after a three-year legal battle, was acquitted on 26 June 2007 for lack of sufficient evidence to convict him. Chia passed away in June 2008.

3. Many have accused the prime minister of not moving on this because of the objection of the upper echelons of the police against its implementation. The IPCMC later morphed into the Special Complaints Commission which was only tabled in Parliament in December 2008.

4. There have a plethora of such cases. Mostly famously, Lina Joy (alias Azlina Jalaini), a forty-three-year old woman was denied her conversion to Christianity when the Federal Court ruled on 29 May 2007 that the word "Islam" could not be removed from her identity card. In another case, in the last week of 2005, the body of thirty-six-year-old Moorthy was claimed by the Islamic religious authorities for burial after a Syariah court ruled he had converted to Islam. Moorthy's wife challenged the decision in a civil court, but to no avail.

5. See internet newspaper *Malaysiakini* <www.malaysiakini.com> 24 July 2006. Among the resolutions passed were: the Federal Constitution and other laws be strengthened to stop attempts to use the courts to weaken the position of Islam; every threat to Islam signifies a threat to the dignity and position and the Malay Rulers who are the heads of Islam in every state, and to the integrity of the Islamic institutions; efforts to overhaul and erode the position of Islam in the Constitution and national laws should be stopped; religious rights and freedoms should be understood in the framework of Islam, not according to individual inclinations; all state and federal legislative assemblies should pass enactments that prevent the propagation to Muslims of religions other than Islam, and these should be implemented immediately.

6. The former PKN was renamed PKR after its merger with the Parti Rakyat Malaysia (PRM). The PRM was originally the Parti Sosialis Rakyat Malaysia (PSRM).

7. For a study of the 12th General Election, see Ooi et al., 2008.

8. See Abdullah Ahmad Badawi (2006, p. x).

9. In Minister Mat Zin's talk, cited earlier, he adumbrated sixteen "features" of Islam *Hadhari*, namely: 1. using Islamic sources, 2. good governance, 3. prosperous livelihood, 4. improving quality of life, 5. strengthening integrity, 6. dynamism, 7. completeness, 8. pragmaticism, 9. self-reliance, 10. freedom, creativity and innovativeness, 11. strengthening scope and focus on family (institution),

12. educational development, 13. economic development, 14. development administration and management, 15. development of science and technology, and 16. agricultural development.

10. The conference held over the week 11–18 October produced the high-sounding Putrajaya Declaration on Knowledge and Morality for the unity, dignity and progress of the *ummah* which, among other things, called for revitalizing of the OIC and a "plan of action" to enhance Islamic institutions such as the Fiqh Academy, and promote Islamic education and the development of science and technology.

11. "Muslim state" seems to be the preferred terminology of the Wisma Putra as opposed to "Islamic state", which is, of course, a more controversial concept. See a statement on the overview of Malaysian foreign policy on the official website of Wisma Putra <http://www.kln.gov.my/>.

12. These remarks were made to the U.S.-ASEAN Business Council on 19 July.

13. He initially escaped to an island near Sabah in November 2001, where he sought political asylum from Malaysia, but was denied.

14. See USIP Special Report (2008), p. 5.

15. The domain covers the whole of the Muslim autonomous region and other areas in Zamboanga del Norte, Zamboanga del Sur, Zamboanga Sibugay, North Cotabatao, Sultan Kudarat and Sarangani provinces, and even Palawan Island and the Sulu Archipelagao (*Manila Times*, 17 December, 2007).

16. The mission was led by Major General Dato' Zulkifeli bin Mohd Zin of the Royal Malaysian Armed Forces (RMAF). According to Jubair (2007, p. 114), he was considered to be a "fine general and seasoned diplomat". His deputy was Brigadier General Mohammad bin Sulong.

17. Japan's role has been focused on the socio-economic aspect of the peace process, while Canada is expected to help in governance of the area.

18. Malaysia officially takes the view that a Palestinian state should be established with East Jerusalem as its capital.

19. The FTA negotiations remain stalled in 2009, apparently on U.S. objections to Malaysia's 'discriminatory' ethnic policies. See section on "Embracing Globalization" in this chapter.

20. See also Chapter 10 where relations with Singapore are cast alongside relations with other neighbouring countries.

21. Based on various newspaper reports and those of the internet paper, *Malaysiakini*.

22. According to the Centre for Independent Journalism (<www.cijmalaysia.org>), the deputy minister's remarks were reported in *Malay Mail* and night editions of Chinese newspapers *Nanyang Siang Pau*, *China Press*, *Guang Ming Daily*, and *Sin Chew Daily*.

23. Among the two most important conditionalities were that Singapore would be allowed to use Malaysian airspace and would be able to import sand.

24. The issue of abandoning the RM1.3 billion CIQ Complex became a bone of contention for detractors of the Abdullah government. However, the government

decided to redesign the complex to link up with the old one and grant a new contract to the builders, Gerbang Perdand Sdn Bhd. See various newspaper reports, including *The Sun*, 15 August 2006.

25. See Singapore, *Water Talks If Only it Could* (no date). Furthermore, Malaysia's obligations were tied down further with the agreement on 24 November 1990 for Singapore to build the Linggiu Dam in Johor to supply treated water to both Singapore and Johor. Under the agreement the Johor government received a compensation of RM320 million for the dam which would be owned by Singapore although treatment plants would revert to Johore in 2061. Singapore's entitlement to water was 250 million gallons per day based on an agreed price structure. See Agreement between the Government of the State of Johore and the Public Utilities Board of the Republic of Singapore (1990).

26. She revealed that from January 2006 till July 2007, there were 196 manufacturing projects with a approved total investment of $1.6 billion from Singapore.

27. Information gathered at a briefing on Iskandar Malayasi which I attended on 16 September 2009 and various publications of the project.

28. Information released by Singapore's Ministry of National Development, <http://www.mnd.gov.sg> on 23 July 2007. It should be noted that on the downside, Minister Mentor Lee Kuan Yew comments on the IDR raised a storm of protest on the Malaysian side in early July 2007. Lee, in an interview with the *Berita Harian* (Singapore), reportedly forewarned Singaporeans not to expect "generous treatment" in the IDR since Malaysia and Singapore were different countries and the Malaysian premier was under pressure from the opposition PAS, as well as Johor UMNO detractors, or words to that effect.

29. See my discussion in Chapter 11.

30. In 2006, Malaysia's external trade just exceeded one trillion Ringgit or US$270.27 billion. This was 10.5 per cent higher that the previous year. Exports were valued at RM588.949 billion while imports totalled RM480.493 billion. (*Bernama*, 2 August 2007).

31. From MITI portal, <www.miti.gov.my> (accessed 21 August 2007).

32. The text of his speech can be found on the MITI portal cited above.

33. From a news report on the stalled fifth round of talks. Also noted was that other sensitive issues included differences over liberalizing Malaysia's services sector, intellectual property rights, labour and environmental issues. *Associated Press*, 13 February 2007.

34. A memo protesting the FTA was posted to the Malaysian cabinet on 14 March 2007.

35. FTA Malaysia website, <www.ftamalaysia.org> (accessed 21 August 2007).

36. The facts of the case are gleaned from various media sources including *Associate Press*, *New York Times*, *BBC* and *CNN*.

37. This was revealed to Parliament by Home Minister Syed Hamid Albar in early 2008.

38. *New York Times*, 25 August 2006.

39. See a *Straits Times* report on this, reproduced by the *Malaysian Insider* <http://

www.themalaysianinsider.com/index.php/malaysia/16053-us-slaps-sanctions-on-scomis-chief> (accessed 16 January 2009).

40. The article "Malaysia's Axis Mysteriously Shifting" is written by Ioannis Gatsiounis, <www.atimes.com> (accessed 29 August 2007). Similar reports have appeared on the internet sites.

41. The U.S. document which lists these companies is *Federal Register* (72, no. 77), 23 April 2007, accessed from internet on 29 August 2007.

42. Koh allegedly diverted the shipments of aircraft parts first to his company Turbo Aviation in Singapore, then to a Malaysian freight forwarder, where a second co-conspirator, Marcus Chua, placed the parts on a flight to Iran. See Press Release of U.S. Attorney's Office, Eastern District of New York, 18 May 2006.

43. From article by Gatsiounis cited above.

44. *Malaysia Today*, 26 September 2006 <http://malaysia-todays.blogspot.com/2008/07/oil-for-food-scandal-revisited.html> (accessed 27 January 2009).

45. The two inquiries are: Charles Duelfer's *Comprehensive Report of the Special Adviser to the Director of the Central Intelligence on Iraq's Weapons of Mass Destruction*, dated 30 September 2004, and Paul A. Volcker's *Independent Inquiry Committee into The United Nations Oil-for-Food Programme (Manipulation of the Oil-for-Food Programme by the Iraqi Regime)* dated 27 October 2005.

46. The account here is gleaned from various Malaysian newspaper reports, including from the internet news portal, *malaysiakini.com*. More specific sources are cited wherever it is deemed fit.

47. The original Kuala Lumpur trial judge, K.N. Segara, was replaced by Mohd Zaki Md Yassin of the Shah Alam High Court. The prosecution team was headed by DPP Tun Abd Majid Tun Hamzah, who heads the civil division of the AG chambers. He replaced DPP Sallehuddin Saidin, who conducted the criminal investigations of the murder. Razak Baginda's lawyer, Wong Chiang Kiat, replaced a well known criminal lawyer Mohammad Shafee Abdullah. Karpal Singh, the renowned criminal lawyer and opposition leader, held a watching brief on behalf of the Shaaribuu family.

48. For example, such was the case in the sensational "Profumo Affair"of 1963 when the eponymous British secretary of state of war of the Harold Macmillan government had to resign when he was alleged to have shared defence secrets with a socialite by the name of Christine Keller. Keller at the time also had an affair with a Soviet naval attaché.

49. According to reports, the Defence Ministry bought three submarines that cost the treasury RM$4.5 billion (US$1.3 billion), for which a company controlled by Abdul Razak Baginda was allegedly paid a commission of RM510 million (US$147.3 million) in a sale that included no competitive tenders, *Asia Sentinel*, <www.asiasentinel.com>, 30 March 2007 (accessed 27 August 2007).

50. The facts of this account are drawn largely from the internet paper, *Malaysiakini*, which posted an expose of the fiasco in a four-part series in June 2007.

10

EXPLAINING RELATIONS WITH NEIGHBOURS
Antipathies of History, Ethnicity, and Intimacy

While all relations of dyads or bilateral relations could also be cast in the themes used for overall foreign policy behaviour, Malaysia's relations with four immediate neighbours perhaps have defining features of their own and deserve a deeper deconstruction. In this chapter we will look specifically at its relations in foreign policy terms with respect to the Philippines, Indonesia, Thailand, and Singapore. Three major tropes tend to inform or structure the construction of relations with these neighbouring states, namely, history, ethnicity, and intimacy. At the same time, they illustrate the extreme tensions and contradictions that affect the relationships. With the Philippines, intimacy and history have meant a close relationship to Malaysia's Borneo state of Sabah, where huge numbers of Filipino migrants reside, many of whom have also become citizens. On top of this, formal relations have been strained from time to time and even severed because of the unresolved Philippine claim to Sabah. With Indonesia, ethnic and historical ties have defined the bilateral relationship from time immemorial and yet a plethora of irritations continue to haunt the relationship. Indonesia is the only state with which Malaysia has gone to war, a development which came in the Tunku years as described in Chapter 4.[1] With Thailand, history has accorded Malaysia a neighbourly relationship that has led to the amicable resolution of a communist insurgency in an amnesty granted by the Malaysian government, which the Thais brokered in 1989. Till today Malayan communists stay in "friendship villages" sponsored by Thailand. However, history and ethnicity plague a relationship in the three predominantly Muslim provinces of Thailand's "Deep South". Crafting relations with Singapore have arguably been the most difficult and complex for Malaysia despite (or because of) the intimate ties of history and ethnicity. Nonetheless, Malaysia's relations across the Johor Straits clearly remain the most limiting and, at the same time, defining of all neighbouring bilateral relations especially in the political and economic realms.

RELATIONS WITH THE PHILIPPINES

Three major issues affect Malaysia's relations with the Philippines, namely, the latter's claim to Sabah, disputed maritime borders and overlapping territorial claims, and the flow of Filipino migrants to Sabah. We need not dwell too long on the Sabah claim which has received treatment in many competent accounts of the issue.[2] As stated in an earlier chapter, the claim was based essentially on the contention that the sultan of Sulu had merely "leased" and not "ceded" the territory in 1878 to the predecessors of the British, the North Borneo Company, from which it was passed on to the British Crown; that sovereignty could be transferred only to sovereigns; and that the Philippine Government was the heir to the sultan of Sulu. The Philippines first made the claim when President Macapagal brought it up in 1962 on the eve of the formation of Malaysia. When Malaysia was formed on 16 September 1963, the Philippines deferred diplomatic recognition although consular relations were established in August 1964. Ferdinand Marcos established diplomatic relations in June 1966 along with the signing of a bilateral anti-smuggling agreement in August 1967 (after ASEAN's formation), but relations remained tense because of the Corregidor affair of March 1968. The Philippines military was forced to suppress a group of Muslim recruits whom Malaysia suggested were being trained for a guerilla war in Sabah. Matters were not helped by the passing of a law in June 1968 by the Philippine Congress confirming Philippine sovereignty over Sabah. After the matter surfaced in an ASEAN meeting, Kuala Lumpur again broke off diplomatic ties with Manila and relations were not re-established until December 1969.[3]

Another matter that continued to sour bilateral relations in the 1970s and 1980s was Malaysia's alleged support and even training of Muslim guerrillas in the Southern Philippines, in particular, those of the Moro National Liberation Front (MNLF). Reports suggest that Sabah Chief Minister Tun Mustafa Harun (1967–76) was behind such moves and Kuala Lumpur did not deem it fit to stop him. Even after Mustafa's departure from state power, an Australian documentary film claimed that Sabah mercenaries were training

Muslim guerillas in Malaysia.[4] Two Philippine presidents, Cory Aquino and Fidel Ramos, tried to lay the Sabah issue to rest by renouncing the claim, but found themselves facing hostile Philippine lawmakers. Ramos turned out to be the more successful of the two and by the early 1990s made a number of bilateral arrangements and cooperative ventures with Malaysia, including the setting up of a Philippine "extension office" in Sabah, and a Malaysian counterpart in Mindanao. In February 1994, Mahathir Mohamed became the first Malaysian prime minister to visit the Philippines and the two states signed a Memorandum of Understanding on defence, "calling for the exchange of information, logistics, and training of both countries' Armed Forces". This action amongst a host of others in the same period seemingly laid the Sabah issue to rest.[5]

However, before long a second set of contentious issues surfaced, revolving around the overlapping claims of both countries in the Spratly group of islands, islets, atolls, and reefs, along with a territorial problem relating to each country's respective continental shelf in the Celebes Sea. Malaysia has to date occupied three of the islets and reefs in the Spratly group, as have the Philippines, which has occupied several others. In 1988, a spat developed over what is known as the Turtle Islands, claimed by both countries. A misreading of a navigational chart led to the accusation that Malaysia had annexed the Turtle Islands, recognized to belong to the Philippines under the Anglo-American Treaty of 1930. A military build-up was announced by the Philippines, but the matter subsided in three days and the navy officer responsible for the mistake was sacked. The episode nonetheless left a bad taste in the festering territorial issue for both countries.

Malaysia's bilateral irritations with its neighbours mostly involve territorial claims made as the result of the publication of its 1979 map, which among other things, extends its continental shelf along the Sabah and Sarawak coast into the Spratlys and includes part of the Kalayaan area claimed by the Philippines.[6] In June 1983, Malaysia occupied Swallow Reef (Terumbu Layang Layang), which was subsequently turned into a tourist resort for birdwatching and diving, complete with an airstrip. The Royal Malaysian Navy protects the islands with its vessels, anti aircraft guns, and other military facilities (Balakrishnan 2002, p. 77). The Malaysian posture has drawn protest not just from the Philippines, but also from Beijing and Hanoi. Undaunted, Malaysia went on to occupy Mariveles Reef (Terumbu Mantani) and Ardasier Reef (Terumbu Ubi). On occupying Swallow Reef, Malaysia deployed three F-5 fighters to Labuan to provide military backing to its claims. In March 1998, Malaysia's deputy foreign minister asserted Malaysia's claims to these territories in the following terms:

The islands and atolls are under Malaysian sovereignty and Malaysia has in the past reaffirmed its jurisdiction ... They are within Malaysia's continental shelf and Malaysian's sovereignty over them has been officially declared through the new Map of Malaysia, published on December 21st, 1979 ... The claim is in line with the Geneva Convention of 1958 pertaining to territorial waters and continental shelf boundaries, and the UN Convention on the Law of the Sea, as well as other international practices. (David 2004, pp. 60–61)

These claims set the stage for the most serious clash with the Philippines to date in April 1988 in an incident which occurred around the Commodore Reef (Rizal Reef for the Philippines and Terumbu Laksamana for Malaysia). The Malaysian navy seized three Filipino fishing boats and arrested forty-nine crew members on the charge of illegal fishing. This was followed by the Philippine accusation in July of the same year that the Malaysian Navy had also chased its fishermen away from the Commodore Reef. Protests from the Philippines implied that Malaysia was using this incident as a bargaining chip for the Sabah claim. In August 1988, the forty-nine fishermen were released without any suggestion that its territorial claim on the Commodore Reef was rescinded. Indeed, Kuala Lumpur announced the construction of a new naval base at Sandakan to control foreign naval activities. Manila, on its part, gave naval escorts to its fishermen and accused Malaysia of border violations in August and September 1988 when the Malaysian Navy was alleged to have fired on Philippine fishing boats.[7] It wasn't until the Ramos-Mahathir overtures and exchanges that relations settled on a more even keel. However, the unresolved Sabah claim remains as an unpleasant political overhang in the bilateral relations. It does not appear that the issue of territorial claims with respect to the Philippines or other littoral states will fade away. Malaysia in 2007 contracted with the Trans Resources Corporation to build a submarine base in Teluk Sepanggar, near Kota Kinabalu, Sabah's capital city. This will cater to two French-made Scorpene-class submarines to be inducted in 2009 and for an Agosta-70 used initially for training.[8]

The issue of illegal Filipino migrants to Sabah continually surfaces in Malaysia. In April 2007, the leader of the Malaysian Opposition, Lim Kit Siang, made the claim that at least one million "illegals" (or undocumented migrants) were present in Sabah.[9] The Sabah government is also clearly concerned about the issue and officials may admit up to half a million illegals are living in Sabah (mainly Muslim Filipinos and Indonesians) who are engaged in local industries such as fishing, plantations, and construction. Malaysia has implemented a number of mass deportations, and in June 2006 held high-level talks with the Philippines over what both sides said was the growing problem of Filipino migrants. From a foreign policy perspective, how Malaysia handles the legal and illegal migrants remains a sensitive and touchy issue with neighbouring countries, especially *vis-à-vis* Indonesia, as we shall in the next section.

In the late 1990s and early 2000s Malaysian-Philippines relations were boosted by the brokering of peace talks by Malaysia over the Southern Muslim problem of the Philippines. The peace talks were initiated by Kuala Lumpur in 1997 soon after the Philippine implementation of the Autonomous Region of Muslim Mindanao (ARMM) collapsed under the leadership and governorship of Nur Musuari of the Moro National Liberation Front (MNLF). Nur Musuari lost control of the MNLF and was later detained by the Philippine government on various charges.[10] While the Southern problem is complicated by the emergence of the militant-terrorist Abu Sayyaf Group (ASG), most observers would recognize that the struggle of the Muslim South has since fallen mostly on the shoulders of the Moro Islamic Liberation Front (MILF) — which broke away from the MNLF in 1977 — with which the peace talks are currently being conducted. According to the United States Institute of Peace (which is an active supporter of the peace negotiations), the important milestones of the talks, negotiations and conflict prevention measures were as follows:[11]

- Agreement for general cessation of hostilities, 18 July 1997
- Tripoli Peace Agreement, July 2001
- Implementation Guidelines of the Security Aspect of the Tripoli Peace Agreement, 7 August 2001
- Implementation guidelines of the humanitarian, rehabilitation and development aspects of the Tripoli Peace Agreement, 7 May 2002
- Operational guidelines of the ad hoc Joint Action, December 2004.

By September 2006, the talks were stalled at the stage of determining the ancestral domains of the Bangsamoro people.[12] Towards the end of 2007, this complex and difficult issue remained deadlocked. Malaysia had maintained a monitoring team of forty-one officers from the Malaysian Defence Forces, the Royal Malaysian Police, and from the Prime Minister's Department. There were also ten military officers from Brunei Darussalam and five from Libya. Malaysia's involvement efforts at peacemaking and peacekeeping in the Philippines grew out of both its ASEAN linkages and its OIC leadership role, and was very much in keeping with its unspoken aspiration to play the role of a regional or middle power. Seen from this perspective, the ties of ethnicity and historical intimacy were like a two-edge sword that could either foil and or help meld fraying relations. Overall, good sense seems to have prevailed in the KL-Manila relationship despite the multiple changes of leadership on both sides.

RELATIONS WITH INDONESIA

In Chapter 3, we have seen how relations with Indonesia were dominated by the war launched against Malaysia in the *Kronfrontasi* period and relations only ameliorated on the eve of ASEAN's formation in 1967.[13] Relations remained on an even keel throughout the 1970s and were capped by the 1980 Kuantan Principle of equidistance to major powers adopted by both countries. By the mid-1980s, during the tenure of Mahathir, a territorial dispute flared up over two islands in the Celebes Sea, Ligitan and Sipadan, off the north-west coast of Sabah. Some writers have also suggested that Mahathir's more prominent presence in international and regional affairs and his eclipsing of Indonesia's putative role in regional and Third World leadership may have irked the New Order regime.[14] On top of this, the protracted Aceh conflict saw the use of Malaysia as a place of asylum for Acehnese rebels, refugees, and even a conduit for weapons (David 2004, pp. 69–71). However, it should be noted that after some initial hesitation, the Malaysian government's official policy was that Malaysia provided no political asylum for any party. Malaysia has also not signed the United Nations 1951 convention on the status of refugees, or the 1961 convention on stateless persons. The Indonesia's request for access to Acehnese refugees was granted in October 1991, but the relationship again soured in 1992 when Acehnese refugees gained entry into the compound of the UNHCR residence in Kuala Lumpur. With the resolution of the Aceh conflict in the mid-2000s, the issue has gone away.

The dispute over Ligitan and Sipadan became the central aspect of deteriorating relations in the 1980s up until its resolution via the International Court of Justice (ICJ) in December 2002 when Malaysia won its claim. In July 1982, Malaysia occupied the two islands to the chagrin of its neighbour.[15] As was the case with Swallow Reef, Malaysia began to develop the islands for tourism. By early 1991 Indonesia started to protest the change in the status quo of the islands. Malaysian fishermen came eyeball to eyeball with the Indonesian Navy in July 1991 after which a joint commission was established. Even so, Malaysia claimed that Indonesian armed forces actually landed on Sipadan several times in 1993, and in 1994 the Indonesian Navy staged a large-scale exercise involving forty vessels and 7,000 troops in the vicinity. By late 1994, Malaysia had proposed arbitration and by 1996 it appeared that Indonesia had reluctantly acceded to Malaysia's suggestion to have the dispute referred to the ICJ, instead of the ASEAN High Council.

Malaysia won its case in the ICJ on the ground of *effectivités*, that is, effective sovereign control of the islands.[16] It is interesting to note that both countries' claims, based on historical entitlement and that the islands were *terrae nullius*, were dismissed by the Court. Instead the Court argued, six judges to one, that Malaysia established *effectivités* regulation and control of the collection of turtle eggs under its Turtle Preservation Ordinance, which had been applied since the 1950s at least. Moreover, British North Borneo constructed and operated lighthouses on both the islands, which revealed the intention to exercise state functions.[17] Observers have noted the psychological impact of the loss of the two small islands to Archipelagic Indonesia with its 3,000 inhabited islands, and thousands more which are uninhabited. The 1999 loss of Timor Leste perhaps adds to this psychology.[18]

Another brewing territorial problem is the "Ambalat" area, also in the Celebes Sea, which is also claimed by both states.[19] According to Schofield and Storey (2005), the dispute resulted from the issuing of exploration licences for two deep-water oil concessions blocks, ND6 and ND7, by Malaysia's national oil company, Petronas Carigali, in partnership with the Royal Dutch Shell Group, on 16 February 2005. The dispute escalated into several minor skirmishes between the two navies. In March 2005, Indonesia accused a Malaysian navy vessel, *KD Renchong*, of ramming into its military ship, *KRI Tedung Naga*. Indonesian Defence Minister Juwono Sudarsono said that the Malaysian Government had apologized for the incident while Malaysian Deputy Prime Minister Najib Razak denied this. The Malaysian Navy had reportedly chased Indonesian fishermen out of Ambalat as well, while Indonesia further accused Malaysia of some thirty-five violations of Indonesian territory. Complicating matters was the fact that both Malaysia and Indonesia have awarded oil concessions to competing oil companies, Shell, Unocal, and ENI, in the area. Several demonstrations against Malaysia erupted on the Indonesia side over the Ambalat issue.[20]

Another major fault line of relations with Indonesia, as with the Philippines, relate to the socio-economic ramifications of migrant labour. The Malaysian human rights organization SUARAM provides the following important information and sometimes disputed statistics on the number of refugees, asylum seekers, and undocumented migrants:[21] As it is quite difficult to have accurate statistics, we produce below the various estimates and contentions:

• According to the government, as of May 2007, there are 28,668 refugees in the country, whereas the UNHCR records 37,920 refugees and asylum seekers as at end of October 2007.

- According to the government, as of June 2007, there were 1.91 million documented foreign workers in country. The Malay language *Berita Harian* reports that this figure did not include 400,000 undocumented migrants, and 10,000 others in immigration detention camps.
- In 2007, whipping was introduced as a punishment for undocumented migrants and the Immigration Act was beefed up to allow for a sentence of five years, RM10,000 fine, and six strokes of the cane.
- The 475,00-strong People's Volunteer Corps (RELA) has been given powers to arrest and detain refugees and illegal migrants. According to reports. 27,770 migrants were detained by RELA in 2007.

The vast majority of illegal migrants residing in Malaysia come from Indonesia and when the issue came to a head, the Malaysian government announced an amnesty period from October 2004 up till 31 January 2005 for illegal migrants to leave the country without penalty. It was estimated that some 340,000 persons, mostly Indonesians, took advantage of this. After the end of the amnesty, a massive operation was conducted, using the police and RELA, to weed out the remaining illegal migrants. There was an early period of amnesty from March to July 2002, when the draconian immigration law kicked in, and it has been reported that some 290,177 illegal workers left Malaysia, comprising 243,772 Indonesians, 18,933 Indians, and 16,648 Bangladeshis.[22] Such actions on the part of Malaysia have invariably sparked emotional reactions, including demonstrations in Indonesian cities and the burning of the Malaysian flag.[23]

In August 2005, hundreds of Indonesians rallied in several cities to demand an apology from Malaysia for the assault by Malaysian policemen on an Indonesian referee for the Asian Karate Tournament held in Nilai, Negri Sembilan, in Malaysia. Protesters invoked the slogan of "Ganyang Malaysia", reviving the memory of *Konfrontasi*. Four plain clothes policemen beat up karate referee Donald Luther Kolobita for no apparent reason as he walked back to his hotel at 2 a.m. In the East Java city of Surabaya, some men searched hotels for Malaysians participating in a badminton tournament there. The four Malaysian shuttlers were flown to Jakarta to avoid an incident. Another flap in relations came in October 2007 when an Indonesian lawmaker called for his government to respond to Malaysia's use of the folk song *Rasa Sayang* in its "Truly Asia" tourism campaign. There was then talk of suing the Malaysian Government for the use of the song which is believed to have originated in Maluku where it has been sung for generations by people to express their love for the environment.

It would seem that, as in Malaysia's relations with the Philippines, geographical proximity, ties of history, and culture have ironically become the bone of contention in relations with Indonesia. Liow's notion of "one kin, two nations" provides an important trope in understanding the Malaysia-Indonesia relationship. This was clearly evident in the parallel notions of "Indonesia Raya" and "Melayu Raya", which had propelled nationalist anti-colonial movements on both sides. But as Liow notes, "it was the advent of nationalism that differences that transcended kin solidarity intensified" (Liow 2005, p. 161). In the 1990s, Mahathir's assertiveness in foreign policy matters led to his reference as a "little Soekarno" by Indonesian commentors. Undeniably an exacerbating psychological factor in the Malaysia-Indonesia nexus is a lopsided economic dependence of Indonesian migrant labour on the more affluent, evidently labour-short, and prospering Malaysian economy. This factor has tended to generate angst on the Indonesian side, and conversely, an unwitting arrogance and insensitvity on the Malaysian side. This said, it is still undeniable that the leadership of both states have remained consistent about maintaining a posture and policy anchored on the the pacific settlement of conflict, as demonstrated by the Ligitan and Sipadan settlement through the ICJ. Realists, however, may interpret that in both the cases of the Philippines and Indonesia, and Brunei as well,[24] "national interests" tend to trump cultural affinities especially with respect to territorial claims and economic issues. A countervailing constructivist interpretaion would be that ASEAN diplomatic norms and socialization have reduced or even eliminated the option for violent resolution of conflict. The fact that violent China-Vietnamese clashes have ocurred over the Spratlys, but none has ocurred between ASEAN states, lends validity to the constructivist view.

RELATIONS WITH THAILAND

As in the two previous sets of bilateral relationships, Malaysian-Thai relations are anchored on ties of history, ethnicity, and conflicting territorial disputes. Historically, four of Thailand's southermost provinces — Narathiwat, Yala, Pattani, and Satun — have been part of the Malay Sultanate of Patani Raya.[25] Malay Muslims constitute some 70 per cent of the population in these provinces. The present state boundaries date back to 1909 when the Anglo-Siamese Treaty conceded Kedah, Kelantan, Terenganu, and Perlis, then under Siamese suzerainty, to British Malaya, and Patani Raya fell on the Thai side. During the Japanese Occupation, from 1943–45, Thailand annexed Kedah, Kelantan, Terengganu, and Perlis and there are pockets of Thais in these Malaysian states up till today. On the other side, Thailand has introduced a policy of cultural assimilation in the Deep South, but the Malay minority, despite speaking Thai, has remained staunchly Muslim in orientation. Signs of problems emerged in the 1960s when various Malay-Muslim separatist and irredentist groups emerged. The most prominent of these were: Barisan National Pembebasan Patani (BNPP or National Liberation Front of Patani), Barisan Revolusi Nasional (BRN or National Revolutionary Front), and the Patani United Liberation Organization (PULO). PULO, formed in 1968, was thought to be the most militant and well heeled, with connections to Saudi Arabia and headquarters in Mecca up until 1984, and was ideologically situated between the orthodox Islamic BNPP and the Socialist BRN.

By the early 1990s, the separatist groups had become severely divided and virtually defeated by the Thai authorities through surrenders and the detention of hundreds of guerillas. The BRN broke up into three factions and the Saudi government closed PULO's headquarters in Mecca in 1984 and deported 700 hundred of its members. However, the conflict in the Deep South had taken a new turn. Daily political violence with incidents of the torching of schools, train attacks, the shooting of monks and school teachers, and bombings of military posts became common, with two major incidents and a mounting number casualties by the mid-2000s. The first serious incident was the at the Kru Se Mosque in Pattani on 28 April 2004 when 105 Muslim youths who holed themselves up there were brutally gunned down by the Thai military. The incident followed close on the heels of the January 4 attack by militants on a military barrack in Narathiwat in which four soldiers were killed. At about that time, twenty schools were also torched. The second major event occurred in Tak Bai, Narathiwat, on 25 October the same year in which eighty-five Muslim demonstrators died either from suffocation or beatings after hundreds were bundled into army trucks with their hands tied to the back. McCargo (2008, p. 4) provides us with the deadly statistics of southern Thailand's conflict. According to his sources, by April 2007, there had been 2,200 deaths and 3,654 persons injured. There were 1,850 incidents in 2004, 2,297 in 2005, and 1,815 in 2006. These incidents have changed the character of the problem from that of a predominantly Islamist separatist agenda, to one of persistent everyday civil strife.[26] Malaysia, from time to time, has been accused by Thai authorities of having trained guerillas and given sanctuary to militants. In particular, the Islamic party PAS does not hide its sympathy for the Thai Muslim cause although its statements have remained ambiguous. The Malaysian Government, on the other hand, has constantly insisted that it offers no support to the Muslim separatists, but still demurs on military cooperation on "all forms of terrorism along the common border" (David 1996, pp. 32–33). In 2005, Malaysia obliged Thailand by repatriating some 131 Thais who had fled to Kelantan in August 2005.[27] Interestingly, a certain

Abdul Rahman Ahmad has been detained under the ISA in Kamunting for his alleged role in bombings in southern Thailand.[28]

Malaysia's cooperation with Thailand with respect to communists guerrillas has proven to be more successful. The Thais brokered an amnesty in December 1989 which ended the communist insurgency in Malaysia which had cost 10,000 lives. David (1996, p. 31) indicates that of the 1,118 communist insurgents, only 494 were Malaysian citizens (including 402 ethnic Chinese), the rest being Thai nationals. Some 338 Malaysians have settled legally in Malaysia and the rest have stayed in Thai "friendship villages" on the Thai side. Another issue that had affected Malaysia-Thai relations in the mid-1990s was that the leader of the Al Arqam movement of Malaysia had sought refuge in Thailand. In 1994 the Malaysian Government banned the movement and claimed that Al Arqam was training militants in Thailand. The Thai Government obliged Malaysia by arresting and deporting its leader Ashaari Mohamed who was then detained by the Malaysian Government.

It would appear that, on the whole, Malaysia's relations with Thailand have been characterized more by cooperation than irritations. The simmering conflict in southern Thailand seems to be the main axis of potential conflict, but to date this has been managed throughout the years with a fairly constructive approach by both sides. Socialization in cooperation *vis-à-vis* communist insurgents may have provided the basis for such an approach. Matters have not been as cordial, however, with respect to fishery rights and Malaysia has been wont to arrest large numbers of Thai fishermen who have strayed into Malaysian waters.[29] Such irritations no doubt have been partially pacified by the 1979 agreement to develop jointly hydrocarbon resources in the disputed territorial area in the Gulf of Thailand via the Malaysia-Thailand Joint Authority (MTJA). Ironically, the MTJA grew out of a territorial dispute over an offshore feature known as "Ko Losin", which Malaysia claimed was on its continental shelf. The 1979 MOU for the MTJA allows for the arrangement to last for fifty years.[30] The project remained fallow for years, but by the mid-2000s, plans for a gas pipeline and the building of a gas separation plant were apparently underway amidst objections from coastal communities.[31]

RELATIONS WITH SINGAPORE

Malaysia's relations with Singapore illustrate both the apogee as well as the most severe constraints of bilateral foreign policy practice. In spite of a history that was conjoined from the outset, relations have suffered the vicissitudes of a relationship bounded by too much history and intimacy. There is no better depiction of this intimacy than when former Premier Abdul Razak opined that it was one of Siamese twins, while Abdullah Badawi in 1991, as foreign minister, averred that even two persons sleeping together could have problems.[32] Singapore's Lee Kuan Yew has embellished this metaphor further by saying that the separation of Singapore from Malaysia on 9 August 1965 was a *talak tiga*, meaning a divorce that is virtually irreconcilable.[33]

At the pinnacle of political convergence was the merger of Singapore with the Federation of Malaya which gave birth to "Malaysia" (with the inclusion of Sarawak and Sabah) on 16 September 1963. At its nadir, the relationship deteriorated into a vicious spiral of irritations over a host of bilateral issues, ranging from the denial of sand export and use of airspace to the island republic, along with a legal territorial tussle over a tiny rocky outcrop with two ridges in the two countries' adjoining seas.[34] As noted in the previous chapter, relations may have entered a new phase of cordiality, thanks to a leadership change on the Malaysian side. Two periods in which relations became particularly acrimonious were during the tenures of the Tunku and Mahathir. Since we have not dealt with the relationship in any systemic way in previous chapters, it may be germane now to recount briefly some of the crucial issues affecting Malaysia-Singapore relations.

Singapore's "Malaysia period", 1963–65, was clearly the source of what observers have termed the historical baggage that plagues relations up till today. Notably, the low point of the period were the racial riots of 1964 in Singapore, involving Malays and Chinese. That Lee Kuan Yew in his first book of memoirs (1998) had blamed the ruling UMNO for the riots itself raised a storm of protest on the Malaysian side, opening up old wounds.[35] The 1964 racial riots occurred when Singapore was still part of Malaysia and began during a procession on the occasion of the birthday of the Prophet Mohammed on 21 July 1964. It occurred at the peak of acrimonious politicking between Malayan and Singaporean politicians. An estimated 20,000[36] Malays and Muslims from some seventy-three organizations had assembled for the traditional parade in the heart of the city. Inflammatory speeches by leaders of the Singapore UMNO preceded the riots, but the situation got out of hand as the procession went through the city and groups of Malays broke ranks and clashed with riot policemen and subsequently were seen to attack Chinese civilians. This sparked Chinese retaliatory attacks on Malays. By midnight, 220 incidents had been reported, 178 persons had been injured, thirty-two of whom were admitted to hospital and four had been been killed. Some houses were also razed. A second riot broke out on 2 September the same year, which after eleven days left thirteen persons dead and 106 injured. Some 1,439 arrests were made by the police.[37]

Given this unfortunate incident, one need not speculate too much on why a break-up between Peninsular Malaysia and Singapore was imminent. However, one should hasten to add that even after the break-up, relations have remained intimate and special. A validation to this observation can be gleaned from the memoirs of Tun Ismail. In an article to the *National Geographic*, soon after Singapore's separation from Malaysia, Ismail wrote: "At the moment both nations, comparatively speaking, are well off. If they can co-exist for some time, each understanding the other's point of view, *the time will come when they will merge again. It is better to wait for this to come because if they do not do so they will sink together* instead of coming together" (Ooi 2006, p. 160, emphasis added). Tun Ismail's biographer Ooi Kee Beng points out that conspiracy theories abounded about the merger and separation, but Ismail remained steadfast in his assertion that separation was "a painful but temporary phase" in the history of the Malaysian federation and, furthermore, Ismail also wrote that in spite of what was believed, the separation was by mutual consent (Ooi 2006, p. 162). Interestingly, the former Singapore premier Lee Kuan Yew (currently Minister Mentor) virtually reiterated Ismail's point in June 1996 when he raised the possibility of a "remerger' with Malaysia when the latter had introduced a system of meritocracy similar to Singapore's.[38] The latter part of the statement was clearly an oblique reference to Malaysia's preferential policy for *Bumiputeras*. As to be expected, Lee Kuan Yew's conditionality for remerger raised strong reactions on the Malaysian side. Prime Minister Mahathir opined that such an eventuality was remote and that "Singapore's re-entry into Malaysia would only be considered after all races in Malaysia had equal ability and capability to compete."[39] This episode and a host of others show that the ethnic factor "overdetermines" Singapore-Malaysia relations.

One of the casualties of this ethnic overdetermination may have been the joint military exercises under the Five Power Defence Arrangement (FPDA).[40] Such military exercises have been off and on over the years and were stopped after the financial crisis of 1997–98, but even in the good years, military aircraft of one country were not allowed to fly mock attacks against installations of the other. As David (1996, p. 82) recounts, typically, bilateral exercises were staged in Sarawak and were on a scale much smaller than exercises between Indonesia and Malaysia. In 1990, these low-key events were further curtailed on the grounds that "the Malaysian Armed Forces was involved in several similar activities with other countries" (David, p. 83). In 1997, Malaysia hosted the largest ever FPDA exercise involving 12,000 personnel, 140 aircraft, and thirty-five warships. However, in 1998, at the peak of the financial crisis and during a particularly bad patch in bilateral relations with Singapore, Malaysia pulled out of the "Stardex" exercise even as ships from Australia, New Zealand, and Britain were steaming towards Singapore. Since 1999 the FPDA exercises have been resumed and have continued, propelled by the post-9/11 political climate.[41]

It seems clear that ethnic considerations on the Malaysian side are also often overlaid with differing foreign policy stances towards Islam, Palestine, and, concomitantly, Israel, which Singapore has recognized, but with which Malaysia still has no diplomatic relations. The implicit trope of an asymmetric Israeli-Palestinian relationship tends to be equated with Singapore-Malaysia relations in the Malay mindset. Indeed, the fact that Singapore has sought Israel advisers for the military training of the Singapore Armed Forces (SAF) and openly adopts Israel as a role model of sorts, further reinforces that view in Malay society and within certain elements of the Malay leadership.[42] The episode that saw an unprecedented outburst of anti-Singapore sentiments was the visit of Israeli President Chaim Herzog to Singapore on 18 November 1986.[43] The visit coincided with a period of Islamic resurgence in Malaysia and Prime Minister Mahathir's anti-Zionist pronouncements and internal strife within the ruling UMNO. Tengku Razalaiegh, who later broke away to form Semangat 46 (Spirit of 46) used the Herzog issue to his political advantage. Other Malay-based opposition parties such as PAS and PSRM were in the forefront of the protests against the visit. When public demonstrations broke out in Malaysia, the ruling UMNO could hardly ignore anymore the outpouring of sentiments,[44] with some opposition parties and UMNO Youth calling for the severing of diplomatic ties with Singapore, cutting off water supplies, transport services, and expelling Singapore from ASEAN. The government responded by recalling its high commissioner to Singapore on 16 November. Indonesia followed suit on 19 November. Even after the visit, there were fanciful allegations on the Malaysian side of a Singapore role in an Israeli invasion of Malaysia and the testing of an Israeli nuclear bomb in the region. By 30 November, Mahathir, fearing that the safety of visitors from Singapore would be affected, ordered the demonstrations to stop in Johor, suggesting that the opposition was exploiting the issue.

Then came a new watermark in irritations, which may be said to have occurred during the late 1990s and early 2000s, when negotiations over outstanding issues in the two water supply agreements of 1961 and 1962 came to a deadlock.[45] The same period saw protracted and unresolved negotiations on the 1990 Points of Agreement (POA)[46] over the Malayan Railway property in Tanjong Pagar, and the holding back of pension (CPF) funds to Peninsular Malaysian employees. The two prime ministers, Mahathir and Goh, in December 1998, had apparently agreed to a "package deal" approach to resolving outstanding issues, including a Singapore accommodation for Malaysia to build a bridge. This clearly did not prove helpful. The point of impasse came in the early 2000s, symbolically represented by the Mahathir government's plan to build a crooked bridge over the Johore Strait, which would bypass the causeway on the Malaysian side. The Singapore Government's objection to the idea on legal grounds was the apparent reason (among others) for the Abdullah government's decision to cancel the Mahathir bridge. Clearly many of these issues cannot be fully comprehended without a reference to the details of each of the points of disagreement. Suffice it to say that all unresolved matters were practically put on hold as long as Mahathir remained the prime minister.[47]

It would not be difficult to show how domestic, in particular, ethnic considerations, could often trump economic and even mutual interests in Malaysia's relations with Singapore. The relationship apparently also fails to avail of strategies that seemed to have worked well in relations with larger powers. It would seem that foreign policy in more intimate bilateral relations tends to be locked into narrow underlying historical tensions, which in the Malaysia-Singapore case, are often further exacerbated by overarching ethnic sensitivities. Thus, even the strictly legal tussle over each country's claim to Pulau Batu Puteh/Pedra Branca can evoke highly emotive responses on both sides. We will now examine more closely this dispute to draw out some insights about the Malaysia-Singapore bilateral relations conundrum.

While the legal dispute over Pulau Batu Puteh (henceforth, PBP), a 500-square metres islet which houses the 1851 Horsburgh Lighthouse, dates to Malaysia's publishing of its 1979 map, the issue only surfaced prominently towards the end of the 1980s.[48] In mid-1989, Singapore established a radar installation on PBP and as all traffic was banned from the surrounding waters, this gave rise to Malaysian leaders in Johor charging that Malaysian fishermen were being chased away from their traditional fishing grounds. Similar protests were lodged in 1991 when Singapore built a helicopter pad on PBP. At about the same time, on 9 August, Singapore's national day, a Malaysia-Indonesia military exercise culminated with the landing of paratroops in southern Johor, codenamed "Total Wipe Out". Taking umbrage, Singapore responded by launching "Operation Trojan" under which its armed forces went on full alert. In an attempt to defuse tensions, in January 1992, Malaysia's justice minister said that the dispute would be resolved amicably in the ASEAN spirit. However, the Malaysian opposition parties PAS and Semangat 46 took the government to task for wavering on the issue and an UMNO Johor politician was quoted as saying that PBP belonged to Malaysia and "if we want to be calculating, even Singapore belongs to us" (Tan 1997, p. 14). In May 1992,

Berita Harian (Malaysia) reported that fishing vessels were being harassed by a Singapore patrol craft while Singapore protested that a Malaysian patrol craft had illegally entered in the waters around the islet on 22 April and that "foreign government vessels, unless on innocent passage, must obtain permission to enter Singapore territorial waters". At about this time, PAS and Semangat 46 announced that they planned to plant a Malaysian flag on PBP, provoking further protests from Singapore.

There was also a report that Johor marine police had seized two Singaporean fishing boats at about the same period. According to the Singapore account, the Johor police had forced at least one of the boats into Malaysian waters. The Malaysian high commissioner was summoned to Singapore's foreign ministry to receive a note of protest and a warning that Malaysian fishermen straying into Singapore waters will not be treated leniently. The Johor authorities rejected Singapore's account and started legal proceedings against the fishermen. In July 1992, Malaysian Foreign Minister Abdullah Badawi stated in Johor that the state should leave it to the federal government to settle the dispute over PBP, warning that the alternative to diplomacy was war and that Malaysia does not want to go to war. Thus in August 1992, the charges against the fishermen were dropped. On 29 June 1992, Malaysia handed legal documents to Singapore to support its claim on PBP. But in April 1993, the issue flared up again when an unidentified patrol vessel allegedly opened fire on three Singapore trawlers. However, in September 1994, after a meeting in Langkawi between Prime Ministers Mahathir and Goh Chok Tong, both sides agreed in principle to refer the issue to the ICJ. The matter lay fallow until 2003 when both countries signed a special agreement referring the dispute to the ICJ for settlement. In May 2007, after the meeting between Prime Ministers Abdullah Badawi and Lee Hsien Loong, it was announced that the ICJ would arbitrate the case in November 2007. Both countries agreed to abide by the ICJ verdict whichever way it went. The ICJ then sat for twelve days, in the period 6–23 November, to hear presentations from legal teams of both countries.[49] The acting president of ICJ, Judge Awn Shawkat Al-Khasawneh, presided over the case at the Peace Palace, The Hague, with a team of sixteen international judges, including two ad hoc judges appointed by Malaysia and Singapore.[50]

The Malaysian delegation comprised an entourage of thirty-two persons led by Tan Sri Abdul Kadir Mohamad, ambassador-at-large, as agent, and Ambassador Dato Nur Faridah A. Rashid as co-agent. Malaysia's international lawyers included Sir Elihu Lauterpacht and James Crawford, both professors in international law at Cambridge University; Professor Jan Schrijver, Leiden University; Professor Marcelo G. Kohen, Graduate Institute of International

Studies, Geneva; and Penelope Nevil of Cambridge University. The team also included Foreign Minister Dato Syed Hamid Albar and Attorney General Tan Sri Abdul Gani Patail. The Singapore team was led by Ambassador Tommy Koh as agent and Ambassador Anil Kumar as co-agent. Its team included Deputy Prime Minister and Professor of law S. Jayakumar and Professor Ian Brownie of Oxford University, Professor Alain Pellet of the University of Paris X-Nanterre, Rodman R. Bundy, New York advocate, and Loretta Malintoppi, member of the Rome Bar.

What is the basis of each country's claims to the disputed islet? Malaysia has argued that the sultan of Johor had exercised full sovereignty over PBP since 1513 when the Johor-Riau-Lingga sultanate was founded by Sultan Mahmud, who fled from the Portuguese after Malacca fell in 1511. Based on the theory of succession, PBP belonged to the Federation of Malaysia because Johor joined the federation in 1957. Thus, according to Malaysia, Singapore's claim that Pedra Branca was *terra nullius* (no man's land) was untenable. Furthermore, Singapore's operation of the Horsburgh Lighthouse did not affect Malaysia's legal entitlement to PBP. Singapore's claim, contrarywise, is that it had full territorial sovereignty and jurisdiction over the islet based on the 1824 Anglo-Dutch Treaty, and because the East India Company, whose legal successor was Singapore, had built the lighthouse which it has operated since 1851. Singapore also argued that no government authority (neither Malaysia nor Johor) laid claim to Pedra Branca until 1979. Thus, for 130 years Malaysian authorities had acknowledged Singapore's sovereignty over the islet. In the twelve days of hearings, both sides evidently stuck to their respective positions, and based on news reports, both sides appeared confident of winning their case.[51] Although no apparent new ground was broken, the presentations were clearly intense and pregnant with insinuations and counter accusations from both sides.[52] For example, Malaysia suggested that Singapore had deliberately concealed Governor Butterworth's 1944 letters of request to the sultan and the *temenggong* of Johor who had consented to the building of the lighthouse, with Singapore refuting that it had such letters. Both sides accused each other of subverting the status quo on PBP, and playing the bully. Moreover, Singapore dismissed as ridiculous Malaysia's claim that Singapore wanted to create a "maritime domain" with Pedra Branca, Middle Rocks, and South Ledge. The issue of aggression of the Singapore Navy also cropped up with Singapore replying that it was Malaysia which had arrested Singapore fishing vessels off the waters of Pedra Branca. Finally, the apparent show of magnanimity by Malaysia offering Singapore the right to continue operating the Horsburgh Lighthouse was dismissed by the latter as an attempt to influence the court with extraneous considerations. Prior to the actual ICJ decision and ruling, the weight of legal opinion appeared to favour Singapore:

> According to the principles of historical consolidation and estoppel,[53] Malaysia has no proof or foundation of any historical legal right to lay claim onto the rock. As adjudicated in the *Legal Status of Eastern Greenland* case, the elements necessary to establish valid title to sovereignty are also the intention and will to exercise such sovereignty and the manifestation of state activity. Malaysia showed neither throughout the twenty years following its independence. (Haller-Trost 1993, p. 27)

The fact that Malaysia and Singapore agreed to ICJ adjudication in the PBP case and that twelve days of hearings at the end of November 2007 did not appear to have stirred too much emotive responses on the part of the two countries was a sign that contentious issues between two countries had been largely ameliorated. On 23 May 2008, the ICJ ruled by 12-4 votes to award sovereignty of PBP or Pedra Branca to Singapore, and by 15-1 votes to award ownership of the Middle Rocks to Malaysia. The main contention of the court on Pedra Branca was that "from June 1850 for the whole of the following century or more", the Johor authorities took no action to establish sovereignty over PBP and that Malaysia's maps of 1960s and 1970s also indicate an appreciation that Singapore had sovereignty. In particular, "It is the clearly stated position of the Acting Secretary of the State of Johor in 1953 that Johor did not claim ownership of Pedra Branca/PBP."[54] As for South Ledge, sovereignty was to be decided once the demarcation of the adjoining territorial seas was determined by both parties. The Court said it had not been mandated by the parties to draw the line of delimitation with respect to the territorial waters of Malaysia and Singapore with respect to South Ledge. Spokespersons of Malaysia and Singapore hailed the decision of the ICJ as a win-win situation.[55] As a confidence building measure, the ICJ adjudication no doubt reinforced the ASEAN bilateral disposition to resolve territorial disputes by pacific means. However, as in the Ligitan-Sipadan settlement, there is no guarantee that the settlement of one territorial issue forecloses the emergence of other bilateral problems.

CONCLUSION

From a foreign policy perspective, several important questions merit answers in Malaysia's relations with its immediate neighbours. How effective and how constructive has been the Malaysian approach to its most proximate dyadic relations? From a theoretical perspective, do Malaysia's bilateral relations indicate the limits to constructivism and the primacy of realism? How have bilateral confidence building measures (CBMs) been engaged to moderate and reduce tensions, and has ASEAN socialization on a multilateral basis been an important basis for ameliorating and reducing conflicts? It seems paradoxical that the accounts of Malaysia's most proximate bilateral relationships illustrate that norms, ideas, identities, and interests tend to coalesce in rather narrow nationalist parameters for itself and its neighbours. This appears to be a validation of the realist perspective that when push comes to shove, core values and interests determine the outcome of the issues, conflicts, and controversies in Malaysian foreign policy practice *vis-à-vis* the Philippines, Indonesia, Thailand, and Singapore. This said, except for the period of *Konfrontasi*, prior to ASEAN's formation, Malaysia has yet to come to blows with its four immediate neighbours. This illustrates yet another irony, that history and intimacy are twin factors in animating conflicts as well as managing them. ASEAN socialization no doubt has added a new dimension to a more constructivist way of addressing conflicts as evidenced by a predisposition, even in the most tense of situations, to settle for non-violent resolution of disputes and conflicts. Such was the case in the handling of the Ligitan, Sipadan, and Pulau Batu Puteh claims. It is to the credit of Malaysia, Indonesia and Singapore that they are the first states in the Southeast Asian region to submit such territorial claims to the adjudication of the ICJ. ASEAN socialization could be assumed to have been a factor here given that other territorial claims in the region involving non-ASEAN states have not followed this path. Be that as it may, the predisposition of ASEAN states to peaceful conflict resolution remains weak at best, given that ASEAN's own mechanism of the Treaty of Amity and Cooperation, involving the setting up of High Council to address such matters, has remained in limbo for the past two decades. Another ideational factor influencing foreign policy has been Islam. Malaysia's policies in the two situations of conflict involving Muslims in the Philippines and Thailand yield yet another interesting interpretation of ASEAN socialization. It has predisposed a Muslim-dominant state such as Malaysia to policies of a third-party intervention and the proffering of good offices to conflict management in Muslim problems affecting both these neighbours. Naturally, whether these conflicts are resolved or even contained, no doubt depends on policies and the politics of the states themselves and Malaysia's approach should essentially be that of middlepowermanship.[56] Overall, it would seem that the overdetermination[57] of cultural factors infuses a unique nuance in Malaysia's closest bilateral relationships that could hardly be explained by a pristine realist interpretation of events.

Notes

1. See the chronology of *Konfrontasi* events provided in Chapter 4.
2. For example, see Milne (1967), Leifer (1968), and Noble (1977). We will draw mostly on the excellent summary of the issue by David (1996).
3. See David, 1996, p. 43.
4. Ibid.
5. Ibid., p. 46.
6. As explained by Balakrishnan (2002, p. 75), Malaysia does not claim the entire Spratly group, but islands located to the extreme south of the Spratlys, thought to be within its continental shelf. Balakrishnan suggests that this is unconvincing because, and as noted by others, waters do not give titles to islands but rather islands confer rights to waters.
7. See David op. cit., p. 61.
8. See Sakhuja (2007) for details and the account of a submarine acquisition race in Southeast Asia apparently to meet the new security challenges of the region.
9. Speech at a DAP Sandakan dinner talk at Tyng Garden Hotel Restaurant, Mile 5, Sandakan on Sunday, 29 April 2007.
10. He initially escaped to an island near Sabah in November 2001, where he sought political asylum from Malaysia, but was denied.
11. We draw from the Special Report of the United States Institute of Peace (2005) for this account.
12. The domain covers the whole of the Muslim autonomous region and other areas in Zamboanga del Norte, Zamboanga del Sur, Zamboanga Sibugay, North Cotabatao, Sultan Kudarat and Sarangani provinces, and even Palawan Island, and the Sulu Archipelagao (*Manila Times*, 17 December, 2007).
13. An in-depth, constructivist study of Indonesia-Malaysia relations is Liow's (2005).
14. See David (op. cit., p. 65) and my own writings, Saravanamuttu (1996, 2004).
15. See Haller-Trost (1995) for details of the incident in which Malaysia and Indonesia tried to play down the event.
16. See Press Release 2002/39 ICJ, from which the facts of my account are taken.
17. It is of interest to note that in March 2001, the Philippines sought to intervene in the case in order to preserve and safeguard their historical and legal rights with respect to the territory of North Borneo. In its judgment of 23 October 2001, the Court held that the Philippines failed to establish an interest of a legal nature that would justify the intervention. See *The American Society of International Law*, 29 January 2003, <http://www.asil.org/ilib/ilib0602.htm> (accessed 15 January 2008).
18. See Schofield and Storey (2005, pp. 39–40) for a treatment of the emotive elements of the claim, especially from the Indonesian perspective.

19. See ibid., for an extended exposition of the dispute and its security and economic ramifications.
20. Based on reports by news agencies, *Bernama* (29 March 2007) and *Antara* (7 March 2007 and 29 March 2007). The crisis may have led to the hacking of the Universiti Sains Malaysia's webpage, where the Soekarno slogan "Ganyang Malaysia" (Crush Malaysia) was inserted.
21. See SUARAM (2007, pp. 16–18).
22. See *Migration Dialogue*, <http://migration.ucdavies.edu> (accessed 17 January 2008).
23. In January 2008, Malaysia announced that 200,000 foreign workers will be sent home by 2009 to open up new jobs for locals. As of 2008, foreign workers make up 2.3 million of the eleven million-strong Malaysian workforce. The government wants to reduce this to 1.8 million by 2009, and to 1.5 million by 2015 (*Straits Times*, 21 January 2008).
24. We have not discussed Brunei's claims in the South China Sea but as in the case of the Philippines, they also overlap with those of Malaysia. See Haller-Trost (1994).
25. We draw mainly from David (1996) unless otherwise mentioned. David's own account draws from the important study by Che Man (1990) and the earlier study of Pitsuwan (1985).
26. I take the view of McCargo (2008) and Liow (2006) who argue that Thailand's problems in the Muslim South are driven more by local factors than a regional or global Jihadist agenda.
27. The group comprised sixty-four men, twenty-four women, and forty-three children seeking refuge in two mosques in Tumpat and Rantau Panjang (*Bernama*, 30 August 2005).
28. According to SUARAM human rights report (2006, p. 27), in January 2005, the authorities arrested Abdul Rahman Ahmad, also known as Deraman Koteh, under the ISA for his alleged involvement in several bombings in southern Thailand.
29. David (op. cit., p. 37) reports that the total number of fishermen detained in Malaysian prisons were about 1,000 in 1988.
30. For a fuller account of the MOU, see Schofield (2007, pp. 291–92).
31. In April 1994, U.S. Troton Oil, the Petroleum Authority of Thailand, and Petronas Carigali signed a series of contracts to develop three production zones in the Malaysia-Thailand Joint Development Area. Progress appears to be slow. As of 2007, reports suggest that the 225-km long pipeline to be situated in Songkhla is about 80 per cent complete. (See David op. cit., p. 35, Schofield 2007, p. 293, and various newspaper reports).
32. As quoted in Lee (1992, p. 220). Abdullah also used the analogy of two neighbours living in a semi-detached house sharing a wall and a roof in his talk to the Institute of Policy Studies in Singapore (Abdullah Badawi 1990, p. 10).

33. See the chapter "Talak, Talak, Talak", in Lee Kuan Yew's memoirs (1998, pp. 14–15). It is possible to remarry someone if the pronouncement is only one *talak*. In Malay-Muslim folklore, the utterance of three *talak*, would require a woman to be remarried and then divorced before the ex-husband could remarry her. The second husband is known by the colourful phrase "Cina buta" (blind Chinese), seemingly derogatory, but perhaps simply meaning a fake marriage.

34. The Pulau Batu Puteh or Pedra Branca claim by both countries was handed over to the ICJ for adjudication in November 2007. The sand ban imposed since 2003 remained in place at the time of writing, while the use of airspace which was curtailed in 1998 was restored in 2001 (See Nathan 2002, p. 404).

35. See Tan (2001, pp. 57–59) for an account of this and other controversies sparked by Lee Kuan Yew's memoirs and Lee's own mention of them in his second book (Lee 2000, pp. 285–86).

36. Lee Kuan Yew mentions a figure of 25,000 (Lee 1998).

37. I have drawn from Lau (1998, pp. 161–210) for this account because of its detailed rendition of events.

38. For a comprehensive account of the remerger debate, see Shamitra Bhanu Abdul Azeez (1998). Lee Kuan Yew (1998, pp. 237–38) in his memoir opines that Tun Ismail was the only Malay leader not prejudiced against Singapore.

39. As cited in Azeez (1998, p. 49).

40. The origins of this military arrangement was the East of Suez policy of the British. The FPDA replaced the Anglo-Malayan Defence Agreement (AMDA) in 1971. As explained by Chin (2004, pp. 173–74), the FPDA was a loose political consultative framework rather than a collective defence system. Singapore considered it to be an important component of its defence architecture, while Malaysia appeared to devalue it progressively.

41. See Tan (2001, p. 72) and Chin (2006, p. 176). I'm also given to understand that during FPDA exercises, there was no restriction for the use of Malaysian airspace by Singapore aircraft, and since 2001, the ban has been lifted (interview with Tan Sri Ahmad Fauzi, 16 July 2007).

42. Cf. Tan 1997, p. 3.

43. Ibid., pp. 3–7.

44. The most dramatic protest was the act of the late PSRM leader Abdul Razak Ahmad lying down on the railway track in Johor Baru to stop a Singapore-bound train symbolically.

45. See Nathan (2002, pp. 396–400) for the details of the dispute which essentially hinged around the impasse over what Kuala Lumpur considers to be the unfair price of water sold to Singapore, which is legally locked until the agreements expire in 2011 and 2061 respectively, even though new negotiations had begun in the mid-1980s. For two official documentations of the major issues relating to the water dispute, see the Malaysian Government's booklet, *Water: The Singapore-Malaysia Dispute: The Facts* (2003), and Singapore's Government publication, *Water Talks? If Only It Could* (2003).

46. The POA was a reworking of the 1918 colonial ordinance which gave the Malayan Railway use of 217 hectares of land in Singapore for 999 years (Nathan 2002, p. 400).
47. See Kesavapany and Saw (2006, pp. 1–11). For various accounts of the bilateral issues afflicting the two countries, see Ganesan (2005, pp. 56–80), Nathan (2002) and Azizah Kassin and Lau (1992, passim, and Chapter 11 by Lee Poh Ping, pp. 219–29).
48. We draw on Haller-Trost (1993), David (1996), Tan (1995) and numerous newspapers and other reports for the recounting of this issue.
49. The complete proceedings are available at the ICJ webpage, <www.icj-cij.org>.
50. ICJ President Judge Rosalyn Higgins disqualified herself as she had represented Singapore prior to her appointment to the Court's top post.
51. See, for example, the report in *The Sunday Times*, 25 November 2007.
52. See, among others, the write-ups in <www.siaaonline.org/news> (accessed 9 January 2008) and <www.malaysianbar.org.my/legal/general_news> (accessed 9 January 2008).
53. An "estoppel" is a bar preventing one from making an allegation or a denial that contradicts what one has previously stated as the truth <dictionary.com>.
54. See ICJ judgment, 23 May 2008, General List, No. 130, p. 75.
55. My impression in attending a closed-door meeting on foreign policy of senior past and present MFA officials at about the time of the ICJ decision was that it was not taken as well on the Malaysian side. There was angst that Singapore would take advantage of this decision and that the Malaysian Government should do its level best to establish its territorial waters and negotiate for ownership of South Ledge. Needless to say, the Malaysian Opposition in parliament played up the government's "failure".
56. The importance of middlepowermanship will be discussed further in the concluding chapter of the book.
57. I used this term in a much more conventional sense than the Marxist scholar Louis Althusser who sees overdetermination as the cultural realm superceding the economic realm, which for Marxists is always "determination in the last instance". For a quick foray into Althusserian and also Freudian thinking about overdetermination, see <http://en.wikipedia.org/wiki/Overdetermination>.

11

THE POLITICAL ECONOMY OF FOREIGN POLICY
Dilemmas of a Developmental State

In this chapter we will examine Malaysia's foreign relations and foreign policy construction from a political economy perspective. Robert Gilpin (2001) has shown persuasively that in the realm of international political economy (IPE), globalization tends to take a backseat to state-centric economic goals of state. This is not to say that globalization does not impact on states, but rather that its significance has been greatly exaggerated.[1] He also illustrates convincingly that "national systems of political economy" exhibit considerable differences in spite of globalization and that these variations can be shown empirically along three important dimensions, namely, the primary purposes of economic activity, the role of the state, and the structure of corporate and private business practices.[2] Thus, according to Gilpin, the American political economy is premised on "market-oriented capitalism" with the primary purpose of consumerism and wealth creation. State intervention in the economy divided between the Treasury, the Federal Reserve, and several powerful agencies, and corporate governance is marked by strong anti-trust and competition policies. In contrast, the Japanese and German systems are characterized by a strong social welfare orientation, addressing the problem of market failure. Furthermore, Japan has been largely neomercantilist with corporate governance largely in favour of large monopolies or *keiretsu*. German "social market" capitalism also differs from that of the Americans or Japanese such as in banking practice where state polices have favoured major private banks such as the Deutsche Bank. Contrariwise, Japanese banking tends to favour and be closely associated with large conglomerates. In the face of the financial crisis and meltdown of October 2008 in the United States and Europe, much may change in terms of how we would in the future depict the American and European forms of capitalism.[3] The Malaysian economic system since the 1980s has tried to emulate Japanese "developmental capitalism", with its broad attendant features and, by and large, has since then joined the ranks of the newly industrializing economies or "developmental states" of East Asia.[4] Loosely following Gilpin, I present below the historical trajectory, as well as the major features, of the Malaysian developmental state.

MUTATIONS OF A DEVELOPMENTAL STATE

To take a historical perspective, capitalist transformation has moved Malaysia from its mercantilist roots to a *laissez-faire* and then to a neoliberal phase. As with most Asian developing countries, its economy transited various economic phases from an import-substitution phase (1950s–60s) to an export-orientation phase (1970s–1980s). Sieh (2000) dubbed the period from the early 80s to just before the financial crisis, as the "Trade and Investment-link Phase", while Jomo (2007) has named three periods in the 1980s till the end of the end Mahathir era, viz. Heavy Industrialization (1981–85), Economic Liberalization (1986–97), and Crisis Management (1997–2003). Under the Abdullah government, the Third Industrial Master Plan for 2006–15 has been launched, which, in my view, continues to open the doors of the Malaysian economy to globalization.

From the perspective of more recent history, it may be said that globalization impacted on the Malaysian economy in the early 1970s right through to the 1980s, through a New International Division of Labour (NIDL) crafted by transnational corporations working in tandem with states. During this phase of capitalist development, the East Asian region was also supposedly further overlaid with a regional division of labour in which Japanese capital was particularly prominent.[5] This phase of Japanese-led capitalist development was known by the colourful phrase, the "flying geese" pattern of development. The concept had its roots in the work of Japanese economist Akamatsu Kaname writing in the 1930s, but was popularized in contemporary times by Okita Saburo and Kiyoshi Kojima.[6] The "flying geese" notion is based on the product cycle view of the migration of industries in the East Asia region whereby the latecomers replicating the development pattern of the earlier industrializers effect an upgrading of industrial capacities. The concept provides part of the explanation to the so-called "East Asian Miracle". Until the 1997–98 financial crisis, the countries of East Asia had been doubling their income every ten years whereas it took Britain and the United States fifty to sixty years to do the same. Furthermore, these countries had rapidly been transformed from initially agricultural economies to manufacture-based economies.

The 1997–98 financial crisis in East and Southeast Asia clearly put the brakes on this sort of transformed Malaysian political economy, as it did to the political economy of all of Southeast Asia. It also exposed the fact that Southeast Asian economies that had become overly dependent on international finance capital and on unproductive profit seeking activities, such as state created rent. Deregulation of the region's economies and privatization policies in the 1990s had facilitated these developments. Patronage characterized these economies and as bankruptcies became widespread, privatized projects got halted, and bailsout attempted, the collusion between the political and the economic elites was exposed. Hence, rather than the problem of total factor productivity being the culprit as highlighted in the Krugman thesis,[7] it was finance capital that finally brought down the curtains on the East Asian miracle. From one point of view, the process began to set in as early as 1971, when President Nixon more or less took the decision to take the U.S. dollar off the gold standard.[8] Further attempts like that of Plaza Accord of 1985 to realign major currencies proved even more fatal for Southeast Asia. Much analysis has been proffered for why the Southeast Asian countries were vulnerable to financial volatility,[9] but most pertinent is the fact that the crisis and economic meltdown may have struck a lethal blow to the developmental state in its original form. For the main Southeast Asian states growth rates plummeted to unprecedented levels in two subsequent years after the crisis and most countries remained heavily indebted and continued to suffer serious socio-economic reverberations. Indonesia saw an economic decline of more than 13 per cent, Thailand, almost 11 per cent, and Malaysia, more than 7 per cent in 1998. Singapore registered next to no growth that year.

Eul-Soo Pang then pronounced that the Asian developmental state had met its demise. He argued that the *dirigiste* state exercising control over national policies would now be a thing of the past since such a state is simply not compatible with the financial globalization that has occurred:

> The new Asian state will have to promote a paradigmatic shift from state-centric to market-driven development; it has to avoid excessive state domination in social, economic, and political life — "the state should not row, but steer"[10] — political actions must not hamper the market, and finally, social solidarity and ethnic cohesion should be preserved and built on economic dynamism and income equity. (Pang 2002, p. 589)

However, a more interesting interpretation of the impact of the economic meltdown is not that it has eliminated the developmental state, but that an enforced mutation occurred. Gilpin holds that there is no substitute for states even in a globalized world and the jury may still be out on the developmental state. Even if the developmental state were dead, one shouldn't escape with the idea that development as a goal will not continue to be pursued, perhaps through the more common "regulatory" state (Jayasuriya 2000). Such a regulatory state already functions famously in the long-established neoliberal orders of Europe and North America, save for a few stubborn social democracies. Furthermore, there is hardly any chance of a rejection of neoliberalism by political elites as it establishes itself fully in the Southeast Asian region. To reject this would be as good as rejecting all the past attainments of industrialization. To be sure, ownership and control of the economy may well change now and in the future, and a greater loosening of national controls over the economy appears inevitable in the current phase of neoliberal globalization. It is in this context of this phase of neoliberal globalization that we now examine Malaysia's post-crisis foreign economic relations, foreign economic policy, and foreign relations. In this chapter, we will look at the following: Malaysia's policies of counterdominance; the economic logic of its trading relationships; Malaysia's major foreign direct investment (FDI) flows, its stances and negotiation positions at the WTO, and its current and ongoing bilateral FTA negotiations in contrast to its current economic policies in ASEAN.

STANCES OF COUNTERDOMINANCE

Malaysia's postures, strategies, and polices of counterdominance and counterhegemony *vis-à-vis* the global economic were already evident during the period of Malaysian second prime minister, Tun Abdul Razak. Drawing from Chapter Five, we have argued that there was a shift during Razak's tenure to a "political economy approach" in foreign economic relations. Malaysia's participation and involvement in UNCTAD saw it championing the causes of the South, along with some of the more radical Latin and African countries. Malaysia also joined the call for a new economic world order in the mid-1970s. On the domestic front, these more radical economic stances coincided with the introduction of the NEP in 1970. As explained in Chapter 5, among one of the effects of the NEP was the drastic reduction of foreign share in the Malaysian economy, which in the 1970s stood at about 60 per cent. By 2004, this had come down to 32.5 per cent of share capital (Ninth Malaysia Plan, p. 339). In Chapter 5, we alluded to Malaysia's two economic stances of "developing world orientation" and "economic nationalism". Among the more significant actions was the establishment of national oil corporation Petronas, which signalled the government's intention of maintaining full control over its national assets. In this sense, while the tenure of Mahathir did introduce a new slew of counterhegemonic stances and policies in economic relations, it was in keeping with existing postures and policies, albeit in a more iconoclastic fashion, as I have argued in Chapter 7. Mahathir's "Look East" policy, his South-South initiatives and his proposal for an East Asian economic bloc or community were clearly counterhegemonic *vis-à-vis* a Western economic dominance often dubbed as the "Washington Consensus". Mahathir's counterhegemonic policies during the 1997–98 Asia financial crisis clearly tried to resist such domination and Malaysia's partial economic recovery no doubt vindicated him in the eyes of many.

However, if one takes a harder look at Malaysia's economic relationships in terms of trade and flows of FDI, it would still appear that the underlying drive for the kinds of relationships that resulted, especially in the post-financial crisis period, have largely been in the context of a globally refurbished neoliberalism. Malaysia's economic system, while unique given its NEP and post-NEP thrusts, is nonetheless that of a modified developmental state. It is this mutated developmental state that has allowed for the policies of economic and "ethnic nationalism" to articulate within the order of a neoliberal world underpinned by globalization. Perhaps ethnic nationalism has also been a factor that has blunted Malaysia's full embrace of globalization. We will now move on to examine Malaysia's major economic relationships, especially during the 2000s.

PATTERNS OF TRADE AND FOREIGN INVESTMENT

Malaysia's political economy has been largely dictated by its changing industrial structure as we have broadly discussed above. However, in spite of whatever changes that may have occurred over the fifty years of Malaysian economic development, there have been some rather stable patterns of investment and trade that are obviously driven by Malaysia's highly externally-oriented economy. Since the 1960s, Malaysia has had a liberal policy of encouraging FDI into the country. In Chapter 4, we saw how Federal Development Industrial Authority (FIDA) now the Malaysian Development Industrial Authority (MIDA) offered various incentives to foreign investors even as the Tun Razak government championed economic nationalism. In later years this policy was further extended and the Investment Act of 1986 was amended in 1991 to promote capital and technology-intensive industries with the offer of pioneer status, investment tax allowances and reinvestment allowances and a plethora of fiscal incentives, ranging from those aimed at the strengthening of industrial linkages, and for computers and information technology assets, research and development, training, disposal of toxic and hazardous waste, to tourism and plantation projects. There were also the added incentives of double taxation agreements and tax exemption under the Income Tax Act for foreign investors (Sieh 2000, p. 64). After the crisis, foreign ownership of the manufacturing industry increased perceptibly. Local content requirements were also removed in line with the WTO Trade Related Investment Measures (TRIMs) Agreement. As pointed out by Lee (2007, p. 232), from 1999–2003, equity in manufacturing projects was distributed as follows: 15.7 per cent *Bumiputera*, 19.3 per cent non-*Bumiputera* and a huge 65 per cent in foreign hands. There were also perceptible changes in the Kuala Lumpur Stock Exchange (KLSE), now known as the Malaysian Bourse, as follows: from 1990–96, the average proportions of new equity issues were 28 per cent in manufacturing, 27 per cent in financial services and 15 per cent in construction but from 1999–2003, equity in financial services constituted 36 per cent while manufacturing stood at 23 per cent and construction at 15 per cent (Lee 2008, pp. 240–42). In 2006, the services sector was estimated to have contributed 58.2 per cent of GDP while manufacturing contributed 32 per cent.[11] The Malaysian economy has been clearly further liberalized at the end of the Mahathir tenure, with foreign ownership regulations relaxed with no limits on foreign equity holdings, irrespective of their level of exports. With the Second Industrial Master Plan of 2002–05, the stress had also been on "knowledge industries" while the Third Industrial Plan, 2006–2015, continues the cluster-based approach to improve industrial linkages in terms of depth and breath and to move up the value chain.[12] The following strategies were stressed in the Third Industrial Master Plan:

• Strengthening and deepening the semiconductor subsegment
• Deepening and widening the development of the ICT value chain
• Intensifying research and development (R&D) and design activities
• Promoting the application of new and emerging technologies
• Integrating domestic companies into the regional and global supply chain; and
• Making available a skilled workforce (*Economic Report* 2007/2008, p. 40)

This approach of improving knowledge industries and moving up the value chase has been reiterated in the Ninth Malaysia Plan, 2006–10 launched by the Abdullah government.[13]

We will now examine Malaysian trade and foreign investment in the 2000s to draw out some patterns and broad generalizations. In 2005 and 2006, Malaysia's major trading partners, ranked in order of the volume of exports, were: ASEAN, the United States, the European Union, China and Hong Kong, Japan, South Korea, and Taiwan. In ASEAN, Singapore took the lion's share of exports with 59 per cent in 2006. The United States was next with 19 per cent, the European Union, 13 per cent, Japan, 9 per cent, China and Hong Kong, 12 per cent, South Korea, 4 per cent, and Taiwan, 3 per cent.[14] This pattern of trade has not changed appreciably since the mid-1970s, if one refers to Table 5.1 in Chapter 5 to make comparisons. Perhaps only the emergence of China as the fourth largest major trading partner and the inclusion of the United Kingdom within the European Union are the major changes. The United States became Malaysia's largest trading partner with 14 per cent of total trade, electronic and electrical (E&E) products accounting for 77.5 per cent of exports. Japan's share, at number three, also declined considerably while United States' share has risen sharply. Malaysia's chronic trade deficit with Japan makes it the largest source of imports. China's rise is also to be noted as perhaps the most significant development in the 2000s. In one year (2005–06), Malaysia's exports to China increased by 21 per cent. Rapid developments in China's ICT sector have fuelled demand for E&E products from Malaysia. ASEAN, excluding Singapore, remains fairly important with total trade in the region of 12 per cent. New export markets include the Netherlands, India, Pakistan, and West Asia.

The flow of FDI apparently remained robust in the early 2000s although inflows have clearly declined proportionally *vis-à-vis* other developing countries in the region. Malaysia is well behind countries such as China, which in 2006 attracted about US$70 billion, Hong Kong SAR (US$41 billion), Singapore (US$24 billion) and India (US$16.9 billion). Malaysia, with an FDI inflow of about US$6 billion was just above Indonesia (US$5.5 billion), but behind Thailand (US$9.7 billion). Malaysia's FDI outflows or investments abroad stood at about US$6 billion, ranking eighth among the top fifteen developing countries. Large established Malaysian corporations in the petroleum and services sectors, through acquisitions and joint ventures, led most investments and found their way to such countries as Indonesia (oil palm, banking, and telecommunications), the Middle East and South Asia (infrastructure, housing, highways), Africa and Central Asia (oil and gas), and China (utilities).

The main sources of FDI inflows (2006) in Malaysia were Japan, the Netherlands, Australia, USA, and Singapore, with the number of projects and total amount of investment as shown in Table 11.1. Although the investment quantities still do not show it too conclusively, Malaysia is clearly taking advantage of its Muslim connections. From 2002–06, there was a total of RM4 billion in approved FDI from the United Arab Emirates.

FDI inflow in the same years was concentrated in the following industries:

- E&E (RM8.6 billion)
- Chemicals and chemical products (RM3 billion)

TABLE 11.1
Sources of Foreign Investment in Approved Projects (2002–06)

Country	2002 No.	2002 Foreign Investment (RM)	2003 No.	2003 Foreign Investment (RM)	2004 No.	2004 Foreign Investment (RM)	2005 No.	2005 Foreign Investment (RM)	2006 No.	2006 Foreign Investment (RM)	2002–06 No.	2002–06 Foreign Investment (RM)
United States	39	2,667,836,406	31	2,181,730,334	27	1,058,826,199	43	5,154,990,909	38	2,476,649,294	178	13,540,033,142
Japan	102	587,386,835	123	1,295,794,177	85	1,010,655,980	84	3,671,721,963	81	4,411,582,988	475	10,977,141,943
F.R Germany	14	5,055,362,309	19	170,309,161	14	4,723,715,759	11	387,722,999	15	232,287,597	73	10,569,397,825
Singapore	146	1,019,191,925	156	1,224,917,366	161	1,515,450,695	130	2,919,868,545	130	1,884,693,675	723	8,564,122,206
The Netherlands	13	606,816,480	15	316,202,479	9	99,248,728	26	1,673,996,910	13	3,284,184,701	76	5,980,449,298
United Kingdom	10	169,879,023	13	3,870,432,484	12	152,748,579	11	99,208,295	17	641,983,444	63	4,934,251,825
United Arab Emirates	1	91,119	2	3,951,774,220	–	–	–	–	1	40,000,000	4	3,991,865,339
Australia	10	108,356,211	20	105,179,213	12	116,529,792	12	155,914,520	20	2,560,053,181	74	3,046,032,917
Korea, Rep.	17	369,276,575	17	446,901,008	25	324,626,110	24	673,592,257	18	437,825,114	101	2,252,221,064
Taiwan	64	251,911,597	57	622,025,078	78	414,544,636	71	430,694,747	70	405,451,042	340	2,124,627,100
Cayman Islands	1	70,000,000	1	1,800,000	3	57,264,065	2	154,086,000	2	860,500,000	9	1,143,650,065
India	5	19,643,716	8	47,010,936	7	291,677,061	8	558,895,477	6	8,317,717	34	925,544,907
British Virgin Islands	3	46,104,920	1	33,400,000	7	138,689,658	3	13,445,250	6	647,665,369	20	879,305,197
Switzerland	3	25,440,000	4	13,488,586	3	121,094,371	6	563,234,355	7	46,109,598	23	769,366,910
China	9	55,262,393	18	247,231,130	19	187,105,378	11	39,584,890	19	134,052,932	76	663,236,723
Lebanon	–	–	–	–	–	–	–	–	1	562,291,898	1	562,291,898
Thailand	1	8,890,000	4	263,585,055	3	36,870,000	5	142,282,216	5	109,462,220	18	561,089,491
Norway	–	–	4	23,009,581	–	–	5	303,178,476	1	114,000,000	10	440,188,057
Indonesia	7	11,786,280	3	48,470,987	2	86,695,999	3	52,476,594	11	214,889,222	26	414,319,082
Hong Kong	10	67,404,270	11	102,653,568	10	51,624,778	17	105,430,448	9	84,460,615	57	411,573,679
France	5	69,632,500	8	43,527,091	10	137,441,276	5	35,277,139	5	85,026,200	33	370,904,206
Italy	5	30,524,655	3	10,491,640	4	30,877,335	2	41,268,480	9	218,628,203	23	331,790,313
Canada	3	1,250,954	2	3,027,363	7	216,267,144	5	70,804,450	4	6,804,184	21	298,154,095
Panama	1	59,500,000	–	–	–	–	1	174,947,077	2	20,907,500	4	255,354,577
The Philippines	1	800,000	2	33,827,457	1	215,416,000	–	–	1	1,000,000	5	251,043,457
Denmark	1	3,749,392	5	8,847,029	1	180,000,000	3	30,613,000	1	7,419,060	11	230,628,481
Portugal	–	–	–	–	–	–	–	–	1	179,775,000	1	179,775,000
Sweden	1	1,233,360	1	33,500,000	4	28,720,250	2	35,860,000	3	43,734,760	11	143,048,370
Bermuda	1	12,078,219	–	–	–	–	2	2,877,519	1	80,000,000	4	94,955,738

continued on next page

Country	2002		2003		2004		2005		2006		2002–06	
	No.	Foreign Investment (RM)	No.	Foreign Investment (RM)	No.	Foreign Investment (RM)	No.	Foreign Investment (RM)	No.	Foreign Investment (RM)	No.	Foreign Investment (RM)
Liechtenstein	1	57,240,000	–	–	–	–	–	–	–	–	1	57,240,000
New Zealand	–	–	–	–	3	53,451,886	1	304,000	–	–	4	53,755,886
Mauritius	1	16,821,600	1	6,013,705	–	–	–	–	3	26,521,952	5	49,357,257
Bahamas	1	9,240,000	–	–	–	–	–	–	1	34,000,000	2	43,240,000
Turkey	–	–	1	646,800	–	–	1	0	1	37,000,000	3	37,646,800
Finland	–	–	1	200,000	1	30,000,000	1	1,460,000	–	–	3	31,660,000
Spain	1	6,330,000	–	–	1	9,676,207	1	9,832,105	–	–	3	25,838,312
Brazil	–	–	–	–	–	–	1	24,457,600	–	–	1	24,457,600
Luxembourg	–	–	–	–	–	–	1	24,125,000	–	–	1	24,125,000
Ireland	1	23,257,693	–	–	–	–	–	–	–	–	1	23,257,693
Russian Federation	2	14,200,000	–	–	–	–	2	7,300,000	–	–	4	21,500,000
Egypt	–	–	1	3,000,000	–	–	–	–	2	17,175,000	3	20,175,000
Austria	–	–	2	5,192,240	–	–	2	12,354,000	1	1,835,400	5	19,381,640
Pakistan	–	–	–	–	3	913,600	1	2,241,530	3	12,052,900	7	15,208,030
Bangladesh	–	–	–	–	–	–	3	9,150,950	–	–	3	9,150,950
Iran	–	–	1	1,900,000	2	4,392,000	–	–	–	–	3	6,292,000
Peru	–	–	–	–	–	–	1	6,114,400	–	–	1	6,114,400
Macau	–	–	1	6,000,000	–	–	–	–	–	–	1	6,000,000
South Africa	–	–	1	5,500,000	–	–	–	–	–	–	1	5,500,000
Cyprus	–	–	–	–	–	–	–	–	2	5,000,000	2	5,000,000
Nigeria	–	–	–	–	–	–	1	4,864,661	–	–	1	4,864,661
Vietnam	1	2,880,000	–	–	–	–	–	–	–	–	1	2,880,000
Myanmar	1	1,500,000	1	270,000	–	–	–	–	–	–	2	1,770,000
Belgium	2	1,621,794	–	–	–	–	–	–	–	–	2	1,621,794
Tunisia	–	–	–	–	1	1,225,000	–	–	–	–	1	1,225,000
Iraq	–	–	1	140,000	–	–	–	–	–	–	1	140,000
Vanuatu	–	–	2	0	2	0	–	–	–	–	3	0
Others	53	120,391,042	99	512,366,138	106	1,854,792,940	89	288,754,331	97	294,543,269	444	3,070,847,720
TOTAL	***	11,572,891,268	***	15,640,364,826	***	13,150,541,426	***	17,882,931,093	***	20,227,884,035	***	78,474,612,648

Notes: ** Expansion of capacities or manufacture of additional products not involving additional capital
*** Figures are not totalled to avoid double counting.
Source: Malaysian Industrial Development Authority, <www.mida.gov.my>.

- Basic metal products (RM2.3 billion)
- Non-metallic mineral products (RM962.2 million)
- Food manufacturing (RM895.4 million)
- Plastic products (RM757.2 million)
- Scientific and measuring equipment (RM664.6 million)
- Machinery and equipment (RM656.9 million)

It is clear from Malaysia's pattern of FDI inflows that electronic and electrical product manufacturing features very prominently. The share of FDI in the E&E industry has increased steadily from 46 per cent in 1985 to 85.8 per cent in 2006. Indeed, this sector is the mainstay of Malaysian manufacturing today and the strategy in the Third Industrial Master Plan and Ninth Malaysia Plan is to move up the value chain in this sector. The share of E&E in manufacturing since 2001 has stood at about 50 per cent of total manufacturing exports. The role and involvement of local manufacturers in tandem with foreign investors is crucial in this process. Evidently the government is aware that Malaysian companies have gained considerable experience in assembly and testing which involves large volumes, but low valued-added activities and that Malaysia still remains predominantly a components manufacturer rather than one specializing in product conceptualization and design. This is in contrast to Taiwan and Korea which have moved up the value chain. The government's efforts in setting up agencies such as the Malaysian Technology Development Corporation, Multimedia Development Corporation, and the Malaysian Biotechnology Corporation, its designation of five "research universities" are all attempts to foster the movement up the value chain. However, it remains to be seen how successful this process will be. Table 11.2 shows that distribution or spread of foreign and local investment in three components of the E&E industry in so-called "new" and "diversified" activities in 2006.

GLOBALIZATION, WTO, AND FTAs

In Chapter 9, we argued that the Abdullah government had embraced globalization, taken to mean the increasing spread of the neoliberal economy on a global scale. We argued that given its strong external orientation, the Malaysian economy has since its early days been subject to the vicissitudes of the global economy, an early form of globalization. We have also argued that Mahathir's polices attempted to confront globalization in various ways, but at the end of the day succumbed to its overwhelming impact. During Abdullah Badawi's tenure, there was a conspicuous shift away from confrontational postures and policies towards a greater accommodation with the forces

TABLE 11.2
Approved Manufacturing Projects in the Electrical and Electronic Products Industry by Subsector, 2006

Sub-sector	New				Expansion/Diversification				Total			
	No.	Domestic Investment (US$)	Foreign Investment (US$)	Total Capital Investment (US$)	No.	Domestic Investment (US$)	Foreign Investment (US$)	Total Capital Investment (US$)	No.	Domestic Investment (US$)	Foreign Investment (US$)	Total Capital Investment (US$)
Consumer Electronics	3	11,482,289	20,997,275	32,479,564	20	15,403,978	28,032,333	43,436,311	23	26,886,267	49,029,608	75,915,875
Electronic Components	22	166,565,771	225,860,071	392,425,842	35	84,207,568	1,594,854,591	1,679,062,159	57	250,773,338	1,820,714,662	2,071,488,001
Industrial Electronics	12	38,152,523	49,518,900	87,671,423	37	25,396,817	279,039,573	304,436,390	49	63,549,340	328,558,473	392,107,813
Electrical Products	22	25,120,583	7,104,251	32,224,834	19	21,195,640	138,318,506	159,514,146	41	46,316,224	145,422,756	191,738,980
Total	59	241,321,166	303,480,497	544,801,663	111	146,204,003	2,040,245,003	2,186,449,006	170	387,525,169	2,343,725,500	2,731,250,669

Source: Malaysian Industrial Development Authority, <www.mida.gov.my>.

of globalization. This notwithstanding, we have noted too that Abdullah continued to pay lip service to South-South forums such as the Group of 77 (Plus China). The prime minister attended the group's Summit at Doha in June 2005, speaking out on the need for a self-empowered "independent developing world" (*Bernama*, 16 June 2005).

This sort of hedging was even evident in the Mahathir period when Malaysia had begun to engage with globalization via the World Trade Organization (WTO), becoming a founding member in 1995. Malaysia then chaired the WTO General Council. The Ministry of Trade and Industry (MITI) indicates that it actively pursues a trade liberalization policy and, having signed Free Trade Agreement with Japan in 2006, was actively negotiating FTAs with the United States, Australia, New Zealand, and Pakistan. The fact that Malaysian external trade has grown immensely[15] has been MITI's rationale for trade liberalization, which was explained in Chapter 9.

As pointed out by Tham (2008), Malaysia has been ambivalent in its negotiations in the WTO and its policies have largely mirrored the stances of the developing countries within that organization. During the Uruguay Round (1986–94), Malaysia, along with other developing countries, committed to implementing stipulated tariff and non-tariff reductions as well as the General Agreement on Trade in Services (GATS), the Agreement on Trade-Related Investment Measures (TRIMS), and the Agreement on Trade-Related Intellectual Property Rights (TRIPS). In post-Uruguay Round developments, a rethinking occurred, greatly prompted by the Asian financial crisis of 1997–98. Developing countries also baulked at what were dubbed "the Singapore issues". In the WTO meeting of 1996 in Singapore, developing countries (Malaysia included) opposed an agreement on investment to establish non-discriminatory and transparent domestic rules on foreign investment, viz. national treatment, investment safeguards, including rules on expropriation, and empowering foreign investors to sue host governments. From their point of view, these attempts at accelerated deregulation and market access and legal protection of MNCs were asymmetric and deprived governments while enhancing investors' rights.

Malaysia joined the "Like Minded Group" of developing countries that was tasked with presentations for the meeting at Seattle in opposition to the Singapore issues.[16] The 1999 Seattle meeting of the WTO was noted for its egregious failure as well as the rise in a plethora of Third World and civil society voices opposing neoliberalism. The WTO subsequently launched its Doha Round in 2001, but negotiations again fell through on many issues and the round has stalled, marked by the collapse of negotiations in Cancun in 2003. According to Tham, who was citing Malaysian WTO Ambassador Dato Superamanian:

Malaysia, like many other developing countries, held the view that more time was needed to study and understand the proposed Singapore issues before they could be tabled for negotiations as they can have far-reaching impact on a country. In particular, the new rules might impinge on the flexibility of the country to implement policies in line with its socio-economic requirements. (Tham 2008, pp. 176–77)

Malaysia, which took a forty-one-member delegation to Cancun obviously took the negotiations seriously, and according to Tham, hedged its position between that of a pristinely developing world stance and that of the developed countries. It participated in the "green room" process that brought together a selected group of developed and developing countries to overcome the sticking points of negotiations. Malaysia also became a member of the Cairns Group of developed and developing countries, which focused on access to the markets of the United States and the European Union. The Post-Cancun Hong Kong meeting of 2005 saw no agreement and the failure of the Doha Round has led countries to move on to the terrain of bilateral and plurilateral trade negotiations.

MALAYSIA'S FTAs

Unlike countries such as Singapore, which has taken an aggressive approach to the negotiation of bilateral FTAs outside of the ASEAN region, Malaysia largely confined itself to working within ASEAN for many years while vaguely targeting only selected countries for bilateral FTAs. According to Tham (2008, p. 179), Malaysia has been unhappy with Singapore, not only because of its support of the Singapore issues, but also its policy of negotiating FTAs outside of the ASEAN umbrella. However, Malaysia's own stance on FTAs took a shift during (or just before) the Abdullah tenure and was clearly demonstrated by the stance of the Ministry of International Trade and Industry, as cited above, namely, to move in the direction of WTO-plus bilateral FTAs.[17] Thus, Malaysia since 2002[18] has been actively pursuing FTAs with Japan, Pakistan, Australia, New Zealand, and with the United States. By the middle of 2008, Malaysia has been successful in concluding only two bilateral FTAs, with Japan and Pakistan.[19]

We have already noted that the Malaysia-U.S. FTA stalled largely on the objections on the U.S. side over government procurement and NEP-related ethnic policies.[20] On top of this, various sections of Malaysian civil society mounted a demonstration against the FTA, such as the Third World Network (TWN), based in Penang, and known for its anti-globalization posture, along with Consumer Association of Penang and Friends of the Earth. The *New*

Straits Times cited then Minister of MITI Rafidah Aziz on 2 February 2007 as saying that Malaysia and the United States needed to resolve some fifty-eight contentious issues, sixteen involving the Domestic Trade and Consumer Affairs Ministry while the rest involved other ministries such as Finance, Agriculture, Human Resources, and the Prime Minster's Department. In November 2007, Malaysia was still confident that the FTA could be concluded in the spring or summer of 2008. However, given the expiry of the United States' fast-tracking Trade Promotion Authority (TPA) bill in June 2008, it became increasingly unlikely that the U.S.-Malaysia FTA would be signed in the near future. The change of the U.S. presidency and Rafidah Aziz losing control of MITI after the 8 March 2008 general election also meant that much negotiation ground would have been lost. This said, in my discussions with senior MITI officials in December 2007, it was emphasized to me that the U.S.-Malaysia FTA was of crucial significance not just because of the United States' economic prominence, but also because of Malaysia's overall economic stance of riding the tide of globalization.[21]

Besides that with the United States, there were ongoing negotiations on other bilateral FTAs with Australia, and New Zealand. Other bilateral FTAs or FTA-type arrangements at various stages of initiation were with India, South Korea, and Chile. The Malaysian-Japanese FTA, which goes by the name Japan-Malaysia Economic Partnership Agreement (JMEPA), was concluded in October 2005 after negotiations began in February 2003. MITI cites the following benefits Malaysia will derive from this agreement:

- The JMEPA would allow Malaysia to maintain, if not expand, its share of the Japanese market for Malaysian exports through preferential tariff treatment and technical collaboration to meet requirements on standards and technical regulations.
- Malaysia would also be able to enhance its position as an attractive destination for FDI, particularly in relation to competition from other investment seeking countries in the region.
- The cooperation and collaboration activities envisaged under the JMEPA would promote the growth of new sectors such as high-tech industries, including biotechnology, services, including manufacturing related services, and ICT and multimedia.
- For SMEs, economic and technical cooperation would facilitate quality enhancement, vendor development, and inclusion of Malaysian SMEs into the manufacturing supply chain of Japanese multinational companies.
- Malaysia's total trade with Japan has increased significantly from RM60.0 billion in 1994 to RM112.9 billion in 2005. Japan accounts

for 11.7 per cent of Malaysia's global trade in 2005 and was its second largest trading partner after ASEAN. Japan, with a GDP per capita of RM106,400, continues to be an important market for ASEAN and Malaysia.

The Malaysia-Pakistan FTA known as the Malaysia-Pakistan Closer Economic Partnership Agreement (MPCEPA) was concluded in January 2008, but the two countries were due to enter into another round of negotiations to fine-tune specific issues in 2009. MITI claims the following mutual benefits of this FTA:

- The agreement will further facilitate and strengthen the two-way trade and investment, as well as enhance bilateral economic and industrial cooperation on a long-term basis between Malaysia and Pakistan.
- The MPCEPA will also facilitate trade through closer collaboration and greater information exchange.
- The agreement provides an excellent opportunity to the business community of both countries to expand further their bilateral trade and investment linkages.
- The agreement will enable the Malaysian business community to use Pakistan as the springboard to expand their business with Pakistan's trading partners in the South Asia region also.
- Pakistan's business community can also leverage Malaysia's strong business links with ASEAN and the Far East to expand their economic interest in the region.

There were also various plurilateral FTAs to which Malaysia was a party. The major ones involved Malaysia as a member of ASEAN. The ongoing ASEAN FTAs proposals at the point of writing were the following: with India, Japan, European Union, Korea, China, and with Australia-New Zealand. The ASEAN-Japan negotiations appear to have gone some distance. Negotiations on ASEAN-Japan Comprehensive Economic Partnership Agreement (AJCEP), which commenced in April 2005, were concluded in December 2007. Accordingly, ASEAN member states and Japan undertook domestic clearance for the signing of AJCEP Agreement, which came into force in February 2009. The highly significant ASEAN-China FTA was still ongoing with several protocols already signed under a Framework Agreement which came into force on 1 July 2003. This is an umbrella agreement which gives a general provision on the establishment of an ASEAN-China Free Trade Area (ACFTA) within ten years by pursuing progressive elimination of tariffs and non-tariff barriers; progressive liberalization of trade in services and investment; strengthening trade facilitation measures; and economic cooperation in other areas of common interest. MITI argues that the ASEAN-China FTA will bring Malaysia the following benefits:

- The establishment of an FTA between ASEAN and China will create an economic region with 1.7 billion consumers, regional GDP of about US$2 trillion, and total trade estimated at US$1.23 trillion. It will be the biggest and largest FTA among developing countries.
- With a population of 1.2 billion, market access opportunities through preferential trade for Malaysian products will increase.
- The removal of trade barriers between ASEAN and China will lower costs, increase intraregional trade, and strengthen the attractiveness of Malaysia and the region as a preferred investment destination.

Along with its various bilateral and plurilateral FTAs, whether concluded or not, Malaysia has evidently worked along with its ASEAN members to move towards concluding the ASEAN Free Trade Area Agreement (AFTA) scheduled for 2015. The AFTA project has gone through considerable metamorphosis and is now anchored on the creation of an ASEAN Economic Community.[22] Economists have made the point that with the proliferation of FTAs in East Asia, ASEAN's own integration appears to be derailed. Economists generally still consider FTAs, whether bilateral or plurilateral, to be only a "second best" strategy of the neoliberal world order. The "noodle bowl" of FTAs may turn out to be counterproductive to such groupings as ASEAN, which may want to integrate regionally into a single market such as the European Union.[23] Malaysia's stance on ASEAN integration is perhaps fraught with such a dilemma. Should it move along with its Southeast Asian economic partners or go it alone and along with the countries with which it has apparent political affinity? Such hedging is clearly evidently in Malaysia's foreign economic relations in general. The example in trade policy was the July 2006 ratification of the Preferential Tariff Agreement (PTA) with eight Islamic countries, namely, Bangladesh, Indonesia, Iran, Malaysia, Egypt, Nigeria, Pakistan, and Turkey. As with FTAs, MITI argues that the implementation of D-8 PTA would enable Malaysian exporters to enjoy preferential tariff treatment for selected products in the market of the participating members, and enable exporters to gain competitive advantage over similar products originating from non-participating countries. It would seem that the major consideration for such a move was political-cultural rather than economic. This leads to our next section on Islamic finance.

ISLAMIC FINANCE, BANKING, AND CREATING A *HALAL* HUB

Malaysia's foray into Islamic banking began in the 1980s and appears to have experienced a healthy expansion. The Islamic banking sector expanded by 8 per cent to RM143.7 billion by the end of 2006, accounting for 12.1 per cent of total banking assets. It captured 12.8 per cent of the market share with concentrations in the household sector. Similarly Islamic insurance or the *"takaful"* industry has been growing, accounting for 8.1 per cent of total premiums. As of July 2007, there were eleven Islamic banks, comprising six Islamic subsidiaries and two domestic banks. Taking advantage of its Islamic credentials, the government in August 2006 launched the Malaysia International Islamic Financial Centre Initiative (MIFC). This is an initiative to provide a linkage between East Asia and West Asia and to reinforce Islamic finance internationally. In March 2007, Bank Negara Malaysia (Central Bank) signed MoUs with the Qatar Financial Centre Regulatory Authority and the Dubai Financial Services Authority. At about the same time, a conference on Islamic finance in Kuala Lumpur saw the participation of some 1,500 participants from fifty countries.

The recent economic move using its Islamic credentials has been to try to turn Malaysia into a *"halal* hub", that is, a trading hub for products and services sanctioned by Muslim religious authorities. Seen and respected as a modern, peaceful, and prosperous Islamic country, especially among OIC member countries, Malaysia has the added advantage of championing the *halal* cause. Malaysia's central position in Asia makes it an ideal trading platform to draw the world's *halal* players in facilitating the sourcing and selling of global quality *halal* products through the Malaysia International Halal Showcase (MIHAS).

This trade fair was pioneered in 2004 and congregates the largest annual gathering of *halal* industry players and entrepreneurs in the effort to ease the sourcing and selling of global quality *halal* consumables, products, and services. It embraces the *halal* concept in all its dimensions, from pharmaceuticals and herbal products, cosmetics and health care to Islamic investment, banking and *takaful* (Islamic insurance). As reported by MITI, the Malaysia International Halal Showcase 2007 (MIHAS 2007) was held from 9–13 May 2007 at the Kuala Lumpur Convention Centre. This event was hosted by the Ministry of International Trade and Industry (MITI) and organized by the Malaysian External Trade Development Corporation (MATRADE), with the cooperation of the Islamic Dakwah Foundation (YADIM) and the Ministry of Entrepreneur and Cooperative Department (MECD). Some 36,792 visitors from the public and trade buyers visited the event. A total of 426 companies, comprising

330 domestic and 96 international companies, participated in the exhibition. Visitors to the exhibition were mainly from Iran, Indonesia, Brunei, Singapore, and China. In conjunction with MIHAS 2007, MATRADE organized an Incoming Buying Mission (IBM) with the objective of:

- providing opportunities for Malaysian suppliers and exporters of *halal* products and services to develop business partnerships and networks with importers from all over the world;
- introducing international buyers to the Malaysia *halal* industry; and
- enabling Malaysian exporters to diversify into new and existing markets of their *halal* products.

Immediate sales generated from business matching were RM209.7 million.[24] To make good its effort to become a *halal* hub, the government established the Halal Industry Development Corporation (HDC) on 18 September 2006 to coordinate the overall development of the *halal* industry. HDC has been tasked to:

- lead the development of *halal* standards, audit and certification procedures in order to protect the integrity of *halal*;
- direct and coordinate the development of Malaysia's *halal* industry amongst all stakeholders — both public and private;
- manage capacity building for *halal* producers and related service providers;
- support investment in Malaysia's *halal* industry;
- facilitate the growth and participation of Malaysian companies in the global *halal* market;
- develop, promote, and market the Malaysian *halal* brand; and
- promote the concept of *halal* goods and services in Malaysia and global market.

Various training programmes and activities have been initiated by HDC, including the Halal Awareness Program, the Halal Industry Program, and the Halal Professional Program.[25]

CONCLUSION

From the perspective of political economy, it can be seen that Malaysia's economic stances and strategies have undergone dynamic developments which are not just due to the changing global environment, but because of its domestic and national political predilections. The transition from Mahathir to Abdullah certainly saw a shift way from counterhegemonic stances and approaches to one more consistent with the winds of globalization. This said, it could hardly be argued that Malaysia's overall policies of foreign investment and foreign involvement in its economy have greatly changed, given its primary status as a developmental state. Furthermore, foreign economic relations have often been geared to take advantage of Malaysia as a Muslim-majority state, as we have shown. This has allowed for balancing and hedging in economic relations seen by the decision making elite as a means to optimize benefits. To some extent, in political economy terms, the Mahathirian "Look East" policy has now shifted in the direction of a "Look Middle-East" policy which, however, has remained somewhat inchoate during the Abdullah tenure. Strategies of Islamic finance and banking predate Abdullah, but the initiation of a *halal* hub is one of his government's initiatives. However, in terms of actual investment quantities, the Middle Eastern countries seem to favour Singapore over Malaysia in the Southeast Asian region.[26]

This said, it should be stressed that Malaysia's primary and most important economic relationships in trade and investment are with the global economic powerhouses of the United States, the European Union, Japan, and increasingly, China. This has meant that in terms of political economy, both its postures and strategies towards these states remained stable. Malaysia's move to negotiate an FTA with the United States should be appreciated in these terms, and so too the conclusion of a comprehensive economic agreement with Japan. Over time China without doubt will feature more prominently in economic policies and actions as we have suggested in this and previous chapters.

NOTES

1. See Chapter 1 of the book (Gilpin 2001, pp. 3–24).
2. See Gilpin 2001, Chapter 7, pp. 148–95 for a full exposition.
3. By October 2008, the U.S. Treasury approved an injection of some US$700 billion in an unprecedented bailout of financial institutions. This sum does not take into account the partial "nationalisation" of some banks. Britain introduced a package of £500 billion to rescue its banks and financial institutions, while the European Union approved a figure of €2 trillion for failing financial institutions. Such hitherto uncharted governmental intervention in the financial order will no doubt change the character or, at least, many dimensions of Western capitalism. Already there are calls for a "Second Bretton Woods" meeting of world leaders.
4. The literature on the developmental state has become voluminous. For an excellent summary of the literature, again see Gilpin 2001, pp. 316–33.
5. See Saravanamuttu (1986, 1988) for an interpretation of how such an NIDL

affected Southeast Asia and for an empirical survey of Japanese penetration in the ASEAN states through a regional division of labour.

6. For an exposition of the "flying geese" concept and its major proponents, see Korhonen (1994) and also Bernard (1996), as well as the work of contemporary proponent Kojima (1977).

7. See Krugman (1997).

8. See Strange (1986, pp. 38–43) for why 1971 saw a vital "non-decision" made on the part of the United States. The 1971 Smithsonian Agreement of that year was supposed to have restored a fixed exchange rate, but instead a lack of U.S. commitment allowed for a "no-rules" financial regime to obtain in 1972.

9. For a summary of the main explanations, see Pang (2002) and Jomo (1998).

10. A quote from Giddens (2000).

11. See *Performance of the Manufacturing and Services Sector 2006*, MIDA, pp. 2–3.

12. See Lim and Ong (2007, pp. 84–85).

13. See *The Ninth Malaysia Plan*, 2006, pp. 14–15, and pp. 24–33. The plan also puts the accent on strengthening agriculture and agro-based industries. See Chapter 3, pp. 81–106.

14. See MIDA, ibid., p. 15. Figures are rounded. Figures are also drawn from the Economic Report 2007/2008.

15. In 2005, Malaysia's total trade increased by 9.9 per cent to reach RM967.82 billion, the second highest growth over the last five years. Malaysia's exports in 2005 expanded by 11 per cent to reach RM533.79 billion from RM480.74 billion in 2004, while imports grew 8.5 per cent to RM434.03 billion from RM400.08 billion in 2004. In 2006, Malaysia's external trade just exceeded RM1 trillion or US$270.27 billion. This was 10.5 per cent higher that the previous year. Exports were valued at RM588.949 billion while imports totalled RM480.493 billion (MITI data and *Bernama*, 2 August 2007).

16. The countries in the group were: Cuba, Dominican Republic, Egypt, Honduras, India, Indonesia, Jamaica, Kenya, Mauritius, Pakistan, Sri Lanka, Tanzania, Uganda, and Zimbabwe. See Tham (2008, pp. 175, 185).

17. Such a position was quite evident from my meeting with MITI officers on 27 December 2007 (interviews with Mohammad Sanusi Abdul Karim, director, Multilateral Trade Policy & Negotiations; and Syed Mohd Faizal Syed Mohd Dardin, principal assistant director, Multilateral Trade Policy & Negotiations, and Firdaos Rosli, assistant director, APEC).

18. The triggering effect was provided by Singapore's successful FTA with Japan in January 2002.

19. Unless otherwise stated, information on FTAs are obtained from Malaysia's MITI webpage, <http://www.miti.gov.my/ekpweb/> (accessed 16 May 2008).

20. See also my earlier discussion of the FTA with the United States in Chapter 9.

21. Interviews with Mohammad Sanusi Abdul Karim, director , Multilateral Trade Policy & Negotiations; and Syed Mohd Faizal Syed Mohd Dardin, principal assistant director, Multilateral Trade Policy & Negotiations, and Firdaos Rosli, assistant director, APEC.
22. For one account, see Severino (2006, pp. 212–55).
23. Cf. Hew (2007, pp. 212–14). Hew suggests that one approach to such proliferation of FTAs would be to "multilateralize" existing FTAs in ASEAN through agreement that ASEAN countries should only sign WTO-compliant FTAs.
24. For 2008 the theme would be "MIHAS Bridging the Global Halal Market" scheduled for 7–11 May 2008. From <http://www.miti.gov.my/ekpweb/> (accessed 16 May 2008).
25. The training on HAP commenced in November 2007. A total of five training sessions were conducted on 5–6 November 2007, 12 November 2007, 12–13 November 2007, 12 December 2007 and 17–18 December 2007. Up to December 2007, HDC had trained forty-nine participants. HDC will roll out HIP training in April 2008 and HPP in June 2008. See <www.hdcglobal.com> (accessed 16 May 2008).
26. This was admitted as much to me in an interview with a very senior Malaysian diplomat (interview with Tan Sri Fuzi Ahmad, 16 July 2007).

12

POSTSCRIPT
The Leadership Change 2009

THE CLOSING OF THE ABDULLAH ERA

After the Barisan Nasional's disastrous showing at the hustings in 2008, Mahathir and Tengku Razaleigh had persistently called for Abdullah Badawi to step down as president of UMNO. The Kelantan politician-prince immediately offered himself a candidate for the UMNO presidency in the UMNO polls. Abdullah managed to resist these calls until his own minister Muhyiddin Yassin also threw down the gauntlet in early May, stating that he was willing to contest one of the two top positions in the December UMNO polls.[1] UMNO provided a face-saving device for Abdullah when it postponed the polls till March 2009. Abdullah had indicated that he would not contest the presidency in March. Before the year ended, Najib Abdul Razak, Abdullah's deputy, had practically won the presidency with 134 nominations out of a possible 191, making him prime-minister-in-waiting. He would assume the UMNO presidency at the general assembly held from 24–28 March 2009 and, by the same act, assume the reins of government as Malaysia's sixth prime minister.

It may be Abdullah's unfortunate fate that history would judge him harshly as the leader who showed more promise than he had the capacity to fulfil. Abdullah who began self-assuredly in foreign policy by debunking some Mahathirist stances and policies, unfortunately ended with scandals, as shown in Chapter 9, and with the personally damaging loss of a piece of territory, Pulau Batu Puteh/Pedra Branca, to Singapore.[2] His own minister for law, Zaid Ibrahim, made a dramatic departure from government, citing Abdullah's failure to allow for legal reform. Zaid had objected to Abdullah's use of the Internal Security Act (ISA) against dissidents. In an open letter to the prime minister on 30 September 2009, Zaid wrote that events of the last three weeks compelled him to review his position within the government and that the way in which the ISA had been used led him to the conclusion that "the government had time and time again failed the people of this country in repeatedly reneging on that solemn promise made by the first prime minister Tunku Abdul Rahman". (*Malaysiakini*, 30 December 2008)

Najib Abdul Razak assumed the reins of government as the sixth prime minister of Malaysia on 3 April 2009. His first action was to free thirteen ISA detainees. The new premier went on to announce a new twenty-eight-member cabinet with seven new faces, while eight ministers were dropped. Predictably, his new deputy was Muhyiddin Yassin, who had won the UMNO (United Malays National Organization) deputy president race the previous month. Prominent among those dropped was Home Affairs Minister Syed Hamid Albar while Sharizat Abdul Jalil, the new women's chief of UMNO, was given the portfolio for Women, Family, and Community Development. The Foreign Ministry went to Sabahan Anifah Aman and the GERAKAN chief Koh Tsu Koon got the new portfolio of Management and Performance. The all-important finance ministry was retained by Najib with the second finance minister post going to newcomer Ahmad Husni Hanadziah. Controversially, the new UMNO Youth chief, Khairy Jamaluddin, received no post, and Azalina Othman, tourism minister under Abdullah, was dropped, suggesting that Najib was instituting a real changing of the guard. Moreover, the defeated UMNO youth chief candidate Mukhriz Mahathir got a deputy minister's job, implying the extension of an olive branch to Mukhriz's father, the severest of Abdullah's critics.

At the point of writing, the new prime minister has made no new substantive initiatives in foreign policy. The fact is that the premier was clearly preoccupied with domestic issues and concerns. As prime-minister-in-waiting, Najib had personally orchestrated a takeover of the Pakatan Rakyat-run Perak government in February 2009. This gave an inkling of the kind of leader the country was to get. The power grab was finessed by the crossovers of two PKR assemblymen and one DAP assembly woman to the BN. This stratagem did not seem to help a fracturing BN which then lost a string of seven by-elections, save for one in Sarawak up until October 2009. The BN finally stemmed the tide of by-election losses by a landslide victory in the state seat of Bagan Pinang on 11 October 2009, when former UMNO Negri Sembilan supremo, Mohd Isa Abdul Samad, roundly defeated his PAS opponent by a majority of 5,435 votes. This notwithstanding, the continued haemorrhaging of BN components parties with interminable leadership struggles in the MIC (Malaysian Indian Congress) and the MCA (Malaysian Chinese Association) put many issues of foreign policy on hold.

NEW FOREIGN MINISTER

The prime minister's appointment of the new foreign minister marked a major departure from tradition in that Anifah Aman is the first East Malaysian to hold that post. Anifah's choice could mainly be surmised as a domestic political move to accord more prestigious appointments to Sabah politicians, given the state's political weight after the 8 March general election outcome. In addition, opposition leader Anwar Ibrahim made it known that he was wooing Sabah and Sarawak politicians over to his camp in his earlier abortive attempt to finesse a parliamentary coup on 16 September 2008.[3] This no doubt influenced Najib's choice.

One the first acts of the foreign minister turned out to be controversial, if not embarrassing, for the government. During his visit to the United States, Anifah held a joint press conference with U.S. Secretary of State Hilary Clinton on 14 May 2009 and made unprepared, off-the-cuff remarks.[4] After the two spokespersons stated their views on the joint efforts of Malaysia and the United States to address various issues of common concern, such as piracy in the Gulf of Aden, Myanmar, the financial crisis, and North Korea, Anifah Aman elected to field a question from a journalist regarding the sodomy trial of Anwar Ibrahim. I reproduce a rendering of the episode below to illustrate how a foreign minister should always be circumspect in the manner he addresses a public audience so as to avoid the proverbial *faux pas* in its conduct of foreign policy.

The question posed by the journalist at the press conference was as follows:

Opposition figure Anwar Ibrahim faces charges again, and I believe a trial later this summer, on charges that the State Department itself in the annual human rights report said are politically motivated. Did you raise his case specifically in your meeting today? And Mr Minister would you care to comment on that and, specifically, with respect to the latter question whether the charges were politically motivated?

The foreign minister answered as follows (almost verbatim, but with my paraphrasing in portions):

I'd like to address the comment on Anwar Ibrahim. You know we have the utmost faith in our judicial system. A few days ago the court has declared that the chief minister of a particular state which comes from the opposition was legitimate and this was a ruling against the government. Insofar as Anwar Ibrahim is concerned — we know him very, very well. And what he has said, especially overseas, most of the things are untrue; for example, like the involvement of our honourable prime minister in the murder of a Mongolian citizen. And he has repeatedly said before the elections that he will provide evidence and yet, until today, he has not given anything. And also just for the information of the audience here, you know, he also said that he will form a government on 16 September and he has changed the dates many times. And he was trying to entice the members of parliament. And I was personally offered to jump into the opposition and offered a very lucrative position, and also told it's like a deputy prime minister. And these are not known to the world at large. And he has started, you know, trying to buy into other, you know, legislative members. And I think what he is doing — he has not accepted the result of the last elections. And we have lost five states and we willingly accept the people's verdict. And all the time we leave it to the people to decide, and which, Anwar Ibrahim has not been able to accept. And it's also my concern and that of our government that it is what he has been doing overseas to tarnish the image of Malaysia, which impinge on trade and indirectly, you know, bring hardship to the people of Malaysia, which he said he's very, very concerned about. And therefore, it is our wish and hope that he will respect the democratic system in Malaysia, which is very open and which, I think, conformed to the wishes of the people. And we have repeatedly told him that if he believes that he is the rightful prime minister, or his party has been sidetracked, then wait for the next election. And he has continuously given the wrong impression and accused all the government officials of being corrupted, which is part and parcel of the system for [inaudible]. And the people have rejected him in Malaysia, and this is proof that he has not been able to accept. [sic]

The rookie foreign minister clearly went beyond the call of duty and his inexperience in fielding a difficult question inadvertently turned out to be a major foreign relations gaffe. While damage control is always possible, mistakes such as these tend to devalue a state's standing in foreign relations. Anwar Ibrahim reacted swiftly by asking his lawyers to file a defamation suit against Anifah who replied defiantly that he would not apologize to Anwar (*The Star*, 17 May 2009).

NAJIB'S FIRST 100 DAYS

In this section we will survey the major events that have marked the new prime minster's foreign relations in his first 100 days as premier and draw some early conclusions about the direction of foreign policy of the Najib government. While making no substantive changes to foreign policy postures and orientations, the new premier undertook a remarkable number of initiatives and foreign policy actions in this short period of time. My narrative below is based on a region-sensitive and chronological categorization of these events.[5]

SOUTHEAST ASIAN RELATIONS

Relations with the immediate region began with a first overseas trip for the premier scheduled on 3 April 2009 to attend the reconvened 14th ASEAN Summit in Pattaya in Thailand. However, the summit was cancelled following massive anti-government protests in Pattaya. Instead of Thailand, the premier set his sights on Indonesia, which he visited from 22–23 April, an event upgraded from a working visit to an official visit. In his meeting with Indonesian President Susilo Bambang Yudhoyono, both leaders agreed to explore two new areas of cooperation, namely, in the defence and energy sectors. As we shall see in the further discussion below that Indonesian-Malaysian relations became rather strained towards the end of 2009 despite this early visit.

Towards the end of April, Najib held discussions with the Sultan of Brunei, Sultan Hassanal Bolkiah in Bandar Seri Begawan on various matters, including the land and maritime boundary between Malaysia and Brunei, where confidence was expressed that the two countries could finalize land and maritime border demarcations although no specific time frame was agreed.[6]

Najib's visit to neighbouring Singapore on 21–22 May came next. This was another step in further bolstering Malaysia-Singapore relations, initiated by his predecessor Abdullah Badawi. Singapore counterpart Lee Hsien Loong opined that legacy problems inherited over the last eighteen years could be resolved, to which Najib responded that the two countries did not have to wait for another eighteen years to solve them. He made particular reference to the Points of Agreement (POA) and the issue of the railway land owned by Malaysia in Singapore, suggesting that is was now time to unfreeze the moratorium on the subject. Najib's trip was reciprocated by a high-profile eight-day visit of the republic's Minister Mentor Lee Kuan Yew to Malaysia in June.[7]

An important breakthrough occurred in 2010 in Malaysia-Singapore relations alluded to above. On 24 May, the Malaysian Premier announced with his Singapore counterpart, Lee Hsien Loong that the impasse over the POA had been resolved. The two governments agreed to the following:

- Relocation on July 2011 to Woodlands of the 78-year-old Tanjong Pagar railway station operated by Keretapi Tanah Melayu Berhad (KTMB).
- The three parcels of land in Tanjong Pagar, Kranji and Woodlands, along with another three pieces of land in Bukit Timah, will be jointly developed and swapped on the basis of equivalent value for pieces of land in two prime Singapore areas.

- A company, known as MS Pte Ltd, will be established no later than 31 December 2010 to jointly develop the parcels of land. Malaysia is to hold a 60 per cent stake in this company under Khazanah Nasional Berhad, while Singapore will have a 40 per cent share held by Temasek Holdings.
- There will be a rapid transit system linking Johor Baru to Singapore by 2018.

On 8 June 2009, Thai Prime Minister Abhisit Vejjajiva visited Malaysia, discussing various issues, related to trade, investments, and the conflict in southern Thailand, with his Malaysian counterpart. The two premiers agreed to visit religious schools in the troubled south of Thailand jointly and were also able to discuss the problem of dual citizenship (*The Star*, 8 June 2009).

RELATIONS WITH EAST ASIA

New Prime Minister Najib initiated a major foreign relations event with a visit to China on 3 June 2009 to celebrate the 35th Anniversary of the establishment of diplomatic relations. Breaking with tradition, Chinese Premier Wen Jiabao took to the public address system after he had presented Najib with a copy of a black and white photograph of second Malaysian Prime Minister Tun Abdul Razak Hussein signing a joint communiqué with the late Chinese Premier Zhou Enlai in establishing diplomatic relations between Malaysia and China in 1974. The Chinese convention was normally to have no speeches after the signing of MoUs. China allowed this in appreciation of Tun Abdul Razak for establishing diplomatic relations with China and subsequently strengthening them, said Malaysian officials accompanying the prime minister's entourage. In response, Najib said he would "dig more wells" to ensure that "the flow of water would be forever bountiful that we can both share for the mutual benefit of both countries".[8]

Just prior to the China visit, on 1–2 June 2009, Najib led a Malaysian delegation to Jeju Island in South Korea, where he, along with other leaders, signed the Joint Statement of the ASEAN-ROK Commemorative Summit. On North Korea's nuclear weapons programme, Najib expressed Malaysia's stand that the region should be free from nuclear weapons, winning appreciation from that remark from South Korea's President Lee Myung-bak.

RELATIONS WITH THE UNITED STATES

On 26 June, there was a much publicized telephone conversation that Najib had with President Barack Obama. As disclosed officially, the two leaders discussed bilateral and international issues of mutual concern, including three major issues, namely, North Korea, Afghanistan, and Iran. The U.S. leader sought Malaysia's help in ensuring a nuclear-free Korean peninsula. Najib agreed to Obama's suggestion on the possibility of Malaysia taking part in the reconstruction process in Afghanistan. Obama also asked Malaysia to play a role in helping to open up dialogue and engagement on a wider scale between Washington and Iran as Kuala Lumpur and Teheran were on good terms.

FOREIGN RELATIONS ISSUES IN 2009

As the year drew to a close, a number of new issues, coupled with some major foreign engagements, took place under Najib's watch. The first important development related to Indonesia-Malaysian relations which perceptibly soured over cultural and territorial claims. We have already discussed the issue of the mutual claims of both states on Ambalat in the Celebes Sea in Chapter 10. In 2009, the issue that surfaced was that Malaysia had plagiarized or stolen Indonesian cultural property and art forms such as songs and dances. Songs such as *Rasa Sayang* (regularly sung by Malaysians at social gatherings) and *Terang Bulan* (whose tune was chosen for Malaysian's national anthem, *Negara-Ku*) were claimed to be Indonesian in origin. The Indonesians were particularly piqued when the *Discovery TV* channel aired a programme which alluded that the *Pendet* dance was Malaysian, when, in fact, this originated from Bali. Various protests, including the burning of Malaysian flags, were staged in parts of Indonesia, and in one instance, the Malaysian Embassy in Jakarta was the scene of a boisterous demonstration. In early September and October, a self-proclaimed group, Benteng Demokrasi Rakyat (Bendera) or People's Defence of Democracy vowed to avenge Malaysia for wrongs committed by setting up illegal roadblocks in parts of Jakarta with the intention to "sweep our streets clear of Malaysians". The group also planned an "invasion" of Malaysian on 8 October. Speaking to reporters in Jakarta, its coordinator Mustar Nona Ventura said that around 1,300 volunteers, including fifty medical personnel, would be departing for Malaysia between 8 and 22 October (*The Star*, 8 October 2009). While Putrajaya issued a statement to say Malaysia was alerted to the event, clearly in the eyes of the Malaysian public, or the Indonesians for that matter, this was more of a stunt than a serious threat.

However, the strained relations were sufficient to force Malaysia to apologize for the *Pendet* mistake and for Indonesian President Bambang Susilo Yudhoyono to drop by formally in Kuala Lumpur on 11–12 November 2009 for talks with Najib before attending the APEC Summit in Singapore. The MFA issued the following statement on the president's visit:

The leaders of both countries are expected to discuss issues of mutual interest including maritime boundaries and Indonesian migrant workers in Malaysia, with the aim to further enhance and strengthen bilateral cooperation and friendship between Malaysia and the Republic of Indonesia. In addition, the visit will enable the leaders to exchange views on regional and international issues of mutual concern and explore opportunities for cooperation through a number of initiatives, such as on food and energy security, and cooperation in counter-terrorism. The visit will also forge closer rapport and understanding between both countries, building upon the strong personal ties between the leaders of both countries, <http://www.kln.gov.my/?m_id=15&hid=1122> (accessed 18 November 2009).

After a closed-door meeting, Yudhoyono and Najib stressed that both countries share common historical and cultural roots, and both leaders pledged to resolve prickly issues swiftly and amicably. Najib gave the assurance that the rights of foreign workers would be protected:

> We appreciate their presence here. We will continue to protect their interest. If there is any transgression of the law, they will be dealt with accordingly. That includes Malaysians who flout the law (and) abuse maids. They will face whatever consequences as per the law in Malaysia, <http://www.channelnewsasia.com/stories/southeastasia/view/1017786/1/.html> (accessed 18 November 2009).

Apart from mending relations with Indonesia, Malaysia also hosted a formal state visit of Chinese President Ho Jintao on 10–11 November, where several agreements on economic projects were made.[9] Ho was en route to the APEC Summit in Singapore on 14–15 November 2009. Malaysia also participated in the APEC meetings under the leadership of its new prime minister, who had his first opportunity to meet with twenty-one heads of states of the APEC economies. Significantly, President Obama of the United States took the opportunity to have a special session with ASEAN members where he raised, among other things, the thorny issue of Myanmar's road to democratization. Together with State Secretary Hilary Clinton, the new Obama Administration had early in the day indicated that America was "back in Asia" and ready for serious engagement with respect to difficult political questions. Along with the other ASEAN states, Malaysia has welcomed this new approach to foreign policy of the United States.

CONCLUSION

In his less than year since the assumption of Najib Razak as prime minister, Malaysian foreign relations has traversed through and engaged in a plethora of issues and events which we have adumbrated above. It has been a seemingly hectic time for a new foreign minister and a new prime minister, who have had to handle foreign visits, acrimonious relations with neighbours, an unstable ASEAN situation, and many changes of leadership in the global environment, not least of all, that in the United States.

This notwithstanding, it is perhaps a testimony to the stable state of Malaysia's foreign policy that no new substantive initiatives, orientations, or policy strategies have been wanting. Malaysia's adherence to its previous tenets and stable practices of foreign relations has been adequate to act as guidelines and signposts for its new leadership.

NOTES

1. See *The Star*, <http://thestar.com.my/news/story.asp?file=/2008/5/11/nation/ 21218890&sec=nation> (accessed 30 December 2008).
2. However, one should note that the agreement to have the Pulau Batu Puteh/Pedra Branca dispute adjudicated by the ICJ was already decided during the Mahathir period.
3. 16 September was the date Sabah and Sarawak joined Malaysia in 1963. The opposition alliance of Pakatan Rakyat needed thirty-one crossovers of parliamentarians which Anwar claimed he had achieved. His stratagem got the government sufficiently exercised to organize a tour for fifty government MPs to Taiwan from 7–19 September. See Saravanamuttu (2009, pp. 180–81).
4. My rendering of this event is based on the viewing of a video recording of the joint press conference of 14 May found at <http://beyond51.blogspot. com/2009/05/blog-post.html> (accessed 17 November 2009).
5. I draw on *Bernama* reports of June and July 2009.
6. It was announced on 3 May 2010 that a disputed oil rich area would be jointly developed by Malaysia and Brunei based on an agreement reached in 2009 under the Abdullah government. Wisma Putra stated that the areas known as Block L and Block M are now recognised by Malaysia to be within Brunei's maritime boundaries under the agreement or exchange of letters signed by then Prime Minister Tun Abdullah Ahmad Badawi and Sultan Haji Hassanal Bolkiah Mu'izzaddin Waddaulah on 16 March 2009. See Wisma Putra statement, <http://www.kln.gov.my/web/guest/pr2010/-/asset_publisher/X9Nx/content/ press-release-:-the-exchange-of-letters-between-yab-dato'-seri-abdullah-haji- ahmad-badawi-prime-minister-of-malaysia-and-his-majesty-sultan-haji-hassanal- bolkiah-mu'izzaddin-waddaulah-english-version only;jsessionid=C34680A6B21 BBE59FC12852AF0350EE8?redirect=%2Fweb%2Fguest%2Fpr2010> (accessed 5 May 2010).
7. The LKY visit was particularly significant given that acrimonious relations during the Mahathir period had seen a hiatus of some ten years in LKY's physical presence in Malaysia. Not to be outdone, Mahathir criticized the visit as that

of a sojourn of a "little emperor" from the "new Middle Kingdom", <http://seelanpalay.blogspot.com/2009/06/mahathir-critisizes-lee-kuan-yews-visit.html> (accessed 18 November 2009).

8. The China visit did see an economic dividend when later in November, it was reported that China was awarded the contract of RM7.5 billion for the construction of the double-tracking railway line of 197 km from Gemas to Johor Baru. There were also agreements signed in November on higher education and another between the Malaysian government and the Beijing Enterprises Water Group to improve the country's sewerage services, <http://www.malaysianmirror.com/homedetail/45-home/18682 9> (accessed 12 November 2009).

9. As stated above.

13

CONCLUSION
Middlepowermanship in Foreign Policy

This book has tried to show how the construction of Malayan and then Malaysian foreign policy throughout its first fifty years and a little beyond has not been just a function of exogenous factors predetermined by a fixed world order. It has shown implicitly, or even explicitly, that foreign policy is attuned to the national needs and interests of Malaysia as defined by the political leadership acting within particular social and cultural contexts whether nationally, regionally, or even globally. This notwithstanding, because of the changing character of the domestic and international environments, the constant flux of ideas, norms, and ideals over the past five decades, Malaysian foreign policy has no doubt been altered or modified along with the global *zeitgeist*. This chapter will further examine Malaysia's relations with respect to particular issues, and with respect to different global and regional contexts and constituencies. Four broad themes of foreign policy practice appear evident over a fifty-year time span, namely postures and policies centred around neutralism or non-alignment from the 1970s onwards; regionalism which emerged in the late 1960s and which intensified in the post-Cold War period; globalization which has impacted on foreign policy and the political economy since the 1980s; and finally, Islam which, while dominant as a subtext even at the time of the Tunku, has emerged as a primary driver of foreign policy from the 1990s onward. These themes translate most significantly into specific foreign policy postures, strategies, and actions, increasingly defined as those of an aspiring middle power. Such policies were crafted *vis-à-vis* East-West relations, important regional actors in Southeast and beyond Southeast Asia, most prominently, in the post-Cold War period, towards East Asia, the Middle East, and the Islamic world generally.

While a constructivist perspective on the subject would certainly sensitize the analyst about the reflexive character of foreign policy in differing contexts, a critical interpretation of foreign policy requires going beyond mere explanation. In particular, with respect to a country such as Malaysia, it would be important to know how foreign policy has served the public interest both in the national or even the global sense. Indeed, it is imperative to have such as analysis given that Malaysia has been thought to have had ambitions, aspirations, and statecraft marked by a deliberate "middlepowermanship". The notion of middle power statecraft[1] lends itself particularly well to a constructivist interpretation of foreign policy as it derives from the postures, strategies, and actions of medium and small states which have tried to "construct" foreign policy to balance, hedge, and countervail the foreign policies of major powers. These foreign policy strategies are also "constructive" in the double sense that they also attempt to ameliorate and mediate the deleterious effects and impact of big power contestations. Middle power statecraft may even be seen to come within the same discursive terrain as the now burgeoning literature on "soft power" which conceives of how hegemonic states such as the United States could be better served by deploying persuasion and "attraction" rather than hard power in foreign policy.[2] The ambitions, aspirations, and stances of being a middle power may be said to have emerged during the tenure of Abdul Razak and had become increasingly prominent during the era of Mahathir.[3] Drawing from the literature, middlepowermanship may be said to involve the following elements in foreign policy conduct:

- the aspirations of a state to increase its own influence in the regional and global environment in the pursuance of interests beyond narrowly defined goals.
- attempts to change the regional and global environment in accordance with certain self-consciously enunciated goals beyond those of mere state survival, that is, beyond the short-range core values of state survival.
- carrying out the above in the face of competition, countervailing pressures, or even conflict with other states, lesser powers, and major powers.
- carrying out any of the above by providing leadership to other states in the pursuance of their own foreign policy objectives.
- a propensity to use international organizations and institutions to pursue the above goals.[4]

It would not be difficult to draw out some of these criteria of middle power statecraft in Malaysian foreign policy, especially in the Mahathir years, as has been done by some authors. For example, Nossal and Stubbs

(1997) posited that foreign policy under Mahathir illustrated the following interrelated characteristics of middlepowermanship: the extended scope of diplomatic interests beyond national boundaries; an activist style seeking to address a range of international concerns; a focus on conflict resolution and conflict reduction *qua* statecraft; and a preference for "forms" and for "forums" which were multilateral rather than bilateral in their approach to statecraft.[5] Drawing on the work of Nossal and Stubbs, and others, Izzuddin has attempted to use the same criteria to evaluate the foreign policy of Abdullah Badawi.[6] It would not be difficult to cite such examples of middlepowermanship particularly evident in the Mahathir era and apparently sustained as well in the Abdullah period.[7] For example, the Langkawi International Dialogue initiated in 1995, when held in August 2007, attracted some 500 participants from forty countries, including ten heads of states and governments. Nossal and Stubbs give the example of the second-track annual Kuala Lumpur Roundtable, first held in 1987 under the auspices of the Malaysian think tank, the Institute for Strategic and International Studies. This event brings together government officials, think tank representatives, and academics in the Asia Pacific region for informal discussions on important issues of the day.

I would add a further point that the behavioural construct of middlepowermanship subsumes some vague notion of military capability although it differs from the more strategically based construct of "middle power", which tends to assume a moderately high level of military capability and hardware. Putative middle powers would also be resource-rich countries such as Australia and Canada while middlepowermanship could even be associated more with much smaller states such as Sweden or Norway. In the case of Malaysia, its military capability has been built up considerably with the modernization of hardware and an impressive beefing up of the strength of its armed forces over the years, but this still compares poorly with neighbouring Singapore, with an admittedly more thorough military agenda.[8] More probing questions relate to whether Malaysian foreign policy strategies as an aspirant middle power were specifically crafted to counter the global status quo and hegemonic global politics and how effective they actually were. It is often also assumed that good international citizenship connotes accountability to the citizenry and society. Beyond its more prominent international concerns, could one say that Malaysian foreign policy was anchored on sound societal norms, needs, and interests? Did it serve the public purpose? Ultimately, could Malaysian foreign policy be said to serve "democratic" ends? We will attempt at the close of this chapter to examine some of these questions from a critical-constructive theoretical perspective.

BALANCING AND HEDGING WESTERN DOMINANCE

Clearly middlepowermanship was not particularly evident in the early years of independence. It was inevitable that the Cold War would plunge the newly independent Malayan state into a dilemma of choices as explained in Chapter 2. The Tunku, despite opposition, was able to put across this case for the Anglo-Malayan Defence Agreement (AMDA) which guaranteed that Malaya's core defence needs were underwritten by the British. AMDA sparked a storm of protest as we have analysed in Chapter 2 and it was not until the Tunku put his leadership of the party on the line that the protests receded. Malaysian opposition parties such as the Labour Party, Parti Rakyat, and the People's Progressive Party, objected to various provisions of AMDA, such as Article 3, which specified Malaya's obligations to Britain. The fear was also that AMDA indirectly tied Malaya to the U.S.-sponsored Southeast Asian Treaty Organization (SEATO). Explaining the Tunku's dilemmas, *The Straits Times* suggested that the Tunku must have allayed the uneasiness over the treaty by disassociating it with SEATO, citing Article 8 of AMDA which required Britain to obtain prior agreement of Malaya before involving the use of its bases for operations (Khaw 1976, p. 84). The AMDA and SEATO controversies show clearly that foreign policy is not divorced from public opinion. Despite the leadership's steering of foreign policy in a pro-Western direction, it could not do this with impunity. Perhaps, the government's other stance of being staunchly anti-Communist was more easily maintained, given the presence of the communist insurgency in Malaya, but even here the issue of Malaya's support of South Vietnam during the Vietnam War tainted its image in the eyes of non-aligned and Afro-Asian countries.

Engaging on one side of the Cold War also meant that relations with the People's Republic of China remained problematic. Rather early in the day, Malaya had chosen not to recognize the PRC although China had "recognized" the newly independent state, but did not see it as full independence because of continued links with Britain.[9] As we have mentioned in Chapter 2, the Tunku condemned China's "occupation" of Tibet and started a "Save Democracy Fund" during the 1962 Sino-Indian clashes. At the United Nations, Malaysia's Tun Ismail took a hard line against China's admission, continuing its support for Taiwan (Nationalist China's) seat at the world body. Relations with China took a further downturn with *Konfrontasi* in the mid-1960s. According to some analysts, the Malaysian leadership saw *Konfrontasi* as something linked and inspired by Peking.[10] As we know, Tun Ismail's "Peace Plan" for Southeast Asia proposed in 1968 signalled the switch towards a more positive view of China. In this plan, Ismail proposed that the major powers, including China, should guarantee Southeast Asia's neutrality. Storey (forthcoming) points out that the announcement of Britain's "east of Suez" policy in 1967, which meant a scaling down of British military presence in Singapore and Malaya, provided the impetus for a warming up of relations with China.

Malaya's early relations with the United States may have been partially stymied by the SEATO membership factor. Pamela Sodhy suggests that the Americans may have wanted to wean Malaya away from the British, but the newly independent country's preference for AMDA over SEATO probably meant that the United States had to be content to let Britain bear the onus of looking after Malaya, especially when the U.S. involvement in Vietnam was becoming increasingly significant (Sodhy 1991, p. 188). In the event, Malaya and the United States signed an investment guarantee agreement in 1959 under he aegis of the U.S. Mutual Security Act of 1954, which put the accent more on economic, rather than political relations. Tun Ismail in his memoir reveals how he tried to court then American Secretary of State John Foster Dulles for a big loan of RM$455 million, but the United States demurred.[11] In the end, the investment agreement seemed to have been the outcome aimed at, spurring American investments with the guarantee that capital flows would be convertible in U.S. dollars. As Sodhy (1991, p. 217) notes, while both the Eisenhower and Kennedy administrations succeeded in making economic inroads into Malaya in the early years in its overall effort to "inoculate" Third World countries against communism, its military aid programme was not very successful with only the conclusion of a limited arms sales. The direct involvement of the United States in Malaysia only came in the *Konfrontasi* years.

We have already mentioned in Chapter 2 that Malaya fully supported the U.S. policy in Vietnam. Because of the ANZUS pact, when Australia and New Zealand were drawn into the defence of Malaysia during *Konfrontasi*, the United States was in theory also obliged to defend Malaya. Furthermore, there was SEATO, which involved not just Australia and New Zealand, but also Britain. While there was no direct military involvement of the Americans, there were many meetings and mission over the issue under the Kennedy and Johnson administrations.[12] The Tunku was then invited to Washington D.C. in July 1964 as U.S. support for Malaysia changed from "reserved sympathy" to active support (Sodhy 1991, p. 256). In the event, the Tunku announced jubilantly in Washington that the United States had agreed to all his requests for military aid, including credit sales at 5 per cent for equipment and military training.[13] At the United Nations in September 1964, U.S. Ambassador Adlai Stevenson called on the Security Council to call for the cessation of armed attacks on Malaysia and for negotiations for ending the dispute. In the event the Security Council motion condemning Indonesia was voted down by Czechoslovakia and vetoed by the Soviet Union (Sodhy, pp. 259–60).

To the chagrin of the Malaysian leadership, Malaysia-U.S. relations during *Konfrontasi* were not without domestic tensions. In Kuala Lumpur in late 1964, anti-U.S. riots broke out, sponsored by the Afro-Asian Solidarity Committee, and the U.S. Information Service library was damaged. After the end of *Konfrontasi* in March 1966, Assistant Secretary of State for East Asian and Pacific Affairs Willian Bundy's visit to Kuala Lumpur was met with some 200 demonstrators condemning "U.S. imperialism". As noted by Sodhy, oppositional groups in Malaysia were perturbed that from 1961 to 1966, Malaysia had helped train some 3,000 Vietnamese officers in anti-guerilla operations, and furthermore, that the Tunku had permited American servicemen to enter Malaysia for "rest and recreation" (Sodhy 1991, p. 264). A further round of anti-U.S. protests and riots broke out when President Johnson visited Malaysia at the end of October 1966.

It is clear that Malaysia's foreign relations during the early Cold War years were choppy under the Tunku. The leadership's furbishing of foreign policy by engaging with predominantly one camp of the Cold War was no doubt driven by historical and internal factors as well as external developments. We have tried to show this in greater detail in Chapter 2. Here, we have demonstrated further that relations with the major Western powers that were Malayan and Malaysian allies (Britain and the United States), and with China (not even diplomatically engaged as yet) entailed a fair degree of foreign policy manipulation. The Tunku and his colleagues were able to maintain strong ties with the West despite a healthy dose of domestic objections which came not only from oppositional forces, but also from within the ruling Malay party UMNO. Some analysts have argued that this shows the strong hand of the leader, but from a constructivist perspective, it could well be argued that even so, the Tunku's latitude for action was limited as can be shown by the non-membership of SEATO. At the end of the day, foreign policy remained anchored to domestic sensibilities. Furthermore, political and societal discomfort with pro-U.S. and pro-Western positions clearly made its mark when towards the end of the 1960s, leaders such as Tun Ismail (the first foreign minister, no less) began to proffer policies which were putatively non-aligned and neutral. Foreign policy norms were also noticeably changed despite Malaysia's successful campaign against *Konfrontasi*. As we have shown in Chapter 3, the easy transition to neutralism was a natural progression for Malaysian foreign policy in the post-*Konfrontasi* years. It is perhaps instructive that in spite of governmental unease over anti-U.S. riots and protests, these actions may have spurred the move to neutralism.

In the Mahathir years, it was to be expected that relations with the West and particularly with the United States would become fractious, given Mahathir's much vaunted and assertive foreign policy postures. This notwithstanding, as noted by Nossal and Stubbs, middlepowermanship as we have defined it above, became a defining trope of the Mahathir period. Postures, strategies, and actions of counterdominance and counterhegemony naturally meant engaging the West, if in a less than cordial fashion, to modify policies and actions constructively, nonetheless. As Pamela Sodhy, a scholar of U.S.-Malaysia relations, has noted correctly, "cooperation outweighs tension" in the overall relationship (Sodhy 1991, p. 517). Mahathir's length of tenure spanned the administrations of four U.S. presidents (one partially) namely, Reagan, George H. Bush, Clinton, and George W. Bush. We already noted that the Mahathir government went along with the United States and the United Nations in the Gulf War of 1991 and rode through the rough times of the Asian financial crisis which saw the removal of Anwar Ibrahim as his deputy. This was arguably the period of highest tension of relations with the United States, but by the time of George W. Bush's administration, Mahathir had made overtures to it and post-9/11 concerns were the order of the day. Another high point came towards the end of the Mahathir tenure in 2003 in the military campaign of the U.S., British and other Western forces in Iraq to oust Sadam Hussein. Mahathir's speeches at the NAM and OIC conferences that year in Kuala Lumpur were unequivocal in the condemnation of the U.S. and British actions. The Mahathir government had consistently argued against U.S. unilateralism or domination ever since the senior Bush's administration's announcement of its plan to create a "New World Order", while sidelining the U.N. Security Council, which Malaysia believed should be reformed to include Third World states and Japan as permanent members.

Mahathir's other contentious quarrels relate to Western policies *vis-à-vis* Bosnia and Mahathir's alleged anti-semitic pronouncements from time to time. Perhaps, arguing on the side of moral righteousness, Mahathir was able to expose the European double standard in dealing with the Bosnia imbroglio and was much admired in many parts of the Third World for such a stance. However, he was on shaky ground when he made his remark on Jewish domination of the world. His 16 October 2003 speech at the Tenth Islamic Summit Conference at Putrajaya focused on the weakness of the *ummah*, but also blamed this on the domination by the Europeans and the Jews.[14] Needless to say, after the transition to Abdullah Badawi, relations with the West settled to a much more even keel as we have noted in Chapter 8. Even so, the political continuity of substantive policies ensured that some irritations in relations remained. This was the case, for example, in the SCOPE affair which we also touched on in Chapter 9.

Much of foreign policy construction and political posturing around the broad policy of neutralism *vis-à-vis* the West in the post-Tunku years were clearly aimed consciously at developing a stronger role for Malaysia in foreign relations. This began in the Abdul Razak period, and particularly during the Mahathir tenure, such a role was consciously cultivated as we have shown. Nesadurai (2004) has argued cogently that even during the fractious period of relations with the United States in the Mahathir years, the relationship had been one of "rejecting dominance, embracing engagement". It may be said that this sort of foreign policy hedging characterizes overall Malaysian foreign relations with the hegemonic Western world. However, it should not be forgotten that middle-range and medium power goals were also dovetailed with the establishment and evolution of ASEAN, which became a pivotal construct for the conduct of Malaysian foreign policy. Let me now turn to this aspect of Malaysian foreign policy.

REGIONAL COUNTERPOISING THROUGH ASEAN

It became rather logical that the post-*Konfrontasi* years would bring about a new political development in Southeast Asia by way of renewed regional cooperation. Malaysian middlepowermanship may be said to have emerged in this period which saw a shift of statecraft from the national to the regional as ASEAN increasingly became the conduit for collective statecraft and policy orientations of engaging the major hegemonic powers, and the instrument for bringing about a new regional political order. There are now many narratives of the ASEAN formation, but central to their story must be that the *raison d'etre* of the regional body lay in the imperative to maintain peace and stability in Southeast Asia. Admittedly ASEAN was born at a point of time when the Indo-China states were still embroiled in a war, but its founding members were forward-looking enough to include in the Bangkok Declaration of 1967 a provision that it was "open for the participation of all states in the Southeast Asian region" subscribing to its aims, principles and purposes.

From the Malaysian perspective, ASEAN's birth served the immediate purpose of putting the seal on the rapprochement with Indonesia and the Philippines, while at the same time, formalizing the growing entente among the five non-communist countries of the region. However, towards the end of 1968, Malaysia-Philippines relations were again temporarily strained over the Sabah issue. In March 1968, the "Corrigidor affair" exposed that a special force of Muslim recruits of the Philippines were supposedly being trained to infiltrate Sabah. Furthermore, a bill passed by the Philippines House of Representatives declared Sabah to be a part of Philippine territory. Malaysia responded by packing off the Philippines diplomatic staff in Kuala Lumpur, but mediation efforts by Thanat Khoman led to a moratorium on the Sabah issue after Malaysia's otherwise disastrous May 1969 general election. By the end of 1969, at the Third Foreign Ministers' meeting held in the cool atmosphere of Malaysia's Cameron Highlands, diplomatic relations were resumed between the two bickering countries and the ASEAN ministers went on to approve all the ninety-eight recommendations put before them, covering projects for cooperation in commerce and industry, tourism, shipping, civil aviation, air services, meteorology, transportation, and communications.[15]

ASEAN provided a renewed credibility to Malaysia's credentials as a Third World developing state. Indonesian Confrontation had been psychologically damaging although it hurt Indonesia more comprehensively. At its height, Malaysia carried out a number of diplomatic missions abroad to bolster its image with countries in Afro-Asia. Although it succeeded in securing a Security Council non-permanent seat in 1964, this proved to be something of a hollow victory and even created more problems for regional relations after Indonesia announced its withdrawal from the United Nations in protest to Malaysia's election. By the middle of 1965, Malaysia had by dint of diplomatic "truth missions" garnered enough support for membership to the Nonaligned Movement (NAM) Conference to be held in Algiers. In the event, the conference was postponed and the birth of ASEAN served instead to reinstate its Third World credibility along with rapprochement with Indonesia and the Philippines. The moratorium on the Sabah issue was in some part due to the fact that ASEAN was already established and Thai good offices could capitalize on a forthcoming meeting of ASEAN in Malaysia.

In short, ASEAN, even in this first period, had become an important instrumentality for Malaysian foreign policy objectives and actions although the organization had by no means assumed any centrality in most aspects of foreign policy as yet. Towards the 1960s, Malaysian foreign policy discourse and practice had tilted definitively towards non-alignment after a long period of close association with the West under the Tunku's leadership. ASEAN's formation provided a smooth transition to this discourse and Malaysia's acceptance as a Third World, non-aligned country. Indeed, it could well be said that after a while, it was Malaysia and Indonesia, more than the other three ASEAN countries, who were known to steer ASEAN further afield from the ambit of major power spheres of influence.

Malaysia was able through the vehicle of ASEAN diplomacy to maintain a balancing act in its relations with the Indo-China states which remained in a state of conflict at the point of time of ASEAN's formation. We have already alluded to the chaos caused by the boat refugees after the end of the Vietnam War and Malaysia's pivotal role in repatriating some 80,000 persons to third countries. Through ASEAN, the Geneva Conference of 1979 was called to deal with the practical aspects of the Vietnamese refugees. Then came the Cambodian crisis and here again Malaysia played a pivotal role in setting up the Coalition Government of Democratic Kampuchea (CGDK). While the formation of the CGKD irked the Vietnamese and its client, the Heng Samrin regime, ASEAN diplomacy kept in check the various political players in the Cambodian conflict by securing the U.N. seat for the CGDK for the most part of the 1980s. This arguably put all the political players of the Cambodian conflict in contention until the peace process took root in the early 1990s. Here again ASEAN played a crucial role in sponsoring the Jakarta informal meetings which we have discussed in Chapter 6. Throughout this period, Malaysia's stances and policies *vis-à-vis* the Indo-China issue followed the tempo and thrust of ASEAN diplomacy. It was clear that ASEAN had become central to Malaysian foreign policy for its regional and global relations, even under the feisty tenure of Mahathir.

The Abdullah government had also followed through the motions of its predecessors in placing ASEAN at the centre of regional politics and foreign relations as we have argued in Chapter 8. The ASEAN push for the construction of three forms of "communities" — security, economic, and socio-cultural — has also been wholeheartedly taken on board by the Malaysian Government along with the ASEAN Charter signed in November 2007 at the 13th ASEAN in Singapore. It is important to see ASEAN as a crucial instrumentality of Malaysia's attempts to use a countervailing and counterpoising foreign policy to handle new issues that have surfaced regionally and globally. Not least of all was the question of Myanmar or Burma, which continued to be the bugbear of the ASEAN states well into the late 2000s.

NEGOTIATING THE EAST ASIAN WAVE

An early phase of Malaysia's middlepowermanship came with policies towards China. The Tunku's strong antipathy towards communism predisposed him against taking any positive steps towards the People's Republic of China. Ironically though, when the Tunku showed some flexibility on the China question, Foreign Minister Tun Ismail initially took umbrage.[16] However, it has been shown convincingly that the Tunku was partial towards Japan despite its occupation of Malaya during the Second World War. In his book on Malaysian diplomacy, Jeshurun (2007) illustrates that the Tunku may have been an early initiator of Malaysia's "Look East" policy rather than Mahathir.[17] It is also no secret that the Malayawata steel plant in Penang and the donation of two frigates by Japan assuaged the Tunku of Japanese indiscretions and atrocities during the Japanese Occupation. Malaya, however, remained cold towards "Communist" China. It was left to Tun Ismail to set the pace belatedly for an eventual Chinese diplomatic recognition, and Tunku's successor Tun Razak to seal it in 1974. Being the first Southeast Asian state to recognize China was an act of middlepowermanship in the sense used in this book, whether it was intended that way or not. Not only was Malaysia ahead of the curve in the region, it was also able to derive much political mileage from the action. The China recognition gave much more credence to its proposal for ZOPFAN and paved the way for a generalized rapprochement with communist states in Asia. It is interesting to note that improved relations with Vietnam and the Indonesian states only came after the Beijing rapprochement.

Without doubt, Mahathir's "Look East" policy first propounded in 1981 and his notion of East Asian regionalism were clearly an attempt to ride the first economic wave that came with the so-called Japanese "miracle" and then the phenomenon of the "little dragons". Wary that his "Look East" policy could be taken to mean emulating the little dragon to the south of Malaysia or the one to the south of China, Mahathir stated in no uncertain terms that Japan and South Korea were Malaysia's role models. Again, notably, this was a vintage Mahathirian strategy to ride a Japanese economic ascendancy to counterbalance the economic dominance of the United States and the West. We have seen in Chapter 7 that as early as 1992, Mahathir foresaw the limitations of ASEAN as an economic entity and argued that only an East Asian Economic Grouping (EAEG) could ultimately serve the needs of the region. While his idea of a grouping was watered down to that of a "caucus" and his objection towards Australian and New Zealand participation was rebuffed, the subsequent formalizing of the ASEAN-Plus-Three grouping and the East Asian Summit, as fruits of ASEAN constructivism, has to some extent vindicated the former Malaysian prime minister.

It has been argued by Liow and Kuik that in the post-Cold War period, Malaysia's relations with China saw a perceptible shift which these two authors see as a form of "hedge diplomacy" (Liow 2005, p. 286, *passim*; Kuik 2008).[18] Mahathir made an important visit to China in 1999, ending with the signing of an MOU which committed Chinese investments to the tune of US$1 billion to Sabah. On the political front, post-9/11, Malaysia's opposition to U.S. unilateralism and the conduct of its war on terrorism resonated with

China's overall posture against American hegemony. Abdullah Badawi as foreign minister visited China in October 2003, a month before assuming the helm of the government. Riding the tide of an economically rising China, the Abdullah government, one may also argue, subsequently took pains to commemorate Malaysia's 30th anniversary of diplomatic relations with China with an official visit in 2004. Liow's overall point about Malaysia hedging U.S. and Chinese relations is even more valid in the Abdullah period wherein Malaysia capitalized on the rise of China's economic and political presence regionally while maintaining stable relations with the United States globally. The early infatuation with a Japan-centric East Asian ascendancy had given way to the more measured ASEAN-sponsored notion of the ASEAN-Plus-Three and the East Asian Summit in the post-Mahathir period as I argue in the next section, which discusses a China-India hedging stance.

NAVIGATING THE CHINA-INDIA ASCENDANCY

As pointed out above, by the end of the 1990s, Malaysia had made important political overtures to China in the aftermath of the 1997–98 Asian financial crisis. In his August 1999 speech in Beijing at the Third Malaysia-China Forum, Prime Minster Mahathir alluded to the common stances the two countries had taken and called for both nations "to work with other East Asian Countries to urge developed nations for a concerted effort to create a new global financial architecture" (Abdul Razak Baginda 2002, p. 243). Towards the later part of Mahathir's tenure a few significant moves were also made in the economic arena to India and China, such as the offer to participate in the RM14.5 billion 329-km double-tracking railway project running between Ipoh and Padang Besar. The project which was awarded to the Malaysian Mining Corporation (MMC) and the Gamuda companies was temporarily shelved when Abdullah Badawi took over the helm of government at the end of 2003. Reportedly, the Abdullah administration revived the project in 2007 and started negotiations soon afterwards with MMC and Gamuda for the northern section, while the southern section, running from Seremban to Gemas, has been awarded to Indian Railway Construction Company (IRCON), the construction arm of Indian Railways, and a local company.[19]

An interesting geostrategic move by Prime Minister Abdullah was his June 2004 visit to China, ahead of both his U.S. and Japan visits. Over the years, Malaysia has become the largest Southeast Asian trading partner with China with a massive US$20 billion in two-way trade in 2003 (*People's Daily Online*, 1 June 2004). Abdullah's visit, which also commemorated the

30th anniversary of diplomatic ties with China, is important as a statement in itself, given Malaysia's large Chinese population and the fact that it was the first ASEAN country to recognize the People's Republic of China in 1974. The "nude ear squat incident", recounted in Chapter 8, showed the lengths that Malaysia was prepared to go not to offend China. Fortuitously, and somewhat to the government's embarrassment, the incident turned out to have nothing to do with a Chinese national.

A similar strategy of paying obeisance to India seems to have emerged in the Abdullah period. The premier made a trip to India in December 2004 where he received an honorary doctorate from the Jamia Millia Islamia University, his first from a foreign institution of higher learning, for his promotion of Islam *Hadhari* or "civilization Islam" which had become the hallmark of his administration. Abdullah in his talks with Prime Minister Manmohan Singh stressed that Malaysia was India's largest trade partner in ASEAN and went on to sign three agreements one between Antrix Corporation Ltd., the commercial arm of the Indian Space Research Organization, and Measat Global to pool their satellite capacities; a letter of intent between Antrix and Measat on the procurement of a Measat-4 satellite; and an agreement for the construction of a new international airport in Hyderabad.[20] Twelve more memoranda of understanding were signed separately between Indian and Malaysian companies at the business forum, including agreements in railways, information technology, and biotechnology. Pointing to the many similarities between India and Malaysia, Abdullah stressed, "[L]ike India, Malaysia is striving to sustain massive economic growth in order to ensure social justice. Like you, we want all our people to benefit from sustained economic growth. Like you, we don't want to leave behind a single citizen because of a lack of opportunity for education and employment. And like you, we want to make an impact internationally at this time of rapid globalisation."[21] Malaysia, he underlined, was keen to invest more to strengthen India's infrastructure and referred to the statement from New Delhi that half a trillion dollars' worth of investment would be required in the next few years.

Malaysia's policy of Western alignment during the height of the Cold War shifted palpably to one of non-alignment for which the diplomatic recognition of China in 1974 proved crucial. Balancing between the more traditional and more cooperative ties with India and the more fractious relations with China was the basis of relations from the 1980s through till the 1990s. It would also be fair to say that Malaysia to a great extent bandwagoned on the rise of Japan-centric East Asia by the end of the 1990s, but the strategy morphed into a more nuanced one of accounting belatedly for the actual and potential ascendancy of China and India by the mid-2000s.

CHAMPIONING ISLAM AND
CO-RELIGIONIST CAUSES

An analyst has argued that "Islam never occupied a central position in Malaysia's foreign policy" while another has said that "Islam has provided direction and content for the foreign policy of Malaysia.[22] It could be that both writers may be correct depending on the context and period of Malaysia's foreign policy. I think we have shown in these pages that Islamic issues and Islam-related factors clearly drove aspects of foreign policy since the time of the Tunku and were in particular capitalized upon during the Mahathir period. During the Abdullah tenure, one could even argue that Islamic discourse became embedded into many aspects of domestic and foreign policy. The systematic work of Shanti Nair, who gives us the second quotation, shows that each of the tenures of four prime ministers before Abdullah bore the mark of Islam and we now draw on some of her main observations.[23] Despite the Tunku's Western leanings, he canvassed for some sort of "Muslim Commonwealth" and initiated the annual Qur'an reading competition. In retrospect, Tunku's policy was one of balancing his Westernism with a strong tilt towards relations with Muslim countries and co-religionist issues. The Tunku managed to win support from twenty-eight countries to attend the NAM conference in Algiers in 1965. Malaysia also played host to international Islamic conferences in the election years of 1959, 1964, and 1969, and after the Tunku's retirement, he was made secretary general of the OIC after its inaugural conference was held in Kuala Lumpur in 1969. Throughout Tunku's tenure, Malaysia supported the Palestinian cause and denied diplomatic relations to Israel.[24]

In the Abdul Razak period, internecine wars and the oil boom in Middle East propelled Malaysia's further attempt to seek out Muslim solidarity. Malaysia hosted the Fifth Islamic Conference in 1974. It gave support to and was able to draw on the Islamic Development Bank (IDB). The influence of PAS then within the ruling coalition may have nudged the government towards greater sensitivity towards Muslim minorities in Southeast Asia, although at that time PAS's regional co-religionist causes also embarrassed the government, as did Sabah's Tun Mustafa's support for Muslim rebels in the Southern Philippines. Tun Mustafa was removed for his alleged plan to take Sabah out of Malaysia. Thus, up until the end of Hussein Onn's tenure, Islamic causes, while largely symbolic, were given great play within Malaysian foreign policy discourse and practice. Malaysia was vocal in condemning the Israeli occupation of Arab territories and the burning of the Al-Aqsa Mosque in 1969. By the time of the Mahathir tenure, Islamic revivalism was at its height fuelled by the Iranian revolution and the Soviet invasion of Afghanistan in 1979. Nair writes that on his assuming power in 1981, Mahathir articulated a redesign of foreign policy with a formal ranking of relations with Islamic countries in the second rung, after ASEAN and ahead of the NAM and the Commonwealth (Nair 1997, p. 80). We have seen in Chapter 7, how Palestine, the first Gulf War (1991), and Bosnia became the dominant issues or Muslim causes in the Mahathir era. Mahathir virtually broke ranks with ASEAN in championing the cause of the Rohinyas, the Burmese Muslim minority. Camroux argues that Mahathir used his ties with Muslim nations to increase Malaysia's exports to the Middle East and gain admission to the International Islamic Chamber of Commerce in Jeddah (Camroux 1994, p. 22). In 2002, The Institute of Islamic Understanding (IKIM) organized an international seminar of "Gold Dinar in Multilateral Trade" with the IDB and launched the Islamic Financial Service Board (IFSB).[25] Thus Malaysia's Islamic tilt was not mere posturing, but had both ideological and economic dimensions.[26]

Furthermore, middlepowermanship was particularly evident in Mahathir's championing of co-religionist causes. By this I mean the pursuit of conflict resolution and management and the use of multilateral instrumentalities for Muslim causes. During Mahathir's tenure, the Malaysian Armed Forces participated in a host of peacekeeping operations of the United Nations, many in Muslim regions; UNTAG, 1989–90 (Namibia), UNTAC, 1992–93 (Cambodia), UNPROFOR, 1993–95 (Bosnia Herzegovina), IFOR, 1995–96 (Bosnia), SFOR, 1996–98 (Bosnia), and INTERFET, 1999–2000 (East Timor). As we have seen, the Bosnia involvement was particularly prominent and, at its height, Mahathir called for the secretary general to step down because of the United Nations' failure to protect Muslims. Malaysia also sent military observer teams to Iraq, Kuwait, Tajikistan, Afghanistan, Eritrea, and Ethiopia.[27] That the Mahathir and Abdullah governments acted as a third-party facilitator in providing good offices for the exploratory talks for a peace agreement in Southern Philippines, and participated as the lead mission of the International Monitoring Team (IMT) in the Bangsamoro conflict in Mindanao is yet another example of this form of middlepowermanship, whether successful or not.

The Abdullah tenure saw the continuation of the Islamic thrust in foreign policy and as we have shown in Chapter 8, the embedding of the *Islam Hadhari* ideological construct by his government. Abdullah maintained a middlepowermanship posture especially in Malaysia's role as Chair of the OIC. This included an unsuccessful bid for the OIC secretary generalship, the holding of civilizational dialogue events profiling a moderate Islam, the pursuit of a *Halal* Hub, even the idea of an OIC peacekeeping force. Abdullah's tenure also saw the continued participation of the monitoring team in the peace process in Mindanao, in the Philippines.[28] On the Palestinian situation, Malaysia repeatedly called on Israel to implement UNSC Resolution 1515 in accordance with the roadmap to peace, and the implementation of the two-state solution. Malaysia in 2005 supported the inaugural Asia-Middle East Dialogue (AMED) as a new diplomatic avenue for preventive diplomacy in the Middle East. In 2006, Malaysia's Institute of Diplomacy and Foreign Relations (IDFR) conducted a special three-week diplomatic training course for Iraqi officers.

FOREIGN POLICY AND DEMOCRATIC PRACTICE

According to Robert Cox's now classic statement on middlepowermanship, it must not be just a preference for internationalism and conflict resolution *per se*; indeed, the role of a middle power is not complete without a "post-hegemonic" approach to foreign policy (Cox 1989). This is taken to mean that middlepowermanship requires not just an external orientation, but the engagement of a state's own societal forces or civil society in foreign policy.[29] Mahathirian foreign policy may tend towards counterhegemonic stances, but was often not post-hegemonic in the sense that it was still not aimed at creating an order devoid of hegemonic dominance of any political bloc. Such a notion did not seem to have been articulated by Mahathir or any Malaysian foreign policy spokespersons for that matter. Second, the exclusion or avoidance of civil society, interest groups, or even parliamentarians in foreign policy formulation is rather conspicuous in the Malaysian case. Indeed, in the Mahathir period, Dhillon (2005) has illustrated that all major foreign policy initiatives ("Buy British Last", "Look East", Antarctica) were virtually personalized decisions of the prime minister and that, not only was the wider society or non-governmental groups not involved, the government's own foreign policy establishment, Wisma Putra, was in the dark about them. While I do not agree with Dhilion that Mahathir's polices were mainly or solely driven by the "idiosyncratic" factor, I do share his view that Mahathir was wont not to consult many on his policies.[30] He had a particular disdain for civil society and social activists. However, there may be some evidence to show that the think tank ISIS did play a substantial role in helping Mahathir formulate some major policies.[31]

As pointed out by diplomatic historian Chandran Jeshurun (2008), in the Tunku era, it was particularly noteworthy that he and Dr Ismail (as then foreign minister) allowed for a full debate of the pros and cons of Malaya's U.N. mission to Congo in September 1960 after the PPP's S.P. Seenivasagam formally tabled a motion for a debate. Indeed, it was common in the Tunku days for issues of foreign policy, such as the apartheid issue and the China diplomatic relations initiative, to be hotly debated in Parliament, a practice that has all but become moribund. Tun Dr Ismail's "Peace Plan", which led to the initiation of the ZOPFAN initiative of the Tun Raznak government, was tabled in Parliament. In the Mahathir tenure and that of his successor Abdullah, there have been hardly any debates in the legislature on some of the most significant initiatives in foreign policy such as the "Look East" policy or Islam *Hadhari*. It is my contention that foreign policy decision making should be ultimately linked to democratic practice and that at the present juncture, the Malaysian foreign making process lacks such an orientation. In his study of the post-apartheid South Africa as a middle power, Van Der Westhuizen (1998) found that non-governmental actors had limited influence on foreign policy despite the ANC's professed commitment towards a democratization of foreign policy decision making. For example, the extension of the Non-Proliferation Treaty (NPT) in 1995 was carried out over the heads of NGOs such as the group for Environmental Monitoring which argued for a system of "rolling extension" to meet some of the demands of developing countries (Van Der Westhuizen 1998, p. 446). Civil society advocates also often argue for white papers to be tabled in Parliament whenever a major foreign policy initiative is propounded or proposed. No white paper on foreign policy has been ever proffered to the Malaysian Parliament on foreign policy questions although there have been some parliamentary debates.

CONCLUSION

In this study, I have found that a critical-constructivist approach serves to provide important insights into the practice and conduct of foreign policy under the tenures of five prime ministers over some fifty years since Malaysia's independence in 1957. Under Prime Minister Tunku Abdul Rahman, policies of alignment prevailed in the political environment of the Cold War. While the Tunku did hedge his policies by championing regional cooperation and causes such as anti-apartheid or "save democracy" in respect of the Indo-China conflict, balancing and countervailing stances *vis-à-vis* the West only became evident in the tenure Abdul Razak, when non-alignment became a formal foreign position of Malaysia. More complex and controversial polices of counterpoising and counterdominance *vis-à-vis* the West and the United States or bandwagoning East Asia emerged in the Mahathir Mohamad era, while hedging the West and more prominent Islamic bandwagoning may be said to have occurred in the Abdullah Badawi period.

By and large, Malaysian foreign policy "constructivism" may be said to have been effective for a small state which in later years clearly aspired towards a middle power role in the Southeast Asian region, and also in terms of its persona as a Muslim-majority nation. During the Tunku tenure, we saw that its small-state foreign policy nevertheless had large-scale ambitions leading to the self-expansion of statehood from a Malaya to a Malaysia. Tunku also began the motions of Southeast Asian regionalism. In the Razak period, constructivism may be said to be at work through vigorous middlepowermanship. The switch to non-alignment, the recognition of China, and the proposal for the neutralization of Southeast Asia, put Malaysia on the global map as an exemplar of global good citizenship and conflict resolution. In the short tenure of Hussein Onn, the middlepowermanship management style was continued with initiatives such as the Kuantan doctrine and the handling of the crisis of the boat people.

The long Mahathir tenure of twenty-two years saw an evolution of a distinctive and definitive style in foreign policy making, its expanding scope, agendas, and counterhegemonic postures. A *prima facie* case could certainly be made for the putative rise to middle power status under Mahathir. However, his combative, personal, and assertive style arguably saw low institutionalization of genuine middle power statecraft in foreign policy. Wisma Putra by all accounts was hardly consulted on the most definitive policies of Mahathir as has been suggested by analysts. There was also little or no engagement of civil society; in fact, there was a deep distrust of civil society forces, which were often Mahathir's political opponents domestically. This notwithstanding, Nossal and Stubbs (1997) have illustrated that the scope, style, focus, forms, and forums of middlepowermanship were all evident during the Mahathir tenure. One could say that there were clear aspirations and ambitions of being a middle power and the record arguably shows many actual achievements. Chief among these were the South-South initiatives, the Antarctica policy, and the many peacekeeping missions under the United Nations. However, Mahathir also had a penchant for stalling and breaking down various bilateral relationships, for example, "Buy British Last", bilateral relations with Australia and Singapore, which are not a typically seen as exemplary of global citizenship or conflict resolution evident in the foreign policy of acknowledged middle powers such as Canada and Sweden.

The Abdullah tenure has seen a more moderate, but weaker leadership and global presence in foreign policy. However, one could argue that Abdullah continued the motions of the scope, forms, and forums of middle power statecraft started under Mahathir. The higher profiling of Islam and maintaining a leadership role as leader in the OIC is Abdullah's claim to the continuation of Malaysia's middle power role. Abdullah's more moderate and open and conciliatory style lends itself to an important aspect of middlepowermanship not developed under Mahathir. Abdullah may be said to have brought into play a greater element of "soft power" in Malaysian foreign policy. The relationship with Singapore could be seen as a prime example of such a soft power approach, so too is Malaysia's relaxing of tensions *vis-à-vis* the United States and Australia. Abdullah has also used his construct of Islam *Hadhari* to valorize the larger global concerns of the Muslim *ummah*. In the later period of his tenure, we argued that Abdullah's "perestroika" in domestic politics may have augured wittingly or unwittingly for a greater role of civil society in politics in general, and by extension, in the foreign policymaking process.

NOTES

1. I take the expression directly from Ping (2005) whose book has Indonesia and Malaysia in its subtitle and a whole chapter dealing exclusively with both countries. The two countries' middle power statecraft is dubbed "precursory" and seen as a form of "hybridised" statecraft. According to Ping, middle powers are inherently hybridizers, selecting forms of statecraft and perceived power most consonant with their intermediate resource base (p. 226). Ping's concepts are refreshing and useful, but I use the term rather more in conjunction with the notion of middlepowermanship as explained in this concluding chapter.

2. The term of course derives from the work of Joseph Nye Jr., who defines soft power as "[T]he ability to get what you want through attraction rather than coercion or payments. It arises from the attractiveness of a country's culture, political ideals, and policies. When our policies are seen as legitimate in the eyes of others, our soft power is enhanced." The quotation is taken from the preface of his shorter work (Nye 2004). See also Nye (1990).

3. We have alluded to this notion in Chapter 1. The term has been attributed to analysts such as John W. Holmes (1979) and Robert Cox (1996), who have applied it to Canada and Japan. See Nossal and Stubbs (1997, p. 149). Mustafa Izzuddin (2007) has also used the term to depict foreign policy in the Abdullah Badawi tenure in Malaysia.

4. Some of these ideas were developed in an unpublished paper on "Indonesia and Malaysia as Medium Powers in Southeast Asia: A Comparison" in my stint as visiting chair of ASEAN Studies at the University of Toronto in 1997.

5. While Nossal and Stubbs have chosen "scope', "focus", "style", and "forms and forums" as the defining terms, I've preferred to use other terms to refer to the same criteria.

6. See his master's dissertation submitted to the LSE (Mustafa Izzuddin, 2007).

7. Izzuddin, cited above, makes the specific point that Abdullah had succeeded in sustaining Malaysia's middlepowermanship.
8. Malaysia has armed forces of 109,000 (Army 80,00, Navy 14,000, Air Force 15,000) and reserves of 51,600 while Singapore has forces of 72,500 (Army 50,000; Navy 9,000 Air Force 13,500) and reserves of 312,500. Just comparing air force hardware, Malaysia possesses 63 combat capable aircraft in contrast to Singapore's 102, which includes 60 F-16C aircraft, which Malaysia does not possess. See *The Military Balance 2007*, pp. 362–64 and pp. 370–72.
9. See Storey (forthcoming 2009) and also Jain (1984, p. 29).
10. See Storey (forthcoming 2009) who cites Yuan-Li Wu (1975, p. 40) as propounding this view.
11. Ambassador's Notes, *Tun Ismail Papers*, Folio 5, pp. 71–72.
12. Of particular importance was the Robert Kennedy Mission of 1964 to Kuala Lumpur, which was followed by a series of tripartite foreign ministers' meetings in Bangkok in February and March 1964 (Sodhy 1991, p. 255).
13. In the end, the United States gave a grant of US$11 million at 3 per cent for arms purchase and a direct loan of US$5 million (Sodhy 1991, p. 261).
14. Mahathir's words exactly, "We are actually very strong. 1.3 billion people cannot be simply wiped out. The Europeans killed 6 million Jews out of 12 million. But today the Jews rule this world by proxy. They get others to fight and die for them." As cited in <http://www.adl.org/Anti_semitism/Malaysia_1.asp> (accessed 4 December 2007).
15. Saravanamuttu, 1983, op. cit., p. 86.
16. See Chapter 2.
17. Jeshurun (2007, pp. 50–52) provides an interesting vignette of the Tunku's "Japan option" when in May 1958 he negotiated for development aid when it was still perhaps controversial to do so with wartime reparations still unsettled. Attending the Tokyo Asian Games as Football Association president, the Tunku was able to strike a deal with Prime Minster Kishi Nobusuke for closer bilateral relations and investment. As Jeshurun correctly observes, Tunku's "Look East" policy was established long before Mahathir's.
18. Kuik (2008, p. 166, *passim*) further decomposes the hedging strategy into a spectrum of risk management stratagems, viz. indirect-balancing, dominance-denial, economic-pragmatism, binding-engagement, and limited-bandwagoning.
19. However, up to the time of writing, there appears to be a shift to China on the double-tracking project. Some new reports surfaced that the Malaysian company YTL Corporation is proposing a bullet train from Kuala Lumpur to Singapore. This appears to be different to the double-tracking project.
20. The consortium of GMR Infrastructure Limited and Malaysia Airports Holdings Berhad has been selected by the Andhra Pradesh and Central Governments following a competitive bidding process to develop a Greenfield international airport through public private partnership in Shamshabad near Hyderabad,

about 20 km from the existing airport at Begumpet. *The Hindu*, 21 December 2004.

21. As cited in *The Hindu*, 21 December 2004.

22. The first quote is from Mohamad Abu Bakar (2004, p. 17), while the second is from Nair (1997, p. 5).

23. See Nair, 1997, especially, pp. 55–83. I've enlisted Nair's use of "co-religionist", which connotes support of Muslim causes in my analysis.

24. It should be noted nonetheless that the Tunku countenanced commercial contact with Israel and allowed for Dr Moshe Yegar, an Israeli diplomat, to be stationed in Kuala Lumpur without accreditation in the early 1960s. The Tunku also met with various Israeli envoys. See the detailed account of Malaysia-Israeli relations by Yegar (2006). Yegar avers that the Mahathir period saw a downturn and rising antagonisms against Israel tantamount to "anti-semitism" by the end of his tenure.

25. As noted in Shaik Mohd Salleh and Suzalia Mohamad (2004, p. 81).

26. On this my analysis differs from Dhillon (2009), cited earlier, about Mahathir's "Islamic posturing". See also my discussion in Chapter 7.

27. See Shaik Mohd Salleh and Suzalia Mohamad (2004, pp. 77–78).

28. In May 2008, Malaysia pulled out twenty-nine members of the monitoring team, while twelve more were to follow suit later. The Malaysian government has been frustrated by the inability of the Philippine Government and the MILF to come to terms on the peace process. See Chapter 9.

29. The second point is further stressed in the work of Van Der Westhuizen (1998) reflecting on South Africa's emergence as a middle power.

30. My many interviews and chats with retired senior diplomats confirm Dhillon's point that many a time the MFA had to carry out "damage control" because of the many pronouncements Mahathir made without any consultation with it. A very senior diplomat made the further point that Mahathir was reluctant to hand over his speeches at the United Nations and elsewhere to the MFA in case it would be altered.

31. This I have gathered from personal association with the former director and CEO of ISIS, the late Dr Noordin Sopiee, and through involvement in some ISIS activities over the years.

BIBLIOGRAPHY

Abdul Rahman, Tunku. *May 13: Before and After*. Kuala Lumpur: Utusan Melayu Press, 1969.

Abdul Razak, Tun. "Radio Malaya Talk on Defence Policy". *Straits Times*, 4 October 1961.

Abdul Razak Baginda, ed. *Malaysia's Foreign Policy: Continuity and Change*. London and Singapore: Marshall Cavendish Editions, 2007.

————, ed. *Malaysia and the Islamic World*. London: Asean Academic Press, 2004.

————. "Malaysian Perceptions of China: From Hostility to Cordiality." In *The China Threat: Perceptions, Myths and Reality*, edited by Herbert Yee and Ian Storey. London, New York: RoutledgeCurzon, 2004.

Abdul Razak Baginda and Rohana Mahmood, eds. *Malaysia's Defence and Foreign Policies*. Petaling Jaya: Pelanduk Publications, 1995.

Abdullah Ahmad. *Dr Mahathir's Selected Letters to World Leaders*. London, Singapore: Marshall Cavendish Editions, 2008.

————. *Tengku Abdul Rahman and Malaysia's Foreign Policy*. Kuala Lumpur: Berita Publishing, 1985.

Abdullah Ahmad Badawi. *Islam Hadhari: A Model Approach for Development and Progress*. Kuala Lumpur: MPH Group Printing Sdn Bhd., 2006.

————. *Malaysia-Singapore Relations*. The Institute of Policy Studies, Lecture No. 2. Singapore: Times Academic Press, 1990.

Acharya, Amitav. *Constructing a Security Community in Southeast Asia: ASEAN and the Problem of Regional Order*. London & New York: Routledge, 2001.

————. "Realism, Institutionalism, and the Asian Economic Crisis". *Contemporary Southeast Asia* 21, no. 1 (April 1999): 1–29.

————. "A New Regional Order in Southeast Asia: ASEAN in the Post-Cold War Era". London: Adelphi Paper No. 279, 1993.

Ahmad Faiz Abdul Hamid. *Malaysia and South-South Cooperation during Mahathir's Era: Determining Factors and Implications*. Selangor Darul Ehsan: Pelanduk Publications, 2005.

Allison, Graham T. *The Essence of Decision: Explaining the Cuban Missile Crisis*. Boston: Little, Brown & Co., 1972.

Amer, Ramses, Johan Saravanamuttu, and Peter Wallensteen. *The Cambodian Conflict 1979–1991: From Intervention to Resolution*. Penang and Uppsala: Research and Education for Peace, School of Social Sciences, USM, and Dept. of Peace and Conflict Research, Uppsala University, 1996.

Antolik, Michael. *ASEAN and the Diplomacy of Accomodation*. Armonk, N.Y.: M.E. Sharpe, Inc., 1990.

Ariff, M. and M.M.C. Yap. "Malaysia: Financial Crisis in Malaysia". In *From Crisis to Recovery: East Asia Rising Again?*, edited by Tzong-shian Yu and Dianqing Xu. Singapore: World Scientific, 2001.

Arndt, H.W. and Hal Hill, eds. *Southeast Asia's Economic Crisis: Origins, Lessons, and the Way Forward*. Singapore: Institute of Southeast Asian Studies, 1999.

Azeez, Shamira Bhanu Abdul. *The Singapore-Malaysia Re-merger Debate of 1996*. Hull: Centre for South-East Asian Studies and Institute of Pacific Asia Studies, the University of Hull, 1998.

Azizah Kassim and Lau Teik Soon, eds. *Malaysia and Singapore: Problems and Prospects*. Singapore: Singapore Institute of International Affairs, 1992.

Balakrishnan, K.S. "International Law and the Dispute over Sovereignty in the South China Sea: Malaysia's Policy". *Journal of Diplomacy and Foreign Relations* 4, no. 1 (June 2002).

Banerjee, Sanjoy. "The Cultural Logic of National Identity Formation: Contending Discourses in Late Colonial India". In *Culture and Foreign Policy*, edited by Valerie Hudson, pp. 27–44. Boulder, Colo.: L. Rienner Publishers, 1997.

Bernard, Mitchell. "States, Social Forces, and Regions in Historical Time: Toward a Critical Political Economy of Eastern Asia". *Third World Quarterly* 17, no. 4 (1996): 649–65.

Boyce, Peter. *Malaysian and Singapore in Diplomacy*. Sydney: Sydney University Press, 1968.

Boulding Kenneth E. "National Images and International Systems". In *International Politics and Foreign Policy: A Reader in Research and Theory*, edited by James N. Rosenau. New York: Free Press, 1969.

Camilleri, Rita. *Attitudes and Perceptions in Australia-Malaysia Relations: A Contemporary Profile*. Bangi: Penerbit Universiti Kebangsaan Malaysia, 2001.

Camroux, David. "'Looking East' … and Inwards: Internal Factors in Malaysian Foreign Relations During the Mahathir Era, 1981–1994". Australia-Asia Paper No. 72, Griffith University, 1994.

Chamil Wariya. *Dasar Luar Era Mahathir* (Foreign Policy in the Mahathir Era). Petaling Jaya: Penerbit Fajar Bakti Sdn Bhd., 1989.

———. *UMNO Era Mahathir*. Petaling Jaya: Penerbit Fajar Bakti Sdn Bhd., 1988.

Chan Heng Chee. "Southeast Asia 1976: The Handling of Contradictions". In *Southeast Asian Affairs 1977*, edited by Huynh Kim Kanh. Singapore: Institute of Southeast Asian Studies, 1977).

Chandriah Appa Rao et al. *Issues in Contemporary Malaysia*, edited by Bruce Ross-Larson. Kuala Lumpur: Heinemann Educational Books (Asia), 1977.

Che Man, Kadir W. *Muslim Separatism: The Moros of Southern Philippines and the Malays of Southern Thailand*. Singapore: Oxford University Press, 1990.

Chee, Stephen. "Malaysia's Changing Foreign Policy". In *Trends in Malaysia II*, edited by Yong Mun Cheong. Singapore: Singapore University Press for Institute of Southeast Asian Studies, 1974.

Chin Kin Wah. "The Five Power Defence Arrangements and AMDA: Some Observations on the Nature of an Evolving Partnership". ISEAS Occasional Paper 23, 1974.

———. *The Defence of Malaysia and Singapore: The Transformation of a Security System, 1957–1971*. Cambridge and New York: Cambridge University Press, 1983.

——— and Leo Suryadinata. *Michael Leifer: Selected Works on Southeast Asia*. Singapore: Institute of Southeast Asian Studies, 2005.

Coleman, William D. and Tony Porte. "Regulating International Banking and Securities: Emerging Co-operation among National Authorities". In *Political Economy and the Changing Global Order*, edited by Richard Stubbs and Geoffrey R.D. Underhill. New York: St. Martin's Press.

Cooper, Andrew Fenton, ed. *Niche Diplomacy: Middle Powers After the Cold War*. New York: Macmillan, 1997.

Cox, Robert with Timothy J. Sinclair. *Approaches to World Order*. Cambridge: Cambridge University Press, 1996.

Cox, Robert W. "Towards a Post-hegemonic Conception of World Order: Reflections on the Relevancy of Ibn Khaldun". In *Approaches to World Order*, edited by Robert W. Cox with Timothy J. Sinclair. Cambridge University Press, 1996.

———. "Middlepowermanship, Japan, and the Future World Order". *International Journal* 44, no. 4 (1989): 823–62.

Dalton, J.B. "The Development of Malaysian External Policy, 1957–1963". Ph.D. Thesis, Oxford University, 1967.

David, Harald. *Tensions within ASEAN: Malaysia and Its Neighbours*. Hull: Dept. of South-East Asian Studies, University of Hull, 1996.

Deutsch, Karl W. *The Analysis of International Relations*. Englewood Cliffs, N.J.: Prentice-Hall, 1968.

Dhillon, Karminder Singh. *Malaysian Foreign Policy in the Mahathir Era, 1981–2003: Dilemmas of Development*. Singapore: NUS Press, 2009.

———. *Malaysian Foreign Policy in the Mahathir Era, 1981–2003*. Ann Arbor, Mich.: University Microfilms International, 2005.

Domingo, Benjamin B. *The Re-making of Filipino Foreign Policy*. Quezon City: Asian Center, University of the Philippines, 1993.

Dzurek, Danies J. *The Spratly Island Dispute: Who's on First?* Durham: International Boundaries Research Unit, University of Durham, 1969.

Falk, Richard. "On Humane Governance: Toward a New Global Politics" (The World Order Models Project Report of the Global Civilization Initiative). University Park, PA: The Pennsylvania State University Press & Polity Press, 1995.

Far Eastern Economic Review (FEER). *Asia 1977 Yearbook*. Hong Kong: *Far Eastern Economic Review*, 1977.

Faridah Jaafar. *Perdana Menteri dan Dasar Luar Malaysia, 1957–2005*. Kuala Lumpur: Penerbit Universiti Malaya, 2007.

Fuaziah Mohamad Taib, ed. *Number One Wisma Putra*. Kuala Lumpur: Institute of Diplomacy and Foreign Relations, 2006.

Funston, John. "Malaysia: UMNO's Search for Relevance". In *Southeast Asian Affairs 2001*, edited by Daljit Singh and Anthony Smith. Singapore: Institute of Southeast Asian Studies, 2001.

Ganesan, Narayanan. *Realism and Interdependence in Singapore's Foreign Policy*. London and New York: Routledge, 2005.

George, Alexander. "'The Operational Code': A Neglected Approach to the Study of Political leaders and Decision-Making". *International Studies Quarterly* 13 (1969): 190–222.

Ghazali Shafie. "Neutralization of Southeast Asia". *Foreign Affairs Malaysia* 4 (1971): 46–53.

———. "ASEAN's Response to Security Issues in Southeast Asia" (Talk delivered at the Centre for Strategic and International Studies during a conference on "Regionalism in Southeast Asia: Problems, Perspectives and Possibilities" in Jakarta, October 1974). Mimeographed handout from the Ministry of Foreign Affairs, 1974.

———. "The Great Domino Fallacy". Text of Radio Malaysia Broadcast, as published in *New Straits Times*, 7 and 8 May 1975.

———. "The Elements of Foreign Policy". *Foreign Affairs Malaysia* 2 (1969): 12–13.

Giddens, Anthony. *The Constitution of Society: Outline of the Theory of Structuration*. Cambridge: Polity Press, 1984.

Gill, Stephen. "New Constitutionalism, Democratization and the Global Political Economy". *Pacifica Review* 10, no. 1 (1998): 23–38.

———. "Knowledge, Politics, and Neo-Liberal Political Economy". In *Political Economy and the Changing Global Order*, edited by Richard Stubbs and Geoffrey R.D. Underhill. New York: St. Martin's Press, 1994.

Gilpin, Robert. *Global Political Economy: Understanding the International Economic Order*. Princeton and Oxford: Princeton University Press, 2001.

Gomez, Edmund Terence. *Chinese Business in Malaysia: Accumulation, Ascendance, Accommodation*. Surrey: Curzon, 1999.

Gomez, Edmund Terence and Jomo K.S. *Malaysian Political Economy: Politics Patronage and Profits*. Cambridge: Cambridge University Press, 1997.

Greider, William. *One World, Ready or Not: The Manic Logic of Capitalism*. Simon and Schuster, 1997.

Gullick, J.M. *Malaysia and Its Neighbours*. London: Routledge and K. Paul, 1967.

Guzzini, Stefano and Anna Leander, eds. *Constructivism and International Relations: Alexander Wendt and his Critics*. London; New York, NY: Routledge, 2006.

Gyngell, Allan. "Looking Outwards: ASEAN's External Relations". In *Understanding ASEAN*, edited by Alison Broinowski. London: Macmillian, 1982.

Haacke, Jürgen. *ASEAN's Diplomatic and Security Culture: Origins, Development and Prospects*. London & New York: RoutledgeCurzon, 2003.

Haggard, Stephan. *The Political Economy of the Asian Financial Crisis*. Washington, D.C.: Institute for International Economics, 2000.

Hale, David. "Is Asia's High Growth Era Over?" *National Interest* 47 (Spring 1997): 44–57.

Haller-Trost, R. *The Spratly Islands: A Study on the Limitations of International Law.* London: The Hague: Kluwer Law International, 1990.

———. *The Contested Maritime and Territorial Boundaries of Malaysia.* London: The Hague: Kluwer Law International, 1998.

———. *The Territorial Dispute between Indonesia and Malaysia over Pulau Sipadan and Pulau Sipadan in the Celebes Seas: A Study in International Law.* Durham: International Boundaries Research Unit, 1995.

———. "Historical Legal Claims: A Study of Disputed Sovereignty over Pulau Batu Puteh". IBRU Unit University of Durhan. Maritime Briefing 1, no. 1 (1998).

Harper, Timothy N. *The End of Empire and the Making of Malaya.* Cambridge: Cambridge University Press, 1999.

Hazra, Niranjan Kumar. "Malaya's Foreign Relations 1957–1963". M.A. Thesis, Dept. of History, University of Singapore, 1965.

Helleiner, Eric. "From Bretton Woods to Global Finance: A World Turned Upside Down". In *Political Economy and the Changing Global Order*, edited by Richard Stubbs and Geoffrey R.D. Underhill. New York: St. Martin's Press, 1994.

Higgott, Richard and Richard Stubbs. "Competing Conceptions of Economic Regionalism: APEC versus EAEC in the Asia Pacific". *Review of International Political Economy* 2, no. 3 (Summer, 1995): 516–35.

Hill, Christopher. *The Changing Politics of Foreign Policy.* New York, NY: Palgrave-Macmillan, 2003.

Hilly, John. *Malaysia: Mahathirism, Hegemony and the New Opposition.* London and New York: Zed books, 2001.

Ho Khai Leong and James Chin, eds. *Mahathir's Administration: Performance and Crisis in Governance.* Singapore: Times Books International, 2001.

Ho Khai Leong and Samuel K.Y. Ku. *China and Southeast Asia: Global Changes and Challenges.* Singapore & Kaohsiung: Institute of Southeast Asian Studies and Center for Southeast Asian Studies, National Sun Yat-sen University, 2005.

Hobson, John M. *The State and International Relations.* Cambridge: Cambridge University Press, 2000.

Holmes, John W. *The Shaping of Peace: Canada and World Order, 1943–1957.* Toronto: University of Toronto Press, 1979.

Holsti, Kalevi J. *International Politics: A Framework of Analysis.* Englewood Cliffs, N.J.: Prentice-Hall, 1967.

Holsti, Ole R. "The Belief System and National Images: A Case Study". In *International Politics and Foreign Policy*, edited by James N. Rosenau. New York: Free Press, 1969.

Hopf, Ted. *Social Construction of International Politics: Identities and Foreign Policies, Moscow, 1955 and 1999.* Ithaca: Cornell University Press, 2002.

Hook, Sidney. *Comparative Foreign Policy: Adaptation Strategies of the Great and Emerging Powers*. Upper Saddle River, NJ: Prentice Hall, 2002.

Horowitz, Donald L. *Ethnic Groups in Conflict*. Berkeley: University of California Press, 1985.

Houghton, David Patrick. "Reinvigorating the Study of Foreign Policy Decision Making: Toward a Constructivist Approach". *Foreign Policy Analysis* 3, no. 1 (2007): 24–45.

Hudson, Valerie M. *Foreign Policy Analysis: Classic and Contemporary Theory*. Lanham, Md.: Rowman & Littlefield Pub, 2006.

———, ed. *Culture and Foreign Policy*. Boulder, Colo: L. Rienner Publishers, 1997.

Hussin Mutalib. *Islam in Malaysia: From Revivalism to Islamic State*. Singapore: Singapore University Press, 1993.

Hwang, In-Won. *Personalized Politics: The Malaysian State under Mahathir*. Singapore: Institute of Southeast Asian Studies, 2003.

Ingles, Jose D. *Philippine Foreign Policy*. Intramuros, Manila: Lyceum of the Philippines, 1982.

Izzuddin, Mustafa. "Malaysia under Abdullah: Sustenance of a Middle Power Role". M.Sc. Thesis, Faculty of Economics/International Relations, London School of Economics, 2007.

Jegathesan, J. "Investment Promotion, FIDA". Paper given at the Malaysia Investment Conference, London, May 1975, Mimeographed.

Jeshurun, Chandran. "The Growth of the Malaysian Armed Forces, 1963–73". Singapore: Institute of Southeast Asian Studies, Occasional Paper No. 35, October 1975.

———. *Malaysian Defence Policy: A Study of Parliamentary Attitudes, 1963–1973*. Singapore: Institute of Southeast Asian Studies, 1980.

———. *Malaysia: Fifty Years of Diplomacy 1957–2007*. Malaysia: The Other Press, 2007.

Jha, Ganganath. *Foreign Policy of Thailand*. New Delhi: Radiant Publishers, 1979.

Jomo, Kwame Sundaram, ed. *Malaysian Industrial Policy*. Singapore: NUS Press, 2007.

———, ed. *Tigers in Trouble: Financial Governance, Liberalization and Crisis in East Asia*. Hong Kong: Hong Kong University Press, 1998.

———, ed. *After the Storm: Crisis Recovery and Sustaining Development in Four Southeast Economies*. Singapore: Singapore University Press, 2004.

———. *Malaysian Eclipse: Economic Crisis and Recovery*. London: Zed Books, 2001.

——— et al. *Southeast Asia's Misunderstood Miracle: Industrial Policy and Economic Development in Thailand, Malaysia and Indonesia*. Boulder: Westview Press, 1997.

Jomo, Kwame Sundaram and Ahmad Shabery Cheek. "Malaysia's Islamic Movements". In *Fragmented Vision: Culture and Politics in Contemporary Malaysia,* edited by Joel S. Kahn and Francis Loh Kok Wah. Sydney: Allen and Unwin, 1992.

Katzenstein, Peter J. *Cultural Norms and National Security: Police and Military in Postwar Japan*. Ithaca, NY: Cornell University Press, 1996.

Khaw Guat Hoon. "Malaysian Policies in South-East Asia, 1957–70: The Search for Security". Thèse No. 227, Université de Genève. Singapore: Singapore National Printers Pte Ltd., 1976.

Khoo Boo Teik. *Paradoxes of Mahathirism: An Intellectual Biography of Mahathir Mohamad*. Kuala Lumpur: Oxford University Press, 1995.

Khoo Khay Jin. "The Grand Vision: Mahathir and Modernisation". In *Fragmented Vision: Culture and Politics in Contemporary Malaysia*, edited by Joel S. Kahn and Loh Kok Wah. Sydney: Allen & Unwin/Asian Studies Assn. of Australia, 1992.

Knorr, Klaus E. *Tin under Control*. Stanford, Calif.: Stanford University Press, 1945.

Kojima, Kiyoshi. *Japan and a New World Economic Order*. Boulder: Westview Press, 1977.

Korhonen, Pekka. "The Theory of the Flying Geese Pattern of Development and Its Interpretations". *Journal of Peace Research* 31, no. 1 (1994): 93–108.

Krugman, Paul. "What ever Happened to the Asian Miracle?" *Fortune* (Internet Text Edition, <http://www. fortune.com>) 18 August 1997.

———. "What Happened to Asia". *Paul Krugman Homepage*, Internet, <http://web.mit.edu/krugman/www/>, January 1998.

Kua Kia Soong. *May 13: Declassified Documents on the Malaysian Riots of 1969*. Kuala Lumpur: Suaram Komunikasi, 2007.

Kubálková, Vendulka. *Foreign Policy in a Constructed World*. Armonk, N.Y.: M.E. Sharpe, 2001.

Kuik Cheng-Chwee. "The Essence of Hedging: Malaysia and Singapore's Response to a Rising China". *Contemporary Southeast Asia* 30, no. 2 (August 2008): 159–85.

Kwan, C.H., Donna Vandenbrink and Chia Siow Yue, eds. *Coping with Capital Flows in East Asia*. Tokyo: Nomura Research Institute, 1998.

Lagos, Gustavo. *International Stratification and Under-Developed Countries*. Chapel Hill: University of North Carolina Press, 1963.

Lebow, Richard Ned. "Thucydides the Constructivist". *American Political Science Review* 95, no. 3 (2001): 547–60.

Lee Hock-Aun. "Cluster Dynamics in Malaysian Electronics". In *Malaysian Industrial Policy*, edited by K.S. Jomo. Singapore: NUS Press, 2007.

Lee Kuan Yew. *The Battle for Merger*. Singapore: Government Printing Office, 1961.

———. *The Singapore Story: Memoirs of Lee Kuan Yew*. Singapore: Times Editions, Singapore Press Holdings, 1998.

———. *From First World to Third: The Singapore Story, 1965–2000: Memoirs of Lee Kuan Yew*. Singapore: Times Editions, Singapore Press Holdings, 2000.

Leifer, Michael. *Singapore's Foreign Policy: Coping with Vulerability*. New York, NY: Routledge, 2000.

————. *Indonesia's Foreign Policy*. London; Boston: Published for the Royal Institute of International Affairs by Allen & Unwin, 1983.

————. *The Philippine Claim to Sabah*. Hull Monograph Series on South East Asia, 1968.

Leo Ah Bang. "Elite Cohesion in Malaysia: A Study of Alliance Leadership". Master's thesis, University of Singapore, 1972.

Lim Chong-Yah. "West Malaysian External Trade 1947–65". In *Economic Interdependence in Southeast Asia*, edited by T. Morgan and N. Spoelstra. Madison: Milwaukee: University of Wisconsin Press, 1969.

————. *Economic Development of Modern Malaya*. New York: Oxford University Press, 1967.

Lim Pao Li and Anna Ong Cheng Imm. "Technology Policy in Malaysia". In *Malaysian Industrial Policy*, edited by K.S. Jomo. Singapore: NUS Press, 2007.

Liow, Joseph Chingyong. *Muslim Resistance in Southern Thailand and Southern Philippines: Religion, Ideology, and Politics*. Washington, D.C.: East-West Centre, Policy Studies 24, 2006.

————. "Balancing, Bandwagoning, or Hedging? Strategic and Security Patterns in Malaysia's Relations with China, 1981–2003". In *China and Southeast Asia: Global Changes and Challenges*, edited by Ho Khai Leong and Samuel C.Y. Ku. Singapore: Institute of Southeast Asian Studies and Centre for Southeast Asian Studies, 2005.

————. *The Politics of Indonesia-Malaysia Relations: One Kin, Two Nations*. New York: Routledge, 2004.

————. "Personality, Exigencies and Contingencies: Determinants of Malaysia's Foreign Policy in the Mahathir Administration". In *Mahathir's Administration: Performance and Crisis in Governance*, edited by Ho Khai Leong and James Chin. Singapore: Times Books International, 2001.

Loh Kok Wah and Johan Saravanamuttu, eds. *New Politics in Malaysia*. Singapore: Institute of Southeast Asian Studies, 2003.

Mahathir Mohamad. *Malaysia: The Way Forward*. Kuala Lumpur: Centre for Economic Research and Services, Malaysian Business Council, 1991.

————. "New Government Policies". In *Mahathir's Economic Policies*, edited by K.S. Jomo. Kuala Lumpur, Insan, 2nd Edition, 1989.

Mak, J.N. "Malaysian Defense and Security Cooperation". In *Asia-Pacific Security Cooperation: National Interests and Regional Order*, edited by See Seng Tan and Amitav Archarya. NY: M.E. Sharpe, 2004.

Malaysia. *Ninth Malaysia Plan 2006–2010*. Putrajaya: Economic Planning Unit, Prime Minister's Department, 2006.

————. *Mid-Term Review of the Seventh Malaysia Plan 1996–2000*. Kuala Lumpur: Percetakan Nasional Malaysia Berhad, 1999.

————. *Petroleum Development (Amendment) Act, 1975*. Kuala Lumpur: Government Printer, 1975.

————. *Economic Report 1974–75*. Kuala Lumpur: Treasury, 1974.

———. *Economic Report 1975–76*. Kuala Lumpur: Treasury, 1975.

———. *Petroleum Development Act, 1974*. Kuala Lumpur: Government Printer, 1974.

———. *Guidelines for the Regulation of Acquisition of Assets, Mergers and Takeovers*. Kuala Lumpur: Government Printer, 1974.

———. *Mid-Term Review of the Second Malaysia Plan 1971–1975*. Kuala Lumpur: Government Printer, 1973.

———. *Second Malaysian Plan 1971–1975*. Kuala Lumpur: Government Printer, 1971.

———. *Malaysia in Brief*. Kuala Lumpur: Government Printer, 1963.

———. *ASA: Report of the First Meeting of Foreign Ministers*. Kuala Lumpur: Government Printer, 1961.

———. *Water: The Singapore-Malaysia Dispute: The Facts*. Kuala Lumpur: Government Printer, 2003.

Malay Mail. *Malaysia Year Book 1973–74*. Kuala Lumpur: Malay Mail, 1974.

Martinez, Patricia. "Malaysia in 2000". *Asian Survey* 41, no. 1 (2001): 189–200.

———. "Islam, Constitutional Democracy, and the Islamic State in Malaysia". In *Civil Society in Southeast Asia*, edited by Lee Hock Guan. Singapore: Institute of Southeast Asian Studies, 2004.

Maznah Mohamad. "Malaysia in 2002: Bracing for a Post-Mahathir Future". In *Southeast Asian Affairs 2003*, edited by Daljit Singh and Chin Kin Wah. Singapore: Institute of Southeast Asian Studies, 2003*a*.

———. "The Contest for Malay Votes in 1999: UMNO's Most Historic Challenge". In *New Politics in Malaysia*, edited by Francis Loh Kok Wah and Johan Saravanamuttu. Singapore: Institute of Southeast Asian Studies, 2003*b*.

———. "The Unravelling of a 'Malay Consensus'". In *Southeast Asian Affairs 2001*, edited by Daljit Singh and Anthony L. Smith. Singapore: Institute of Southeast Asian Studies, 2001.

McCargo, Duncan. "What's Really Happening in Southern Thailand?" Paper prepared for ISEAS Regional Forum, Singapore, 8 January 2008. ISEAS webpage, <http://www.iseas.edu.sg/rof08.htm> (accessed 31 October 2008).

Means, Gordon P. *Malaysian Politics: The Second Generation*. Singapore, Oxford, New York: Oxford University Press, 1991.

Miller, Harry. *Prince and Premier*. London: G.G. Harrap, 1959.

Milne, R.S. *Government and Politics in Malaysia*. Boston, Houghton Mifflin Co., 1967.

Milne, R.S. and Diane K. Mauzy. *Malaysian Politics under Mahathir*. London and New York: Routledge, 1999.

———. *Malaysia: Tradition, Modernity, and Islam*. Boulder: Westview Press, 1986.

Milne, R.S. *Government and Politics in Malaysia*. Boston: Houghton Mifflin Co., 1967.

Mohamad Abu Bakar. "Islam in Malaysia's Foreign Policy: The First Three Decades (1957–1987)". In *Malaysia's Foreign Policy: Continuity and Change*, edited by

Abdul Razak Baginda. London and Singapore: Marshall Cavendish Editions, 2004.

Mohamed Ariff and Michael Meow-Chung Yap. "Financial Crisis in Malaysia". In *From Crisis to Recovery: East Asia Rising Again?*, edited by Tzong-shian Yu and Dianqing Xum, pp. 305–45. Singapore-New Jersey-London-Hong Kong: World Scientific Publishing, 2001.

Mohammed Azhari et al. *Malaysian Foreign Policy: Issues and Perspectives.* Kuala Lumpur: National Institute of Public Administration, Malaysia, 1990.

Mohd Ridzam Deva. "No Longer the Envy of the Diplomatic World". *New Straits Times*, 21 June 2009.

Mohd Yusof Ahmad. *Continuity and Change in Malaysia's Foreign Policy, 1981–1986.* Ph.D. Thesis, Tufts University, 1990.

Morais, Victor, ed. *Strategy for Action: The Selected Speeches of Tun Haji Abdul Razak.* Kuala Lumpur: Malaysian Centre for Development Studies, Prime Minister's Department, 1969.

————, ed. *Blueprint for Unity.* Kuala Lumpur: Malayan Chinese Association, 1972.

Nair, Shanti. *Islam in Malaysian Foreign Policy.* London and New York: Routledge. (Issued under the auspices of the Institute of Southeast Asian Studies, Singapore, 1997).

Nathan, K.S. "Malaysia: 11 September and the Politics of Incumbency". In *Southeast Asian Affairs 2002*, edited by Daljit Singh and Anthony L. Smith. Singapore: Institute of Southeast Asian Studies, 2002.

Nelson, Joan M., Jacob Meerman and Abdul Rahman Embong. *Globalization and National Autonomy: The Experiences of Malaysia.* Singapore: Institute of Southeast Asian Studies, 2008.

Nesadurai, Helen E.S. "Malaysia and the United States: Rejecting Dominance. Embracing Engagement". Institute of Defence and Strategic Studies, Singapore, Working Paper No. 72, December 2004.

————. "Attempting Developmental Regionalism through AFTA: The Domestic Politics-Domestic Capital Nexus". Institute of Defence and Strategic Studies, Singapore, Working Paper No. 31, August 2002.

Netto, Anil. "Abdullah Badawi: Malaysia's Tinker Man". *Asian Times* (Online Version), 25 November 2003.

Noble, Lela Garner. *Philippine Policy Toward Sabah: A Claim to Independence.* Tucson, Ariz.: Published for the Association for Asian Studies by the University of Arizona Press, 1977.

Noordin Sopiee, Mohamad. *From Malayan Union to Singapore Separation: Political Unification in the Malaysia Region 1945–1965.* Kuala Lumpur: Penerbit Universiti Malaya (University of Malaya Press), 1974.

Nossal, Kim Richard and Richard Stubbs. "Mahathir's Malaysia: An Emerging Middle Power?". In *Niche Diplomacy: Middle Powers After the Cold War*, edited by Andrew Fenton Cooper. New York: Macmillan, 1997.

Ooi Kee Beng. *Lost in Transition: Malaysia under Abdullah*. Petaling Jaya and Singapore: SIRD and Institute of Southeast Asian Studies, 2007.

―――. *The Reluctant Politician: Tun Dr Ismail and His Time*. Singapore: Institute of Southeast Asian Studies, 2006.

Ooi Kee Beng, Johan Saravanamuttu, and Lee Hock Guan. *March 8: Eclipsing May 13*. Singapore: Institute of Southeast Asian Studies, 2008.

Ott, Marvin C. "Foreign Policy Formulation in Malaysia". *Asian Survey* 12, no. 3 (March 1972): 225–39.

―――. "The Sources and Content of Malaysian Foreign Policy, toward Indonesia and the Philippines 1957–1965". Ph.D. dissertation, John Hopkins University, 1971.

Pang, Eul-soo. "The Financial Crisis of 1997–98 and the Fall of the Asian Developmental State". *Contemporary Southeast Asia* 22, no. 3 (December 2002): 570–93.

Pathmanathan Murugesu and David Lazarus. *Winds of Change: The Mahathir Impact on Foreign Policy*. Kuala Lumpur: Eastview Productions, 1984.

Pathmanathan, Murugesu. *Malaysia and World Affairs: The Mahathir Impact*. Petaling Jaya, Selangor Darul Ehsan, Malaysia: Economic Research Associates, 1990.

―――. "The Straits of Malacca: A Basis for Conflict or Co-operation?". In *New Directions in the International Relations of Southeast Asia*, edited by Lau Teik Soon. Singapore: Singapore University Press for Institute of Southeast Asian Studies, 1973.

Pauly, Louis W. *Who Elected the Bankers? Surveillance and Control in the World Economy*. Ithaca and London: Cornell University Press, 1997.

"Perjanjian Persahabatan di antara Persekutuan Tanah Melayu dengan Republik Indonesia (1959)" [Treaty of Friendship between the Federation of Malaya and the Republic of Indonesia (1959)]. In *Perjanjian Kerajaan Malaysia dengan Kerajaan Asing*. Malaysia: Kementerian Pelajaran, Arahan Pejabat bil.13, Kuala Lumpur, 1973.

"Perjanjian Persahabatan antara Kerajaan Malaysia dan Kerajaan Republik Indonesia (1970)" [Treaty of Friendship between the Government of Malaysia and the Republic of Indonesia (1970)]. In *Perjanjian Kerajaan Malaysia dengan Kerajaan Asing*. Malaysia: Kementerian Pelajaran, Arahan Pejabat bil.13, Kuala Lumpur, 1973.

Pillay, Subramaniam. "Politics, Economics and General Elections". *Aliran Monthly* 19, no. 6 (1999): 2–4.

Ping, Jonathan. *Middle Power Statecraft: Indonesia, Malaysia and the Asia-Pacific*. Aldershot, UK and Burlington, US: Ashgate, 2005.

Pitsuwan, Surin. *Islam and Malay Nationalism: A Case Study of Malay-Muslims of Southern Thailand*. Bangkok: Thai Khadi Research Institute, Thammasat University, 1985.

Poulgrain, Greg. *The Genesis of Konfrontasi: Malaysia, Brunei, Indonesia, 1945–1965*. Bathurst, N.S.W. and London: Crawford House and C. Hurst, 1998.

Rao, Chandriah Appa and Bruce Ross-Larson. *Issues in Contemporary Malaysia*. Kuala Lumpur: Singapore: Heinemann Educational Books, 1977.

Rau, Robert Lincoln. "Singapore's Foreign Relations, 1965–1972: With Emphasis on the Five Power Commonwealth Group". Ann Arbor: University Microfilms (1975) Thesis (Ph.D.), University of Michigan, 1974.

Rengger, N.J. *International Relations, Political Theory and the Problem of Order*. London and New York: Routledge, 2000.

Roff, Margaret. "The Politics of Language in Malaysia". *Asian Survey* 7 (1967).

Rosenau, James N. *The Scientific Study of Foreign Policy*. London: F. Pinter, 1980.

————, ed. *International Politics and Foreign Policy: A Reader in Research and Theory*. New York: Free Press, 1969.

Rosenberger, Leif Roderick. "Southeast Asia's Currency Crisis: A Diagnosis and Prescription". *Contemporary Southeast Asia* 19, no. 3 (1997): 224–51.

Ruggie, John Gerard. *Constructing the World Polity: Essays on International Institutionalization*. London and New York: Routledge, 1998.

Rüland, Jürgen. "ASEAN and the Asian Crisis: Theoretical Implications and Practical Consequences for Southeast Asian Regionalism". *The Pacific Review* 13, no. 3 (2000): 421–51.

Sakhuja, Vijay. "Submarine Frenzy in Southeast Asia". Commentary, *Asian Defence & Diplomacy*, July 2007.

Salazar, Lorraine Carlos. "Privatisation, Patronage and Enterprise Development: Liberalising Telecommunications in Malaysia". In *The State of Malaysia: Ethnicity, Equity, and Reform*, edited by Edmund Terence Gomez. London: Routledge, 2004.

Saravanamuttu, Johan. "Tun Ismail — Early Architect of Malaysian Foreign Policy". *Journal of Diplomacy and Foreign Relations* 9, no. 1 (2007): 1–16.

————. "Iconoclasm and Foreign Policy — The Mahathir Years". In *Reflections: The Mahathir Years*, edited by Bridget Welsh. Washington, D.C.: Southeast Asian Studies Program, SAIS, 2004*a*.

————. "Malaysian Multicultural Policy and Practices: Between Communalism and Consociationalism". In *The Challenge of Ethnicity: Building a Nation in Malaysia*, edited by Cheah Boon Kheng. Singapore: Marshall Cavendish International, 2004*b*.

————. "Globalisation, Capital and Governance in a Newly Industrialising Plural Society: Malaysia during the 1990s". In *Crises of Governance in Asia and Africa*, edited by Sandra J. Maclean, Fahimul Quadir and Timothy M. Shaw. Aldershot, England: Ashgate, 2001.

————. "The ASEAN Model for Regional Cooperation". In *Asian Peace: Security and Governance in the Asia-Pacific Region*, edited by Majid Tehranian. London & New York: I.B. Tauris, 1999.

————. "The Southeast Asian Development Phenomenon Revisited: From Flying Geese to Lame Ducks?". *Pacifica Review* 10, no. 2 (1998): 111–26.

————. "ASEAN in Malaysia's Foreign Policy Discourse and Practice, 1967–1997".

Asian Journal of Political Science 5, no. 1 (June 1997, Special Issue on ASEAN): 35–51.

———. "Malaysia's Foreign Policy in the Mahathir Period, 1981–1995: An Iconoclast Come to Rule", *Asian Journal of Political Science* 4, no. 1 (June 1996): 1–16.

———. "Manoeuvrings for Middle Power". *ISEAS Trends, Business Times*, 26–27 March 1994, No. 43.

———. "Looking Beyond Looking East". In *Southeast Asian Perceptions of Japan*, edited by Renato Constantino. Tokyo and Manila: Zenzei Publishing and Karel Inc., 1992*a*.

———. "The Indochinese and ASEAN Roles in the Cambodian Peace Process: A Regional Perspective". Paper presented at the Conference on "Peace in Asia towards the 2ist Century", Fukuoka City, Japan, 2–3 August 1992*b*.

———. "Militarization in ASEAN and the Option for Denuclearization in South-East Asia". *Interdisciplinary Peace Research* 2, no. 1 (1990).

———. "Look East Policy: The Real Lessons". In *Mahathir's Economic Policies*, edited by K.S. Jomo. Kuala Lumpur: Insan, 2nd Edition, 1989.

———. "Japanese Economic Penetration in ASEAN in the Context of the International Division of Labor". *Journal of Contemporary Asia* 18, no. 2 (1988): 139–69.

———. "The State, Authoritarianism and Industrialization: Reflections on the Malaysian Case". *Kajian Malaysia* 5, no. 2 (December 1987).

———. "Malaysia's Foreign Policy, 1957–1980". In *Government and Politics of Malaysia*, edited by Zakaria Haji Ahmad, pp. 128–60. Singapore: Oxford University Press (issued under the auspices of the Southeast Asian Studies Program, Institute of Southeast Asian Studies, Singapore).

———. "Imperialism, Dependent Development and ASEAN Regionalism". *Journal of Contemporary Asia* 16, no. 2 (1986): 204–22.

———. "Malaysia's Look East Policy and Its Implications for Self-Sustaining Growth". In *The Malysian Economy at the Crossroads: Policy Adjustment or Structural Transformation*, edited by Lim Lin Lean and Chee Peng Lim. Kuala Lumpur: Malaysian Economic Association/ Organisational Resources Sdn Bhd., 1984.

———. "Malaysia: Middle-Class Affectations of a Democratizing Multicultural Society". In *Values and Life Styles in Urban Asia: A Cross-Cultural Analysis and Sourcebook Based on AsiaBarometer Survey of 2003*, edited by Takashi Inoguchi, Miguel Basanez, Akihiko Tanaka and Timur Dadabaev. Institute of Oriental Culture, University of Tokyo, Mexico: SIGLO XXI Editores, 2005.

———. "Is there a Politics of the Malaysian Middle Class?". In *Southeast Asian Middle Classes: Prospects for Change and Democratisation*, edited by Abdul Rahman Embong. Bangi: Penerbit Universiti Kebangsaan Malaysia, 2001.

———. "The State, Ethnicity and the Middle Class Factor". In *Internal Conflict and Governance*, edited by K. Rupesinghe. New York: St. Martin's Press, 1992.

————. *The Dilemma of Independence: Two Decades of Malaysia's Foreign Policy, 1957–1977*. Penang: Universiti Sains Malaysia, 1983.

————. *The Content, Sources and Development of Malaysian Foreign Policy, 1957–1975*. Ph.D. Thesis, University of British Columbia, Vancouver, 1976.

————. "Southern Bargaining in North-South Trade: The Case of Tin Agreements". Master's Thesis, University of British Columbia, 1972.

Santaputra, Charivat. *Thai Foreign Policy 1932–1946*. Thai Khadi Research Institute, Ph.D. Thesis, Thammasat University, 1985.

Saw Swee Hock and K. Kesavapany. *Singapore-Malaysia Relations under Abdullah Badawi*. Singapore: Institute of Southeast Asian Studies, 2006.

————, eds. *Malaysia: Recent Trends and Challenges*. Singapore: Institute of Southeast Asian Studies, 2005.

Schofield, Clive. "Unlocking the Seabed Resources of the Gulf of Thailand". *Contemporary Southeast Asia* 29, no. 2 (2007): 286–308.

Schofield, Clive and Ian Storey. "Energy Security and Southeast Asia: The Impact on Maritime Bondary and Territorial Disputes". *Harvard Asia Quarterly* IX, no. 4 (2005): 36–46.

Scott, James C. *Political Ideology in Malaysia*. New Haven: Yale University Press, 1968.

See Seng, Tan and Amitav Archarya. *Asia-Pacific Security Cooperation: National Interests and Regional Order*. NY: M.E. Sharpe, 2004.

Searle, Peter. *The Riddle of Malaysian Capitalism: Rent-seekers or Real Capitalists?* St. Leonards and Honolulu: Allen & Unwin and University of Hawaii Press, 1999.

Severino, Rodolfo C. *Southeast Asia in Search of an ASEAN Community*. Singapore: Institute of Southeast Asian Studies, 2006.

Shaik Mohd Saifuddeen Shaik Mohd Salleh and Suzalia Mohamad. "Malaysia and the OIC". In *Malaysia and the Islamic World*, edited by Abdul Razak Baginda. London: Asean Academic Press, 2004.

Shamsul, A.B. "The Battle Royal: The UMNO Elections of 1987". In *Southeast Asian Affairs 1988*, edited by M. Ayoob and Ng Chee Yuen. Singapore, Institute of Southeast Asian Studies, 1988.

Sharma, Archana. *British Policy Towards Malaysia, 1957–1967*. New Delhi: Radiant Publishers, 1993.

Sieh Mei Ling. *Taking on the World: Globalization Strategies in Malaysia*. New York/Kuala Lumpur: McGraw-Hill, 2000.

Silcock, T.H. "Development of a Malayan Foreign Policy". *Australian Outlook* 17, no. 3 (1963): 42–53.

Simbulan, Roland. *The Continuing Struggle for an Independent Philippine Foreign Policy*. Manila: Nuclear Free Philippines Coalition, 1991.

Simon, Sheldon W. *Asian Neutralism and U.S. Policy*. Washington, D.C.: American Enterprise Institute for Public Policy Research, 1975.

Singapore. *Water Talks? If Only it Could*. Singapore: Ministry of Information, Communications & the Arts, 2003.

————. *Agreement between the Government of the State of Johor and the Public Utilities Board of the Republic of Singapore*, 24 November 1990.

Sodhy, Pamela. "Malaysia-US Relations". In *Malaysia's Foreign Policy: Continuity and Change*, edited by Abdul Razak Baginda. London and Singapore: Marshall Cavendish Editions, 2007.

————. *The US-Malaysian Nexus: Themes in Superpower-Small State Relations*. Kuala, Lumpur: Institute of Strategic and International Studies, 1991.

————. "Passage of Empire: United States — Malayan Relations to 1966". Ann Arbor, Mich.: University Microfilms International (1986), Ph.D. Thesis, Cornell University, 1982.

Soros, George. *The Crisis of Global Capitalism: Open Society Endangered*. London: Little, Brown and Company, UK, 1998.

Statement of Malaysian Committee for International War Crimes Commission on the Gulf War on "Why Malaysia Supported Security Council Resolution 678 leading to the Outbreak of Gulf War on January 17, 1991", 5 pp.

Stiglitz, Joseph. *Globalization and Its Discontents*. London & New York: Penguin Book, 2002.

Storey, Ian. *Southeast Asia and the Rise of China: The Search for Security*. London & New York: RoutledgeCurzon, forthcoming.

Stubbs, Richard. "The Foreign Policy of Malaysia". In *The Political Economy of Foreign Policy in Southeast Asia*, edited by David Wurfel and Bruce Burton. London. Macmillan, 1990.

Stubbs, Richard and Geoffrey D. Underhill, eds. *Political Economy and the Changing Global Order*. New York: St. Martin's Press, 1994.

Subhan, Malcolm. "ASEAN-EEC Relations". In *Southeast Asian Affairs 1977*, edited by Huynh Kim Kanh. Singapore: Institute of Southeast Asian Studies, 1977.

Subky Latif. "UMNO: 30 Years After". In *Southeast Asian Affairs 1977*, edited by Huynh Kim Kanh. Singapore: Institute of Southeast Asian Studies, 1977.

Sukma, Rizal. *Islam in Indonesian Foreign Policy*. London: Routledge, 2003.

Suryadinata, Leo. *Indonesia's Foreign Policy under Suharto: Aspiring to International Leadership*. Singapore: Times Academic Press, 1996.

Syed Hamid Albar. *Issues in Malaysian Foreign Policy and Diplomacy: Selected Speeches by Syed Hamid Albar*. Kuala Lumpur: Institute of Diplomacy and Foreign Relations, 2007.

Tan, T.H. Andrew. *Problems and Issues in Malaysia-Singapore Relations*. Canberra: Strategic and Defence Studies Centre, Australian National University, 1997.

Tan Tai Yong. *Creating "Greater Malaysia": Decolonization and the Politics of Merger*. Singapore: Institute of Southeast Asian Studies, 2008.

Tawfik Ismail and Ooi Kee Beng. *Malaya's First Year at the United Nations: As Reflected in Dr Ismail's Reports Home to Tunku Abdul Rahman*. Singapore: Institute of Southeast Asian Studies, 2009.

Tham Siew Yean. "Trade Liberalizsation and National Autonomy: Malaysia's Experience at the Multilateral and Bilateral Levels". In *Globalization & National Autonomy*, edited by Joan M. Nelson, Jacob Meerman and Abdul Rahman

Embong. Singapore: Institute of Southeast Asian Studies with Institute of Malaysian and International Studies, 2008.

Thongpricha, Vimolvan. "Malaysia and the Commonwealth". Washington: American University, 1970. M.A. Thesis, American University, 1970.

Tilman, Robert O. *Malaysian Foreign Policy*. Report RAC-R-62-2, Washington DC, Strategic Studies Department, 1969*a*.

————. "Malaysia Foreign Policy: The Dilemmas of a Committed Neutral". In *Public Policy*, edited by J.D. Montgomery and A.D. Hirschman. Cambridge, Mass.: Harvard University Press, 1969*b*.

Tow, William T. "Alternative Security Models: Implications for ASEAN". In *The 2ⁿᵈ ASEAN Reader*, compiled by Sharon Siddique and Sree Kumar, pp. 303–09. Singapore: Institute of Southeast Asian Studies, 2003.

Tun Ismail Papers. Folio 5 (1 & 2). Notes by the Ambassador (Confidential).

Tunku Abdul Rahman. *May 13: Before and After*. Kuala Lumpur: Utusan Melayu Press, 1969.

United Nations. Conference on Trade and Development. Proceedings of the United Nations Conference on Trade and Development, Geneva, 23 March–16 June 1964, Vol. 2. New York: United Nations, 1964.

Veltmeyer, Henry, ed. *New Perspectives on Globalization and Antiglobalization: Prospects for a New World Order?*. Aldershot, U.K. and Burlington, US: Ashgate, 2008.

Wain, Barry. *The Refused: The Agony of the Indochina Refugees*. New York: Simon and Schuster, 1981.

————. *Malaysian Maverick: Mahathir Mohamad in Turbulent Times*. Houndsmills: Palgrave Macmillan, 2009.

Wallerstein, Immanuel. *The Modern World System*. New York: Academic Press, 1974.

Waltz, Kenneth A. *Theory of International Politics*. New York: McGraw-Hill, 1979.

Weinstein, Franklin. 1976. *Indonesian Foreign Policy and the Dilemma of Dependence: From Sukarno to Soeharto*. Ithaca, N.Y.: Cornell University Press, 1976.

Weinstein, Franklin B. "The Uses of Foreign Policy in Indonesia: An Approach to the Analysis of Foreign Policy in Less Developed Countries". *World Politics* 24 (1972): 356–81.

Welsh, Bridget. "Tears and Fears: Tun Mahathir's Last Hurrah". In *Southeast Asian Affairs 2004*, edited by Daljit Singh and Chin Kin Wah, pp. 139–55. Singapore: Institute of Southeast Asian Studies, 2004.

Wendt, Alexander. *Social Theory of International Politics*. Cambridge: Cambridge University Press, 1999.

————. "Constructing International Politics". *International Security* 20 (January 1995): 71-81.

————. "Collective Identity Formation and the International State". *American Political Science Review* 88, no. 2 (1994): 384–96.

————. "Anarchy is What States Make of It: The Social Construction of Power Politics". *International Organization* 46, no. 2 (1992): 391–425.

Widmaier, Wesley. "Kenynesianism as a Constructivist Theory of the International Political Economy". *Millennium* 32, no. 1 (2003): 87–107.

Wilairat, Kawin. *Singapore's Foreign Policy: A Study of the Foreign Policy System of a City-State*. Ann Arbor, Mich.: University Microfilms International, 1976, 1985.

————. *Singapore's Foreign Policy: The First Decade*. Singapore: Institute of Southeast Asian Studies, 1975.

Wolfers, Arnold. *Discord and Collaboration*. Baltimore: Johns Hopkins University Press, 1962.

World Bank. *The East Asian Miracle: Economic Growth and Public Policy*. New York: Oxford Univerity Press, 1993.

Wurfel, David. "Philippine's Foreign Policy". In *The Political Economy of Foreign Policy in Southeast Asia*, edited by David Wurfel and Bruce Burton. New York: St. Martin's Press, 1990.

————. *Philippine Foreign Policy: Strategies for Regime Survival*. Toronto: Joint Centre on Modern East Asia, University of Toronto-York University, 1983.

Wurfel, David and Bruce Burton. *The Political Economy of Foreign Policy in Southeast Asia*. Houndsmills and London: McMillan Press, 1990.

Van Der Westhuizen, Janis. "South Africa's Emergence as a Middle Power". *Third World Quarterly* 19, no. 3 (1998): 435–55.

Yegar, Moshe. "Malaysia: Anti-Semitism without Jews". *Jewish Political Studies Review* 18, no. 3-4 (Fall 2006).

Yu, Tzong-shian and Dianqing Xu, eds. *From Crisis to Recovery: East Asia Rising Again?* Singapore: World Scientific, 2001.

Zainal Abidin Sulong. "Early Diplomacy." In *Number One Wisma Putra*, edited by Fauziah Mohamad Taib. Kuala Lumpur: Institute of Diplomacy and Foreign Relations, 2006.

Zakaria Haji Ahmad. "Malaysian Foreign Policy and Domestic Politics: Looking Outward and Moving Inward?". In *Regional Dynamics: Security, Political and Economic Issues in the Asia-Pacific Region*, edited by Robert A. Scalapino, et al. Jakarta: Centre for Strategic and International Studies, 1990.

Zakaria Mohd Ali. "Normalization of Relations with China". In *Number One Wisma Putra*, edited by Fauziah Mohamad Taib. Kuala Lumpur: Institute of Diplomacy and Foreign Relations, 2006.

INDEX

ABOUT THE AUTHOR

Johan Saravanamuttu is currently a Visiting Senior Research Fellow at the Institute of Southeast Asian Studies (ISEAS), Singapore. He was formerly professor of political science at Universiti Sains Malaysia (USM) in Penang where he served as Dean of the School of Social Sciences (1994–96) and as Dean of the Research Platform on Social Transformation (2003–06). In 1997, he was the Visiting Chair in ASEAN and International Studies at the University of Toronto. His published works include the first major study of Malaysia's foreign policy (1983), ASEAN regional non-governmental organizations (1986) and the nexus between industrialization and the institutionalization of authoritarian regimes in Southeast Asia (1991). More recent publications include *New Politics in Malaysia* (2003, edited with Francis Loh), "Political Islam in Southeast Asia", Special Issue (guest editor), *Global Change Peace & Security* 16, no. 2 (June 2004), and *March 8: Eclipsing May 13* (2008, with Ooi Kee Beng and Lee Hock Guan). His latest publication is as editor and contributor of *Islam and Politics in Southeast Asia* (2010).